There is a growing view that intelligence evolved as a product of social interdependence. The unique development of human intelligence was probably linked to the use of spoken language, but language itself evolved in the context of social interaction, and in its development it has shaped – and been shaped by – social institutions. Taking as their starting-point the social production of intelligence and of language, scholars across a range of disciplines are beginning to rethink fundamental questions about human evolution, language and social institutions. This volume brings together anthropologists, linguists, primatologists and psychologists, all working on this new frontier of research.

D1457614

Social intelligence and interaction

Social intelligence and interaction

Expressions and implications of the social
bias in human intelligence

EDITED BY
ESTHER N. GOODY
University of Cambridge

CAMBRIDGE
UNIVERSITY PRESS

Published by the Press Syndicate of the University of Cambridge
The Pitt Building, Trumpington Street, Cambridge CB2 1RP
40 West 20th Street, New York, NY 10011–4211, USA
10 Stamford Road, Oakleigh, Melbourne 3166, Australia

First published 1995

Printed in Great Britain at the University Press, Cambridge

A catalogue record for this book is available from the British Library

Library of Congress cataloguing in publication data
Social intelligence and interaction: expressions and implications of
    the social bias in human intelligence / edited by Esther N. Goody.
        p.   cm.
    Based on papers presented at a workshop sponsored by the
Wissenschaftskolleg zu Berlin, held in the spring of 1990, with the
theme Some implications of a social origin of human intelligence.
    ISBN 0 521 45329 1. – ISBN 0 521 45949 4 (pbk.)
    1. Intellect – Social aspects.   2. Social intelligence.
3. Sociolinguistics.   I. Goody, Esther N.
    BF431.S617   1995
    153.9 – dc20   94–8853   CIP

ISBN 0 521 45329 1 hardback
ISBN 0 521 45949 4 paperback

SE

Contents

Part III Genres as tools that shape interaction

Part IV Expressions of a social bias in intelligence

Contributors

Nurit Bird-David Department of Anthropology, University of Tel Aviv, Israel

Penelope Brown Max Planck Institute for Psycholinguistics, Nijmegen, The Netherlands

Richard W. Byrne Scottish Primate Research Group, Department of Psychology, University of St Andrews, Scotland

Michael Carrithers Department of Anthropology, Durham University

Paul Drew Department of Sociology, University of York

David Good Faculty of Social and Political Sciences, University of Cambridge

Esther Goody Department of Social Anthropology, University of Cambridge

Brian Hazlehurst Departments of Anthropology and Cognitive Science, University of California, San Diego

Edwin Hutchins Department of Cognitive Science, University of California, San Diego

Stephen C. Levinson Max Planck Institute for Psycholinguistics, Nijmegen, The Netherlands

Thomas Luckmann Fachgruppe Soziologie, Universität Konstanz, Germany

Jürgen Streeck Department of Speech Communication, The University of Texas, Austin, Texas

David Zeitlyn Wolfson College, Oxford

Conventions used in transcripts

CAPS	spoken loudly
underlined	spoken with emphasis
:	extended sound
(h)	soft inbreath
.hhh	audible inbreath
.kh	inbreath with other audible sounds
[	two speakers speaking simultaneously: position of bracket indicates point of overlap onset
=	short transition time (no pause between lines of speech)
—	word broken off
>	speeding up
(---)	unintelligible
( )	bounds uncertain transcription
(( ))	bounds transcriber's comments
→	indicates target turns referred to in text
(0.1)	pause (in seconds)
(.)	micropause

Preface

It is both a hazard and a delight of anthropological fieldwork that the more completely one becomes immersed in a society and culture totally different from one's own, the more similar people seem to kin and friends at home. Despite the manifest, subtle and profound differences there is a level on which people seem to feel and act in basically similar ways.[1] The dynamics of this dialectic between socio-cultural uniqueness and common humanity lie in part at the intersection between cultural forms and inter-personal interaction. This is an area I first explored in papers on the links between greeting, giving and constraining (1972) and on questioning (1978a). However these two problems raised more general issues concerning the inferring of intentions in interaction, and thus the significance of social roles for making interaction more predictable (1978b). Ethologists are now suggesting that primate intelligence was directly linked to the challenges of social interdependence. This insight places the problems of greeting, questioning and inferring intentions in an even wider context. What can we learn about the nature of human society by taking seriously the possibility that human intelligence is in this fundamental sense *social* intelligence?

It is difficult to know where to begin with such a general problem, particularly if there is a commitment to a firm empirical base. The Working Papers were essays directed at particular aspects: the implications for primate social intelligence of an emerging spoken language; the new potentiality of language for meeting the challenges of social interdependence; language and the emergence of institutionalized gender roles; language and the emergence of rules. During my attempts to pull together these several themes it became clear that these very preliminary ideas needed the challenge of scholarly debate, and exploration in a range of empirical contexts. The Wissenschaftskolleg zu Berlin made this possible by sponsoring a workshop on *Some implications of a social orgin of human intelligence* in the spring of 1990 to which the contributors to this volume were invited. Each had already begun to explore some aspect in their own work, though not necessarily under the rubric of social intelligence. A set of the draft Working Papers in Social Intelligence was circulated to participants with the invitation to respond with a paper related to their own research. Since the present volume grew out of papers written for this workshop it seems appropriate to begin the Introduction with themes from the Working Papers. Discussion during the Workshop and during revision of the individual papers has led to several issues being more fully worked out, for which grateful thanks to stimulating colleagues.

In several ways this volume owes its existence to the Wissenschaftskolleg zu Berlin. First, because it gave the editor a year of peace, marvellous facilities and stimulating colleagues which made it possible to pursue background reading and to draft further Working Papers for the social intelligence project. Second, because their funding of the workshop on social intelligence made it possible to bring together scholars from several fields who were working already on issues related to social intelligence. And finally because, in the setting of Berlin in May, our discussions of the exploratory papers led to unanimous agreement that we should publish revised papers and so extend the debate.

Particular thanks are due to Wolf Lepenies and Joachim Nettelbeck who were willing to believe that it would be worthwhile to find funds and facilities to bring participants from far and wide for the Social Intelligence Workshop to talk about such an amorphous topic. Stephen Levinson and Penny Brown, who were in Berlin launching the Max Planck Projectgruppe für Kognitive Anthropologie, gave generously of time, ideas and enthusiasm during the planning of the workshop. Dr Stefan Strohschneider of the Projectgruppe für Kognitive Anthropologie acted as scribe.

Particular thanks are also due to a number of individuals who let me talk to them about social intelligence and said it was all worthwhile: First, to Jack Goody, whose patience is matched only by his willingness to lend a hand to innumerable chores; and to John Barnes, Michael Cole, Elizabeth Duvan, Maurice Godelier, Ward Goodenough, John and Jenny Gumperz, Robert Hinde, Stephen Hugh-Jones, Phyllis Lee, Skip Rappaport, and S.J. Tambiah.

The logistics of putting together a manuscript from individual papers can be daunting; they were made bearable by Sarah Green's skill with a word processer and preparation of the index, and by Sue Kemsley's diligence with the bibliography. Sandy Anthony's sub-editorial sharp sight has made the final stages surprisingly untraumatic.

Several participants admitted later that they had wondered whether it would be possible to find common ground across such disparate disciplines. In fact we were repeatedly surprised at the ease with which topics

and issues crossed subject boundaries. The problematic of the implications of intelligence as social provided a common perspective – though
by no means unanimity!

Note

1 There are certain key ethnographies which explore this question in relation to
emotions, a direction not pursued here but which is part of the wider puzzle:
Briggs's *Never in anger* (1970); Rosaldo's *Knowledge and passion* (1980);
Reisman's two books on the Fulani, *Freedom in Fulani social life* (1977), and
First find your child a good mother (1992).

ESTHER GOODY

Introduction: Some implications of a social origin of intelligence

Recent work in ethology persuasively argues that the striking advance in primate intelligence over that of lower mammals is a product of social interdependence. This finding raises two kinds of questions for students of human society. In the first place, if the constraints of social interaction generated primate intelligence, what was the ratchet that led to the emergence of incomparably greater hominid intelligence, that is to *Homo sapiens sapiens*? For reasons outlined below, this stimulus seems likely to have been closely related to the gradual emergence of spoken language. Although discussion of the role of language in human evolution can, for the present at least, be only speculative, the problem has a fascination which justifies such exploratory thinking. We need to ask how language might have altered primate social life in ways that demanded, and rewarded, more complex intelligence.

A second question looks forward, not back; it concerns the contemporary nature of human intelligence. If human intelligence evolved in response to the challenges of social living, what are the implications for understanding thought, interaction and social forms? This introduction outlines some of the dynamics likely to be related to both questions in a way that is intended to raise problems for further analysis and research.

Themes from Working Papers

1. Primate intelligence as a response to social interdependence

In a seminal paper, 'The social function of intellect', Nicholas Humphrey (1976) has argued for a social origin of primate intelligence. He begins by noting that the higher primates, and particularly chimpanzees, are on many measures highly intelligent. Yet there is nothing in their life as foraging animals which demands such a level of intelligence. In this, he says, they are comparable to what we know of early man from studies of hunter-gatherer society. For both species, foraging follows customary patterns and the use of tools is very limited, both being based on imitation of others, or trial and error. Innovation requiring 'higher-order' or

1

'creative' intelligence – that is, the ability to make inferences from novel conjunctions of events, is rare. The stone tools of *Homo erectus* appear to have hardly changed at all over one million years. This is a problem for ethologists because it is inconceivable that a creature would develop skills that are seldom or never used. Indeed, their assumption is the opposite: that skills only develop in response to pressures from the environment, such that the emergent skill makes a significant contribution to improved chances of reproductive survival. So what use is higher-order intelligence to anthropoid apes and stone-age man, if it doesn't provide an advantage in dealing with the natural environment?

Humphrey suggests that the most difficult problems facing chimpanzees are other chimpanzees; that it was in dealing with the social environment that creative intelligence evolved. This suggestion makes sense once one recognizes the peculiar situation of interdependence that characterizes both ape and human society. Both live in groups. And living in groups requires being able to pursue individual goals effectively without alienating one's fellows, breaking up the group, or creating a situation of conflict within the group so that it becomes vulnerable to outside attack.

Thus social primates are required by the very nature of the system they create and maintain to be calculating beings; they must be able to calculate the consequences of their own behaviour, to calculate the likely behaviour of others, to calculate the balance of advantage and loss – and all this in a context where the evidence on which their calculations are based is ephemeral, ambiguous and liable to change, not least as a consequence of their own actions (Humphrey 1988:19).

Acting on such models of the behaviour of others involves social transactions; there is a constant trading off between partners. If one animal or person wishes to change the behaviour of another he must take into account the other's goals and tactics. So in addition to the cognitive skills required to perceive the current state of play (low-level intelligence), the social gamesman, like the chess player, must be capable of a special kind of forward planning. As each move may call forth several alternative responses, and ego's own response choice must vary accordingly, this situation generates a decision-tree model.

In short, effective social living requires anticipation of the actions of others, calculation of short- and long-term costs and gains, and close attention to signals about the consequences of one's own behaviour. The higher primates, and man, have the ability to model this interdependence of one's own and others' behaviour at the cognitive level.[1] In order to facilitate thinking about this kind of thought it is useful to give it some kind of representation; for convenience it might be termed *anticipatory interactive planning*, or AIP.

Anticipatory interactive planning was a response to social living among primates. In turn, AIP set challenges which generated progressively increasing intelligence in the hominid line (Jolly 1966a; Humphrey 1976; papers in Byrne and Whiten 1988).

2. *Hominids, or at least* Homo sapiens, *were able to utilize spoken language in the representation of their own and others' contingent responses. Language clearly facilitates AIP in several ways, and must have made it very much more powerful. The emergence of language, then, may have been critical in the generation of hominid intelligence*

Social intelligence itself cannot account for the emergence of *Homo sapiens*, since it is shared with many higher primates. If spoken language is found only in humans, how is this related to the emergence of our species? How might social intelligence have led to, and been enhanced by, the development of language?

Progressive increase in cranial capacity through the *Homo* species to *Homo sapiens* suggests a continuing increase in intelligence during hominid evolution. This accelerates markedly with *H. erectus* and early *sapiens*.[2] Until recently it had been thought that language occurred suddenly through a mutation ('a unique genetic event') in which grammar and syntax were 'wired in' (Chomsky 1968, 1980; Premack 1986). However, several authorities have recently argued that language must have appeared in two stages: Lyons suggests that a gestural language preceded the emergence of human spoken language (1988). Recently Donald has proposed a protolanguage based on gesture and mime related to a mimetic form of cognition (1991). He sees both this protolanguage and cognition as distinct from spoken language and its related cognitive structures. Bickerton (1990) proposes a spoken protolanguage consisting essentially of a simple lexicon, perhaps later augmented by grammatical elements which were, however, quite independent of the grammar and syntax of 'true language' that appeared only with a genetic mutation. Thus these authorities retain the Chomskian premise that 'true language' was the result of a unique genetic event rather than developing gradually on the classic Darwinian model. This position makes it difficult to view early protolanguage as preadaptive for more complex forms since it is the disjunction between them that is stressed. In Bickerton's case this difficulty is ironic, since his insightful discussion of the emergence of grammatical elements in response to challenges for more clarity and specificity of reference is a model for an adaptionist account of the emergence of grammar and syntax.

Other scholars are beginning to pursue an adaptionist model that seeks to relate the initial emergence of spoken language to such primate features as the evolution of hemispheric specialization for both manual function and language, bipedal posture and tool use.[3] In such a view early protolanguage could have been extremely crude permitting only simple reference, with phonemes, grammar and syntax very gradually emerging as particular responses to specific problems of using spoken language (e.g. tense, negation, thematic roles). In their several papers and joint book (forthcoming) Lindblom, MacNeilage and Studdert-Kennedy persuasively argue the general case for a Darwinian view of gradual emergence of spoken language, laying out in detail how phonemes fit such a pattern, and addressing the critical issue of the structural and behavioural acquisition of the ability to produce speech. Based on his studies of primate and human structures Lieberman has long argued that spoken language must have evolved through progressive modification of the vocal tract and associated cognitive specialization (1968, 1991). The current picture suggests that early *Homo erectus* already had a vocal tract differing significantly from the apes and *Australopithecus* species. As there would be no reason for such modification without the advantage of spoken language,[4] the clear implication is that hominids have been using some sort of spoken language for over one million years.[5]

Robin Dunbar (1993) proposes another, very persuasive link between hominid intelligence and spoken language. He argues that primate group size and intelligence can be shown to increase in parallel, supporting the Humphrey, Jolly, Byrne and Whiten view that social living was the critical challenge; as primate groups got larger, demands of cognitive representation multiplied. But Dunbar points out that many sub-human primates rely on mutual grooming for the servicing of social relationships, and that for large groups this mechanism ceases to be effective, since it is time-consuming and a one-to-one interaction. Even a simple language, on the other hand, would have permitted the 'servicing' of many social relationships – simultaneously, and at a distance. Indeed, he suggests that initially instrumentally focused information may have been of secondary importance.

In accounting for the emergence of early language, Dunbar retains the premise that ecological constraints were primary in hominid evolution. He suggests that conditions for securing subsistence required early hominids to live in groups too large to be socially maintained through grooming. Thus, being forced to live in large groups, early hominids evolved 'gossip' to service social relationships. The argument for a social facilitation function of early language is very strong. Anthropologists since Malinowski (1927) have recognized its continuing significance.[6] However there is no real argument made for ecological constraints as the initiating factor, and it is in any case superfluous. We know that some primates use complex vocal signals (e.g. Cheney and Seyforth 1990). It seems quite probable that human protolanguage developed from such a base. An alternative hypothesis would be that some early hominid group(s) began to elaborate vocal signals in a way that facilitated the servicing of social relations in groups larger than those possible using grooming alone. The challenge of using protolanguage in larger groups may well have driven the first simple regularities of usage, precursors of grammar and syntax.

If, as it seems probable, the long-term intimacy of mother–infant–child–sibling communication is central to the transfer of language skills between generations, then this posed the problem for early hominids of how children of different mothers (and different matrilines) understood each other. Mothers who were themselves matri-siblings might transmit the same language usages to their children, but there must be a point at which the group becomes too large for this to balance changes of usage. Perhaps initially protolanguages were shared only within small groups. Larger groups of the sort Dunbar identifies as truly depending on spoken language for maintaining social relationships might then have been possible only after rudimentary grammars emerged which could cross boundaries of domestic bands.

The invisibility of social behaviour, especially spoken language, in the archaeological record has inevitably led to a focus on 'bones and stones', skeletal fossils and tools. Clearly both indirectly reflect social forms, but not without conjecture. If sociality does prove to be central to hominid cognition, then an evolutionary account must also give it a key role. A parallel development of hominid intelligence and of language invites us to ask in what ways early language might have facilitated social intelligence. Among the most obvious effects would be:

(a)   Reference by name to things and actions permits joint attention, and thus coordination of complex activities.

  (i)   This reference would then have to be mentally represented.
  (ii) The processes of coordinating joint activity would also have to be mentally represented.

(b)   The emerging structures of grammar and syntax permit much more complex and more rapid conversation.[7]

  (i)   These grammar and syntax structures have to be cognitively represented.
  (ii) Grammar and syntax processes have presumably become standardized, then routinized and finally automatized,[8] as has the motor control of speaking. We are not aware of how we articulate and produce the sounds in our speech (How *do* you say 'feather'?) Nor are we conscious of whether we put subject or verb first in a sentence. Automatization appears to free many complex processes from awareness, as car drivers are often startled to realize (see Velmans 1991 and comments).

(c)   Bickerton argues that a major vector of animal evolution is the complexity of representational system. He distinguishes between Primary Representational Systems (PRS), based on processing and representation of sensory input, and Secondary Representational Systems (SRS) in which the output of the PRS is mapped onto an externalized language. Species having only a PRS still respond to their environment in systematic ways which show they have 'tacit concepts' – like a frog's response to a fly. But a SRS permits the *labelling* of tacit concepts so that they become explicit (1990).

What difference does it make that concepts are labelled? There are important processes nested within the use of reference in spoken language. Reference (by name or words) permits classification of things, actions, feelings, events, etc. by making it possible to be explicit about the categories to which they belong. Such classification is built into languages so that we use it automatically (animal > dog > terrier > my terrier Spot). Cognitive psychology suggests that this must have had important consequences for the organization of perception and memory. If we can process, organize and recall categories then we can handle hugely more information than if we must deal with particular instances. This must have represented a major advance in human cognition.[9]

The very process of establishing common meanings for lexical items places them in the domain of shared knowledge, as a part of what Hutchins and others have called distributed intelligence (see Hutchins and Hazlehurst, Chapter 2, this volume). A shared lexicon represents the coordination of *meanings* which makes the coordination of actions possible on a quite new level compared with what is possible on the basis of private inference.[10] Another way of putting this social reality of language is to note that a Secondary Representational System does far more than multiply the power of the individual's primary representational system; it gives every individual the power to enter into the linguistic representations of others, and to use these shared secondary representations to model cognitively the understandings as well as the intentions of others. And of course the fact that we use language to influence others means that we can move from cognitive AIP models incorporating reference to using these categories in speech to seek to implement AIP strategies. Language as a SRS bridges individual cognitions through cognitive modelling using shared meanings. At the same time it makes possible the coordination of joint action between individuals by speaking about common goals, instrumental means etc. using these shared meanings.

(d)   Classification in turn is a prerequisite for the emergence of social roles (see below) and social rules (see below) which were necessary tools for the construction of even the simplest institutions of human social living. Both roles and rules now become elements in AIP representations, simplifying them in some ways, but also making them more powerful. At the same time roles and rules constrain the behaviour of others, making it more predictable.

(e)   Language permits the individual to act much more effectively on his social world in two modes: information and control.

   (i)   The cognitive modelling of the contingent actions of others, anticipatory interactive planning, depends on information about how others will act. While past experience may give clues for inferring responses, this process is obviously limited. Language permits the explicit exchange of information. (If I want another to help me get food it is useful to know whether he is hungry. He may have mentioned this, or I can ask him. Or I can ask someone else if he is hungry, or . . .)
   This raises the issue of distortion of information as one AIP strategy. Ethologists have seen deception as the key to primate social intelligence, as suggested in the title of a recent important book *Machiavellian Intelligence* (Byrne and Whiten 1988) and further discussed in Byrne's contribution to the present volume. Barnes's study of lying (1994) pursues this theme in human social life. The linguist Grice proposes that effective use of language depends on our being able to assume that others speak truthfully. Indeed deception is powerful precisely because we are so dependent on correct information for modelling our own and others' actions. AIP models of others' intentions can include the intention to deceive, their perception of our awareness of this deception, and our own counter deception, and so on. In Chapter 6, Good suggests that the ambiguity of conversational exchange may be one way of preserving the freedom to respond appropriately to deception.
   (ii)   However, AIP is not an end in itself but a means towards reaching our goals. AIP strategies must be implemented. The other mode of acting upon the world which language profoundly enhances is that of control. The use of language to manage relationships with others is extremely powerful, and dauntingly complex. On the simplest level commands both organize action and express dominance. Successful commands are probably the most effective AIP strategy of all, since they secure direct compliance with one's own goals without the need for calculating alternative strategies or engaging in negotiation. But of course language also permits social cooperation and negotiation of joint strategies. Conversational analysis reveals, on a less explicit level, the subtle nature of the cooperative negotiation of meanings in ordinary daily life. And the identification and analysis of speech acts has led to the recognition that speech often conveys several kinds of message simultaneously. The contributions of Streeck, Drew and Good in Part II of this volume present current thinking on key aspects of interactive negotiation in conversation.[11]

It is clear that information and control tend to be merged in most use of spoken language; language is used to manage social relations at the same time that it conveys information. However, management of relationships is probably the single most central use of language. Malinowski noted its importance long ago when he pointed out that communication apparently carrying no content whatever (which he termed 'phatic'[12]) was still important for maintenance of social life. Greeting forms are the most familiar example (see E. Goody 1972). Indeed Dunbar suggests that spoken language may have begun as companionable chatter with minimal referential content ('gossip') which served to maintain social integration (1992a). The formal constraints on use of language represented by institutionalized avoidance and joking relations (E. Goody 1978b), and by the universal politeness forms (Brown and Levinson 1978, 1987) reflect points where social relationships can be threatened by casual use of language. Garfinkel's experiments (1967) with altering expected responses in interactions between associates show again how fragile are the routines we construct to give meaning to our normal use of language, and how threatening is any deviation from what we expect. We depend on customary use of language to give constant evidence of the social validity of our relationships.

(f)   Finally, language makes possible the objectification of belief (Rappaport 1988; Goodenough 1990). With language we construct social worlds that have ultimate reality. The totemic world of the Australian Aborigines, the layered world of Hindu reincarnations, the medieval realms of heaven and hell – these exist only through the complex representations made possible by language. It is the *sharing* of these beliefs, impossible without language, which makes them real.[13] And it is this reality which in turn sets premises for shared goals which make possible joint social action at least part of the time.

Language and AIP together generated the complexity of mental representations which characterize the cognition of *Homo sapiens*.

3.   *Language was essential to the awareness of the embedding of intentionality which distinguishes* Homo sapiens *(Dennett 1983, 1987)*

The awareness of the self as both actor and object is probably dependent on language. Mead has given a brilliant account of how hearing ourselves speak brings about this recognition. Among the higher primates only chimpanzees have been shown to recognize themselves in a mirror, but mirrors are not a part of the natural chimpanzee world. Even if they occasionally catch sight of themselves in a pool of water, chimpanzees cannot represent this 'self' to others in speech; it cannot be objectified. If primate creative intelligence is based on the capacity to represent mentally the reciprocal contingency of one's own and others' actions, perhaps language has made it possible for *Homo sapiens* to become at least partially aware of this process of representation. In AIP terms, awareness of the 'self' could be seen as the recognition by the 'I' of the planning of interactive strategies in which the self is also one of the actors ('me'). Linguistic representation of intentions may also have been critical in the development of the human skill in pretending. Leslie (1987) has suggested that pretending requires the capacity simultaneously to maintain two levels of belief; one knows the way the world 'really is', and at the same time one posits a different state of the world and manipulates this, for play or fantasy. Children with the mental deficit of autism appear to be unable to sustain such dual levels of representation. Again there is some evidence that chimpanzees engage in pretence in play. But they do not represent this pretence to themselves, or to other chimpanzees, as a basis for alternative hypothetical worlds. Only with language can pretence be socially objectified.

With language, *Homo sapiens* is able to objectify the self as well as others in representation of AIP strategies.

4. The capacity to learn from others is enhanced by language in several ways. Homo sapiens *depends on learning rather than instinct for the transmission of adaptations between generations; effective learning on the scale necessary for the transmission of culturally developed adaptations depends on language*

The Vygotskian view sees learning as based on activity carried out jointly by novice and expert.[14] The novice begins by watching, then joins in with the simplest tasks, then gradually takes responsibility for the whole activity. In carrying out the activity together with the 'expert', the novice establishes routines which form the basis for mental schemata of the activity. These schemata model both the actions of the novice and of the expert. At first the novice need not 'understand' what s/he is doing, since the expert organizes and guides the process. As the novice comes to understand, and to master component skills, s/he is able to take responsibility for parts of the activity, and eventually for the whole. Vygotsky argued that cognitive processes take place first on the social plane, and that these joint processes are internalized to become the individual plane. During the learning process there is a 'space' where the novice is able to cooperate, but not to take responsibility – this has been termed the zone of proximal development (Vygotsky 1978:84–91; Wood, Bruner and Ross 1976; Cole 1985:154–9; Rogoff 1990). This view implies that the novice can jointly perform an activity before s/he is able to do it alone. Some chimpanzee learning is clearly of this sort, as with the use of straws to extract termites. What does language add to this process of social learning?

(a)   When learning is accompanied by speech, the schemata are objecti-fied. The task may be discussed, corrected, elaborated. The activity being learned can become an explicit object for learning. The Utku Inuit have partly verbal routines between parents and infants which act out fearful-ness, and the appropriate response of conciliatory dependence. These routines 'teach' the child to control anger at all times, and control of anger is a prerequisite for membership in an Utku community (Briggs 1970).

(b)   With language, skills can be explicitly identified with roles, and indeed tend to form a central component of the social definition of roles. The ubiquity of a sexual division of labour as a core premise of every society is a paradigmatic instance of this process. Many authorities have noted that tasks which are culturally specified as gender-specific often lack any features objectively restricting them to that sex (e.g. LaFontaine 1978). It seems likely that once *terms* for gender roles based on physiologi-cal differences are in use, activities typical for that gender come to be referred to by these terms and to be regarded as 'naturally' gender-specific in the same way as physiological differences themselves. In this way language enters into the social construction of reality (E. Goody n.d.).

(c)   Many simple societies have not institutionalized formal teaching/learning roles beyond the expert/novice distinction integral to coopera-tive activity between adults and children, and the modelling and control implicit in the relationship of parents to children (E. Goody 1982, 1989, 1993; Rogoff 1990). However with language, teaching roles become possible because learning can be objectified. Many simple societies link teaching with role transitions, usually heavily embedded in ritual, as in 'initiations' at puberty. What is taught, and learned, tends to be a blend of deference to the authority of seniors and the rights and obligations of adult roles (cf. Richards 1956).

(d)   With language, culturally developed skills become cultural capital, to be transmitted, shared, or restricted. Skills become objectified.

With language, the schemata on which AIP depends can be more effectively taught through joint activity; culturally developed skills can be transmitted between generations, both through joint activity, and through explicit teaching.

5.   *The social nature of learning replicates, and objectifies, the social character of AIP in which one's own actions are represented as contingently interdependent on others' responses. With language, AIP representations come to be expressed in internal dialogue.*

Vygotsky (1962) argues that thought is internalized speech. Initially the infant participates jointly, apparently passively, with adults and older children in speech acts; mothers of newborn babies have been found to hold conversations with the infant in which they also supply responses.[15] Mothers of older babies engage in play routines which scaffold the learning of vocabulary and apparently of syntactic frames (Bruner and Sherwood 1976). The child's increasing competence in speaking is expressed in conversation with those around her, but also in conversations with herself (egocentric speech) to which every new parent listens with awe. Older children continue to use egocentric speech, for instance when confronting a difficult problem where the steps of a solution are uttered verbally as self-instruction. Egocentric speech is 'a form found in the transition from external to inner speech' (Vygotsky, quoted in Wertsch 1985a:108–28). Gradually, at about the age of seven, egocentric speech disappears as the child comes to internalize it as inner speech, which nevertheless retains its regulative force (see also Luria 1979:chs. 5 and 6; 1981).

For Vygotsky the significance of inner speech is that it 'enables humans to plan and regulate their activity and derives from previous participation in verbal social interaction' (quoted in Wertsch 1985a:111). This model of human planning and regulation maps neatly onto our model for primate AIP, with the addition, of course, of spoken language. A basic axiom of Vygotsky's theory is 'that development . . . occurs through the decontextualization of mediational means'. For ape AIP the mediational means must be some form of cognitive representation, but presumably highly contextualized, anchored in the immediate here and now. Language is the prime mediational means for action between humans, and is also central to cognitive representations. However as a Secondary Representational System, language is decontextualized; shared lexical meanings must hold across contexts. Unfortunately we cannot know what form is taken by apes' inner thoughts. But it cannot include a shared verbal lexicon, which means that ape plans cannot include labelled concepts, or the possibility of basing AIP strategies on explicitly shared meanings. Nor can ape inner thoughts be self-regulatory in the sense of 'talking to oneself' – internalized egocentric speech – which explicitly represents intentions to oneself.

The use of inner speech in planning and regulating human actions gives AIP a concreteness not possible without language. However the fact that inner speech at times gives us awareness and control over AIP is probably misleading. For introspection forces one to admit that intentional modelling of contingencies and planning of strategies is intermittent at best. Or better, we move between levels of awareness. At times attention is sharply focused on a problem arising from social interdependence and we intentionally work out alternative solutions; at other times we muse on such problems, but attention is directed elsewhere; yet again we are engrossed, perhaps in music or a technical problem, and totally ignore any social dimension.[16] Just as apes were using AIP without language, so humans seem to continue to monitor social interdependence on non-verbal levels at the same time as we make use of linguistic representation.[17] Although we are seldom aware of doing this, conversation itself appears to involve constant monitoring and moment-by-moment adjustments of each speaker to what the other says and the way it is said. This reciprocal monitoring is so integral to conversation that often the meaning which emerges from this mutual contingency of response was neither anticipated nor intended by either speaker (Chapters 4, 5 and 6 in this volume).

Both through inner speech, which is a sort of dialogue with ourselves (between me and I), and through our close attention to conversational partners, spoken language seems to have constructed a dialogue template for social cognition. In inner speech and in conversation, dialogue and the dyad are built into human cognition. This dyadic premise and the dialogue template can be seen to underlie the human reliance on prayer as 'supplicatory speech addressed to some external force or being'. It is also expressed in the social construction of unseen mystical powers and the personification of good and evil which form the basis of religions.

When language transforms thought into internal dialogue, internal dialogue provides a mode for responding to cognitive problems.

6. *The AIP structure of thought which incorporates mental representations of others' responses to one's own actions is itself a model for reciprocity in social relations*

If the way we think already includes the linking of our actions to the responses of others, then the expression of this in giving and receiving 'things' is an externalization of thought processes. This highlights the complexity of AIP, which must both model contingent responses and model strategies for securing actions from others which are favourable to ego's goals. AIP moves constantly back and forth between modelling and strategic action. Thus 'giving' in its most basic form is the bestowal on another of something expected to favourably influence behaviour. This would fit with the fact that as well as giving 'things', we 'give' actions: respect, affection, offence . . . (E. Goody 1972).

It is also consistent with the 'mystical' quality of the gift to which Mauss drew attention; the giver of a gift is somehow still linked to it, the act is incomplete until a return gift is made.[18]

The power and ubiquity of the gift in human societies can be seen as related to its capacity both to represent the contingency of social relations, and at the same time to permit manipulation of this contingency.

7.   One implication of the view that thought models reciprocal socially contingent actions is that 'logical' thought is 'artificial'

Formal logical thought requires finding a way to represent events that does not involve the AIP format of action and response, interpersonal cause and effect. The role of writing seems to be critical in the emergence of such logic, as Jack Goody has argued (1977, 1987). It permits externalization of thought apart from the individual's goal strategies. One can see Plato's use of the dialogue as a vehicle for demonstrating the truth of his propositions as transitional between conversation and writing. Writing makes possible, though obviously it does not necessitate, the representation of information separately from the conditions of goal-realization (E. Goody 1978a). Levinson's chapter in this volume (Chapter 11) explores evidence for and implications of a separation between interactive (social) intelligence and logical reasoning.

Formal logical thought employs conceptual tools developed through literacy, and is not inherent in human cognitive processes.

8.   The constraints of social interdependence on which language built to produce hominid intelligence may also be central for the emergence of human social institutions. When language enhanced predictability, information and control, the result may have been the emergence of social roles and rules

What are the implications of the view of intelligence as fundamentally social for the construction of social institutions on which *human* society depends? One way to look at this is to ask what factors AIP depends on for efficacy. On the most general level these seem to include predictability of others' actions, information concerning the meaning of others' actions, and control over our own and others' actions.[19] If predictability, information and control were critical constraints in the emergence of spoken language, they probably also shaped social institutions.

The forms of social institutions vary greatly across human societies. So great is this variation that some anthropologists have argued that it is futile to seek regularities in their form and function; that rich description can be the only legitimate goal. While this is certainly true at the level of an attempt to compare total institutions, successful comparison has always depended on using analytical concepts that represent common features. Thus very useful studies have been made of joking relations, cross-cousin marriage, descent-group dynamics, gift giving, legal institutions, the feud, ritual, etc. It is a question of matching the conceptual tools to the level of process being examined. In working at the level of the emergence of social institutions, there are good reasons to consider as basic the constructs of social role and rule. Our question then becomes, how do social roles and rules mediate between individual AIP cognition and social institutions?

Social roles

One of the possibilities created by the use of reference in speech is the naming of categories. Categorization has basic effects on both perception and memory (e.g. Miller and Johnson-Laird 1976). Some insight into the implications for social institutions is provided by recent attempts to model the significance of the emergence of the role of 'father' in human societies (Wilson 1980, Fortes 1983). Both authors argue that the social recognition of the father marked the beginning of human society. Yet neither discusses the role of language in this transition. Their arguments in fact presume spoken language. Wilson writes of the power of the promise as a commitment to future action; but promises presume complex spoken language which permits representation of obligation, and of the future. Fortes links the emergence of the role of the father with the internalization of rules, without which people cannot live together in society. But it is hard to see by what process rules could be formulated or invoked, let alone internalized without spoken language. Further, the kind of rules Fortes is discussing refers to categories of actors and actions; not to one particular father only, but to the role of father; not to the sin of sleeping with a particular female, but to the sin of sleeping with a 'mother' or a 'sister'. Indeed it seems probable that it is the very extension of norms generated in domestic relationships to other kin which is paradigmatic of both social roles and social rules. It is surely worth reflecting on the fact that one of the few true universals in human societies is some form of kinship terminology linked to kin roles.

Another of these rare universals is a division of labour based on sex. The emergence of a complex sexual division of labour must also have depended on language and the capacity to categorize behaviour. While the actual tasks assigned to each sex vary widely across societies, the grouping of tasks into those appropriate to one sex or the other appears to be universal (E. Goody n.d.).

The naming of regularities of behaviour associated with positions in a social structure as roles entailing recognized rights and obligations is thus a feature of all human societies. In this way roles provided a powerful new kind of information for AIP. Roles of this kind create frames for predictable behaviour, associated with sanctions. Further, they define behaviour in dyadic terms – a maternal role implies a child role, and it is the interdependence of the two roles which is delineated by the rights-duties-sanctions complex. Thus a definition of appropriate role behaviour includes both the proper behaviour of ego, and the proper reciprocal responses of the role partner. In this way it makes AIP more powerful, since acting in a clearly defined role makes the behaviour of both members of the dyad more predictable. Indeed, their behaviour is predictable not only to the participants, but to others (in the same society).

Roles also facilitate AIP through increasing predictability on another level by implying sanctions if one or other member of the dyad does not behave in the correct, predictable way. Thus roles include a control element that facilitates the AIP cognition of all members of the society.

The classifying and labelling of role behaviour has an added significance at the level of the social system because sanctions are part of the mechanism for learning and maintaining 'social structures' and 'social capital'. Roles lead out from individual behaviour to the reproduction of the social structure.[20]

Rules

'Rule' is one of a fuzzy set of terms for regularities of behaviour. Other terms include 'routines', 'regularities', 'norms' and 'laws'. These terms have in common the fact that they refer to an apparent regularity in behaviour in a specific domain. But they differ profoundly in the extent to which the regularity is (a) intentional (routines need not be intentional, and may not be subject to conscious awareness); (b) socially sanctioned (as in norms); (c) explicitly formulated (as in rules); or (d) embedded in legal institutions (as with laws). These regularities of behaviour vary on two dimensions at least: they vary in their degree of explictness, and the formality with which they are formulated; and they vary in how deviations are sanctioned. At one extreme, routines are sanctioned only by those who participate regularly in them, and the sanction may be unconsciously produced and subliminally perceived (as when another's frown expresses unacknowledged discomfort at an unfulfilled expectation, and warns the actor of his departure from the normal routine, perhaps again without his being aware of it). Other forms of sanction range from complaints and protests, to punishments, divine retribution, or rebellions. Sanctions can, of course, be positive as well as negative, and either individual or social.

As Garfinkel has demonstrated, once a regularity of interactive behaviour becomes established, failure to follow the expected pattern makes participants feel uncomfortable; a failure is also understood to be a statement about the relationship. Such behaviour has meaning attributed to it, whether or not that meaning is 'intended', whether or not it is 'correct'. As AIP-users, we depend on predictability in order to construct our mental representations of plans based on anticipated responses. Whatever the origin of predictable patterns of behaviour (whether roles, rules, or personal relationships), when our expectations are violated we feel uncomfortable and, unless under some form of constraint, we do something to cause the wayward behaviour to return to 'normal'. Norms, rules and laws are terms used to refer to the kind of regularity that is publicly defensible. In this way they are indicators of expected regularity, and their defensibility asserts their social legitimacy. Norms, rules and laws have to do with the synchronizing of actions of individual actors in socially defined forms. They are about the transformation of individual attempts to reach goals through cooperation with or the coercion of another individual into socially constrained forms of action. The mechanisms of this synchronization, this transformation, are not always clear, and indeed should be far more central to our study of society than they are.[21]

The general mechanisms by which routines shape individual interaction as reciprocally interdependent must draw on and be represented in AIP modelling. The processes by which such routinized expectations come to be more widely shared as norms, rules or laws, are social rather than cognitive, but they must also be cognitively modelled. Such social processes clearly include the use of language to categorize and label, the linking of labels to roles, the sharing through language of expectations as norms, the explicit framing of rules and laws, the creation of cultural representations (such as mystical beings, totemic myths, and kinship systems), and the framing of cultural premises of causation, obligation and morality. The single feature that all these processes would seem to share in addition to the dependence on language is that their products are the result of social interdependence. These products – norms, beliefs, institutions and cultural premises – are emergent from, constructed through, the mutual negotiation of predictable patterns of behaviour. In Heritage's terms (1984), people are made accountable for their actions in social settings. This accountability produces, literally, accounts – to ourselves and to others – of our actions. It is these accounts which constitute the shared stuff of beliefs and institutions.

The cognitive modelling of others' contingent responses (AIP) seems likely to have driven the dramatic growth in primate intelligence. Ultimately AIP concerns the modelling of intentions, both my own intentions and what I deem to be the intentions of others.[22] Spoken language constitutes a uniquely powerful tool, both for modelling intentions and for seeking to influence them. Language, increasingly as grammar and syntax began to evolve, also proved to be a tool for constructing reality. More complex language made it possible to tell stories about the past, and about distant people and places; it made it possible to ask, and try to answer, questions about how and why things happen; language made it possible to map understanding of intentionality onto imagined worlds.

Themes from individual chapters

The original invitation urged participants to bring even rough drafts to the Workshop on Implications of a Social Origin of Intelligence, since this was intended as an opportunity to explore ideas. At the conclusion of the Workshop all agreed that we wished to pursue these questions by publishing papers; the present volume is the result. The contributions fall naturally into four sets focusing on different aspects, and different levels of social intelligence. The chapters in Part I concern what might be termed primary structures or processes. Part II concentrates on the implications for an hypothesis of social intelligence of the interactive negotiation of meaning in conversation. The two chapters in Part III describe how communicative genres are both shaped by wider institutional and historical processes, and yet act as tools with which individuals can manage interaction. Finally, Part IV includes papers which discuss ways in which the social bias in human intelligence is expressed in reasoning, in interaction, and in social institutions. Some chapters of course speak to more than one of these domains, and all address other issues as well. Here I pick up themes which are central for the general problem of the implications of an intelligence which is social in origin and in dynamics.

Part I   Primary processes

The stimulus to reformulate our understanding of human intelligence as profoundly social came from ethologists' reassessment of the development of primate intelligence. Richard Byrne's contribution to this volume (Chapter 1) provides an account of the current state of this exciting work, and argues for the central importance of the capacity for deception in the rapid increase in primate intelligence. Deception in social relation has the special quality of challenging the other to outwit the deceiver. Transactions built on deception thus are not closed, modelling and planning must always allow for revision to take account of further deception. The ape who was most skilful at deception literally outwitted the others in competition for scarce resources, resulting in selection pressure towards increasing deceptive skill. Byrne sees hominid intelligence as the result of yet more deception, i.e. of the continued operation of this same mechanism.

It is in the nature of AIP to model alternatives contingent on varied responses to ego's actions; this is evident in Humphrey's use of the chess game as a model for social intelligence. We would expect strategies for action, and for conversation, to reflect this need for flexibility. Perhaps during the evolution towards the hominidae there was a progression from modelling others' current actions, to modelling likely future actions, to modelling alternative possible future actions. The fact that others were also modelling with increasing complexity would drive the sort of escalation posited for Machiavellian intelligence. Here the element of deceit would be an aspect of goal-directed behaviour rather than the goal itself.

Byrne argues that in contrast to monkeys, there is evidence that apes model *intentions* of others as well as their immediate behaviour. Hence AIP has to include representation of possible intentional states as well as of instrumental actions; the possibility of deception would drive the modelling of intentional states of others. The need to model intentional states in others must have been directly linked to the recognition of intentional states in oneself, and chimpanzees' ability to recognize their own reflections suggests that this is so. Vygotsky would see recognition of our own intentional states as growing out of the practice of modelling others' intentions.

However, the capacity for anticipatory interactive planning provided a basis for cooperation as well as deception. Quite complex primate cooperation has been documented, both at the level of alliance against a more powerful individual (Harcourt and deWaal 1992) and of the males of a band against a hunted animal (Boesch and Boesch 1989). Stephen Levinson (Chapter 11) argues that cooperation is more difficult than deception since it requires mutual coordination of several individuals. It is clear that spoken language provided a many-faceted tool for forging and utilizing cooperation. Language facilitates cooperation at the level of the communication of shared meanings, and by controlling coordination of actions across considerable space, in the dark, and for the future. Critically, language permits *joint* planning, transforming individual AIP into a social process, and individual AIP strategies into social – cooperative – action. If there is an answer to the puzzle of the hominid transition, it may well lie in the power of the tool of language to transform individual AIP strategies into cooperatively planned and executed social action.

However the establishment of shared meanings is a problem. Bickerton (1990) considers reference to be the first of two major achievements which led to 'true' language. Levinson's chapter outlines in detail the difficulties in knowing what others mean by our words (and of course vice versa). This is the background to Edwin Hutchins's and Brian Hazlehurst's model for establishing shared meanings for a lexicon (Chapter 2). Critically, this model only works if there are two (or more) actors to exchange words and establish meanings. Each confirms the meaning for the other by responding appropriately and 'sending it back to him' in later exchanges. This is indeed an appropriate model for social intelligence itself. It only 'works' because there are two or more actors; and it 'works' through each actor taking account of information provided by the other to model contingent AIP strategies. The shared meanings which are the product of this process are social in the special sense that they cannot be constructed by an individual alone; they cannot be the product of any single cognitive process by itself, however brilliant the mind. If there *is* anything 'wired in' about human cognition, it may be the 'other' slot required for establishing common meanings and for the cognitive modelling of social interdependence. Recent work on infants' attunement to maternal signals suggests that this faculty develops virtually from birth (e.g. Trevarthen 1988).

This model for the construction of a lexicon could also be used to represent Vygotsky's view of how a child learns through joint participation with an 'expert' (Vygotsky 1962; Goody, Chapter 10, this volume). Since differential skills/knowledge among participants would be a feature of even the simplest hominid society, it would be interesting to incorporate this into the Hutchins and Hazlehurst model.

Mead's account of the recognition of self as both object and agent through hearing one's own speech, and observing others' response to it, takes on new meaning here. Indeed there is a sort of parallel between the duality of 'speaker' and 'hearer' and that between self as subject and as object. When we speak, we hear what others hear, and judge its meaning partly by how they respond. So the 'circuits' between speakers are, literally, replicated internally within each speaker. This argues strongly for spoken language as having played a central part in the emergence of self-consciousness as objectifiable both for each individual, and in human social formations.

The sensitive and original work of Nurit Bird-David (Chapter 3) with the Nayaka gatherer-hunters of south India has given new depth to our understanding of social life in tiny, face-to-face communities living at this lowest level of economic subsistence. Although of course they have spoken language, in fact she found that these people speak little among themselves. Relations between people who are in intimate proximity without pause, year after year, are patterned by spheres of avoidance and silence as well as by talk. With this strong sensitivity to individual privacy, ways of calling to and of addressing people take on special importance. Kin terms may be used like names, for address, as well as to attract a relative's attention. This, she points out, is a basis on which members of the community come to take alternative perspectives of one another. The individual one person calls to as 'father' is another's 'mother's brother'. We see here the emergence of social roles.

Instead of formally explicit roles and rules, Bird-David describes (with difficulty, as they are implicit in nature) *de facto* patterns which are a focus of feelings of obligation or uneasiness. She calls these 'quasi-norms', a term which nicely reflects their partially binding, unframed character. What she describes is an (open) set of individuals who have identicial life-styles, living in close proximity, and who somehow recognize that they feel the same way – approving or disapproving – about certain patterns of behaviour. Clearly here quasi-norms emerge from the constraints of daily practice. And in this tiny society individuals interact with sufficient frequency and stability that such norms 'need not' become explicit.[23] The picture which results is not of a Machiavellian society, but rather of simple but basic forms of cooperation, both in daily activities and in the management of social relationships themselves.

Although they do not speak a great deal about feelings, plans or the meaning of what they do, Nayaka use speech to manage many sorts of social action. Perhaps the Hutchins and Hazlehurst model for the establishing of a lexicon also fits the way in which the Nayaka establish common meanings for patterns of avoidance, *de facto* roles and quasi-norms. There are clearly important continuities between the emergence of lexical terms and implicit patterning of action.

The chapters in Part I highlight a number of primary processes: the challenge posed for cognitive modelling by deception, but also the power of cooperation; a model for establishing shared meanings for a lexicon which depends on systematic reciprocal exchange and confirmation of information between individuals; the emergent nature of *de facto* roles and implicit rules. These are not the only primary processes involved in social intelligence, but they do appear to be basic to many of the particular forms discussed in later chapters.

Part II   The negotiation of conversational meaning

These three chapters deal, at different levels, with the fine-grained analysis of informal conversation. They follow in a tradition based on the work of Garfinkel, Schegloff, Sacks and their colleagues in ethnomethodology and conversational analysis, which seeks to identify the routines and conventions which structure everyday interactions. These studies have shown that ordinary everyday life is not the casual, haphazard affair we often assume it to be. Instead, even very ordinary behaviour like taking turns in conversation follows surprisingly precise patterns, and people become highly agitated at any deviation. Increasingly researchers are asking fundamental questions about the way these implicit patterns emerge, how they influence the way in which people manage interaction, and how they influence the construction of meanings within this interaction.

A central point in Paul Drew's contribution is the importance of distinguishing between cognitive strategies and strategies for interaction. Close analysis of ordinary conversations reveals complex links between the two. These links tend to be mediated by conversational micro-routines such as the 'prefatory components' analysed by Streeck (Chapter 4) and the 'repairs' described by Drew (Chapter 5).

On the basis of his very detailed analysis of the sequencing of gesture and speech in conversations, Jürgen Streeck has isolated what appears to be a very general 'design feature of human action' – a prefatory component, expressed in speech and in gesture, which precedes overt action. Prefatory components ('pre's') prefigure intended actions by projecting indications for others to recognize. Such 'pre's' enable others to anticipate intended actions and to respond accordingly, thus synchronizing understandings of the participants. In their very nature, 'pre's' are tentative initial formulations of more important issues. They can be picked up or ignored by the partner in interaction 'off-stage', i.e. without any formal rejection of the overture. Because they are tentative, 'pre's' can easily be subsequently redefined without challenging the validity of the original form. As an example of their function in avoiding possible conflict in interaction, Streeck discusses an invitation made (tentatively) in 'pre' form which was ignored and never followed through.

Paul Drew uses formal conversational analysis to look at the relationship between conversational forms, cognitive strategies, and strategies for interaction. He identifies several types of interaction sequence: teases, the conversion of disagreements into agreements, and 'pre-requests'. In each case he distinguishes between the structural organization of the sequence, and the procedures through which it is utilized. An interaction sequence involves a patterned exchange of a certain form between speakers. A tease, for instance, challenges the validity of a prior statement in a gentle way which requires what linguists call 'repair' – that is, a revision of the original comment so that it avoids the initial 'error'. All these sequences are ways of carrying through a given conversational goal (of the individual) while maintaining the joint enterprise of the conversation itself. Thus the actual outcome is a product of joint interaction.

The several specific analyses of conversational sequences raise a number of critical issues for understanding the fit between individual cognitive modelling and the interaction between two (or more) different people. One such issue is the location of the synchronization of individual cognitive modelling within the interdependence of joint conversation routines and procedures. It would seem that procedures for conversational sequences are culturally framed and also linguistically patterned. Routines like a tease or a pre-request can be seen as tools available both 'to think with' and 'to interact with'.

Another issue concerns the level of awareness in the use of conversational sequences. In one sense sequences are emergent in conversation, as when one person's comment is interpreted as meriting a challenge which takes the form of a tease, leading to a repair of the original comment. AIP modelling here may be at the general level of an intention to maintain a given style of conversational interaction; hence the choice of a tease rather than a more direct challenge. But because the tease response is available as a routine, detailed planning is not required for its execution. It seems likely that routinization tends to reduce the level of awareness with which interactions are planned and executed. Levinson explicitly suggests this for what he calls 'heuristics' of spoken language (Chapter 11). Routinization of procedures requires recurrent practice and cultural framing. Both conditions seem to occur where a given conversational task is frequently encountered, as with the need for repair, avoidance of disagreements, and securing cooperation with individual goals.

The distinction between cognitive strategies and strategies for action is useful for thinking about both these issues. The synchronizing of AIP modelling of plans and goals of two (or more) individuals can be seen to occur both with cognitive strategies, and with strategies for action. Routines must be modelled at some level, whether with awareness or not. As routines are both linguistically and culturally framed, different actors are using more-or-less the same model for their cognitive strategies. Thus when these are brought into action strategies, the turns specified in the procedures are familiar to both participants, and the sequence can unfold smoothly.

The work of both Streeck and Drew provides striking evidence for the patterning of interaction on a level of which we are not aware. We see the cognitive modelling of AIP to be accompanied by communicative micro-strategies which permit delicate adaptation to each other's responses. To follow a formulation used by Thomas Luckmann (Chapter 8), the micro-communicative strategies of prefatory components of conversation permit the 'mutual adjustment of perspectives' necessary for effective solution of any communicative problem. Intuitively one feels that the modelling of cognitive strategies moves between levels of awareness depending on many factors, ranging from attention, to routinization of sequences, to degree of complexity, to whether responses of the other are as expected, to whether a given cognitive strategy is to be translated into action. This is clearly an area which needs further working out.

The inclusion of gesture in Streeck's work has a special relevance to the role of language in *Homo sapiens'* social intelligence. John Lyons (1988) and Merlin Donald (1991) have suggested that a language of gestures may well have preceded spoken language. A central aspect of this argument is the continuing importance of gesture in contemporary human conver-sation, and indeed the grammatical and lexical complexity and richness of sign languages used by the congenitally deaf. Streeck's evidence that gesture is used in the subtle negotiation of topic and intention is clearly consistent with the view of the importance of gestures in early hominid language. The contention of both these authorities that gestural language was prior to and separate from the emergence of the earliest spoken language seems extreme. If indeed spoken language emerged very gradually it may have been intimately linked with gesture from the beginning, at the time when the vocal tract was not yet specialized for complex speech.

If the power of language to structure the close coordination between interacting individuals is revealed in the conversational analyses of Chapters 4 and 5, in Chapter 6 David Good shows that there is still pressure to maintain individual freedom of action and the determination of meaning within the framework for cooperation constructed by and for conversation. The empirical starting point for his discussion is the observation that conversations are inherently ambiguous, and subject to constant reinterpretation and shifts of meaning. He argues that a critical difference between the use of AIP by primates and *Homo sapiens* arises from 'the way the language transforms the nature of time'. Here Good is not simply talking about the possibility of referring to past and future events; by describing again what has already happened, spoken utterances can give many interpretations, and later reinterpretations, to the same event. This retrospective reappraisal becomes as important as prospective planning: 'Foresight becomes focused on what hindsight can do' (p. 140). This creates the need to include in cognitive modelling both future and retrospective planning, and therefore makes different and much greater cognitive demands on AIP.

This possibility of restructuring meanings as a conversation progresses means that participants can slide out of ostensible social contracts, a Machiavellian realization of AIP in spoken language. It now becomes advantageous for each participant to maintain sufficient ambiguity to permit shifting meanings favourable to his objectives; at the same time each tries to constrain possible future re-interpretations by others.

Good is here delineating the implications of the full potential of spoken language for cognitive modelling of alternative strategies. When language has been incorporated into ways of thinking (about time, and about new understandings of past events), and ways of managing the use of conversation to achieve goals, the complexity of AIP increases dramatically. While he points out the potential this provides for deception, it is at the same time true that the whole enterprise of conversation itself rests on the elaborate cooperative synchronies described by Streeck and Drew.

Part III   Genres as tools that shape interaction

We have seen that close analysis of conversation reveals complex patterning linking cognitive strategies with strategies for interaction. Micro-routines like prefatory components and repairs often act as bridges between cognition and action. Indeed they tend to become routinized as

solutions to particular communicative problems such as avoiding conflict, and establishing and controlling meanings. Good suggests that
control over meaning can itself be the object of conversational strategies,
which can obscure and may even reverse meanings as talk proceeds.

This management of meanings as strategy in interaction can be seen in
the utilization of communicative genres such as politeness forms (Brown
and Levinson 1978, 1987), questions (E. Goody 1978a) or irony as
discussed in Chapter 7 by Penelope Brown. The Brown and Levinson
analysis of the linguistic and performative uniformities in politeness
across cultures has marked a paradigm shift in sociolinguistics, and
together with the Humphrey paper led to framing the notion of anticipatory interactive planning outlined in this Introduction. This early work
threw into sharp relief the importance of modelling intentions. To be
effective the modelling of others' possible actions must incorporate
assessment of their intentions – 'we positively seek out intentions in what
people say and do. There seems to be a universal premise that other
people's behaviour will be goal-oriented; . . . Very often this results in the
imputation of intention where no clear intention message is provided' (E.
Goody 1978b:12). This premise of intentionality makes interaction risky,
since our intentions are always apt to be interpreted in terms of other
people's goals rather than our own. Thus our actions easily are seen as
threatening others' self-esteem or their capacity to reach their own goals.
The genre of politeness is a mode of engaging in interaction (usually, but
not necessarily through conversation) which signals our intention not to
threaten either self-esteem or others' goals. But the power of the Brown
and Levinson model lies in its including factors influencing the ability to
facilitate or impede others' goals: power, social distance and ways in
which self-esteem and competence might be vulnerable. As Brown says
here 'This model ... makes very strong assumptions about humans'
abilities to reason reflexively about each others' desires and intentions'
(p. 154). Speakers have to be able to modify their communicative
expression of intentions accordingly, as hearers must 'be able to read such
modification as evidence that the speaker is inferring particular things
about their own views, desires and intentions' (p. 154). And she notes that
communication of this elaborateness seems so complex as to be impossible. Use of conventional forms – e.g. for politeness – is clearly one way of
cutting through these layers of reflexive inference. And indeed this is
presumably how such conventional forms emerge in every society.
Because Brown's analysis is so fine-grained she is able to show that Tzeltal
irony has become normatively stabilized around three sub-modes, off
record and ambiguous, negatively polite and positively polite; as well as
being able to convey the intention to be impolite. However her analysis
shows definitely that conventional forms in turn come to be used in

nuanced ways which depend on the understanding of presumed intentions in this particular context. Further, choice of how irony is used is strongly influenced by social role. Women frequently use irony to emphasize shared opinions and understandings, and to elicit sympathy. Where normally women stress solidarity and suppress anger, in the context of confrontation in a court the same genre is, as it were, inverted to convey hostility.

We see at work here the emergence of routines for handling particular tasks, but the use of these routines then itself becomes an element in the cognitive and strategy modelling. It is as if where there is a premise of cooperation, as among kin, friends and other women, irony is employed to express solidarity; where there is a premise of hostility, as in the antagonistic confrontation of a court case, irony is used to express hostility; and where the relationship is ambiguous the use of irony achieves at least a surface agreement, and 'provides a negotiated end to the topic' (p. 169). As Good argues, there are situations in which such tools will be employed to maintain ambiguity, and thus enhance control over emergent meanings (Brown's 'ambiguous case').

Thus we see that Tzeltal use of the ironic genre does not so much focus on problems of sustaining communicative interaction, as on problems of managing meanings and social relationships themselves. In a final twist to the story, Brown finds that irony is unusually elaborated in this Amerindian society which, for the 500 years since the coming of the Spaniards, has been in a subordinate position in its own land; and that within Tzeltal society it is structurally subordinate women who make the greatest use of irony. Irony, she argues, is a common strategy for the underdog since it permits off-the-record complaints that can be innocently disavowed if necessary. It seems that where a society or social segment is structurally subordinate, routines which are individually effective may come to be culturally elaborated as a widely shared genre.[24]

The fundamental question for Thomas Luckmann (Chapter 8) is how communication and effective interaction are possible between discrete individuals. (This is, in another form, the problem of establishing shared lexical meaning discussed in Chapter 2, and reflects Levinson's puzzlement over the possibility of mutual understanding, in Chapter 11.) The answer lies, he believes, in mechanisms for the reciprocal adjustment of perspectives, which in turn both requires and permits patterning of communication. This occurs on many levels ranging from the 'givens' of phonology, morphology, semantics and syntax, through linguistic styles and dialects, to the implicit and explicit shaping by roles, rules and institutions.

Adjustments of perspective may take place automatically when situations are clearly predefined. Here one might say that AIP planning has become routinized. At the other extreme, where background knowledge is faulty, or doesn't work, 'almost everything . . . must be negotiated "locally"' through trial-and-error explorations of perspectives of the participants. Luckmann sees genres as emerging from replicated experiences of solving communicative problems of the same kind falling between these two extremes of routinization and trial-and-error. Specific communicative problems are normally solved in communicative repair procedures (cf. Streeck and Drew, Part II). It is the normal mutual assumption of actors that social models exist for this. 'When such modelling reaches a high degree of structural "closure", and when it is associated with intersubjectively recognized formal constraints, we are in the presence of comunicative genres' (pp. 179–80). Thus communicative genres are socially constructed models for the solution of specific types of communicative problems. They become part of the stock of shared social knowledge of a particular society at a particular time. The general nature of such communicative problems is in the form of conversational dialogue. 'The elementary function of communicative genres in social life is to organize, routinize and render (more or less) obligatory the solutions to recurrent communicative problems' (p. 182).

Genres emerge because the underlying fundamental problem in communicative processes is the reciprocal adjustment of perspectives. (This reciprocal adjustment of perspectives is also a prerequisite for effective AIP modelling of interaction strategies.) Genres assist in the reciprocal adjustment of perspectives in two ways: by providing easily recognizable markers for the mutual adjustment of perspectives (e.g irony, politeness forms); and because genres help to maintain interlocking perspectives in the production and reception of communicative interaction.

Just why the attribution of intentions should be so central becomes clear in the view of human intelligence as essentially social. The modelling of others' possible responses to one's own actions (AIP) *depends* on judgements of others' intentions. The 'face wants' of the Brown and Levinson politeness model are fascinating and fundamental. The concept of negative politeness refers to 'the desire not to be impeded in one's actions'. This is indeed basic to all AIP strategies; they are about how to reach goals with minimum interference. In this sense it is prior to particular strategies.

The desire to be approved of, liked, admired, validated – which is seen to underlie 'positive politeness' – is surely a universal human characteristic. It is so familiar we take it for granted. We are so accustomed to living with, and managing, this need to be approved that despite the considerable literature on 'face' (beginning with Goffman's classic *The Presentation of Self in Everyday Life* (1962)) it has not really been addressed. But *why* should this matter so much to us? Perhaps because any expectation that others will cooperate with our AIP strategies depends on their valuing us sufficiently to do so. If we feel approved, liked, then it is possible to expect that the other will be prepared to recognize *our* goals as valid as well as his own. Of course if the other really values us, then cooperation will become his own goal, and he too will seek the negotiation AIP strategies that are jointly advantageous. If we sense that we are not approved of, not taken as valid, then we expect 'our acts to be interfered with' and the interaction takes on a confrontational form. An AIP strategy must take account of this. Levinson argues (Chapter 11, this volume) that cooperation is more complex than competitive, agonistic relations, and has been more fundamental in the emergence of human society. Indeed it seems likely that we tend to attribute a general 'cooperative' or 'antagonistic' stance to others first, and that this then shapes more specific attributions.

Part IV   Expressions of a social bias in intelligence

The final part is concerned with ways in which contemporary human intelligence can be seen to express the social bias originally identified in work on sub-human primates. The analyses of conversational interactions in earlier parts are clearly also about social bias. They document finely the intricacies of the interdependence of speakers in the microdynamics of conversation, and the emergence of culturally idiomatic communicative genres for managing interaction. And indeed the chapters in this section draw also, in one way or another, on the way in which spoken language is employed to solve problems of social living. Prayer and narrative clearly depend on speaking, and express in this sense the social bias of what Luckmann terms 'dialogic form'. And in a new approach to understanding divination, David Zeitlyn shows that this too can be seen to use a dialogue template.

However these authors are also concerned with social bias rooted in the cognitive modelling of contingent interdependence itself. They argue, in different ways, that this leads to a concern with understanding and explaining our experience in terms of our motivations and the intentions we attribute to others. What happens to us is understood as the result of purposive action, and we tend to explain what happens by the attribution of appropriate intentions to the agents – whatever they may actually have intended (E. Goody 1978b).

Such a primacy of intentionality is consistent with our cognitively modelling the constraints of social interdependence (AIP). For knowledge of what another intends to do can only enhance the accuracy of our model. Zeitlyn (Chapter 9) and Levinson (Chapter 11) argue that the social bias of attributing intentionality to events which are in fact random influences the very way in which we define problems and understand solutions. Both Levinson and Michael Carrithers (Chapter 12) see human thought as preoccupied with making sense of experience using social relations and intentionality as an explanatory model. Carrithers's term narrativity refers to our need to organize our thinking, as well as our talking, so as to construct a story which makes sense of our experiences as this is defined in our particular society and culture. And of course by telling stories to each other, we establish common understanding of shared experiences, yet another expression of the Hutchins and Hazlehurst model in Chapter 2. Prayers employ the dialogic mode to actually seek to change the way the world is. We may use prayer to seek to influence the intentions of spiritual powers; and we may in part do this by asserting the excellence of our own intentions. Social bias then involves the use of social interdependence as a model for thinking with.

David Zeitlyn analyses his detailed transcriptions of Mambila divination sessions as though they were conversations between *Nggam* (divination itself) and the local diviner. Since the effectively random movements of the burrowing crab used in Mambila divination yield contradictory answers to the questions posed by the diviner, this seems to support the view that such divination cannot provide rational solutions to problems. The diviner, however, does not treat the responses as contradictory, but as indicating that he must formulate the questions differently or include a wider range of factors. In fact there is experimental evidence that when sophisticated westerners are given contradictory answers to personal problems they too succeed in rationalizing these in very similar ways. In both cases the questioner assumes that the one answering must be giving knowledgeable and rational replies; that the problem lies in the way he is framing the questions or interpreting the answers. Empirically it seems that there is a 'premise of intentionality' underlying divination which matches the constraints which make dialogue possible (Grice 1989).

The premise of intentionality underlying divination is also consistent with a view of social intelligence based on the modelling of causality in terms of contingent interaction between actors. It is as though there is an 'other' slot in our cognitive model in which we represent the responses and plans of those with whom we interact. The underlying question in Esther Goody's chapter on prayer is 'Why, when there is no direct evidence of anyone listening, do people pray?' Of course on one level prayer reflects the cultural construction of cosmologies around deities demanding prayer. However there are religions like Buddhism which formally reject prayer, in which, nevertheless, prayer plays a major role. And there are individuals who say they do not believe in religion, but who turn to prayer in time of crisis. Within the framework of social cognition, prayer 'makes sense' as a way of solving problems *as though* they were caused by a social other. Through speaking/praying to the other we seek to account for our own actions, to understand His intentions, and solicit His help. The blissful peace which accompanies deep meditation may indicate a suspension of the AIP modelling process, with its demands of representing multiple contingencies and elusive intentions.

A number of studies have reported that otherwise highly intelligent people demonstrate 'a curious inability to use logical reasoning'. In Chapter 11, Stephen Levinson brings together a wide range of material to confront this paradox, arguing that people tend to use forms of reasoning which are effective for solving problems arising out of social interdependence, and they prefer these forms, even when presented with 'logical' problems. This is indeed a 'social bias in intelligence'.

Parallel with this account of social biases in human thought, Levinson pursues the problem of how it is possible for humans to successfully use language. How can we possibly know what is meant by gestures, and even words? (This problem is also central for Hutchins and Hazlehurst, and for Luckmann.) He considers several previous explanations of this puzzle and finds them inadequate. Instead he suggests that understanding is only possible through following signals which indicate the speaker's intentions, and that these greatly restrict the otherwise incomprehensible range of meanings that might apply. If we depend on such heuristic signals to interpret each other's speech and actions, then in learning to speak and understand we must learn to think of causation as embedded in meanings and intentions. It is precisely such assumptions which experimental subjects do in fact make when they fail to 'think logically'. Thus, Levinson argues, in order to make sense of the actions and talk of those we interact with, we have had to learn to take account of their plans and intentions. We have learned, in effect, a premise of intentionality, and we apply this way of thinking even to those events which are quite random. Both the discussion of divination in Chapter 9 and of prayer in Chapter 10 offer evidence of the human reluctance to accept that events occur by chance.

In focusing on the narrative mode of understanding, 'the ability to create, narrate and comprehend stories' (p. 261) Michael Carrithers may appear to be abandoning an interest in social intelligence for folklore. However the cognitive psychologist Jerome Bruner has recently argued that there are two distinctively different sorts of thought, the logical mode and the narrative mode; and that 'narrative deals with the vicissitudes of intention' (1986:17). Carrithers broadens the concept of narrativity by pointing out that it functions simultaneously on the cognitive and on the social plane, enabling us to both understand the flow of social events, and to convey this understanding to others. Further, he suggests that sharing stories is a 'particularly powerful form of interactive planning' because it brings together accounts of the past and of present events in a way that makes possible planning for future joint action. We might add that narrative brings the individual planning of AIP out into the arena of shared action; planning becomes a social product. In the case of Kaluli stories the describing of past events vividly recalls both the social dynamics – witchcraft, a fight, calling brothers-in-law to plant bananas – and the associated emotions. It is the combination of the meaning of past events and the evoking of associated emotions which makes plans for the future seem to follow necessarily from what has already happened. Like David Good, Carrithers stresses the power of spoken language to transform our experience of time. There are also interesting resonances here with Good's stress on conversational ambiguity, potential reversibility and contests for control over meanings.

To emphasize the socially dynamic nature of story-telling Carrithers offers the term 'confabulate', for 'together making a story'. However, he suggests that in making their stories, people also confabulate – make together – their social worlds. This confabulation creates several kinds of reality: for the individual it creates an account of personal experience that makes 'sense', and can continue to structure past and future experience; for the set of people who together make the narrative it creates a *shared* view of past, present and future to which they are all in some measure committed, since they contributed to its creation; and for both individuals and the group what is made is social action, perhaps an exchange of pigs, perhaps a vengeful attack.

This discussion of narrative raises again the issue of how shared meanings are established. But where Hutchins and Hazlehurst model a possible basis for naive strangers to develop shared meanings, in our real worlds narrative is built on 'cultural scenarios', templates for meaningful relationships between certain actions and certain consequences.[25] Carrithers also stresses the particularity of personal experiences in narrative. This not only provides 'news value' but as it were anchors the story in our immediately shared world; it is *our* story. If the story is to legitimately make social action, then it has to be certified relevant. For ultimately it is the joint participation in 'doing confabulation' which gives it its power to create shared meaning and plan action.

Notes

1 This modelling ability seems to underlie what Sperber and Wilson (1986; Sperber 1990), refer to as *inferential communication* in which 'communication is achieved by producing and interpreting evidence' without resort to a linguistic 'code' (1986:2).

2 See Bickerton 1990, ch. 6; Phyllis Lee, personal communication.

3 See especially MacNeilage, 'The evolution of hemispheric specialization for manual function and language' (1987); MacNeilage, Studdert-Kennedy, and Lindblom, 'Primate handedness reconsidered' (1987); Greenfield, 'Language tools and brain: the ontogeny and phylogeny of hierarchically organized sequential behavior' (1991).

4 Hominid adaptations of the primate vocal tract for speaking are costly; both breathing and swallowing are less efficient, choking is not uncommon, and there is a strong possibility that cot deaths in human infants are linked to these changes (Lieberman 1991:53–7; Phyllis Lee, personal communication).

5 The evidence from fossil hominid endocasts suggests a radical difference in the structure of the brains of *Australopithecus* and *H. habilis*, with the latter having an enlargement of the parieto-occipito-temporal junction (POT) which has been identified as 'the association area of association areas' (Geschwind 1965, quoted by Wilkins and Dumford, 1990:763). It has been argued that the presence of a developed POT is the basis of the ability for spoken language. If this datum and the related arguments are substantiated by subsequent archaeological finds then even *habilis* may have used an early form of protolanguage (Wilkins and Dumford 1990). Such a protolanguage might well have combined gesture and vocalization (*pace* Bickerton and Donald – neither of whom offers a convincing argument as to why early protolanguage need have used a single channel). It need not have required changes in the vocal tract; Lieberman has argued that the ape vocal tract would be adequate for a simple spoken protolanguage *if* they had the necessary neural structures to support it (1991).

6 Malinowski, writing on language use in the Trobriand Islands in relation to meaningful communication noted what he termed 'phatic communion' – conversational forms which actually conveyed little information but which he saw as critical for managing social relationships.

7 Lieberman has stressed the significance of speed of speaking and of decoding speech for the transmission of long messages within the constraints of human short-term memory and information processing (e.g. 1991:38); the linguists' paradox of the human ability to produce an infinite number of new sentences from a finite language corpus is due to the recombinative potential of syntax.

8 'The general process of *automatization* . . . allows us to learn to rapidly execute complex goal-directed patterns . . .' It 'converts a series of *learned* motor instructions into a "sub-routine" that is stored in the motor cortex and executed as a complete whole' (Lieberman 1991:48). The concept refers specifically to the learning of motor control subroutines. Lieberman is discussing the automatization of speech production which combines planning of what to say and how to say it. Grammar and syntax similarly involve combinations of what is said and how it is said, though the 'how' has shifted from the motor cortex to the areas responsible for planning speech. If learned motor instructions can be automatized, why cannot learned grammar and syntax instructions also be automatized?

9 The implications of classification for cognitive complexity are discussed by, among others, G. Miller (1956), Miller and Johnson-Laird (1976) and Goodenough (1990).

10 The difficulty with the Sperber–Wilson discussion of the opposition between inferred and coded meaning lies in the problem of how individuals know what to infer from others' behaviour. The implication is that coded meanings exist 'out there in language' (but are cognitively decoded) while inferred meanings exist in others' behaviour and are also made sense of cognitively. However, most of the clues on which we base social inference are either partly cultural (in which case they too have a culturally coded meaning, it just isn't in words), or they take their meaning from shared experience, as it were a private code. The Chomskian stress on language as code masks the important fact that language constantly creates a shared focus of attention and shared meanings in a far more explicit way than where communication is based on inference from non-linguistic behaviour.

11 The term 'mands' has been used to represent this generic aspect of control in conversation (Whiting and Edwards 1988).

12 'Phatic' presumably from 'emphatic' meaning 'forcibly expressive' from the Greek *emphaino*, an appearance, a declaration; this appears in Malinowski's contribution to Ogden and Richards's pathbreaking *The Meaning of Meaning* (1927).

13 A private totemic world would be a psychotic delusion; but shared by others it becomes the basis for birth, marriage and death – for social reality.

14 There is a large recent literature on 'activity theory' in relation to learning. The interested reader may gain an overview by looking at: Vygotsky (1978), Luria (1979), Wertsch (1985a), Rogoff (1990).

15 Reported by Ryan in the UK and Goody in northern Ghana, cited and discussed in E. Goody (1978a).

16 The relationship between intentionality and awareness, how these relate to goal-directed behaviour, and in turn to routinization and automatization is, to say the least, problematic. The work of Leslie (1987), Velmans (1991) and Dennett (e.g. 1983, 1988) indicates the range involved and some of the issues. The planning of social intelligence (AIP) is probably best seen as shifting between levels of intentionality and awareness in achieving socially constrained goals.

17 The work of Argyle on gaze and Hall and his colleagues on body language and response to cultural variations in patterns of proximity and touching are particularly interesting examples (Argyle 1968, and Hall 1959).

18 There is a huge anthropological literature on 'the gift'. Apart from Mauss's original article, the single most significant contribution is probably Marilyn Strathern *The Gender of the Gift* (1988).

19 This theme is developed in the 'Working papers on implications of a social origin of intelligence', E. Goody n.d. [1990; 1993].

20 This view draws heavily on S.F. Nadel's discussion of role in relation to the articulation of individual and social institutions (1957).

21 The recent prominence of vigilanti movements in places as far apart as Tanzania and New York reminds us that this process is never finished; new problems of synchronization are likely to lead to the emergence of new mechanisms. See R.G. Abrahams 1989.

22 Bruner's discussion of narrative intelligence begins by proposing that intention constitutes a primitive category system in terms of which experience is organized, indeed one even more 'primitive' than causality (1986:18–19). This is exactly what we would expect with a social intelligence based on modelling actions of others, which is dependent on their intentions.

23 One wonders what is the significance for this non-framed implicitness of norms of the total absence of formal authority roles which might back up assertions of what is right. Perhaps if there is no 'might', there is no 'right'. See E. Goody 1987.

24 The cultural elaboration of the insult in early modern Italy as described by Peter Burke is another instance of genre shaped by 'local' constraints – here class, status and concept of honour (1987).

25 The cultural shaping of templates for narrative is of critical importance for establishing shared meanings. This can be particularly problematic for children of different sub-cultures in early schooling. See Heath 1983 and Michaels 1986.

PART I

Primary processes

RICHARD W. BYRNE

1 The ape legacy: the evolution of Machiavellian intelligence and anticipatory interactive planning

There appears to be a yawning gulf in sophistication and complexity between the subject matter of social anthropology – ritual, language, religion, negotiation, taboo, obligation – and the behaviour of a group of monkeys. But unless one takes the view that the possession of language utterly changed the mental life and cognitive structures of our ancestors (and such a view will see any research on the origin of human mentality as a fruitless task), there must *be* an evolutionary connection.

In order to know in what spheres of human activity this connection might become visible, and what form any legacy of our evolutionary heritage might take, it would help first to know how our ancestors came to be intelligent: what selection pressures led to the evolution of human cognition? While the traditional view has emphasized the impact of tool-making, ever since suggestions were made of an alternative, social, pressure towards high intelligence (Jolly 1966a; Humphrey 1976), there has been interest in developing social models of human intellectual evolution. Perhaps more surprisingly, there is considerable evidence supporting the basic idea (see papers in Byrne and Whiten 1988). Primates display remarkable social complexity in their social manipulations. Since the ends of these manipulations are – at least in non-humans – always selfish, even where the means involve some cooperation, and since the process often appears impressively cunning, Byrne and Whiten (1988) named this Humphrey–Jolly hypothesis 'Machiavellian intelligence'.

Distinguishing among the alternative theories depends on finding phylogenetic differences in intelligent behaviour among animals other than humans, and this chapter will sketch the evidence that some non-human primates differ intellectually from other animals. In the first place, these data make a case in favour of accepting social complexity as the evolutionary pressure that started the chain of increasing intellectual sophistication that led, ultimately, to the stuff of social anthropology. But the same data, when viewed comparatively, can also suggest what mental faculties were possessed by those species ancestral to humans.

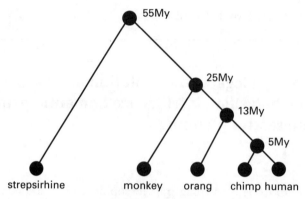

Figure 1.1 Modern evolutionary taxonomy of primates. The diagram is a cladogram, showing the pattern of shared ancestry of the five primate groups referred to in the text. The evidence comes largely from molecular taxonomy, including immunological distances, DNA hybridization and especially the comparison of detailed sequences of large fragments of DNA – the genetic 'code'. All these methods agree on the basic pattern, and there seems no room for any doubt that this is correct. The dates of each split (and thus of the inferred common ancestor of the modern forms) are less certain. However, those given here are consistent with recent sequencing of large strings of both mitochondrial DNA and of a pseudogene, an unexpressed portion of nuclear DNA. The patterns thus found have been calibrated with the most reliable ape fossil now known, an ancestral form of orangutan (*Sivapithecus*) from 13 million years.

It was in an animal with these faculties – and in no other – that language and all other uniquely human skills developed, and so there is every reason to suppose that modern modes of human cognition *required* these ancestral skills, or at least that modern thinking *accommodated* to primate skills rather than replacing them. Thus the chapter can also serve to chart the legacy of intelligence's evolutionary origin in social manoeuvring: the styles of thought that no being whose intellect was evolutionarily derived via a non-social route would possess. As such, its aim is to allow any such 'residues' to be identified the more easily, if they do indeed occur in human thinking.

Classifying primates

It will be useful first to divide the modern primates into three groups, of differing relatedness to human beings (see Figure 1.1). Firstly, there are *strepsirhine* primates such as lemurs, galagos and lorises (for purposes of using the comparative method to derive the 'best-bet' characteristics of ancestral species, this grouping replaces prosimians, a category which also included the tarsiers – now classified with the monkeys). Strepsirhines are separated from humans by around 55–90 million years of independent evolution (R.D. Martin 1990), and in many ways appear similar in form to the earliest primates known from fossils. The rest of the extant primates (which are called haplorhines), can be conveniently divided into the monkeys and the apes. *Monkeys* includes tarsiers, New World monkeys and Old World monkeys, taxa which split off from the line of human descent at various times, the most recent of which was 25–35 million years ago.

However, humans themselves are part of the other group, the *apes*, and among the apes it is now certain that humans are much more closely related to some species than others. There are many uncertainties in attaching even an approximate time-scale to any of the measures of evolutionary similarity (*ibid.*), but there is now no doubt that the African apes (chimpanzees and gorillas) are more closely related to humans than are the Asian apes (Oxnard 1981; Sibley and Ahlquist 1984) – indeed, from the chimp point of view, humans are a closer cousin than orangutans! As an illustrative example, taking the Old World monkeys to have diverged from apes at 30 million years and using immunological similarity, gives the last common ancestor of human and chimpanzee a date of 5 million years, not long before the earliest known *Australopithecines*, while the orangutan is separated by 10 million years (Sarich and Wilson 1967).

Comparing primate brain sizes

In contrasting these three groups, use will be made of brain size as well as behavioural data. The reason for using such an indirect measure of intellectual ability, which tells us nothing about the type of intellect and anyway itself needs to be validated as a measure, is a certain desperation. There is a long history of work in comparative psychology, trying to find out how animals differ in their intellectual abilities by testing them with problems set in the laboratory (see review by Warren 1973). Over the years, many of the differences that have been hailed as due to intelligence have been found merely to reflect differences in the ease of motivating different species, or in the sensory and motor aptitudes of the animals. Indeed some would go so far as to say that the general picture shows no intellectual differences between any animal groups (Macphail 1985). Certainly, we now realize that intelligence is such a slippery concept to define and quantify fairly that it seems less unreasonable – and it is often done – to take the brain size of the animal as an indirect measure of it – one which at least can be accurately estimated.

To compare brain sizes properly, it is necessary to take account of two characteristics of growth and form. Larger animals, in general, have larger brains; this is not particularly surprising, since for most mammals, much of the brain is taken up with sensory and motor processes. Secondly, as the absolute size of living things changes, so the relative proportions of their parts is liable to change. In this case, absolutely larger animals have relatively smaller brains than one would expect from linearly enlarging smaller animals. A technique that takes account of both of these difficulties is called *allometric scaling*. In it, a double logarithmic plot of something, in this case brain size, is made against body size for the given group of animals. This forces the species points onto an approximate straight line. Then we can see whether any particular animal in the group lies above the line (has a relatively larger brain than one might expect), on the line (has average brain size), or below the line (has a relatively small brain). This technique has limitations (see below), but it is the one used standardly now to compare animals' brain sizes.

When we apply allometric scaling to brain sizes of mammals, we find that primates as a whole are larger brained than most other groups (Jerison 1973). And using the same techniques, we find that humans have brains three times as large as we would expect from even a monkey of human size (Passingham 1982), which of course tends to give us confidence in the relationship between relative brain volume and intelligence! But when we separate the strepsirhine primates from the rest, the strepsirhines emerge as a perfectly typical group of mammals (Passingham and Ettlinger 1974): in other words, in general they have brains about the size one would expect from their body sizes. The monkeys and apes, however, have brains twice as large as normal mammals of their size. What are they using these large brains for?

Comparing intelligence among primates

Primates have an everyday reputation for greater cleverness than most mammals, but can we quantify this? Certainly monkeys and apes do not emerge as outstanding when intelligence is measured in the laboratory (see review by Passingham 1982). The best that can be said is that when animals of various groups are trained on the same task, it frequently turns out that monkeys are able to reach the required criterion very much *quicker* than rats, cats, squirrels, or whatever (Passingham 1981). Conversely, when animal *curiosity* is tested, for instance by presenting novel objects to animals housed in a zoo, monkeys remain interested in the objects for longer than other animals (Glickman and Scroges 1966).

These differences in curiosity and mental speed are matters of degree, and fairly minor degree at that. However in recent years there have been a number of suggestions that the lack of species variation is an artifact of the tasks used (Jolly 1966a; Humphrey 1976). If the increase in brain size of monkeys and apes was promoted by social needs, and the resulting intelligence was therefore shaped for social skill, then the gadgetry of the laboratory will be a very blunt instrument for its assessment. Have we let our own technological superiority, perhaps largely developed since language evolved, mislead us into believing that this was what intelligence was all about?

Socially smart monkeys

In the social arena the distinctiveness of monkeys from strepsirhine primates (and from non-primate animals) is more striking. This is apparent in several ways.

Most animals interact in dyads with one other animal at a time, but in monkeys interactions are frequently *triadic*, with a third party crucially affecting what happens in the dyad. Not only may the third party choose to intervene, but the interactants sometimes visibly take this into account: for instance, a threatened female hamadryas baboon may run to and sit in front of her harem-leader male, so that any threat directed to her is necessarily also directed to the male (Kummer 1967).

While many animals compete with fighting strength or weaponry, monkeys rely far more on social *alliances* to give them power and influence in social groups (see review by Harcourt 1988). These alliances may often be among close kin, but in addition long-term *friendships* are found (Ransom 1981; Strum 1983; Smuts 1985); these friendships persist over a number of years, and confer mutual benefits – sometimes the rewards are of different kinds for each participant, as in a barter system. In building up friendships, or merely putting together a temporary alliance, the 'trade currency' that is used among monkeys is *social grooming*. As a result, monkeys groom each other far more than would be necessary for health purposes.

Primatologists analyse the social dynamics of monkey societies in terms of patterns of kinship, friendship, and rank. Recent work has shown that the monkeys themselves do the same: monkeys are *socially knowledgeable* as well as socially complex. In both macaques and baboons, individuals who have been attacked aim 'redirected' aggression to innocent parties, but the choice of victims shows that they are well aware who the relatives or friends of their persecutors are (Judge 1982; Smuts 1983), a sort of monkey vendetta. In experimental tests, monkeys easily learn and use the concept of 'mother of' (Dasser 1988). And a series of experiments (Seyfarth and Cheney 1988; Cheney and Seyfarth 1988), playing back pre-recorded calls to vervet monkeys to study their reactions under controlled conditions, has shown that they have knowledge of dominance relations of third parties as well as their kinship, and even know the membership of vervet groups which they have never themselves entered. This knowledge shows up in the strength and type of their reaction to calls which are not specifically directed at them, yet convey information about other individuals. For instance, individuals normally do not react much to the calls of vervets who are not members of their group. But when a call is artificially manipulated to suggest that one of these animals has transferred groups (so now calls from an unexpected direction), the hearer's reaction shows its surprise. It should be noted that, while monkeys show knowledge of one another's kin and friends, they may not distinguish *between* these concepts: in most cases, and all those experimentally tested, the relationship could be subsumed under some rubric like 'looks after', and exactly why monkey A looks after monkey B may not be clear to the monkey.

Finally, monkeys also differ from strepsirhine primates in the way that they use tactics of *deception* with some regularity to achieve goals in their everyday lives (Byrne and Whiten 1990, 1992). For instance, a female monkey, living in a small group with a powerful male who prohibits her social or sexual contact with other subordinate males, may use a number of tactics to give her the freedom she desires. She may simply 'get left behind' so that she is fully out of sight of her leader male before she socializes or copulates; she may carry out her actions with unusual quietness, for instance suppressing the copulation calls that she would normally make; or, perhaps most subtly of all, she may remain partly in the sight of her leader, but adjust her position so that she can carry out prohibited acts which cannot be seen from his viewpoint. All monkey groups sometimes use tactical deception, but the African savannah baboons do so significantly more than others (*ibid.*).

All this implies that monkeys are in some way 'better' than most animals, including the 25 per cent of primates classed as strepsirhines, at certain kinds of learning – and in particular they are *better at representing socially relevant information about conspecifics and using this information to gain rewards in group living*. It seems unlikely to be a coincidence that this enhanced ability to learn and plan, which largely shows up in social contexts and in taking account of the social attributes and typical reactions of other players, occurs in animals whose brain volume is also much larger than would be expected in animals of their weight.

Empathic apes

But how do humans compare intellectually with their much closer relatives, the great apes? In terms of relative brain size, apes do not notably differ from monkeys (Clutton-Brock and Harvey 1980). However one must add two caveats to that statement. Firstly, the method of working out a relative brain size assumes that the extra volume, over that minimally required to service the bodily needs of sensory and motor systems – in other words the 'computational part' – is some multiplicitive fraction of total volume. So, 5 per cent extra brain is equally useful for intelligence in a 5kg animal or a 50kg animal, even though the extra brain tissue is far larger in the second case, and contains far more neurons. This is a very odd assumption for anyone used to computational machines, since these are chiefly limited in power by the number of their elements.

One can instead make a different assumption, that of additive volumes, in which what matters is not the percentage of the total that is in excess, but the absolute volume free for computation (and the number of neurons, which also scales allometrically with brain volume at a different slope). This assumption is less tractable mathematically, but on it the living great apes all have more 'extra neurons' than those of any monkey (Jerison 1973), since they are much larger animals than monkeys. (Fortunately for our egos, humans both extant and extinct turn out to have considerably larger numbers of extra neurons than do modern apes.) The great apes also have a generally larger 'neocortical ratio', the ratio of neocortex to the rest of the brain, than do monkeys (Dunbar 1992b), and it is the neocortex which has chiefly enlarged during primate evolution.

The second caveat is that there are problems in trying to compare allometrically the brains of animals which differ in diet type: a larger gut makes the abdomen larger but requires little brain expansion, so it may be invalid to compare species adapted for different diet qualities. Scaling against body length instead of weight helps a bit, but the length of primate bodies is still heavily influenced by gut size. Though all great apes have a broadly similar type of gut, they do vary in their adaptedness to coarse food, i.e. in the size of their large intestines. In fact, the gut sizes rank gorilla > orangutan > chimpanzee > > human. This is exactly the inverse of their relative brain sizes!

In any case, there is little doubt in most researchers' minds that in fact apes are at least as adept socially as monkeys. Yet this has been less studied in the case of apes, apparently because apes are less easily manipulated into test situations. Many of the tests of monkey social knowledge have used field playback of calls, a technique which has only been done successfully with apes in the very simplest and most obvious of ways. Perhaps the very difficulty of experimentally manipulating apes should tell us something about their intelligence! Where there is evidence for the apes, it is consistent with the idea that apes are just as socially smart as monkeys.

Chimpanzee and gorilla societies show female transfer (and in general they are patrilocal), so the monkey hallmarks, of power groups consisting of extended matrilines and the acquisition of female rank by the support of relatives, seldom occur. In the few cases where chimpanzee and gorilla females have remained in their natal groups, they have gained rank from the support of their mothers, just like monkeys do (Goodall 1986, for chimpanzees; personal observation for gorillas). Male rank is also attained largely by social support in chimpanzees, but in a different way. In a number of known cases in the wild, the younger of a pair of brothers close in age gains the highest rank with the support of his elder sibling. Where such obvious kin support is lacking, the particular ways that chimpanzees use grooming to forge friendships, and use friendship and alliances to gain power (deWaal 1982; Nishida 1983; Goodall 1986), suggest that they have even greater sophistication than monkeys in social manipulation. Direct comparisons have been made to the recommendations of Niccolò Machiavelli, as regards the benefits of rising to power with the support of many weak allies rather than a few strong ones, and the use of the special status of a 'kingmaker' to gain the ultimate power without ever possessing the strongest resources.

So apes too are generally considered to be socially adept; but increasingly, information is emerging that implies more than this. Converging lines of evidence suggest that the knowledge and understanding of the great apes (or at least some of them) are of a quite different *type* to that of monkeys, going beyond the enhanced learning and complex planning of monkeys.

Understanding mirrors

Most animals, when confronted with a mirror in which they can see themselves, give an initial reaction that is appropriate to a strange member of their species, and then habituate or get bored and show no further reaction to mirrors. Monkeys are unusual, in that they can learn to use mirrors, for instance to see round a corner and identify another monkey there (Anderson 1984). But they systematically fail to understand their own reflection in a mirror, and continue to react to it as if it were a stranger (Gallup 1970). By contrast, many chimpanzees and several orangutans (and recently also a gorilla: Patterson and Cohn, in press) are able to interpret their reflection in a mirror correctly. Under anaesthetic a coloured mark is made on the animal's face. When it recovers, as soon as it catches sight of its face in a mirror it immediately reaches and touches the spot. Gallup has used mirror understanding as an indication of whether an animal has a self-concept, and it can be argued that an understanding of oneself is a necessary basis for the understanding of another individual's mind (Humphrey 1983).

Imitation

Despite the popular belief that monkeys are the great imitators of the animal kingdom, and indeed despite a considerable tradition in primatology and psychology of attributing various monkey behaviours to imitation, attempts directly to test monkeys' ability to imitate have all failed (Visalberghi and Fragaszy 1990). Instead, these experiments have shown monkeys to be quick at learning, and to benefit from the social context by enhancement of trial and error learning. This now appears fully adequate to explain the innovation and spread of the special feeding techniques so famous in Japanese macaques. Some would even go so far as to deny that imitation has been well demonstrated in apes (Tomasello *et al.* 1987), yet the ability of the captive chimpanzee Viki to understand a command which meant 'copy the action that I am now doing', shows clearly that at least one ape species can truly imitate (Hayes and Hayes 1952). The fact that home-reared chimpanzees, orangutans and gorillas routinely pick up unrewarded motor skills, such as teeth brushing and tying shoelaces, would also be very hard to account for in an animal which could not imitate action patterns. Bruner has long argued that the ability to imitate requires that the mimic is able to put itself into the mental position of the model (Bruner 1972): in contemporary terms, to represent mentally the knowledge and plans of another individual.

Theory of mind

A series of experiments by Premack and Woodruff presented a captive chimpanzee with short film clips, each of which depicted a human with a problem (Premack 1988). For instance, a shivering man was seen in a bare room with an oil heater, but no matches with which to light it. The ape was given no formal training, but merely shown several photographs, yet it spontaneously chose the photograph of the object that would solve the problem – in the example given, a box of matches. The researchers termed this emphatic understanding of the needs of another individual 'theory of mind', and the concept of theory of mind is now used in understanding the deficits of autistic children (Baron-Cohen *et al.* 1985).

Pretend play

Kittens chase balls of wool as if pretending that they were prey. This can be most parsimoniously explained by saying that the characteristics of the object elicit a hunting response, because of an overlap in features between the appearance of an unwinding ball of wool and an escaping mouse. Such a simplistic explanation cannot apply to pretend play when the consequences of the pretence are elaborated and used in the play. Leslie (1987) has argued that this form of pretence requires the holding of simultaneous mental representations of two conflicting sets of knowledge or belief, and as such is logically equivalent to knowing that another individual's knowledge or belief is different to one's own. It is therefore of interest that several apes have shown pretend play. The classic example was again the chimpanzee Viki (Hayes 1951), who not only acted as if she were trailing a pull-toy on a string but showed consternation and appropriate strategies to free the toy when it became snagged on a (real) object! Other chimpanzees have apparently invented imaginary monsters with which to frighten their conspecifics (Savage-Rumbaugh and McDonald 1988), and publicly available film of these individuals (Savage-Rumbaugh 1986) also shows them eating imaginary food and one of them having its finger bitten by a child's doll. Kanzi, a captive individual of the closely related pygmy chimpanzee, often acts as if he is holding an object which does not exist: he may hide this invisible object and retrieve it later, all as if it were real (Savage-Rumbaugh and McDonald 1988). In gorillas too, there are some data of a similar kind: the home-reared Koko has used signs to refer to a rubber hose as an elephant's trunk in play (Patterson and Linden 1981), and a wild gorilla, Maggie, was seen to collect up moss and carry the bundle as if it were a baby, and then, when she had made a nest, to cuddle and fuss over her imaginary baby for many minutes (Karisoke Research Centre, unpublished records). Pretend play has not been recorded in monkeys.

Teaching

After the death of her own baby, Washoe, the chimp taught to sign American Sign Language, was given an infant chimp whom she adopted. The human caretakers did not teach the infant Loulis to sign, and stopped signing at all in her presence. Washoe used both demonstration (with attention to Loulis's gaze direction) and physical moulding of Loulis's hands to teach her to sign – with considerable success (Fouts et al. 1989). Recently, wild chimpanzees too have been seen teaching their infants, in this case to impart a technique of cracking hard nuts using a hammerstone with another stone as an anvil (Boesch 1991). Mothers sometimes perform actions slowly and in full view, paying close attention to the eye-gaze of the infant and performing the action only when it is watching. 'Scaffolding' has also been seen, the mother setting up the physical situation so that the infant is easily able to achieve the final goal, at a stage of development when it could not perform all the necessary constituent acts or sequence them correctly.

Table 1.1 *Distribution of the behavioural indicators of imagination in apes*

	imitation	pretend play	mirror	theory of mind	deceit attribution	teaching
orangutan	Yes★	Yes★	Yes	?	Yes	?
gorilla	Yes★	Yes★	Yes★	?	Yes	?
pygmy chimpanzee	Yes★	Yes★	?	?	Yes★	?
chimpanzee	Yes★	Yes★	Yes	Yes	Yes	Yes

Note: ★Strong evidence comes only from individuals home-reared by humans.

Attribution of intentions

Recent work on tactical deception in primates has thrown up a number of ways in which animals can in principle show us that they are capable of attributing intentions to others (Byrne and Whiten 1991). That is, in certain cases tactical deception can sometimes be shown to be 'lying'. (In many other cases, the acts match what in humans we would assume to be lying, but it is also possible plausibly to account for the tactic's acquisition by reinforcement without invoking an understanding of another's intentions.) As one example, a chimpanzee which evidently suspected (and quite rightly) that another was concealing the location of food, hid behind a tree and peeped out to unmask the deception. Here is the use of a tactic of *counterdeception*, with no possible opportunity to learn by trial and error since it relies on an appropriately designed *novel action*. Other diagnostics include the *righteous indignation* that is visible evidence that an animal has understood that it has been deceived; suppressing the *anticipated behaviour* of another animal before it could happen and so become a nuisance; and in general, cases of deception where it is known that there has been *no previous opportunity for trial and error learning*. Almost unknown in monkeys, this sort of evidence has been found repeatedly with all great apes species (Byrne and Whiten 1992).

The origin of imagination

Examples of this collection of phenomena have variously been found in orangutans, gorillas, pygmy chimpanzees and common chimpanzees (see Table 1.1), but not in monkeys. What they have in common is that in each case *the animal must imagine another 'possible world'*, in which things differ from what it knows to be really the case at the moment. This possible world varies in whether it is the current belief of another individual, another version (an untrue one) of the current world as viewed by the self, or a potential future state of the world that may or may not be desired.

Imagining other individuals' minds has been given various labels, as well as Premack's 'theory of mind': 'second-order intentionality' (Dennett 1983), 'mindreading' (Whiten and Perner 1991), 'first-order belief attribution' (Wimmer and Perner 1983).

The argument of this chapter is that a single common aptitude underlies the wide range of behaviours catalogued above, and that the great apes, but no other group of animals, possess this ability to imagine other possible worlds than the current perceived truth. This ability is lacking in monkeys, and – it seems – in autistic children (Baron-Cohen *et al.* 1985). The data on tactical deception have shown that, whereas monkeys can not apparently represent mentally what other animals *know*, they are able to react appropriately to what other animals can *see*, when it differs from what they can see themselves. At first sight this seems a hair-thin distinction to make. Yet it turns out that autistic children also have no difficulty with tasks that require them to anticipate a physical view from another individual's position (Hobson 1984), and only systematically fail when the task involves understanding the knowledge of another person.

Whether it is a coincidence that the one ape which has shown that it is able to understand its reflection, imitate, pretend, empathize with others, teach its infants and attribute intentions to others, is also the one which routinely makes tools in the wild, must be left as an interesting unsolved question for the moment. We simply cannot rule out the possibility that this is merely a matter of sampling bias, when chimpanzees have been so much more studied than any of the other apes. Equally, variations across the apes in the basic ability to imagine possible worlds cannot be ruled out. If present, this variation could tell us more precisely how and when the human imagination developed in our evolution. Thus the issues of clarifying exactly which ape species are capable of which mental skills, and at what dates their lines of descent diverged from our own, are crucial ones for future research.

Interpretation of actions: a double standard?

Accepting apes as able and monkeys as unable to attribute intentions to others and imagine other possible worlds than the current reality, has consequences that will worry some: a sort of 'double standard'. Consider a gorilla and a vervet monkey, both described as executing a sequence of actions that has the effect of socially manipulating a conspecific to the actor's advantage. The sequence has the same pattern, and in neither case is a full history of its ontogeny available (as in fact is true for many records of infrequent but interesting primate behaviours collected on an *ad lib* basis by skilled observers). Imagine that in both cases it is possible to construct an elaborate *post hoc* account in behaviourist terms – the social situation acted as a stimulus array and controlled the behaviour, with no need to invoke intention attribution – but the accounts are so elaborate and seemingly contrived as to be dismissed by any social psychologist whose data was of *human* action. Then in the monkey case we should still accept the behaviourist account, but for the ape behaviour we would now use an intentional explanation *even though in the given case intention attribution was unprovable*.

For a real example, consider what we should make of this observation of gorillas by Dian Fossey (Byrne and Whiten 1990: 72):

The majority of the group were day-nesting within a 25ft radius, with low-ranking Quince at the edge of the group. After intently gazing at Poppy [a one-month old infant, Effie's daughter; adolescent gorillas are strongly attracted to babies] from the side-lines, Quince stares in the opposite direction, circles and begins bending down branches for a nest. After momentarily sitting in the nest, Quince, with gaze averted from Poppy, gets up and moves a few feet closer to repeat the act of 'nest-building'. After roughly 40 minutes and 6 'nests' later, Quince was sitting next to the dominant female Effie and gazing directly at infant Poppy.

The record itself contributes no evidence of attribution, yet once it is accepted that gorillas *have* such an ability then an intentional interpretation becomes rather compelling. Quince, adolescent and unrelated to the highest rank female Effie, could not simply walk up to Effie and sit down to gaze at her new infant: only Effie's own daughters can do such a thing (present tense, since Effie is still the highest ranking female of this group today, and is no more permissive with non-relatives than in 1976!). Yet if at any point Effie had screamed in threat at this approaching female, the silverback leader who would rush to intervene would see that Quince had 'only been building a day-nest', and would be expected to intervene against Effie. The behaviour remained at all times *ambiguous* and liable to be misinterpreted – by anyone, that is, except Effie who could hardly have failed to realize what we call the 'true' motive (see Good, Chapter 6, this volume, for consideration of related cases where the 'future retrospective' interpretation is crucial).

If Quince had been an inarticulate and working-class adolescent, approaching a well-to-do lady's baby in an expensive pram but 'checking her shopping list' throughout, a similar interpretation of intended ambiguity would be uncontroversial. The girl *could* have been asked her motive for continual re-checking of the same list, of course; but would she have been honest in her reply, or even (since I described her as inarticulate) able to explain? In general we find it unproblematic that people cannot or will not explain what we attribute to be their 'real' motives (see also Drew, Chapter 5, this volume, for similar dilemmas of interpretation). Instead, gaining predictive power over their future behaviour is our everyday criterion of understanding. (If the well-to-do lady picked up her baby, smiled at the teenager, and offered her a chance to hold the child, we might predict that the girl would not return to list-checking afterwards.)

This is the same criterion that any behavioural scientist would adopt, and the issue is simply one of whether such intentional accounts make more wrong predictions than other theories do. Since gorillas' non-verbal communication is less subtle than humans', I suspect that we will make fewer errors of prediction for gorillas than for humans. A radical behaviourist would take a different line, on principle rejecting intentional explanations for humans' *and* animals' actions even-handedly, treating all as 'operants' under stimulus control, which is at least fair. But this approach has yet to explain which stimuli might have controlled Kim Philby's everyday behaviour, for instance.

Evolutionary implications

The implications of this chapter are as follows. The earliest primates were no more intelligent or socially sophisticated than other mammals. However, at some point between 55 and 25 million years ago (or 90 and 25 million years at the other extreme of estimation) the monkey and ape line of descent was exposed to a strong selection of pressure (presumably a need for greater social or Machiavellian aptitude). It responded with a much greater ability at learning and using social knowledge, and consequently an increased brain size – despite the energetic costs of the metabolically expensive and fragile brain. This probably occurred early rather than late in the time-band, since most monkey groups show at least some tactical deception and all are large-brained.

One branch of their descendants, the apes, acquired the remarkable ability to imagine alternative possible worlds, for instance the knowledge and intentions of another individual. Although it is obvious that this ability vastly increases the scope for social manipulation, it is quite unclear what selection pressure could have promoted it. The problem is just why such a useful trick should have evolved in apes but *not* monkeys, who appear to have equal need of it. It is likely that the basic ability was present in apes before 10–20 million years ago. By 5–8 million years, at the time of the last common ancestor of human and chimpanzee, that ancestor's ability to attribute intentions to others and imagine alternative worlds would have been sufficiently sophisticated to permit success at all the purely behavioural tests of it that psychologists have yet been able to devise.

In the full sense of the term (Goody, Introduction to this volume), these animals were capable of 'anticipatory interactive planning'. What they lacked was language and its consequences. As far as we know, only the *Homo* line of their descendants made this final step, but it may be argued that anticipatory interactive planning was a necessary precursor to it. Would any species unable to take account of an interlocutor's current intentions and needs be capable of benefiting from linguistic communication, anyway? And from an understanding of another's intentions it is perhaps a small step to that of understanding true communication, in which a speaker takes account of the hearer's belief that the speaker intends to pass information to the hearer. Modern apes may completely lack the formalizing systems of language, but they do not lack the understanding of what this kind of communication is all about. From this perspective, we can predict that when the heated arguments over 'ape signing' experiments have finally died down, it will be acknowledged that apes understand and use true communication, even if they never double-embed a relative clause.

The idea of Machiavellian intelligence

Does this mean that the social or Machiavellian intelligence hypothesis is to be accepted? The problem with answering this question is that 'social intelligence' is not just a little vague, it is multiply ambiguous. At least three senses (and thus answers) can be distinguished. Firstly, there is the hypothesis that an overriding selection pressure for the evolution of primate and human intelligence was the need to live in societies and yet maximize individual benefits, and that subtle manipulation of conspecific group members was the best way to achieve this. The finding of increasing intelligence in the social domain as one looks from strepsirhine to monkey to ape, is consistent with this idea (and indeed predated it), but does not prove it. The current popularity of this idea owes more to the paucity of well-developed alternatives – never a strong basis for faith – and it is anyway unlikely that a single factor was crucial in selecting intelligence over a span of 55 million years. The energetic constraints on large brains, for instance, cannot be ignored: diet must be a part of a full explanation (see Milton 1988).

Secondly, there is the claim that primate intelligence is more 'advanced' in social domains, that the social factor of intelligence has advanced ahead of any other. In one sense this is simply redescribing the data. Monkeys sensitive to demographic changes in other troops of conspecifics appear not to notice bizarre behaviour by hippos and waterbirds, as simulated by playbacks, or even obvious signs of the presence of predators (Cheney and Seyfarth 1988), and children demonstrate an understanding of concepts like seriation earlier in social interaction than they can be shown to possess them in conventional tests

Smith 1988). In another sense the claim is bizarre and untestable. We are not all-knowing beings able to catalogue the facets of intelligence in the absolute; we can only notice how monkeys or children deviate from our own, adult norm. Not only is there no metric on which to compare intelligences, but we know that all supposed factors of human intelligence correlate with each other.

The legacy

The third meaning of the Machiavellian intelligence hypothesis, and the one of most interest for this volume, is the idea that all descendants of the first anticipatory interactive planners carry a distinctive legacy. Human intelligence includes abilities which are certainly not unique to language-using humans. The monkeys and apes, like their human relatives, have considerable social knowledge and an ability to plan effectively in complex and socially subtle situations, in order to achieve their ends. And modern apes have the ability to imagine the intentions, needs and beliefs of other individuals, and to understand how these differ from their own. Certainly we still rely on these skills (see Brown, Chapter 7; and Streeck, Chapter 4, in this volume, for impressive examples). But perhaps human intelligence is, as a result of its evolutionary origin, biased towards dealing with *all* problems as if they were social problems. It is evident that in everyday life humans are poor at predicting the lawful, probabilistic results of random processes. Is this because they insist on treating all processes as intentionally caused? (See Levinson, Chapter 11 in this volume.) If so, then could this explain the odd tendency to reason with and see communicative meaning in things which are wholly unpredictable and unaffected by human actions? (See Goody, Chapter 10; and Zeitlyn, Chapter 9 in this volume.) Suggestions like these have been made before (Humphrey 1976), and it has long been a matter of amusement that people treat inanimate objects such as cars, computers and houseplants as interlocutors in a dialogue. Now that we understand a little more of the background to this peculiar trait, it is time to take the idea as a serious subject of study.

EDWIN HUTCHINS AND BRIAN HAZLEHURST

2 How to invent a shared lexicon: the emergence of shared form-meaning mappings in interaction

Recently, we have been exploring a new approach to cognitive anthropology. We've been trying to push the boundaries of a genuinely cognitive unit of analysis out beyond the skin of the individual. Ever since symbolic and cognitive anthropology embarked on their ideational odyssey in the 1950s, they have proceeded without the material and the social. Of course, many people are interested in *social cognition* where the social world is the content of cognition. And in fact, there are good arguments for believing that human intelligence developed in the context of reasoning about social situations (Byrne and Whiten 1988; Byrne, Chapter 1, this volume; Levinson, Chapter 11, this volume). This kind of relationship between the social and the cognitive is important, but it is still centred on the notion of the individual as the primary unit of cognitive analysis. The social world is taken to be a set of circumstances 'outside' the individual about which the individual reasons.

What we intend instead is to put the social and the cognitive on an equal theoretical footing by taking a *community of minds* as the unit of analysis. This permits us to do three things that are not possible from the traditional perspective. First, we can inquire about the role of social organization in the cognitive architecture of the system and may describe the cognitive consequences of social organization at the level of the community (Hutchins 1991; in press). Second, we can treat symbolic phenomena that are outside the individual as real components of the cognitive unit of analysis. This we take to be the position pioneered by Sperber (1985). Third, we can account for the emergence of shared symbols or form-meaning mappings; something that cannot be explained by reference to the processes operating in individual minds alone.

Making this move also presents an opportunity to view language in a new way. Cognitive science generally takes the existence of language as a given and concerns itself with the sorts of cognitive processes that must be involved when an individual processes language; in production and comprehension. From the perspective of the community of minds as cognitive system, language – its information-bearing capacity, its structural properties, the conventions of its use, etc. – becomes the determinant of the cognitive properties of the community because it in part determines where and when different kinds of information move through the system. This attention to the movement of information in the larger system necessarily brings the social and material back into play since, having acknowledged symbols outside the head, we now must take seriously their material nature and their use for organizing behaviour in social integration (cf. J. Goody 1977).

The existence of shared language is one of the central facts of human existence. Language appears to be closely tied to most high-level cognitive activities. It mediates most of the social interactions among the members of the most social of all species. Once a language exists, it is not difficult to think of means by which it could be maintained and propagated from generation to generation in a population. But without anyone to tell individuals which language to speak, how could a language ever arise? How could something structured come from that which is unstructured? It's a puzzle.

Here we are not thinking only, or even primarily, of the historical origins of human language. There is, of course, a vast speculative literature on the origins of language which we will not attempt to treat here. Rather, we are thinking more modestly in terms of the development of sets of local lexical distinctions such as may arise in small groups engaged in shared tasks. In this chapter we outline a scheme by which a shared lexicon emerges, the material components of one kind of form-meaning mapping. Shared form-meaning pairs, which we will call symbols, emerge from the interactions among members of a community. The set of public forms used in interaction by the members of this community constitutes the lexicon.

This is certainly not a model of the development of a human language, but it does demonstrate how simple shared form-meaning mappings can arise where none existed before. In the presentation below we will refer to the forms as though they are words, terms, descriptions, or patterns of acoustic features. There is, however, no strong commitment to any particular level of linguistic representation here and the structures described might just as well be thought of as patterns of denotational or even relational features.

The model is based on six central theoretical assumptions.

1. No mind can influence another except via mediating structure. (The no telepathy assumption.)
2. No social mind can become appropriately organized except via interaction with the products of the organization of other minds, and the shared physical environment. (The cultural grounding of intelligence assumption.)

3. The nature of mental representations cannot simply be assumed, it must be explained. (The 'shallow symbols' assumption – in contrast with the 'deep symbols' assumption which brings symbols into the language of thought as an article of faith rather than as a consequence of cultural process.)

4. Symbols always have both a material and an ideal component. The material component is what makes forms, structure, and difference possible. The ideal component is a function of the stance that organized individuals take toward these material forms. (The material symbols assumption.)

5. Cognition can be described as the propagation of representational states across representational media that may be internal to or external to individual minds. (The distributed information-processing assumption.)

6. The processes that account for the normal operation of the cognitive system should also account for its development through time. (The no developmental magic assumption.)

Below we present a computer simulation that is an implementation of these assumptions. It turns out to be a very robust procedure by which a community of individuals can develop a shared set of symbols. It is the simplest possible scheme that captures the essential properties of the system being modelled. The models are much too simple to be taken as representations of human cognition. They simply demonstrate that a particular kind of process is capable of producing a particular sort of outcome, in this case, a community with a shared lexicon.

The constraints on a shared lexicon

The central problems of inventing a lexicon can be stated in terms of a description of the outcome. Consider two individuals, A and B, and a set of phenomena in the world numbered 1, 2, 3 . . . m. Let the word that an individual uses for a phenomenon be denoted by the concatenation of the letter designating the individual and the number of the phenomenon (i.e. 'B5' denotes the word that B uses for the fifth phenomenon). Now, if the lexicon is to be *shared*, the word that A uses for any particular phenomenon must be the same as that used by B. In notation: $A1 = B1, A2 = B2, . . . Am = Bm$. Simultaneously, if the lexicon is to be a lexicon at all, there must be differences between the material forms of the words used by each individual for different phenomena. In notation: $A1 \neq A2 \neq . . . Am$; $B1 \neq B2 \neq . . . Bm$. It won't do to have a lexicon for m phenomena that consists of m homonyms.[1] These two constraints must somehow be simultaneously satisfied in any process that is to develop a shared lexicon. For our purposes, *a shared lexicon is a consensus on a set of distinctions*.

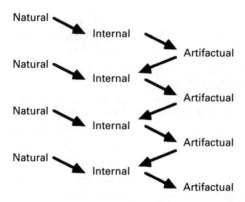

Figure 2.1 The relations of environment, internal and artifactual structure. The arrows represent the propagation of constraints. Constraints
may be propagated by many means. We use the cover term 'coordination' to refer to the satisfaction of constraints no matter the mechanism
by which constraint satisfaction is achieved.

Before turning to the simulation, we need to say a few more words
about the theoretical stance. The six theoretical assumptions described
above can be assembled into a model of socially distributed cognition as
shown in Figure 2.1. Our inventory of representational structure includes
natural structure in the environment, *internal structure* in the individuals,
and *artifactual structure* in the environment. Artifactual structure is a
bridge between internal structures. Artifacts may provide the link
between internal structures in one individual and those in another
individual (as is the case in communication), or between one set of
internal structures in an individual and another set of internal structures
in that same individual (as is the case in using written records as a
memory, for example). Internal structures provide bridges both between
successive artifactual structures and between natural and artifactual
structures. Following Sperber (1985:76) we may say that 'A representation [artifactual structure] is of something [natural structure] for some
information processing device [internal structure].'

In the past five years, developments in computational modelling have
made it possible to think in different ways about the relations between
structure inside a system and structure outside. Connectionist networks
of a class called 'autoassociators' have particularly nice properties with
respect to the problem of discovering and encoding structural regularities
in their environment.[2]

Autoassociator networks learn to duplicate on the output layer the
pattern of activation presented to the input layer. Figure 2.2 shows a
simple autoassociator network. It consists of three 'layers' of units. Input

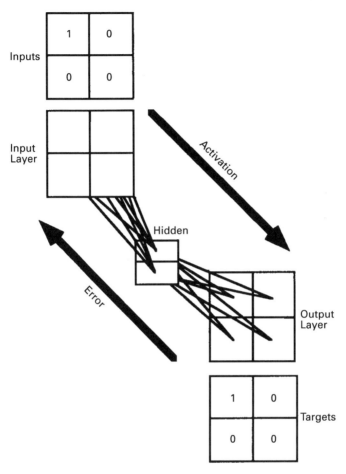

Figure 2.2 A typical autoassociation network and learning scheme. See text for explanation of network components.

units on the left, output units on the right, and 'hidden' units in the middle. 'Targets' are real valued vectors which are structurally similar to the output and input layers but, like inputs, are thought of as information external to the network – these are part of the environment which the network is made to learn (see below).

Limitations on space make a full description of this kind of information-processing system impossible. The following sentences will hopefully convey the style of computation entailed, if not the details.

Every unit in the input layer of a network has a unique connection to every unit in the hidden layer, and every unit in the hidden layer has a unique connection to every unit in the output layer (see Figure 2.2). The strengths of these connections can be adjusted. The activations of the input layer are set by external phenomena. The activations of the other units are determined by the activations of the units from which they have connections and on the strengths of those connections. The task for the network is, starting from random connection strengths, to discover a pattern of connection strengths that will produce the desired output in response to a given set of inputs. Incremental improvement in accomplishing this task is referred to as 'learning'. The networks modelled here use a procedure called the 'back-propagation of error' to find an appropriate set of connection strengths. In this scheme, the output produced is compared to the target[3] and the difference between output and target is an error in the network's ability to perform this input–output mapping. The connections are then adjusted to reduce this error on future trials at this task. The problem for the network can be viewed as one of finding a set of connection strengths which simultaneously meets the constraints imposed by all of the input–output mappings it is made to perform.

Rumelhart, Hinton and Williams (1986) have shown that under certain conditions the activations of the hidden layer units of fully trained autoassociator networks converge on efficient encodings of the structural regularities of the input data set. That is, the connections between input and hidden units must produce activations at the hidden layer which can be used by the connections between hidden and output units to produce the target, under the constraints of the function which propagates activation. For example, given any four orthogonal input patterns and an autoassociator network with two hidden units, the hidden unit activations for the four input cases should converge on $\{(0\ 0)\ (0\ 1)\ (1\ 0)\ (1\ 1)\}$. This is because the network must use the activations of the hidden units to encode the four cases and the encoding scheme attempts to distinguish (optimally) among the cases. Producing these efficient encodings is equivalent to feature extraction. That is, the networks learn how to classify the input data in terms of distinctive features or principal components.

Imagine an autoassociator folded in half. The hidden units still produce efficient encodings of the input data set. Since the patterns of activation on the hidden units encode the features of the input set, they can be seen as representations of the world of experience. If we make these representations 'public', so that they become a part of the shared material world of interaction, then they serve as this individual's descriptions of the input data.[4] These public hidden layer encodings produce one of the properties we want in a lexicon; distinctions among representational forms. In Figure 2.3 we have relabelled these units 'verbal input/output' units.

If we take the remaining parts of the network to be a simple visual system – capable of classifying scenes in the environment – then the verbal

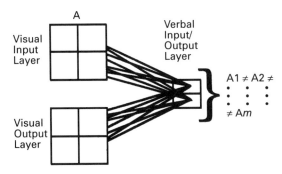

Figure 2.3 A modified autoassociator, with 'public hidden units'. By 'folding' an autoassociator back on itself, we create a system capable of generating referentially meaningful (i.e. distinct) representations of the *m* scenes.

input/output layer is capable of generating patterns of activation in response to each visual scene encountered, and these patterns are (or become) maximally different from each other. Regarding network A's descriptions for the *m* scenes, this satisfies the constraints: A1 ≠ A2 ≠ ... A*m*.

Virtually all work in connectionist modelling today models aspects of the cognition of *individuals*. Our theoretical stance suggests that it might be useful to consider the properties of *communities* of networks. Of particular interest here is the fact that in traditional connectionist modelling, the programmer constructs the world of experience from which the networks learn. In a community of networks the behaviour of *other networks* might also be an important source of structure from which each network could learn. Connectionist programmers refer to the output patterns to be learned as the 'teachers' for their networks. With a community of networks, we can let an important part of the teaching be embodied in the behaviour of other networks. Thus, where traditional network modelling is concerned only with the relation of structure in the environment to internal structure, a model of interactions in a community of networks adds the universe of communicational artifacts to the picture.

It is easy to show that consensus among two networks (say A and B) can be achieved by taking the output of each as the teacher for the other. This satisfies the constraints that A1 = B1, A2 = B2, ... A*m* = B*m*.

Implementation

The simulation proceeds via interactions – one interaction is one time-step in the simulation. An interaction consists of the presentation of a chosen scene (from the set of *m* scenes) to two chosen individuals, a

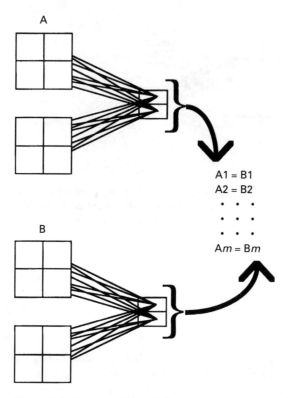

Figure 2.4 A scheme for evolving consensus on a set of distinctions. By reciprocally constraining autoassociators at their hidden layers, consensus about the representations used to classify the m scenes can be achieved.

'speaker' and a 'listener' (from the set of n individuals). The functions which do this 'choosing' determine what we call the 'interaction protocol' of the simulation. The typical functions simply implement random selection from the domains of scenes and individuals, respectively. One of the individuals chosen (say A) responds to the scene by producing a pattern of activation on its verbal output layer (A 'speaks'). The other individual (say B) also generates a representation of what it would say in this context but, as 'listener', uses what A said as a target to correct its own verbal representation. The listener (B) is also engaged in a standard learning trial on the current scene, which means its own verbal representation – in addition to being a token for comparison with A's verbal representation – is *also* being used to produce a visual output by feeding activation forward to the visual output layer. The effects of this learning on B's future behaviour can be stated as: (1) in this context produce a

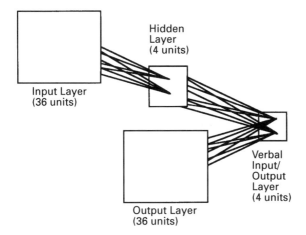

Figure 2.5 Network architecture for the simulation. (Not all of the connections between layers are shown.)

representation at verbal output more like what A said, and (2) produce a representation at visual output more like the scene itself.

By randomly choosing interactants and scenes, over time every individual has the opportunity to interact with all the others in both speaking and listening roles in all visual contexts. The effect to be achieved is for the population to converge on a shared set of patterns of activation on the verbal output units that makes distinctions among the m scenes. That is, we hope to see the development of a consensus on a set of distinctions.

The small network architecture described above is a simplification of the architecture actually used in the simulation reported below. In this simulation, each individual is an autoassociator network consisting of thirty-six visual input units, four hidden units, four verbal output units and thirty-six visual output units, as shown in Figure 2.5. Notice that an additional layer of four hidden units appears in these networks. These additional resources were required by networks in this simulation in order for the community to converge on a shared lexicon.[5] The scenes to be classified are twelve phases of a moon, represented as patterns in the 6×6 arrays shown in Figure 2.6.

Results

Developing consensus on a set of distinctions appears to be a highly likely final stable state of this dynamical system. Since the initial connection strengths of individuals are small and randomly assigned, early verbal representations do not differentiate among the scenes represented. Figure

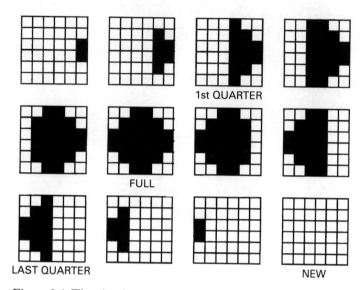

Figure 2.6 The visual scenes utilized in the simulation. These can be thought of as representations of the visual field associated with sight of the moon in twelve different phases.

2.7 shows the activation levels of the four verbal output units in response to the twelve scenes for some typical individuals, early in a simulation run. It is easy to see that there is little variation in the response of any individual to the different scenes.

Figure 2.8 shows the same individuals after an average of 2,000 interactions with each of the other individuals in the five-member community. For the most part, individuals now respond *differently* to each of the twelve scenes, and all of the individuals *agree* with each other on how to respond. That is, we have consensus on a set of distinctions. Due to the random starting weights of the networks, and the random interaction protocol functions which organize their learning experiences, there is no way to predict *which* lexicon will develop – but the procedure is robust in the sense that *some* well-formed lexicon or another develops nearly every time.

The need for a critical period of language learning

We have also experimented with adding new individuals with randomized nets ('babies') to communities that have already developed a lexicon. Depending on the size of the community, the addition of the new individual may have quite different effects. A new individual added to a large community with a highly shared lexicon will be entrained by the community and will learn the shared lexicon. A new individual added to a

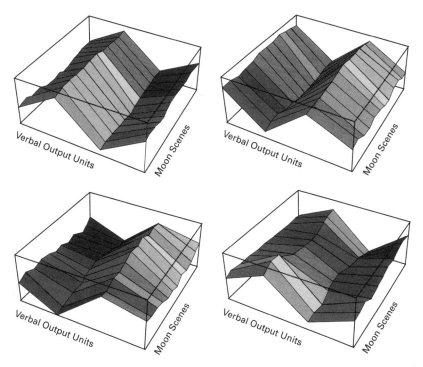

Figure 2.7 Four individuals of a five-member community at the start of a simulation run. The surface represents the value of each verbal output unit in response to each moon scene.

smaller community may completely destroy the previously achieved solution. After such an event the community may or may not be able to relearn a lexicon with the new individual.

In running these simulations, we found ourselves wishing that there was some principled way to reduce the learning rate once individuals had learned the language. In particular, one would like to reduce the learning rate at the point where individuals are likely to encounter many interactions with disorganized individuals. This would amount to implementing a critical period for language learning so that individuals learn less from the linguistic behaviour of others once they have reached sexual maturity. Perhaps evolution has engineered something like this into our species. We did not implement a critical period, however, because to do so seemed arbitrary and a violation of one of the core premises: that the processes that account for normal operation of the system should also account for its development through time. In more complex situations, like that of biological evolution where adaptive searches are conducted in parallel at many levels of specification, it may be reasonable to expect violations of this premise.

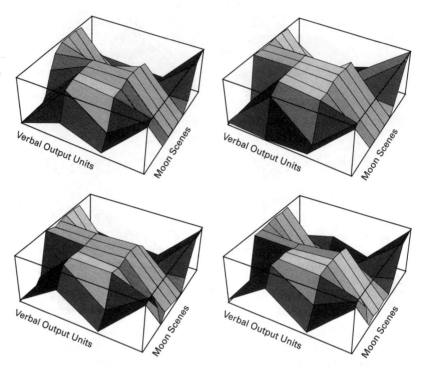

Figure 2.8 Four individuals of a five-member community after 50,000 interactions. Each individual has had (on average) 2,000 interactions with each of the other four individuals. Half of these were in the role of 'listener' and half in the role of 'speaker'. The surface represents the value of each verbal output unit in response to each moon scene.

Discussion

The model explicitly represents the interactions of the three kinds of structure discussed earlier: natural, internal and artifactual. The patterns representing phases of the moon are the 'natural' structure. The connection strengths in the networks are the internal structure that provides coordination between the two kinds of external structure. The patterns of activation on the verbal input/output units are the 'artifactual' structure. We see this as the smallest first step toward a system in which artifactual structures invoke the experience of that which is not present in the environment.

As we have seen, no individual can influence the internal processing of another except by putting mediating artifactual structure in the environment of the other. However, by putting particular kinds of structure in each other's environments, they all achieve a useful internal organization.

It would be possible for each individual to achieve an internal classification scheme in isolation – after all, that is what autoassociators are known to do by themselves. But such a classification would be useless in interaction with others. That is, idiosyncratic distinctions may be useful, but not as useful as shared ones. By forcing the individuals to learn from the classification behaviour of others we ensure that each individual can only become internally organized by interacting with the external products of the internal organization of others. The effects of this kind of system enable individuals to tap the resources of an entire group (and ancestors of the group), enabling cognitive performance not achievable by individuals alone. This is the foundation upon which human intelligence is built (Hutchins and Hazlehurst 1991).

Although this simulation is too simple to claim to address the issue of symbolic thought processes directly, it suggests a way in which shared symbols that could subsequently come to serve internal functions could arise as a consequence of social interaction. Such symbols are outside the individual first as pieces of organized material structure – in the behaviour of others – before they have explicit internal representations. Undoubtedly, such shared public forms can be given internal representations, as can any structural regularity in the environment whether natural or artifactual. This perspective in which symbols are in the world first, and only represented internally as a consequence of interaction with their physical form is what we mean by the 'shallow symbols' hypothesis. In this view, symbols and symbolic processing may be relatively shallow cognitive phenomena, residing near the surface of functional organizations resulting from interaction with material structures.

The computations performed by the networks are well characterized by the propagation of the representational state. The universe of inputs is propagated through the networks and re-represented at the output. This general notion of computation comes from Simon (1981:153) who says, 'Solving a problem simply means representing it so as to make the solution transparent.' Simon may not have intended quite so broad a reading of his definition but it seems to capture well the behaviour of this system. The structure of the natural world is fixed in this model, but the internal structures and the artifactual structures co-determine each other and co-evolve in the development of the lexicon. In the broadest sense, the solution arrived at was determined by the structure of the natural world as manifested in the phenomena encountered and in the random initial configurations of the internal states of the individuals in the community. The process of developing a lexicon in this model is a process of propagating transformed representations of naturally occurring structure throughout a system that contains artificial structure as well. At the outset, the structures of the 'minds' of the individuals are 'natural', having been given by nature. At the end of the simulation, these same structures are 'artificial' in the sense that they are organized by structure created by other individuals.

Finally, even when two networks are in complete agreement with each other about the structure of the lexicon, each has a unique internal structure. Through learning from each other the individuals become functional equivalents, not structural replicates, of each other. That is, constraints on public form do not uniquely specify internal structure so long as shared form-meaning pairs are established.

Clearly, this generation of shared form-meaning pairs is not limited to acoustic forms of symbolic behaviour – what we have characterized in this simulation as words of a lexicon. Words are a particularly salient vehicle for symbolic processes, as they are representations which are easily recorded and objectively characterized. What of the meanings we attach to other social behaviours? Or the meaningful activities of the incumbent of a recognized social role? The same sorts of processes are certainly at work in establishing the sharedness and consistency of these forms and meanings as well (cf. Barth 1966; Goffman 1959). Roles and the meanings of those roles – including norms which legitimate and motivate constellations of social behaviours – may come into being together as the result of constraints on the building and maintenance of consensus through social interactions. Although the current simulation does not address this level of complexity of social interaction, it does suggest possible candidates for the foundational mechanisms involved.

Acknowledgement

Research support was provided by grant NCC 2–1591 to Donald Norman and Edwin Hutchins from the Ames Research Center of the National Aeronautics and Space Administration in the Aviation Safety/Automation Program. Everett Palmer served as technical monitor. Additional support for the first author was provided by a fellowship from the John D. and Catherine T. MacArthur Foundation.

Notes

1 This model does not deal with either homonyms or synonyms.
2 The best background work in connectionism is the two-volume set *Parallel Distributed Processing* by Rumelhart and McClelland (1986). The behaviour of autoassociator networks is thoroughly analysed in Chauvin (1988).
3 For an autoassociator, the target is identical to the input, thus reducing the problem to an identity mapping on the input set.
4 We thank Elizabeth Bates (personal communication, February 1991) for coining the term 'public hidden units' for this construction.

5 It is a well-known result from connectionist history that two layers of weights are required to perform nonlinear mappings from input to output (Rumelhart, Hinton and Williams 1986). The range of verbal representations that individuals are attempting to map in this simulation apparently constitute a nonlinear set, which requires the extra hidden layer to perform properly. Another reason for the required extra layer has to do with the large compression of data from input to verbal output layers. This compression tends to 'swamp' the verbal output layer with large values reducing the amount of useful information here, and limiting the usefulness of these values as targets for other individuals.

3 Hunter-gatherers' kinship organization: implicit roles and rules

This chapter offers an analysis of the emergence of explicitly institution-alized roles and rules based on kinship (Kinship roles and rules) among Nayaka.[1] They provide a case of 'hunter-gatherers',[2] with the simplest known social organization called band-organization. While analysis of this kind of organization has been traditionally informed by an ecological-evolutionary paradigm, the present analysis is informed by Berger and Luckmann's *The Social Construction of Reality* (1966). The analysis was inspired by Goody's AIP project, which calls for examining human practices in relation to evolutionarily programmed anticipatory interactive planning (AIP). The analysis aims to contribute to the project, in reciprocity, a perspective on hunter-gatherers that can raise hypotheses about the possible contribution of AIP to the emergence of human roles and rules.

I shall first outline the conceptual links that lead from the AIP idea to the analysis. Then I shall examine the Nayaka social scene, and their kinship system (terms, cooperation, and avoidance). Finally, I shall offer a comparative perspective, and reflect back on AIP concerns.

Theoretical links

The AIP idea started from primate research. Challenging the traditional view that goes back to Darwin and Wallace, students of high primates recently suggested that the principal selective pressure behind the evolution of 'higher intellectual faculties' lay not in technical dealings with the physical environment but, instead, in everyday dealings with social associates (Byrne and Whiten 1988; Humphrey 1976; Jolly 1966a). They argued that living within social groups, early hominids had – like chess players – to foresee others' actions in order to preempt or exploit these actions to their own advantage. Furthermore, they had to adjust their plans to the actual deeds of others, who equally planned their actions strategically. This complex situation generated selective pressure for intellectual prowess.

As Goody recognized, pursuing further this primate-based evolutionary argument, it follows that anticipatory interactive planning is evolutionarily programmed into human intelligence. If so, it should have bearings upon cultural practices and institutions and be expressed in them. Goody explored this hypothesis at great depth in her work on questions, politeness and praying (1978a,b; Chapter 10 in this volume). She briefly noted other areas in which it could be explored – among them, the emergence of roles and rules.

It would have been best to follow this last-mentioned avenue in relation to hunter-gatherers: seen as ethnographic examples of the simplest human social organization, or – much more problematically – as a source of insight on evolutionary processes. However, hunter-gatherers have been traditionally viewed within a (naturalistic) ecological-evolutionary paradigm. Conventionally, this paradigm views their institutions in relation to their dealings with the physical environment (rather than their dealings with each other); in terms of functional subsistence needs (rather than inter-personal interaction and communication). Therefore, the existing ethnography would not have done for the purpose.

A fresh perspective on hunter-gatherers is required in order to pursue the AIP hypothesis – a perspective informed by a paradigm that does view institutions in relation to inter-personal interaction and communication. Berger and Luckmann's *The Social Construction of Reality* (1966) is an obvious choice. Its first chapter, based on Alfred Schutz and Thomas Luckmann's work (1973) – separate from the rest of the book and less well known – is particularly useful. It deals with the 'prototypical case of social interaction' that takes place in the 'face-to-face situation'. In this situation, it is argued, individuals know each other 'vividly' and as 'fully real'. Their interaction is predominantly directed towards the concreteness of the other. As a result, typificatory schemes are more 'vulnerable' to personal interferences than they are in 'remoter' forms of interaction where there is a greater amount of anonymity. Relationships are highly flexible. It is comparatively difficult to impose rigid patterns on them. The dialectic development of institutions is held at bay (Berger and Luckmann 1966:28–34).

Phenomenologically complex, this argument can be read more simply and then brought to bear on what anthropologists commonly called 'band organization'. The latter involves living in very small groups – twenty-five individuals on average – under material conditions that preclude privacy. However, 'face-to-face' has been traditionally used by anthropologists to describe situations wherein individuals interact with each other in diverse roles (almost the opposite of Berger and Luckmann's 'face-to-face situation'). Moreover, under Goffman's influence, 'face' has come to be associated with a representational mask (again, almost the opposite of Berger and Luckmann's 'face-to-face'). Therefore, instead of 'face-to-face', yet paraphrasing it, I use 'person-to-person'. This terminological change also signals a departure from the full phenomenological connotations of the concept (discussed at length by Schutz: see 1970).

To conclude, *The Social Construction of Reality*'s perspective, especially the discussion of the pre-institutionalized 'person-to-person' situation, provides a framework within which to analyse hunter-gatherers in a way which will make it possible to use their important case for exploring AIP-related ideas, especially with reference to the emergence of roles and rules.

A case study

This perspective will be brought to bear on kinship among hunter-gatherers with 'immediate-return systems' (Woodburn 1980, 1982). These are hunter-gatherers with the simplest known social organization, comprising among others, the !Kung of the Kalahari, the Hadza of Tanzania, the Pygmy of the Ituri forest in the Congo, the Negrito Batek of Malaysia, and the Hill Pandaram, Paliyan and Nayaka of South India. In general, they have few and simple roles and rules (Woodburn 1980). Division of labour, if at all, is by sex and age alone. As for their Kinship – on which the analysis will focus, not least because its institutionalization is argued to have been crucial in the genesis of human society (e.g., Lévi-Strauss 1969; Fortes 1983) – Woodburn has already argued that it 'regulates so little' (1979:257). However, he left many questions open – why? how? can it really be so? – questions which could not have been explored within the conventional ecological-evolutionary paradigm. My argument will be that this state of kinship has to do with the 'person-to-person' situation which dominates their social life; a situation which hinders the dialectic development of Kinship roles and rules.

The analysis refers specifically to Nayaka. They inhabit tropical forests in the north-western slopes of the Nilgiris in South India. This is a border-area between Tamil Nadu, Kerala and Karnataka, and their composite dialect reflects the three languages spoken there: Kanada (being traditionally dominant); Malayalam (rapidly increasing its influence); and Tamil (having a steady minor impact).

The total population of Nayaka is estimated at about 1,000. In practice, they are distributed in enclave local communities, each of which is almost autonomous. My own work was done among one local community – whom I call the Gir Valley group. I stayed with them during 1978–9, and re-visited them in 1989.[3] They numbered (in 1978) 69 individuals (22 men, 24 women, and 23 children), who were further dispersed in five residential clusters ('hamlets'), at a distance of two to ten kilometres from each other, one to five families living in each. For a living, they gathered wild fruits, nuts, tubers and the honey of wild bees; they fished and hunted occasionally (mainly deer and monitor lizard); they engaged on a casual basis in wage work and in trade in minor forest produce; and occasionally grew some fruit around their huts.

The social scene

What is social life like in a band organization? One's imagination is frequently coloured by one's own conditions of sociality (in itself attesting to Goody's AIP hypothesis!). Therefore, westerners often find it difficult to imagine. To my students I often suggest that they imagine themselves spending the twenty-four hours of the day, each day, from birth to death, almost exclusively, with the neighbours (who are relatives as well) in a sixteen-flat building, without the material partitions which provide privacy. Here, I rather sketch the daily routines of an 'average' Nayaka (arbitrarily female living with a man and young children).

She lives in a hut constructed in a small forest clearing surrounded by a thick tropical jungle on the sloping side of the Gir valley. The hut stands next to several other huts (ranging from one to five) at a distance of two to five metres from them. She occupies in this hut – with her family – a small living space (at most two by two metres); and the hut may also contain other living spaces (at most two), each for another family. The internal partitions, if any, are clumsily built, and often are crude signals of partitions. The external walls are made of strips of bamboo, interwoven either thickly – in which case they block out vision but not audition, or thinly – in which case they bar neither. Under these conditions, she overhears almost everything uttered in the hut, and much of what is said in the hamlet, whether it is said to her or to others. She also sees a great deal of what her neighbours do (in the hut and within the hamlet generally).

At any rate, during the dry seasons (in this local monsoon climate) she spends most of her day outside the hut, at leisure, eating or sleeping by the side of an external fireplace. Her fireplace is only a few metres away – in the open – from other fireplaces, where other people spend their time. None of them pretends to be outside the sight and hearing of the others. They often talk to each other across space (and in the hut, across partitions), each remaining by their own fireplace (or in the hut, in their own living space).

Our Nayaka bathes and draws water from a nearby stream, going always to the same stretch of water together with the other Nayaka in her hamlet – frequently during the same early and late hours of the day. She goes on forays, normally with her family, but they are often in close proximity to other families, since all follow the same spatial trajectory of seasonal variations. Occasionally, she goes to work in the plantation, or the local timber company, but there she is designated tasks commonly given to Nayaka, and therefore works alongside her Nayaka neighbours.

Occasionally she goes on visits to other hamlets in the locality, staying there for weeks or several months at a time; while others come for visits to her hamlet. However, since there are only five hamlets in the close locality, with fewer than fifty adults altogether, she gets to know them, through repeated visits over the years, in almost the same immediate way I have just described.

The local community itself is not totally cut off from other local Nayaka communities and, occasionally, single young persons leave for, or come from, other communities. The 'immigrants' settle in, often upon marriage to a local person, and within a year or two our Nayaka get to know them pretty well, in an immediate sort of way. Or they leave after a while and, remaining outside the zone of everyday social life, they are rarely mentioned, if at all. It seems that when they are out of everyday social reach, they are also out of everyday concerns and expressed consciousness. Likewise, the 'emigrants' either remain away, effectively abolished from collective memory, or they return after a while (with or without a spouse) and become re-absorbed into the intimately known local community. At any rate, these young persons constitute a negligible proportion of the local community, at any given point in time (for example, only two came, and none left during 1978–9).

All in all, the Nayaka woman spends the greater part of her life in the way I have just described, sharing the 'here and now' in all domains of life with the same few adults who, at diverse degrees of relatedness, are also all her relatives. She also grew up with many of them.

Thus, we can conclude[4] that our Nayaka's (inter-Nayaka)[5] interaction is largely confined to people with whom she has ongoing relationships. Furthermore, and this is important, she constantly witnesses their ongoing interactions with each other. In other words, this is a highly close-meshed intimate network. Moreover, she is familiar with their routines in most domains of life, their idiosyncrasies, and most of what has happened, and is happening, in their lives. In short, her principal and regular field of (inter-Nayaka) social interaction comprises people who she knows vividly, immediately, and in a manifold way. We can say that her social world is predominated by 'the person-to-person' situation.

In this situation, how is kinship expressed and what does it do? Through the two-stage detailed description which follows, I want to show that while people classify kin and use kinship terms extensively in everyday communicative acts, they neither formalize nor discuss Kinship roles and rules. They do not expect distinct categories of kin (spouse excluded) to behave in any distinct way.

Kinship and communication

Kinship terms are used extensively in everyday communicative acts. One can constantly hear Nayaka using them interchangeably with personal names. They use twenty-seven Dravidian kinship terms (most of which come from Kanada, but a few are from Malayalam). They also use twenty-seven names (commonly used in the region by people of other ethnicities as well), twelve of which are clearly of recent origin (see Bird 1983a).

This intermingled use of kinship terms and personal names varies according to the life-cycle. Young babies do not receive names at all. My host explained it in a simple, if somewhat pragmatic, way. One woman, for example, said to me: 'He [her baby] cannot respond to a name, so I do not call him.'

Young children are then called either by the name Kungan (for a boy) and Kungi (for a female), or by the kinship terms *maga(n)* (son) and *maga(l)* (daughter). All of them are called by these same names or kinship terms – by any adult, including the parents. It seems that, familiar with individuals' voices and idiosyncratic routines in this 'person-to-person' situation, Nayaka easily identify by context which of the children – few in any case – is being referred to or hailed in any instance.

Adolescents, compared with all others, are frequently addressed and referred to by distinguishing nicknames. These are names drawn from the limited list of twenty-seven, with prefixes which relate to diverse attributes, for instance, relative age (e.g., Cik Mathen; 'cik' means junior), place of origin (e.g., Munderi Mathen; 'Munderi' is a place) and biographic detail (e.g., Chikkari Mathen; 'chikkari' is a hunting guide). The nicknames are frequently changed. Furthermore, any given individual can be simultaneously called by diverse names. I remember asking informants in 1978 to list Nayaka by name. To my surprise – and at the time also suspicion – they hailed my subjects of inquiry and asked them 'how they were called now' then passed the replies on to me. During my follow-up survey in 1989, some of them then asked me what they were called in 1978. (Other local non-Nayaka – for example, employers and traders who keep accounts of transactions with Nayaka for their own needs – also stabilize the use of names in out-Nayaka communication).

The use of nicknames almost ceases in adult life, whereupon kinship terms are used almost exclusively. Although the kinship terms are Dravidian, Nayaka use them in a distinct way, sometimes in stark contradiction with the logic of the Dravidian kinship system. They learn which kinship terms to use – as the examples which follow illustrate – within the context of everyday communicative acts. My hosts always explained to me how they arrived at any particular kinship term in these ways. Firstly, 'He (or she) [often a person from ascending generation] calls me "x" so I call him (or her) "y": for instance, he calls me *tamma(n)* [younger brother] so I call him *anna(n)* [older brother].' Secondly, 'My so-and-so relative calls him (or her) "x" so I call him (or her) "y": for instance, my *appa(n)* [father] calls this man *tamma(n)* [younger brother] so I call him *cikappa(n)* [father's younger brother – literally, junior father].' Finally, 'My spouse calls this woman "x" so I call her "y" (or sometimes "x" as well): for instance, my spouse calls her *tanga* [younger sister] so I call her *nadini* [younger sister in-law] – or sometimes *tanga* as well.' Thus, they learn kinship terms by hearing older people using them to address and refer to other present people. They learn them from persons who directly address them by kinship term. And they learn them from their spouses.

In the obverse, the width and depth of Nayaka genealogical knowledge is confined to the zone of everyday person-to-person interaction and communication ('the zone of bodily manipulation' in Berger and Luck-mann's terms). My hosts, for example, could not specify genealogical relatives beyond the third ascending generation. They said matter-of-factly that 'they were not there'. Likewise, they could not specify genealogical relatives of the second and third ascending generation when the individuals concerned had died or emigrated when they themselves were young. They said 'they were not here when I came to know things so I did not know them'. Thus, they learned about their kin – who they were and how they related to them – through interactive use of kinship terms in place of personal names.

It is noteworthy that, in the first year or so, my hosts did not address or refer to newly arrived Nayaka, who married someone locally, by kinship terms. They could have reasoned out the appropriate kinship through the ways specified above, but chose not to in favour of names. As Mathi explained it, when referring to a young 'immigrant' who had married her sister's daughter: 'I do not know how to call him. I am shy to call him because I do not know him'. This suggests that they use kinship terms only in reference to Nayaka who, in the course of time, they come to know in a 'person-to-person', 'vivid' and 'fully real' sort of way. (And it is then, in fact, that we can understand how a general kinship term – like *tamma(n)* (younger brother) – being called across the hamlet, reaches its exact addressee.)

Kinship and cooperation

Using twenty-seven kinship terms so extensively in everyday communi-cation, the importance of Nayaka linguistic classification of kin cannot be doubted. However, I shall now attempt to show that this linguistic classification does not go with a behavioural classification. My hosts did not talk about linguistically distinguished relatives in terms of what they 'should do' and 'do' in interaction with them. Conversations with them about how one should behave with a particular category of relative, say *cikappa(n)* (father's younger brother), or even about how they themselves behave towards a specific person who is a *cikappa(n)*, always came to a short end. It seems they do not associate clusters of rights and obligations, or even kinds of habitualized cooperation, with linguistically distinguished kin. But can this really be the case?

Even when the same is reported for other comparable groups (Woodburn 1979, 1980; see below), it can still be counter-argued that the ethnographer (and her colleagues as well) simply failed to find out everything there is to find. To fend off such criticism one can substantiate the claim by further ethnographic observations – which I shall do next – and, since even further data cannot conclusively make the point, one can at least explain *why* roles and rules are not fully institutionalized in the 'person-to-person' situation – which I shall do subsequently.

Starting then with the former, I describe life-cycles and special events which in most other societies, constitute a stage for demonstrating and affirming Kinship roles. However, in this case they *do not*: it can be seen from the following examples which are concerned, respectively, with marriage, burial, the annual celebration, sharing of large game, disputes, and the division of labour – all stages *par excellence* for Kinship performances.

Marriage

Though couples often simply start to live together, they sometimes celebrate it with a meal. The meal is rarely planned in advance, and is given to people who happen to be around at the time. For example, in the most elaborate case I have on record, a messenger went to another hamlet, the evening before the meal, and returned the next day with a few additional guests. The father of the bridegroom, a widower, was in neither of these hamlets, and he did not attend the celebration.

Burial

Burial is carried out on the day of death. Those who happen to be in the hamlet carry the body to a place, several walking-hours away from the hamlet, where all Nayaka are buried. The spouse and the children, and then other attendants, take what they want for remembrance, and the rest of the possessions are buried with the deceased. A person, even a close relative, who happens to be away, does not participate in the event, nor 'inherit' anything from the deceased.

The annual celebration

A celebration is held almost every year in each of the hamlets, staging communitas with local ancestral and natural spirits. Lasting twenty-four hours, it involves shamanistic conversations with the spirits, dances, the playing of music, and a communal meal at the end of the day. The preparation of the communal food is done by a resident couple – not a group of relatives. Furthermore, when the food is dished out, each nuclear family takes its share and sits to one side to eat it. Moreover, the families spend most of the twenty-four-hour communal occasion standing by themselves at some distance from others. Only occasionally do 'married' men and women part to join single-sex dancing circles, kept going by young 'unmarried' dancers.

Sharing large game

Large game, hunted by dogs and killed by knives, or rescued from the claws of other forest predators, is distributed among all who happen to be present in the hamlet. Everyone present during the distribution gets a share, irrespective of particularistic kinship ties, or duration of stay in the hamlet.

Disputes

Individuals do not intervene in the internal affairs of their close kin. For example, in an exceptional case I have on record of a husband who maltreated his wife (a very uncommon occurrence), her brothers did not interfere, although they lived in the same hamlet.

Division of labour

Conjugal spouses (accompanied by their young children, if any) cooperate with each other – not with respective relatives – in most subsistence and domestic activities. They go on most subsistence pursuits together; they jointly build and repair their hut; they carry firewood together; they sometimes cook together; they often share care (and carriage) of their young children; they look after each other during times of illnesses (see Bird 1983a for a fuller description).

All in all, it is clear that Kinship does not play a major role in regulating Nayaka life: Kinship roles and rules are neither discussed and formalized by Nayaka nor manifested in everyday and kinship-prone occasions. Relationships between kin are 'weak' in material and moral content in the sense that they do not involve kinship-located obligatory economic transactions, nor conspicuous instances thereof. Furthermore, they do not involve kinship-located obligations to help, avenge, or take part in life-cycle events.

Following *The Social Construction of Reality*'s first chapter, I now want to argue that the 'person-to-person' situation impedes the dialectic development of Kinship roles and rules. Nayaka know 'vividly' and 'fully' most (if not all) of the people in their (Nayaka) social world – including most (if not all) of their own and others' relatives of any given kinship category. For example, they know in a 'person-to-person' way, say, all their own *cikappa(n)*, and all the *cikappa(n)* of anybody else. There is no *cikappa(n)* they can think about in typical terms divorced from concrete personality. Their interactions with diverse *cikappa(n)* are flexible and influenced by idiosyncrasies and shared 'here and now', respectively. Thus, to put it shortly, kinship does not dialectically develop into Kinship.

Kinship and avoidance

Hopefully, there is a more convincing case now for the claim that 'kinship regulates so little' – at least as far as cooperation between kin is concerned. Is kinship associated with something else in this 'person-to-person' situation? I want to suggest now that it is: while Nayaka neither discuss, nor formalize cooperation with kin in relation to linguistically distinct kinship categories, they do so – at least in a quasi-manner – in relation to avoiding kin. Furthermore, on occasions they actually *avoid* interaction with close kin.

My hosts commonly mentioned *nachika*. Translatable as shyness, or reticence, *nachika*, they said, would bring them to avoid certain interactions, for example, direct physical contact, frontal encounter, joint stay in enclosed space, and joking. They suggested a rough correspondence between the degree of avoidance and the closeness/proximity of the relative. For example, strong *nachika*, they said, is felt with respect to one's parent-in-law of the opposite sex who lives nearby, and, to a lesser degree, with one's own parent. For example, one avoids joking with either of them; but one steps out of one's path only when one sees one's mother-in-law coming towards one.

Though somewhat faintly, *nachika*-related behaviour resembles what the literature on tribal societies commonly associates with the rule-bound non-joking relationship (distinguished from the joking one). However, my hosts insisted that they do not follow any Kinship rule but behave this way because, to diverse degrees, they *feel nachika* towards these kin. Indeed, the *nachika*-related behaviour they speak about was neither stylized, nor conspicuous in other ways.

Concern with habitualized avoidance behaviour is seen elsewhere: Nayaka say that one must not refuse requests for sharing: if someone asks one for something they say one 'ought' to give it. The closer the kinship tie, the more this applies; one should refuse nobody, but least of all close kin who live next to one.

All this means that cooperation with close kin in domestic and subsistence activities is sensitive and trouble-prone. And indeed, conjugal pairs – who mostly pursue domestic and subsistence activities jointly – rarely cooperate with other couples. Occasionally, they only cooperate with single (unmarried) persons – and then avoid those who are close kin (see detailed analysis in Bird 1983a).

Why do Kinship roles and rules develop – or quasi-develop – with respect to avoidance rather than cooperation? A commonsensical explanation first offers itself. Given a social scene which is dominated by the 'person-to-person' situation – rather than one characteristic of large societies, which are dominated by alienated, anonymous situations – concern with avoidance is understandable. The band organization throws people into involuntary proximity, immediacy and intimacy with each other. Therefore, their major concern lies with ways of maintaining interpersonal space.

Over and above this, it can be argued that there are fewer personal 'interferences' to the dialectic development of roles and rules than there are in the context of cooperation; for, by definition, avoidance involves disengagement from the other person. Therefore, idiosyncrasies and personal attributes do not interfere as much. In simple words, it does not matter much if one avoids this *cikappa(n)*, who has this particular personality, or that *cikappa(n)* with his idiosyncratic personality – the avoidance remains the same. Whereas the cooperation with each one of them can be significantly different, depending on their personalities.

However, whatever the reason may be, we can conclude that while Nayaka neither formalize, nor discuss Kinship roles and rules in relation to cooperation, they do so to a modest degree in relation to avoidance.

A comparative perspective

Notwithstanding differences in degree (see below), Nayaka are similar in broad terms to other hunter-gatherers on all the major points that emerged from the analysis above. Most importantly, the 'person-to-person' situation dominates social interaction among hunter-gatherers generally. They are band societies – this is one of their most distinguishing common characteristics (Lee and DeVore 1968:8) – who live dispersed in small groups. The common size of the band – called the 'magic number' by Lee and DeVore (1968) and never since contested while almost everything else has been – is twenty-five. Its members are attached to a particular location – much more than was realized in the early 1970s – but at the same time frequently visit others. Huts are casually built – often more crudely than Nayaka huts – and they are also constantly reconstructed and relocated, placing people in relations of immediate neighbourhood with diverse others. Thus, on the whole, people live within the 'bodily manipulative zone' of a significant number of their fellows (I would say, even, the critical mass thereof), far more, in any case, than they would in settled communities.

Secondly, many hunter-gatherers use kinship terms extensively and universally within the group (Barnard 1981; see also Woodburn 1980:105).

Thirdly, nevertheless, kinship 'regulates so little'. As Woodburn further elaborated, kinship relationships are typically not 'load bearing'; they 'do not carry a heavy burden of goods and services transmitted between the participants in recognition of claims and obligations' (1980:105). 'Kinship . . . [only provides] a broad idiom for friendly rather than hostile relations and a set of rough and ready expectations for appropriate behaviour' (1979:257). More generally, 'people often do not, at least explicitly, seem to value their own culture and institutions very highly and may, indeed, not be accustomed to formulating what their custom is or what it ought to be' (1980:106).

Finally, hunter-gatherers are commonly distinguished by a lack of, or minimal, cooperation between people in general, and kin in particular (P. Gardner 1966; Woodburn 1980). Families and individuals are highly autonomous (P. Gardner 1991). They often sanction refusal of explicit requests to share (e.g. Myers 1982; Ingold 1987). Many of them deal with disputes by 'voting with their feet', not through kinship-related channels (e.g. Turnbull 1968).

Though similar in broad terms, there are differences in degree between hunter-gatherer groups on all these four points – and the differences are of equal interest to us. Take for example the !Kung, as reported in the detailed studies of Marshall (e.g. 1976) and Lee (e.g. 1979).

Firstly, they are larger in number than Nayaka. With an estimated population of 6,500 (Lee 1979:35), the number of !Kung is more than sixfold that of the 1,000-strong Nayaka. Compared with the 69 Nayaka of the Gir locality, the Dobe !Kung (counted by Lee in his 1964 study) comprise 379 'residents' (who mostly, but not always stay in the Dobe) and 87 'marginals' (who spend less than six months in the area, and in some cases only a day (1979:43)). Each !Kung hamlet (or camp) is larger than the Nayaka equivalent. While the Gir Nayaka are distributed in five residential clusters, the much larger Dobe !Kung are distributed around nine water-holes. Moreover, being confined within highly populated

South India, Gir Nayaka have little contact with Nayaka in other communities, while Dobe !Kung maintain extensive links with other !Kung communities, and occasionally come into contact with relatively anonymous and even stranger !Kung. All in all, it can be said that anonymity is more apparent in !Kung life – though, on the whole, they also mostly interact with other !Kung in the 'person-to-person' situation.

Secondly, !Kung use kinship terms and personal names in everyday communicative acts, much as Nayaka do, but have a more elaborate system (see Marshall (1957) and Lee (1984) for detailed descriptions). Names are given, each to a number of people (of the same sex), and establish between them namesake relationships. In a unique way, these name-relationships implicate kinship relationships: for example, a woman who bears the same name as one's sister is referred to as a sister – even if she is a stranger. Indeed, when a 'Kung arrives at a new unknown group, he locates bearers of names identical to names of close relatives in his home group and establishes corresponding kinship relationships with them' (Marshall 1957:24–5).[6]

Thirdly, !Kung have significantly more kinship-located rights, obligations and economic cooperation than Nayaka do (though still few in comparison with non-hunter-gatherer societies). For example, men customarily work for their wives' parents for some years after their marriages, and are, later, obliged to always give the in-laws specific shares of hunted game. In addition !Kung maintain extensive networks of *hxaro* relationships – involving exchange of gifts and hospitality – and frequently (at times weekly) gather for communal medicine dances.

It is most interesting that kinship-located behaviour goes in tandem with kinship terms; the latter are applied to others – even strangers – through the name-relationship practice and entail a corresponding behaviour. Thus, a !Kung who, through similarities of name, calls a stranger 'sister' also behaves towards her as towards a sister.

Finally, !Kung practice various avoidance behaviours with respect to close kin, including (among others) parents, parents' siblings and spouses' parents (see Marshall 1957: 19–20; Lee 1984: 65). These avoidance practices seem to be more elaborate and more fully formalized than among Nayaka.

The differences between Nayaka and !Kung, I suggest, can be explained within the terms of this analysis adapted from *The Social Construction of Reality*. It can be argued that, with the greater anonymity that exists among !Kung, relating in turn to social and demographic scales, the dialectic development of Kinship roles and rules goes further, impeded less by the 'person-to-person' situation.

The emergence of roles and rules: AIP and evolutionary reading

Hopefully, the analysis shows how hunter-gatherers' kinship practices are embedded in inter-personal social interaction and, furthermore, how the emergence (or lack thereof) of Kinship roles and rules is influenced by patterns of social interaction. Kinship terms, it has been shown, are learnt within the context of social interaction; and roles and rules 'rise and fall' depending on the predominant mode thereof.

Over and above this conclusion – which, in a way, achieves the purpose of this chapter by itself – the analysis invites thoughts about the possible evolutionary emergence of human roles and rules. Of course this is highly problematic. We cannot overlook the considerable problems that are involved in reading contemporary hunter-gatherers evolutionarily, and comparative ethnographies precessually. However, this has been traditionally done by scholars seeking insight and information on evolutionary questions – for lack of better alternatives as much as for other reasons – and the present chapter, notwithstanding the problems, will follow this tradition. It will depart from it in one significant respect, however: the rationale of the exercise will not lie in presuming continuity of a deterministic mode of production (between contemporary hunter-gatherers and early humans) as the orthodoxy maintains, and is currently heavily criticized for.[7] Rather, it lies in presuming a suggestive similarity in demographic and societal scale (at least relative to other contemporary examples) which can help us to imagine what social life in emergent small societies could have been like. But it has to be emphasized that in this exercise we no longer talk about the Nayaka, the !Kung or other contemporary tribal minorities we collectively call hunter-gatherers. We 'think with them' on evolutionary questions, trying to say something – conjectural at that – on evolution.

Based on primate research, the naturalistic scheme for the evolution of roles and rules would have been this: roles and rules evolved because it was advantageous to make intents explicit, and behaviour predictable. Once behaviour standardized, it was labelled and subsequently institutionalized (see E. Goody 1978b; n.d.). Does human-based research suggest otherwise?

Given a language-able human, three hypotheses can be drawn from the above ethnographic examination (and comparison):

Firstly, linguistic objectification of kinship links (i.e., kinship terms) existed *before* fully developed Kinship roles and rules. The Nayaka show us how it could have been. What could have been the evolutionary rationale of kin classification? Its use – a universal phenomenon after all – could have demonstrated (and reproduced) inter-relatedness, which was important for social group-based life. Furthermore, the terms could have served for human individuals to initiate interaction with others from a distance. One can imagine how, wanting to attract someone's attention, they turned to verbal signs for biographic relationships (meanwhile usefully emphasizing bonding inter-relatedness). Or in the dialectic obverse, how distinct sounds they used for the purpose came to be interpreted as symbols of kinship links. It is harder to conjure up how, instead, they started to use objective, detached names.

Secondly, the emergence of roles and rules started with avoidance (not cooperation) rules. For as individuals became aware of their individuality, so they became concerned about inter-personal social space. At the same time, they would be concerned to avoid disruptions within the group. Group disruption was dangerous and, at the same time, highly likely in group-based social life.

Thirdly, as groups grew and dispersed, anonymity entered the world, yet people remained aware of kinship relatedness, expressed in the communicative use of kinship terms. Thus, kinship terms played an instrumental role in the dialectic development of Kinship roles and rules. It is probable that general social interaction, in which kinship terms were applied to group-recognized but personally unknown individuals (as among the !Kung), were modelled on the interaction with personally known kin. With this sort of demographic dispersal, the 'person-to-person' situation would no longer impede the dialectic development of Kinship roles and rules.

Compared with the naturalistic scheme, this three-stage sociological one is, at the very least, more plausible. For the naturalistic scheme is logically inconsistent. It posits an overall selective pressure for predictable behaviour – yet predictable behaviour is advantageous to others, not to oneself; it is, in fact, *disadvantageous* to oneself. Furthermore, the naturalistic scheme implies that (human) roles and rules are biologically programmed, yet history and personal experiences, no less than the ethnographic record on hunter-gatherers, speak strongly against this. In contrast, the sociological scheme, following *The Social Construction of Reality*, posits that language, social interaction and group-awareness suffice for the dialectic development of roles and rules. The potential was released and realized with demographic growth and the decreasing dominance of the 'person-to-person' mode of social interaction.

The sociological scheme adds a subtle yet consequential role to AIP thinking in the evolutionary emergence of Kinship roles and rules. Firstly, language, which strongly reflects on AIP (see other contributors, this volume), was imperative in the evolutionary process, not just a label-provider. Secondly, kinship terms, particularly crucial in the process, evolved within an interactive context involving anticipation and planning. Finally, minimizing group disruption concurrent with maximizing private gains (as posited by the scheme) called for more sophisticated AIP thinking. It called for anticipatory interactive planning in view of two aims which often contradict each other and, therefore, had to be weighted against each other. Such a situation generated selective pressure for a kind of intelligence which enabled humans to arrive at novel solutions by playing variations of old and socially accepted ones. It generated their ability, as the phrase goes, 'to play within the rules'.

Conclusions

This chapter has, I hope, provided an AIP-compatible perspective on hunter-gatherers, with particular reference to Kinship roles and rules. It also illustrates, I hope, the scope of spin-offs from the AIP project. The latter led, in this case, to a fresh perspective on contemporary hunter-gatherers, and to an explanation of their otherwise enigmatic Kinship. In turn, to add to *The Social Construction of Reality*, it offers an ethnographic illustration of a 'prototypical case of institutionalization'; a case which Berger and Luckmann themselves left unexplored, being concerned with the developed form, and, more important, unfamiliar with band societies.

Acknowledgements

I am indebted to Esther Goody for recognizing the seeds of the ideas expressed here in my doctoral dissertation; and for her comments on earlier drafts. I also thank G. Kunda, Y. Shenhav, Y. Peres, A. Gopher and E. Illuz for their comments on early drafts.

Notes

1 Since 1992, when this chapter was written, I have developed some of the ideas contained in it. The results appear in Bird-David (1994).
2 The term is problematic, not least because it confuses early and contemporary populations, both called indistinguishably by the same term.
3 For financial assistance during the first spell of fieldwork I am indebted to Trinity College, Anthony Wilkin Fund, H.M. Chadwick Fund, Smuts Memorial Fund, the Wyse Fund and the Radcliffe-Brown Fund of Cambridge; and for the second spell of fieldwork to the Horovitz Institute for Research in Developing Countries, Tel Aviv, and to the Jerusalem Foundation for Anthropological Studies.
4 A few Nayaka occasionally live in the fringe of the locality, in huts constructed near villages or places of employment. They visit close friends once or twice a year for several days each time.

5 Some non-Nayaka people live in and around the Gir valley. Nayaka maintain a regular contact with them, however this lies outside the concerns of the present chapter (but see Bird-David 1988).
6 !Kung also occasionally change names – like Nayaka – and then the name-based network of kinship relationships change accordingly.
7 See Solway and Lee (1990) and Wilmsen and Denbow (1991) for summaries of the opposing views on the issue.

PART II

The interactive negotiation of meaning in conversation

JÜRGEN STREECK

4 On projection

The topic of this chapter[1] is a varied class of phenomena, most of them small if not tiny, some elaborate and large, which occur in all kinds of visible and audible shapes in all kinds of contexts in human talk and interaction. What is common to all of them is that they occur as prefatory components to bigger things to come. Prefaces range from rather minimal units such as *uh*, *well*, or micro-moments of silence, to fully developed pre-sequential utterances such as *can I ask you a question?* (Schegloff 1980). Gestures also are quite often performed in prefatory slots. The role of prefaces – or *pre*'s (as conversation analysts have fondly nicknamed these pet phenomena) – is to 'foreshadow' or 'project' (Sacks *et al.* 1974) something that comes after them, to bring it into play and 'prepare the scene' (Schegloff, 1984b). They allow other participants a certain premonition as to what this actor might be up to next.[2]

Vague as it is, this description is not likely to yield a neatly bounded set of phenomena. The collection I describe is eclectic at best. The chapter is loosely organized around a sequence of talk between two nurses from Thailand who discuss weather conditions and proper attire in Germany. This sequence was chosen because it nicely illustrates the theme that runs through all of the examples, namely that interactional units foreshadow one another: moment by moment, the speaker's gestures prefigure the next moment, allowing the participants to negotiate joint courses of action until, finally, a communication problem is solved collaboratively. Pre's, it is suggested, are at the very heart of social collaboration in talk and interaction. The various projections made within this sequence lead us radially to other interaction samples, each of which instantiates a similar type.

The interest in these small phenomena with respect to the investigation of social intelligence and anticipatory interaction planning is that many of the behaviour artifacts that humans have created to be used in interaction (deception and other secondary stratagems excluded) are shaped in ways that enable 'foresight' (see Good, Chapter 6, this volume). In all their diversity pre's seem to point to an underlying organization, a design feature of the human interaction order itself (Goffman 1983). It is argued here, in line with Drew (Chapter 5, this volume) and Heritage (1990/91) that 'socially intelligent' action formats – ones that give recipients immediate and maximum opportunities for social adjustment – can not be attributed to actors' pro-social motives. Rather, social intelligence resides as much in the cultural resources that interactants routinely and automatically employ. They are among the 'prothetic devices' that make up culture (Bruner 1990). The issue of where social intelligence lives – whether it is 'in the mind' or 'around us', will be taken up at the end of the chapter.

Action projection: pre's and possible trajectories

The term 'action projection' was introduced by Schegloff in an article on 'preliminaries to preliminaries' (1980).

Extract 1

→	B	I like tuh ask you something	11
	A	Shoot.	12
	B	Y'know I'ad my license suspended fuh six	13
		munts,	14
	A	Uh huh	15
	B	Y' know for a reason which, I rathuh not mention tuh you, in	16
		othuh words – a serious reason, en I like tuh know if w'd talk	17
		tuh my senator, or- somebuddy, could they help me get it back,	18

In this extract, B announces a question. But he then does not ask it, but gives a *report*, which then turns out to be preliminary to the question. The main action (question) is 'doubly displaced' (p. 106). The preface-question indicates that what is to follow will be a preparation; everything said between the preface and the action will be understood to be part of this preparatory work.

There are other ways in which preface-questions are used; often they are indeed followed immediately by *the* question. In these cases, the pre marks the question as 'delicate':

Extract 2

PAM	H'llo::,	9
VICKY	Hi:. Vicky.	10
	(0.4)	11
VICKY	You ra:ng?	12
PAM	Oh hello there yes I di::d	13

	.hh um I nee:d tuh ask you a	14
	questio:n?	15
	(0.4)	16
PAM	en you musn't (0.7) uh take	17
	it personally or kill me.	18
	(0.7)	19
PAM	I wan to know (0.7)	20
	whether you: will (b) would	21
	be free:, (.) to work o:n um	22
	tomorrow night.	23
	(0.4)	24

A preface question, then, does not unequivocally show its character as a pre or pre-pre. Recipients may mistake one for the other. Pre's only project *possible* courses of action. Not only is the meaning-in-context of the preface underspecified – a 'prefiguring' rather than a 'figure' – but the course of action sequences is always open to unforeseen contingencies; participants can take unanticipated actions that alter the projected sequence course. While pre's enable a bit of foresight, occasionally only hindsight will reveal the prefatory role of an utterance or utterance-component.

Preface questions can engender *pre-sequences* (Drew 1984).

Extract 3

→	J	So who'r the boyfriends for the week.	1
		(0.2)	2
	M	.k.hhhh- Oh: go::d e-yih this one'n that	3
		one yihknow, I jist, yihknow keep busy en	4
		go out when I wanna go out John it's nothing .hhh	5
		I don' have anybody serious on the string,	6
→	J	So in other words you'd go out if I:: askedche	7
		out one a'these times,	8
	M	Yeah! Why not.	9

J's question turns out to be a *preinvitation*, and M may or may not have heard it this way in the first place. This kind of ambiguity is essential to the design of prefaces: they are designed to foreshadow possibilities, which are often enough cancelled or redefined. Pre's are noncommittal for good reasons. Their role is to 'point forward to possible patterns of perception', to give a 'prescription of the path to a more precise determination' (Husserl, quoted in Liberman 1985:182).

Let us now take a first look at the mundane sequence of Thai conversation at the Berlin Goethe Institute: who could have known this is what they call summer, not a chance to wear these clothes. We will look especially at the gestures. Each one seems to foreshadow something and to give the hearer an orientation, until eventually, a rapidly delivered movement triggers the hearer's response. She becomes active and helps out in a word-search.

Extract 4

```
                ((wiggle))
                 └──────┐
A  Mâi kôi dâi prà yò:t. (.)                                   1
   You can rarely use it.
     ((scratches face))
┌──────────┬──────────────┐
     Arai là man uh- (---------------)                        2
     What it is uh-
                  ((clapping))
              ┌──────┤
     man mâi mâi mâi mâi mâi mòh-=                             3
     it's not not not not not suit-

┌─────────┐                      ((folds hands))
B  Mâi mòh gàb agàrt.                  │                       4
   Not suitable in this weather        └──────────────┐
  │                                                    │
A  Mâi mòh gàb spâb tang ní loei.                             5
   Not suitable in this climate.
```

Figure 4.1

Figure 4.2

Figure 4.3

Figure 4.4

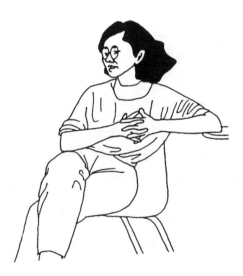

Figure 4.5

This sequence culminates in *joint action*. The collaborative action is the 'shared saying' at lines 4 and 5. It is brought about via a series of steps which typologically fall under the category of 'repair activities'. The term 'repair' in conversation analysis designates all those activities by speakers and recipients which deal with (actual or virtual) problems in speaking and understanding: speaking errors, lack of memory, failure to hear an utterance or identify a referent, etc. 'Repair actions' are those that address – or are made out to address[3] – these problems: self-correction, word-searches, asking for and providing clarification, etc. A useful distinction separates 'retrospective' repair (e.g., correction) from 'prospective' repair, i.e. repair on a (potentially) upcoming problem.[4]

Speaker A initiates repair on her turn at line 5, but at this point, repair is already in play: the turbulences in line 3 mark her problems. Throughout this sequence, the speaker makes a series of gestures, each of which addresses the trajectory of the sequence in a different way: first she foreshadows 'vagueness'; then she indicates that there is a 'problem'; next she produces a gesture indicating a 'fit' – arguably a spatial representation of the concept she is searching for, 'suitable'; finally, when the search is completed, she folds her hands.

Let us examine a few other instances of joint action in which the mechanics of this format are more transparent. A rather transparent example is extract 5; it is a 'unison'. Three children, two girls and a boy, in an American elementary classroom argue over an assignment. At this point, one of the antagonists (Leola) is about to present her opponent (Wallace) with evidence: she is about to read out loud the instructions that are printed on the work-sheet. But while Leola initiates the moves, she and her friend Carolyn end up reading these instructions in unison.

Extract 5

```
              1         2          3
LEOLA     You see. Here it say. Ho:w man. How many words
                                          [
CAROLYN                                   How many words
LEOLA     can you make out of those five letters.
          [
CAROLYN   can you make out of those five letters.
```

The unison is prepared in a series of three prefaces (marked by numbers above the text). First, Leola suggests a particular cognitive orientation for the reception of her subsequent utterance (*you see*); then she projects reading (*here it say*) – this is the action projection 'proper', finally she begins to read (3), but immediately self-interrupts to then resume: she thereby transforms the beginning of the action into an action-preface and thus not only informs her friend that she is going to read, but also affords her another opportunity to join her. In fact, restarts often *solicit* co-participation (Goodwin 1981). The reading-in-unison, then, is a carefully prepared-for event.

Extract 5 has the format

[action, action abandoned→joint action]

This format can be observed in many, rather diverse interaction domains. For example, pre-enactments often occur in 'juncture activities', i.e. activities accomplishing or taking part in a more embracing 'recalibration' of an encounter. Among the actions typically engaged in during such moments are posture shifts and activities dealing with a participant's bodily needs (e.g. drinking, self-touch, clothing adjustments etc.).

A posture-shift is frequently pre-initiated by one party – by a small 'pre-shift' – and then carried out collaboratively and simultaneously by two or several parties. A frequent format for drinking is that one party lifts the cup or glass but then puts it back down. Thereafter, both parties simultaneously lift their cups and drink. One of the social functions of such joint activities at moments of juncture may be that by engaging in symmetrical and identically constructed actions, the participants sustain a state of engagement while no particular framework for the interaction is selected. Yet another kind of action that is frequent during moments of interactional juncture is self-touch: people in interaction become peripherally involved with themselves when involvement with the other decreases. Often, however, another participant will 'mirror' the self-involvement, thereby turning it into a display of mutual engagement. Responding to self-touch with self-touch in return enables a participant to demonstrate to another that, although currently not involved *with* one another, they are nevertheless involved in the interaction *in the same way*. And again, frequently a participant who initiates self-touch without observing self-touch in return by the other, will discard the activity to then resume it; and the restart of self-touch is then done jointly, in synchrony, by both parties. In other words, self-touch – considered to be an instance of self-involvement – is often constructed in a way that secures joint engagement in it.

The 'shared talk' in the sequence of Thai conversation, then, is brought about via a very routinized, very widespread interaction design.

Possible repair pre-initiation

In contrast to body actions, talk is generally not carried out by two parties simultaneously, but turn-by-turn, with a minimum of overlap. Extended simultaneous talk is rare. However, collaborative talk does occur in *repair* segments and sequences, in particular in word-search repair, of which the Thai sequence is an instantiation.

Repair is another domain of conversational organization in which action projection can be observed. Self-initiated repair is often initiated only after a pre-indication of 'trouble ahead' has been given. Within the *repair-segment* proper, the speaker, by manipulating sounds and other language units, can indicate what kind of audience-participation is sought, whether or not the audience's support in dealing with the trouble is wanted. Typically, there is a shift from non-collaborative to collaborative organization: at first, self-repair is preferred; audience collaboration is invited only after one or more attempts at self-repair have failed. Schegloff (1984b) has described the initiation of repair in American conversation and specified 'the first signs in an ongoing flow of talk that repair is upcoming' (p. 268). Most common are 'cut-offs' (glottal stops) when a word is in progress, and 'uh's' when not. Sometimes there are repair 'pre-initiators', indications of trouble ahead, e.g. hitches or sound-stretches before the actual repair is initiated, as in extract 6.

Extract 6

$$1 \quad 2 \quad 3$$

ROBIN She hadda wait up the:re fo:r u-she:s been there
        since eight uh' clock this morning

Two sound-stretches (1 and 2) pre-indicate the initiation of repair (at 3). Schegloff points out that the more removed these 'harbingers' are from the 'trouble source', the more problematic it is whether they are, in fact, harbingers: even when repair is prefigured, it can subsequently be 'cancelled' (p. 269). In other words, 'harbingers' are only *possible* repair pre-initiators.

There are interesting cross-linguistic variations in repair-initiation and pre-initiation (and, by implication, in the organization of collaborative talk). In conversations among speakers of Ilokano in the Philippines, for example, 'cut-offs' and 'uh's' are unlikely repair-initiators, 'uh's' being virtually absent from speech; by far the most likely initiators are sound-stretches (Streeck 1989b).

Extract 7

A Ngem dagsan gasat ta::– ti sumagmamano nga aldaw nagarirulos 1
   But after several days had passed
   ti::::: Disyembre.   2
   in::::: December
   [
B   Disyembre   3
   December

Thus, sound-stretches are not only used as repair-initiators, but also – as in American-English conversation – as 'harbingers' of such initiations.

Ilokano sound-stretches, thus, are structurally ambiguous things: they can be heard as harbingers of later repair, or as initiations of current repair, or, when the talk quickly progresses, as (for all practical purposes) 'nothing at all'. What the sound-stretch amounts to, on any given occasion, is to be determined by 'recipient's work'. These sound-stretches can go to very considerable length, creating larger and larger 'opportunity spaces' for such negotiation; the longer the stretch, the more compelled the recipient may feel to treat it as a 'repairable', thereby securing the 'contiguity' (H. Sacks 1986 [1973]) or 'progressivity' (Schegloff 1979) of the conversation.

Similarly, speakers who have initiated repair can then actively pursue the audience's co-participation and turn the sequence into a collaborative one. This often takes place in word-searches.

Trajectories of a word-search

Once a speaker has initiated repair on a current utterance, he or she can overtly mark the repair *type* as a word-search. The 'parts' with which this is commonly done include *pauses* and 'recycles'; the element recycled is the last unit of talk prior to the trouble source.

When entering into a pause, speakers engaged in a word-search commonly withdraw their gaze from recipients. They thereby display that they are currently 'non-listeners' in the moment's conversation and – by implication – indicate that co-participation is dispreferred.[5] When no solution is found, gaze is returned to the recipient, and the 'preference for self-repair' is relinquished or relaxed in favour of the 'progressivity' of the conversation: co-participation is now invited. In the Thai sequence, the speaker withdraws her gaze from the listener just before she enters into the pause; she returns it just before she resumes speech.

Speakers of trouble sources can actively pursue collaboration. One way in which this is done is to recycle the last morpheme prior to the trouble source. These units project grammatical features of the 'target'.

In the following extract from a conversation between two speakers of German, the recycled unit is *son* (*so + ein*), a fusion of a deictic and an indefinite article, indicating that the target is a noun and that information relevant to the solution can be gleaned from the environment, in this case from the gesture (Figure 4.7).

Extract 8

    B Also ich hatte- ich hatte letztens w- irgendwo a äh äh ähm aufm   1
          Well, I had- I had- the other day wh- somewhere- uh uh uhm at the
          Arbeitsamt?oder (.) was das war. Da hatte ich ge- äh äh   2
          Labor Office or (.) whatever that was. I had (ge-) uh uh

→   mal son son son son son son Merkblatt äh inner Hand?   3
          one time this this this this this flier uh in my hand?

Figure 4.6

Figure 4.7

Figure 4.8

In extract 9 – an Ilokano morpheme (*in*) projects grammatical information which is taken up by the recipient in her attempt to help with the word-search.

Extract 9

> A Inkabil ko ti telepono idiay kwa:;- idiay sa:1a, kunak a.   1
>   I had put the telephone in the what- in the living-room, I said
>   Sa in- kwak- **in**- in- in- in- in- uhh-   2
>   And then (in-) I what-
>   [
> B   Hmm.   3
> B Insaram didiay ruangan?   4
>   You had closed the door?

Recipients may or may not opt for and/or be able to volunteer candidate solutions. Similarly, candidate solutions can be treated by the primary speaker as appropriate or as non-solutions. Recipients who volunteer candidate solutions, in constructing them, make use of the materials provided by the pre. The pre becomes a component of the solution – like in the Thai sequence (extract 4) where the negation morpheme *mâi* is incorporated in the solution.

> man mâi mâi mâi mâi mâi mòh-=   3
> it's not not not not not suit-

B mâi mòh gàb agàrt.   4
  not suitable in this weather
[
A mâi mòh gàb spâb tang ní loei.   5
  not suitable in this climate.

Gestures as trajectory components

I now want to extend the range of phenomena subsumed here under the category 'projection' yet a bit further, by addressing the incorporation of visual components – *gestures* – into turns-at-talk. For 'projection' also describes the communicative effects of many visual utterance components: they often precede speech-components and thereby 'prepare the scene' for them (see Schegloff 1984b). Gestures – especially iconic gestures – are often components of word-search sequences. For brief moments, sense-making is primarily accomplished by the speaker's hands. Both speaker and recipients *attend to* these manual symbol constructions; that is, they temporarily shift their attention to them. This shift in orientation is itself prepared.

Four successive gestures appear in the Thai fragment (see Figures 4.1–5 above). Each gesture is constructed differently, and not all occur at the same spatial location. The first is carried out in the neutral space where most descriptive gestures are done: in front of the speaker's torso. It is a slight horizontal rotation (Figure 4.1). It conveys a sense of ambiguity, indecisiveness, vagueness. The second visual act (at the beginning of line 2) involves self-touch: the speaker looks away and rubs her face (Figure 4.2). Interestingly, as Goodwin (1986) has shown, facial touch tends to be disattended by recipients – it 'drives their gaze away'. Thus, by rubbing her face in the course of a word-search, the speaker in effect discourages the listener from attending to or even becoming involved in her current action; she thereby secures the possibility of self-repair (the 'preferred' repair solution). The speaker then returns her gaze to the listener and brings her hands into a position from which she can execute a gesture (Figure 4.3), and immediately produces a series of claps (Figure 4.4). These are synchronized with the recycling of the function word *mâi*. I regard these motions as, on the one hand, vaguely iconic displays of a 'fit', and thus as projections of 'suitable', and, on the other, as acts of self-stimulation (which are not uncommon during moments of speech-production problems). Finally, when the recipient begins to offer a solution (line 5), the primary speaker freezes the gesture and, once the search comes to completion, she returns her hands to her lap and folds them (Figure 4.5). These gestural trajectory components all instantiate 'types'; their organization is not idiosyncratic. We will describe how these gestures work by looking at a few more examples; they represent 'iconic gestures' and what one might call 'action projectors'.

An iconic gesture's trajectory

Iconic gestures commonly *precede* their 'speech-affiliates'; they unfold – and often decay – before the word arrives. This makes them interesting phenomena for a study of projection in interaction.

Extracts 10 and 11 are from a conversation between two Japanese women who tell each other about car-accidents in which they were involved. In extract 10, the speaker verbally encodes a motion: *supin* (the loanword 'spin'), lexicalizes a rapid circular movement; the gesture visualizes the same conceptual profile, but further specifies it as a motion on a plane.

Extract 10

                              1
T .h nichiyoobi datta shi ne (---) kuruma suiteta shi h   1
   But, well, it was a Sunday and, you know, the car was empty and .h
   (2.0)
                  2
   supin shite   2
   it spun around

The speaker begins the gesture during a pause in her turn (1), before she utters the verb. She looks at the gesture. She then returns her gaze to the recipient, after uttering the verb (2). Thus, while gesture and speech share a semantic profile, the gesture nevertheless 'projects' that profile *prior* to the speech.

In the second instance (11), taken from the same compound utterance,

Figure 4.9

Figure 4.10

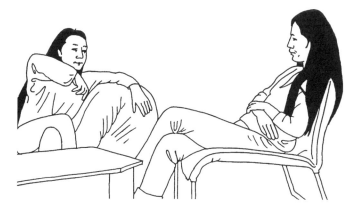

Figure 4.11

the speech unit – the noun *gaadoreru* (the loanword 'guardrail') profiles a long, horizontal object ('rail') as well as its function ('guard'). The gesture, in contrast, profiles a thin, round, vertical object, a *part* of the object – the pole. There is thus a remarkable division of labour between speech and gesture; each supplies a different *partial* conceptual profile. In this instance, the part of the object selected for representation by gesture is not a salient semantic component of the lexical unit *guardrail*. But it is salient in the course of this story, because it is the pole that was hit by the car (Figures 4.12–13).

Extract 11

T watashi no hoo no seki ga ano hora (----------) are   1
  the seat on my side, you know, look (----------) there
  aru ja na (---) gaadoreru   2
  was a guardrail

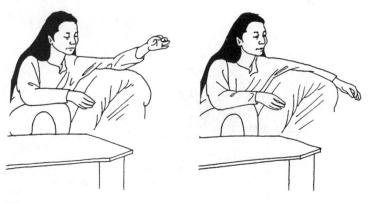

Figure 4.12   Figure 4.13

Again, the gesture is initiated far before the speech-unit to which it 'belongs'. This is the characteristic place of gestures in turns-at-talk: they *preface* speech units and *prefigure* the concepts communicated by them. They thus enable recipients – in varying degrees and depending upon contextual information provided by prior talk – to *anticipate* conceptual profiles of subsequent talk. The semantic relationships between the profiles supplied by the gesture and those encoded in lexical units are manifold. In these two examples, one gesture (in extract 10) overlaps with the lexical concept 'spin' but additionally encodes a horizontal plane; the gesture in the second example (extract 11) highlights a feature of the object which is not a prominent feature of the lexicalized gestalt. The gesture thus supports the story by prefiguring a component (the guard-rail's pole) that will be relevant in the further course of events. The speaker then moves on to show, by gesture, how the car hit and wrapped around the pole. By virtue of both their placement and their specific conceptual profiles, gestures afford recipients opportunities for anticipatory understandings.

Iconic gestures are symbolic constructions, equally motivated by the speaker's analysis of the *signifié* and by her analysis of the local requirements for understanding. They make use of established symbolic conventions and of prefabricated parts; but gestures at the same time allow local, idiosyncratic elaborations. Iconic gestures are designed to communicate; they provide imagery, kinaesthetic profiles. But given their regular place of occurrence – as prefaces to speech – they only 'point forward to *possible* patterns of perception' give a 'prescription of the *path* to a more precise determination' (Husserl, quoted in Liberman 1985: 182; my emphasis).

While iconic gestures prepare the scene for upcoming linguistic representations, they, too, arrive on a prepared scene. In order for gestures to receive the attention of the listener and to thereby become components of conceptual understanding, listeners must be pre-alerted to the gesture's occurrence. A common way in which speakers solicit the audience's attention to a gesture is the use of a deictic particle which *points* to the movement. This item is incorporated into the talk at the moment when the gesture begins. In the following example (from Goodwin 1986), the 'pointer' is the demonstrative *this*.

Extract 12

> A Ma::n she's <u>this</u> wi::de.

In extract 13 it is the demonstrative *som*.

Extract 13

> A Sie stand unten? Mit som weißn R̲ock nur?
> She stood d̄own below? In this ski̅rt only?

Words, thus, establish the gesture's relevance to the talk.

Secondly, speakers who produce iconic gestures withdraw their gaze from the recipient and briefly focus it on their own hands. Depending upon the gesture's placement in the listener's field of perception, the recipient also shifts her gaze. Speaker and recipient thus share in a momentary orientation to the gesture, which thus becomes the primary medium of communication (Streeck 1993, 1994).

This is also the design of gestural communication during word-searches. When the speaker has difficulty finding an appropriate word, he or she can opt for gesture as subsidiary symbolism, and the visual image – along with other contextually available information – can then be used by the recipient in formulating a solution. The speaker uses deictic participles and gaze to orient the recipient to the gesture and, characteristically, recycles a grammatical morpheme while he or she produces the gesture.

Extract 8 above – although completed by the primary speaker – has design features similar to the Thai sequence. Two German postgraduates discuss the difficulties of finding employment. B describes a visit to the employment office. He wants to relate how he read something in a flier; flier (*Merkblatt*) is the target of the search. As he moves into the search, the speaker lifts his hands and shows the shape of a booklet. He looks at his hands, thereby displaying 'reading'. The recipient's gaze follows his hands. When the speaker completes the search he – like the Thai speaker – folds his hands (see Figures 4.6–8 above).

There is thus a very systematic, apparently transcultural organization to the use of iconic gestural symbols in human communication. Speakers and recipients utilize the projective potential of manually produced images, and they use yet other communicative modalities (gaze and speech) to highlight the local relevance of the manual mode.

Action projectors

Not all gestures in interaction are of the iconic type, representing visible features of real-world objects and events. Another way in which gestures are used is the prefiguration of *linguistic action*, e.g. of the construction features of a subsequent utterance, the speech act about to be performed, the type of response proposed, etc. Only little research has been done on these uses of gesture, and the following remarks are tentative.

One place in unfolding interaction sequences where gestures project upcoming speech actions are 'transition places' between turns-at-talk. Participants who intend to take the turn sometimes demonstrate this intent gesturally, while another participant is still talking. Intending next speakers can also prefigure aspects of the action-type for which they solicit the turn (i.e. a gesture can be a recognizable 'pre' to a 'telling').

Turn-transition is a rather specific environment in conversation. The very circumstances of the task – turn-taking – occasion the use of the visual mode. Using gestural displays, intending next speakers can make their claim to the floor known and show what they plan to do with it – without interrupting the current speaker and without subjecting their own premature talk to overlap. Preliminary research on gestures used during turn-transition (Streeck and Hartge 1992) suggests that these are highly conventionalized, less formally elaborated than iconic gestures, and often metaphorical.

Turn-exit is another place where gestures that project actions are used. The task they are occupied with is the specification of the response-type sought. Gestures are occasionally appended as 're-completors' to turns. For example, shoulder shrugs are sometimes appended to the end of a story-telling. Story endings are interactionally underspecified: audiences have considerable leverage in selecting a type of response. Shoulder shrugs are commonly done when no immediate response is given, and display that no specific type of response is proposed.

Another place for visual displays during turn-endings is before the 'utterance-completor'. Often, a micro-pause makes room for the enactment. Gestures or displays thus positioned can solicit an 'early response', e.g. applause. In extract 14, a talk-show guest frames the 'keyword' of a punchline by a facial display. The guest, the comedian Richard Jenni, talks about his childhood and youth in Brooklyn.

Extract 14

And plus I had- no, I was into different things, I wa:s-   1
            1
and my particular neighborhood wa:s, you know (.)   2
        2
very into: uh (.) cri̲me I guess is the word.   3

In this extract, the arrival of the keyword (crime) is projected by a 'broad smile' (2) which proposes 'laughter' as an appropriate type of response; the smile, however, is itself projected by a brief eyebrow-flash (1). This sequence is a good illustration of the ways in which projection contributes to the rapid fine-tuning that is characteristic of human interaction. Speakers consistently foreshadow their next moves, and while this foreshadowing does not specify all features of this move but only projects a silhouette, it nevertheless prepares the audience and often enables them to initiate a response before the act to which they respond is actually completed. Action images and bodily displays of human states are frequently used as dramaturgical devices in narratives. In extract 15, the speaker talks about her always depressed roommate; here she describes in what state she finds her roommate when she comes home.

Extract 15

                    1
    A und Sibylle. (.) mit Grabesstimme und so.   1

        and Sibylle with a voice like from like a grave
        ((voice shift)) .hhh Was ganz Schreckliches passiert.   2
                    Something terrible happened.

The facial display (1) is a 'mouth of sadness'. By making the display the speaker enables her listener to 'meet' Sibylle before 'listening to her'. The speaker recreates the temporal structure of the event she describes.

We can now return to the sequence with which we began this survey of action projection and summarize the different 'paths' or 'trajectories' that eventually culminate in a collaborative completion. The path towards a word-search initially comes into play when turbulences appear in the utterance. The possibility of imminent trouble that is projected by these hitches is then specified when the speaker makes a first gesture which – in this context – can quite readily be identified as a projection of vagueness. At this point, a formulation problem is clearly in play. The speaker then addresses the trouble with a face-rub, a 'monitor' (Scheflen 1972) not uncommon in troubled interaction environments. By touching her face and at the same time withdrawing her gaze from the listener, the speaker invites the listener to disattend the problem, that is, *not* to become involved in the search. In other words, the speaker's visible actions project *self-repair* as the preferred trajectory for this sequence. But the speaker then reorients to the listener and initiates a series of iconic gestures. She thereby invites the listener to aid her in the search. Once the word-search is collaboratively completed, the speaker displays that successful completion by folding her hands. Each move thus prefigures a possible path for navigating through the sequence.

Language and such: socially intelligent shareware

In this chapter, a haphazard collection of interaction units has been described; each item in the collection in one way or another foreshadows shapes of things to come. 'Things to come' includes varied appearances ranging from posture shifts to nouns (which can be premarked for gender, number, case and so on). The term 'trajectory' has been used to describe the unfolding of symbolic and interaction units from a first indication that something is 'in play', to the unit's completion and ratification as a social act. The underlying theme has been the suggested need for a description of language and behaviour as phenomena *in progression, unfolding towards (possible) completion.*[6] The hallmark of pre's is that they pre-indicate default courses of action. It appears that this design is an imprint of a rather generic social intelligence.

But *where* does this intelligence live? As far as pre's are concerned, when we pre-decline an offer, do we each exercise our individual sensibility, or do we just do 'what everyone does?' In this case the social intelligence of our action is owed to the common resource, the socially available conventional 'format for declination'. So when we ask, 'where does social intelligence live, in our heads or in the world around us?', the answer must obviously be: in both (and in other places as well). Reviewing only the odd collection of moments illustrated here, it appears that social intelligence resides partly in our bodies: a tendency to go along with another organism's 'intention movement' (as in the posture shift ex-amples), or a tendency to inhibit certain acts (and to restrain associated affects (D'Andrade 1984)), as in the case of delayed antagonistic actions. To what extent this intelligence is not only embodied but also innate, and to what extent it is traditional and learned, is not completely clear. The boundary between these classes of phenomena might well be fuzzy. Certainly, innate impulses are generally shaped into traditional mean-ingful forms. In either case, the effect is a tendency within interaction processes towards avoidance of antagonistic action and towards maximiz-ing opportunities for collaboration and solidarity (Heritage 1984: 277). Much embodied social knowledge needs other, interlocking 'bodies of knowledge' to become alive and to function. (This is true of all competencies relating to entrainment phenomena such as shared speech and movement rhythm (Stern 1977; Trevarthen, 1979a, b).)

Then there are the many kinds of knowledge that we have acquired as competent individual members of a society or culture; much of this knowledge presumably resides in our separate minds/brains. (The latter is what is commonly studied under the terms 'knowledge' and 'cognition'.) As far as pre's are concerned, some also may occur because their users possess certain items of *propositional, cultural* knowledge, for example that 'one doesn't say no to a request for a favour'.

And finally (to simplify matters drastically), social intelligence is embodied in the symbolic *resources* that we share, in particular our languages, in their structural design. Simply by using their normal forms, the ones that the grammar wants us to use (by making them easy to master), we gravitate towards civility in our interactional dealings with one another. Not acting upon the consensus presupposed by the normal forms takes a little bit of extra constructional effort. This share of the corpus of knowledge belongs to the traditional, evolved interaction *forms*, not to individual users. All that people have to do is 'plug in' to the public shareware in a routine fashion and take it from there. To an extent at least, one can be fully unconscious and still act intelligently. Symbolic and interactional resources are always open to clumsy and refined, to naive and self-reflexive uses. But just participating in conversational interaction has a mildly civilizing effect.

Hence, to be able to describe even the most trivial and mundane moments of symbolic interaction, we must acknowledge that knowledge and intelligence are *distributed* across a variety of 'locations': bodies, individual minds, other minds, cultural symbolisms and external memory systems. How bodies of knowledge are represented depends on where they reside, how they are used, and what purposes they have.[7] But any modelling of intelligent activity as a mere externalization of individual mental knowledge resources is false and misleading; even when we silently talk to ourselves our communicative intentions are shaped by the conceptual schemata that our common languages offers us (Bruner 1990).

While the computer metaphor for the human mind has perhaps caused more confusion than enlightenment, it is aptly used by Donald (1991: 17) when he suggests that 'the cognitive architecture of humans . . . is similar to providing . . . a computer . . . with a link to a network'.

If a computer is embedded in a network of computers, that is, if it interacts with a 'society' of other computers, it does not necessarily retain the same 'cognitive capacity' . . . As part of a network, the computer can now delegate computations beyond its own internal capacity . . . It can store its outputs anywhere in the network . . . The point is, in a true network the resources of the system are shared, and the system functions as a unit larger than any of its individual components.

(Ibid.: 310)

The link to a network is for us humans primarily provided by language, which is not only a code of communication but also an *external memory store*. Thus, we cannot properly point to a location in space when asked where knowledge is located.

In his well-known essay on speech genres, Bakhtin (1986 [1952–3]: 88) wrote:

The words of a language belong to nobody, but still we hear those words only in particular individual utterances ... Any word exists for the speaker in three aspects: as a neutral word of a language, belonging to nobody; as an *other*'s word, ... filled with echoes of the other's utterance; and, finally, as *my* word, ... already imbued with my expression.

Communal ownership extends not only to words as form of self-expression, but also to the meanings inherent in them, to the conceptual matter or 'conventional imagery' (Langacker 1987). Language, including grammar, is conceptualization, a vast symbolic resource for making sense of our experiences in the terms in which generations before us have made sense of theirs (D'Andrade 1990; Lakoff 1987).

Grammatical structures ... are inherently symbolic, providing for the structuring and conventional symbolization of conceptual content. Lexicon, morphology, and syntax form a continuum of symbolic units, divided only arbitrarily into separate 'components' – it is ultimately as pointless to analyze grammatical units without reference to their semantic value as to write a dictionary which omits the meanings of its lexical items (Langacker 1987: 1–2).

But linguistic structures are not only responsive to cognitive (conceptual) and communicative demands. In interaction contexts, the places where languages come to life, they also meet with the demands of rapid, open-textured, sometimes risky social situations. The highest chances of surviving in the primary forests of human interaction belong to those conventionalized formats that meet the two kinds of requirements concurrently. But for them to reveal themselves, a descriptive language will be needed which evokes the *progressional* character of language in talk-in-interaction (Lerner 1987). Perhaps a language of 'gestalt' and 'appearance' is best suited to the emergence of grammatical-semantic units over time. Whatever the eventual shape of the descriptive language, 'projection' cannot be explained unless we assume that grammatical constructs are structured wholes, rather than bottom-up products of compositional syntax (Langacker 1986). In the origin and deployment of language schemata out of which interactional turns can be constructed, conceptual and social intelligence meet.

Pre's are simple but artful upshots of forward-looking utterance design. Clearly, they are part of *langue*, and any specification of their proper use must take account of the social and syntactic fact that pre's belong at sentence and/or utterance beginnings. To properly describe language units we must constantly remind ourselves that 'the natural environment of language use is talk-in-interaction ... The natural home environment of clauses and sentences is turns-at-talk' (Schegloff, 1992c). It is irrelevant whether we are dealing with items such as *uh* or *well*, or schematic constructions (e.g., 'left dislocation'): the phenomena clearly fall into the domain of traditional grammatical description, but they are equally clearly interaction-motivated phenomena, some of them exclusively so. Abstracting them from either force deprives them of their beauty: the density, economy and transparency of natural symbols.

Pre's are humble things, and they may come from humble beginnings. They could well be 'vestiges' from pre-human stages of evolution (Darwin 1964 [1859]).[8] They can be traced to an initial recognition by social animals that 'individuals can benefit not just from obtaining information from each other, but also from making it available to each other', because 'the information ... might ... reduce the ambiguity in a developing social interaction' (W. Smith 1977: 9). Mead (1967 [1934]) has defined his concept of 'gestures' similarly: a gesture is an early phase of a social act, 'that phase ... to which adjustment takes place on the part of other individuals in the social process of behavior' (p. 46). The gestures 'serve their functions [by] calling out the responses of the others, these responses becoming themselves stimuli for readjustment, until the final social act itself can be carried out' (p. 44). In Mead's view this 'conversation of gestures' was the breeding ground for symbolization and the human mind.

Social intelligence is very, very old, much older than humanity. Some ancient, pre-human intelligence has survived from times before our own species emerged. It is alive and well in our modern interactions, distributed across various kinds of locations. Some of this intelligence is certainly deeply buried in our bodies, inherited by nature and unbeknown to us, but experienced, nevertheless, in the form of feelings (embodied social cognitions (M. Rosaldo 1984)). But a lot of it, interestingly enough, lives in our artifacts, our symbolic inventions. Its place is the 'network', the 'shareware', the 'tribal encyclopedia' (Havelock 1963). Exposed to the stormy weathers of moment-to-moment interaction, miniscule objects such as pre's 'acquire the precision of continuously refined exterior devices' (Donald 1991: 11).

Language – *any* language, in effect, any word – is entangled in an unbroken tradition of talk in interaction. Like life, language is always in progression, a 'transitory [yet] enduring thing' (Humboldt 1988 [1836]). That is why we moderns, in our urban, self-reflexive ways, still draw upon the wisdom of *Homo erectus* when it comes to the nitty-gritty of moment-to-moment interactional life. Luckily, there has been no gap in the oral tradition.

Notes

1 This chapter owes a lot to conversations with Robert Hopper, about 'trajectories' and 'possible trajectories'.
2 Among the many conversation analysis studies devoted to forms of pre's and/or action projection are Drew (1984); Goodwin (1986); Heritage (1990/91); Jefferson (1992); Kendon (1976); Pomerantz (1984); Schegloff (1979, 1980, 1988b); Streeck (1992); Streeck and Hartge (1992); Terasaki (1976).
3 See Jefferson (1975) about repair as social camouflage.
4 Schegloff, Jefferson and Sacks (1977) give a typology of repair.
5 See Goodwin's (1986) analysis of the role of gaze in the negotiation of participation in word-searches.
6 Conversation analysts make much of the need to say '*possible* completion' because, in order to capture the progressional nature of talk and language, it is necessary to envision and conceptualize everything from the reference point of an idealized *now*. The future appears as a horizon of possibilities which, the more apparent they become, the more likely they are to be preempted.
7 See the beautiful study of 'The dialectic of arithmetic in grocery shopping' (Lave *et al.* 1984). See also D'Andrade 1981; Goodwin 1993; Hutchins and Klausen 1990; Lynch and Woolgar 1988.
8 This is how Donald (1991:3–4) summarizes his modern variant of Darwin's thesis: 'The essence of my hypothesis is that the modern human mind evolved from the primate mind through a series of major adaptations, each of which led to the emergence of a new representational system. Each successive new representational system has remained intact within our current mental architecture, so that the modern mind is a mosaic structure of cognitive vestiges from earlier stages of human emergence. Cognitive vestiges involve the evolutionary principle of conversion of previous gains and are similar in principle to the many other vestigal behaviors we possess – for instance, baring the teeth in anger, or wailing in grief.'

PAUL DREW

5 Interaction sequences and anticipatory interactive planning

In this chapter I shall consider some relationships between sequential patterns or organizations in talk-in-interaction, notably in conversation, and that aspect of social intelligence which Goody has termed 'anticipatory interactive planning' (hereafter AIP). Social intelligence consists, in part anyway, of cognitive models of action which might underlie the production and interpretation of 'meaningful' communicative behaviour among social beings (humans, and possibly some primates; see Byrne, Chapter 1, this volume). AIP highlights the reciprocity of communication in social relations, incorporating as it does the mental representation of alter's responses to ego's actions (Goody, Introduction to this volume). Goody is thereby suggesting that AIP concerns the possibility that, via their cognitive models of action, interactants have ways of predicting that if they make a given verbal 'move' (and from now on I shall refer exclusively to those actions which are verbal), this will engender or facilitate a subsequent verbal action by either themselves or their recipients. The predictability of some contingent subsequent action(s) is part of 'mentally modelling' the likely behaviour/responses of their co-interactants, which hence underpins the strategic nature of selecting a current action.

The ability to anticipate subsequent verbal actions, performed in turns at talk, and to select or design a current action (turn) accordingly, would seem to rest on the cognitive representation of *sequences* of actions. I mean by 'sequences of actions' the discernible shapes, patterns, organizations or regularities which may be associated with, or which may be the products of, the progressivity of participants' decisions about 'what to say next' in response to what was just said. (An extended account of the progressively unfolding character of contributions to talk, from the perspective of those participating in the talk, in real time, is given in Streeck's chapter in this volume; hence it is unnecessary to say more about that here.) Thus, underlying AIP is some mental representation of interaction sequences. For this reason I shall focus here on the ways in which sequential patterns might be associated with AIP, and particularly on whether a current turn-at-talk might be produced with an eye to an anticipated future slot or move in a sequence.

I am going to be considering whether a case can be made for the possibility that AIP may involve the conscious use by speakers of knowledge of sequential patterns, in attempts to generate subsequent environments or slots in a sequence in which favoured or unwanted actions may be, respectively, performed or avoided. However, it should not be supposed that the relationship between social intelligence and manifest verbal behaviour is one which necessarily involves consciously planned action. Communicative strategies do not need to be located at the conscious level of intentionality of speakers; nor do the other concepts associated with AIP such as 'planning', 'anticipation', 'predictability' and 'control'. It is perfectly consistent with AIP to regard the 'mental imaging' of interactive sequences as cognitive procedures for action and interpretation, and not as part of the overt social knowledge which speakers may possess in order consciously to model the contingent responses of their co-interactants. It is thus not necessary to account for sequential patterns in terms of these being the products of speakers' conscious knowledge of the organizations that inform their conduct (Heritage 1984: 241; 1990/91). Whilst participants may orient to stable patterns of talk-in-interaction (and hence recognize the planned, predictable and rational character of communicative actions), this does not imply that particular speakers on particular occasions engage in consciously planning their utterances. Social intelligence may consist of social procedures for action and interpretation, without these procedures becoming the objects of conscious articulation (in the mind, at least) on the occasions of their use.[1] We are not, then, required to find evidence of conscious intentionality in order to sustain the view that 'anticipatory planning' involves interactants' representations – at a cognitive level – of the organized contingencies generated by the selection of actions.

Indeed, the very business of considering what evidence there might be for the conscious or intentional use of sequential strategies might appear to risk confusing interactants' attributions of intentionality to one another with an analyst's version of participants' intentions (in something like a reconstructed narrative conversation). When participants engage in a conversation, any move or turn in that conversation is accountable; that is, inferring what an utterance means and selecting an appropriate response involves ascribing intentions to our co-interactants. The case for the centrality of intention-attribution in making 'rapid interactional moves in an ongoing sequence of actions structured at many levels' is elegantly argued in Levinson's contribution to this volume (Chapter 11, p. 221). Indeed, Levinson defines social intelligence as 'just and only the core ability to attribute intention to other agent's actions, communicative or otherwise, and to respond appropriately in interdigitated sequences of actions' (n. 1). Thus it might appear that the focus of enquiry ought to be fixed on co-participants' attributions of intentionality to one another's actions. To do otherwise might risk missing the domain of interactional accountability for participants in the conversation itself.

Certainly our investigations of the social organization of talk-in-interaction should continue to focus primarily on participants' analyses of one another's conduct, their understanding of what each other means/intends, and on the consequent sequential progressivity of talk. Nevertheless, we might also consider whether participants, under certain circumstances and for certain sequential patterns, may consciously 'orient to' knowledge of those patterns and employ that knowledge in an intentionally strategic sense. Whilst the planning, anticipation, control, strategy and prediction which are associated with AIP may be cognitive operations, there might be evidence that on occasions these are conscious operations of sequential management.

There are plainly certain respects in which conversationalists consciously orient to sequential patterns. For example, the structure of greetings exchanges is well enough known for people to anticipate what they should do in a particular slot when they come to greet someone (e.g. should they kiss or shake hands?), or in the course of a greeting, to choose the appropriate moment for the performance of an anticipated move in the exchange.[2] Knowledge about such 'ritualized' exchanges, and how to behave with propriety during them, is of course so much part of the vernacular that they may be taught to children as rules of social conduct.[3] Furthermore, such knowledge is a resource for deception: for example, in a telephone greeting a caller may design his/her opening turns in the greeting exchange so as playfully to deceive the person s/he has called into believing that s/he (the caller) is not known to the called, when in fact s/he is (for an analysis of which see Drew (1991)).

But there are more complex sequences which might manifest the intentionality of conduct. For instance, Jefferson (1993) reports that in circumstances where a recipient has apparently misunderstood a question, and replied about something which was not asked, the speaker (i.e. the one who asked the question) may refrain from correcting the recipient; instead the speaker first responds appropriately to the answer, and then re-asks the original question. So the speaker allows an error to go uncorrected: but the subsequent move of re-asking the question (in a manner which has a 'first time' appearance) demonstrates that the speaker understood that an error had been made (i.e. the error was observably relevant to the speaker, and did not simply go unnoticed) and puts things to rights. Such instances involve more than the (cognitive) orientation to a procedure: the sequence is evidence of the speaker recognizing the recipient's error, refraining from correcting it, but remedying the error by choosing to ask the question again – all of which manifests the speaker's consciousness of the error, and the intention to pursue the original question.

So what I am beginning to consider here is whether there is evidence, in the sequential management of talk, for participants' conscious orientation to sequential patterns or procedures. If there were such evidence, then the procedures or organizations which underlie what Levinson refers to as 'interactive intelligence' could be employed at a conscious level of anticipatory planning of subsequent moves or turns in a sequence. If so, we could add a level of consciousness in actors' representations of their own actions and the contingent responsive actions of others – envisaged by AIP – to the cognitive imprinting of the procedures for producing and interpreting conduct. The issue is whether the knowledge of sequential patterns which underlies mental representations of action may be consciously exploited in interaction.

A couple of caveats, very briefly. First, undoubtedly there are many other areas of research into the organization of conversation which have a close bearing on social or interactional intelligence and to AIP, but which will not be touched upon here. Such areas as 'recipient design' and the organization of self- and other-repair are, for instance, quite evidently related to anticipatory planning: Streeck touches on these phenomena, especially self-repair, in his analysis of 'projection' (Chapter 4, this volume). I shall not be considering the details of the design of particular speaker turns, except insofar as the action which a speaker selects to do in a turn has sequential consequences. Second, I shall not be concerned with the larger or more diffuse goals which participants might have in conversing (such as the order of priority in the day's business, cementing a friendship or securing the other's co-operation), or in choosing to raise a particular topic in the conversation. Although the pursuit of such goals is certainly to be considered part of AIP modelling, I do not deal here with how far such goals may be evident in particular conversational sequences (but see particularly the various contributions to Tracy (1991) for a consideration of goal-directedness in conversation). The discussion which follows is focused just on the management and planning of local sequences (or types of sequences), involving local sequentially constrained goals.

Some types of sequential patterns in conversation

It was noted above that certain sequences are so conventionalized as to be part of the vernacular, for instance in instructing children how to behave properly: so children are taught to say 'thank you' when given something, to answer questions and to say 'hello' when greeted by another. Such sequences as greetings–greetings and questions–answers are instances of what have been termed in conversation analysis 'adjacency pairs': this is a large class of sequences in which the production by one speaker of a first action (e.g. a question, request, offer, greeting, invitation, accusation etc.) occasions the relevance by the recipient of a paired next action (e.g. an answer) or one from alternative paired actions (e.g. acceptance/rejection, granting/rejection). The conventionalized expectation that if a speaker's turn or utterance is hearable as the first part of such a pair, then the recipient should enact the second paired response, is a demonstrably 'strong' normative sequential constraint on what a recipient should appropriately do in the next turn (Atkinson and Drew 1979: 46–61; Heritage 1984: 245–60; Levinson 1983, ch.6; H. Sacks 1986; Schegloff and Sacks 1973). The projectability of relevant next paired actions is a quite elementary but perhaps fundamental mechanism for anticipating alter's response (i.e., *class* of response), and hence is most important for AIP.

However, in sequences of adjacently paired actions, only one move ahead – the adjacent next action by speaker B, in response to the first pair-part by speaker A – can be projected or anticipated. Whilst the conditional relevance associated with adjacency pairs provides for strong constraints controlling 'next position', it appears that the sequential organizations for conversation are relatively weaker in terms of there being structures which control or project actions beyond that.[4] Research in conversation analysis (and from other perspectives for the analysis of discourse) has identified very many sequential patterns of three or more turns or moves: but these patterns are, I think, not all equivalent forms of organization with respect to participants' sequential management of talk, and in particular to the projectability of future turns in the sequences.

This can be illustrated by considering three kinds of sequential patterns which have been discerned in conversation.

Teases

The first is a pattern associated with 'po-faced receipts of teases', a phenomenon in which recipients of teases overwhelmingly respond to the tease in some serious fashion (Drew 1987). Even in cases where recipients do respond to the humour in a tease, for example by laughing, they almost always do so either as a preliminary to or in the course of making a serious response.[5] The following is an instance; Nancy has called Emma to tell her about a man she met the previous evening at the home of a close friend (Martha).

Extract 1   (NB:II:4:14)

NANCY: But he's ni:ce looki:ng a::nd ah just a rea:l nice:
= PERsonable, VERY personable, VERY SWEET. .hhh
VE:RY: (.) CONSIDERATE MY GOD ALL I HAD
TO DO WAS LOOK AT A CIGARETTE AND HE
WAS OUT OF THE CHAIR LIGHTING (h)IT
YhhhOU KNO(h)OW =

EMMA: = I: KNO:W IT

NANCY: .hehh.hh One of those kind .hhhhh =

EMMA: = Yes

NANCY: A::nd so: but we were

　　　　　　[

→ EMMA: 　　　　　　THEY DO THAT BEFORE AND A:FTER

NANCY: 　　　　　　　　　[　　　　　　　[
　　　　　　　　　　　　　eeYhhehee 　　AHH

EMMA: THEY DO:n't.

NANCY: HAH HAH.hhh

→ NANCY: NO:?e-MARTHA HAS known Cli:ff, … ((a good 30 years
and he's an absolute boyscout))

In response to Emma's somewhat sexually laden tease 'THEY DO
THAT BEFORE AND A:FTER THEY DO:n't', Nancy begins by
laughingly agreeing: but she then rejects the teasing proposal with
[No] + [Serious Account], 'NO:?e-MARTHA HAS known Cli:ff …'.
This phenomenon of serious responses to humorous teases (in only a very
few instances did recipients respond to the humour alone) is partly
accounted for by the sequential environment in which teases occur. In all
the instances I collected, in the turn(s) immediately preceding the tease
the person who is subsequently teased has been complaining, extolling/
praising or bragging in an *exaggerated* or overdone fashion. Space
prevents illustrating the extent to which in extract 1 Nancy had been
extolling the attractions and virtues of the man she met. But a flavour of it
is conveyed in her first turn in the extract; and this comes at the end of an
extravagant report of this man's comparative youthfulness (Nancy is well
into middle age), that he was a senior officer in the marines, that he has a
responsible job, his easygoing manner, his intelligence, how well they hit
it off and so on.

The sequential context in which teases occur is, then, typically one in
which the recipient has gone on extolling something or someone, has gone
on complaining or been self-pitying. The subsequent tease, conveying
some scepticism about what the teased has said, has a social control
function insofar as it may be considered a mild form of reproof for a minor
conversational transgression. The sequential pattern associated with
teases, and which is illustrated in extract 1, can be summarized thus:

A: Exaggerated Extolling/Praising/Complaining
B: Tease
A: Serious Response

Preference for agreement

The second kind of pattern that I want to consider is associated with an aspect of the organization of the preference for agreements with assessments, and a dispreference for disagreements (Pomerantz 1984; see also H. Sacks 1986). Pomerantz documented how the dispreferred character of disagreement is evident in such actions being withheld or delayed: a recipient may delay disagreeing with the first speaker's assessment either by the design of a turn (by prefacing the upcoming disagreement with an agreement component) or sequentially – or the recipient may withhold a response. In the following two cases recipients withhold their response to the first speakers' assessments.

Extract 2   (NB:III:6)

> FRAN: Oh::::. Wih gee isn'at funny gee I'm going down t'see
> somebody they're going do:wn the end a' this month et
> twunty seven hundred- .hhh Ocean Fro::nt.
> (0.7)
> FRAN: Is that a diffrent pla:ce then Newpo:rt?
> TED: M-hm I gue:ss, this is, Balboa Penninsula.

Extract 3   (G.L.2: from Frankel 1983)

> PATIENT: This- chemotherapy (0.2) it won't have any lasting effects
> on havin' kids will it?
> (2.2)
> PATIENT: It will?
> DOCTOR: I'm afraid so.

In extract 2 Fran's assessment is conveyed in 'gee isn'at funny', a claimed coincidence that people she's going to be visiting are staying in, as she thinks, the same vicinity as Ted. In extract 3 the patient's question conveys an evaluation (by selecting 'It won't have . . .', rather than asking 'Will it have . . .'). In each case, following the pause in which the recipient does not respond, the speaker (respectively, Fran and the Patient) apparently recognizes that she had it wrong, and offers instead a revised position, with which now the recipient straightaway agrees. Thus silences may be oriented to as potential disagreements, with the interactional consequence that 'It is not only that what would be a disagreement might

not get said, but that what comes to be said may be said as an agreement'
(Pomerantz 1984: 77). A simplified version of the sequential pattern
which emerges from this orientation to recipient silence post-assessment
is:

A: Assessment
      Silence
A: Backdown/Modified Position
B: Agreement

Pre-sequences

The third kind of sequence relevant to a preliminary consideration of the
possible relationship between AIP and sequential organizations will also
be familiar: it is conversational pre-sequences, such as pre-invitations,
pre-requests and such like. These are questions or enquiries which are
made on behalf of a next action, contingent upon the response to the
enquiry (Atkinson and Drew 1979: 141–8; Levinson 1983: 345–64;
Schegloff 1980). The following instance is particularly transparent, and –
what is most to the point here – is particularly transparent to the recipient
(Jim) of the pre-sequence enquiry.

Extract 4   (Holt:2:14)

```
        JIM:    J.P.Blenkinsop good morning,
                (.)
        SKIP:   Good morning Ji:m,
                (0.5)
        SKIP:   Uh it's Skip.
        JIM:    Hiyuh,
        SKIP:   You coming past the doo:r,
        JIM:    Certainly?
                (0.8)
   →    JIM:    What time wouldju like the car Sah. =
        SKIP:   -Uh well ehhh hhehh hhhehh hhehh .hh Oh that's
                m:ost unexpected of you hhh::: n(h)o it's v(h)ery
                nice'v you to offer huhh uh-heh heh-u-hu-.ehh
                Thanks very much. .hhh
                                    [
        JIM:                        Eh:m I wz planning tih leave
                here at just about twenty . . .
```

The enquiry 'You coming past the doo:r,' is treated by Jim as a prefatory
enquiry, as leading up to something. His recognition that Skip 'wants
something' is particularly evident in his humorous response to the
enquiry: 'What time wouldju like the car Sah' humorously mimics what a

chauffeur might ask – but it is also an offer (of a lift to work). As such, it displays Jim's understanding that Skip's enquiry was made in the service of requesting a lift, a request which does not now need to be made. Thus, whereas the usual pattern or 'standard sequence' associated with pre-sequences is

A: Pre-request enquiry
B: Response
A: Request
B: Granting,

here the sequence is attenuated in a way which commonly happens when the recipient, recognizing what the enquiry is leading to, opts to address the projected action directly (i.e. without waiting for the request to be officially or formally made).

A: Pre-request enquiry
B: Offer
A: Acceptance

These then are three examples of the kinds of sequential patterns or organizations which have been uncovered in conversation analytic research. They are each an instance of what might be regarded as 'conversational routines' (Coulmas 1981a). But they have, I think, rather different potentials for the role of *projectability* in 'anticipatory interactive planning'. I have selected these to illustrate or represent, in a preliminary fashion, some of the ways in which sequential patterns may or may not be associated with conscious 'strategy', or the ability to plan for subsequent moves in a sequence.

The first sequential pattern, associated with teases and po-faced responses to them, does not appear to involve projectability at any stage in the sequence. The exaggerated complainings, praising etc. only 'initiate' the teasing sequence insofar as the recipient responds (sceptically) to the overdone version. It is plainly no part of the design of the complaint/ praise to generate or provide the occasion for a tease. Likewise, the tease is not designed to generate the third stage in the sequence, the serious response/denial (indeed there's every reason to treat teases as designed *not* to be taken seriously). And both the tease and po-faced response are 'backward-looking' responses to prior actions;[6] they are not themselves designed to project any next actions. So whilst there is a discernible sequential pattern associated with teasing, no individual move in the sequence seems to be part of any manifest strategic repertoire. At each stage participants are oriented to a prior turn, and not to some projected subsequent turn. The overall 'shape' of the sequence is not what either was aiming to exploit.

There are, I think, many examples of sequential patterns of this kind, in which the overall organization of the sequence is not being oriented to by co-participants. Their shape is discernible to the analyst; and of course the regularity of the sequential pattern is the product of common interactional problems or goals which participants manage, or find solutions to, in typical ways/moves. But the project of participants is not to design a current turn with an eye to any projected action in the sequence. The sequential pattern is the product of a turn-by-turn progression through a series of 'typical' interactional contingencies (e.g. dealing with an exaggerated version of a complaint). It is not the product of participants' mental representation of a projected sequence, and the exploitation of a move within such a sequence.[7]

The other sequences illustrated above, associated with speaker modifications/backdowns post recipient withholding, and with pre-requests, seem to be rather different organizations, inasmuch as they do manifest participants' orientation to projectable next slots or moves.[8] In the former, that orientation is quite implicit; and the turn projected is that adjacent next turn. In the latter, in pre-sequences, that orientation may be explicit; it need not be explicit but, as extract 4 (above) illustrates, participants can and do overtly display their understanding that the business of a current turn is some projected action in the sequence. And in this case the projected action is not restricted to the adjacent next turn: the pre-sequence enquiry is designed – and recognized by the recipient as designed – with a view to both the next-but-one turn (the request), and the turn after that (the response to the enquiry indicating the likelihood of the request being granted, and the making of the request being contingent upon such a 'promising' response).

Pre-sequences seem then to sit opposite the kind of patterns illustrated in teasing sequences. Pre-sequences are manifestly initiated with an interactional goal in view, to see whether a request – if it were made – would be received favourably, or (as in extract 4) to elicit an offer. And the fact that the shape of the sequence – what the pre-sequence enquiry is recognizably leading to etc. – is part of the speaker's conscious design or strategy is evident in the playful way Jim exposes that design.

The pattern of speaker backdowns post recipient silences lies somewhere between 'non-projectable organizations' and the designedly strategic nature of pre-sequences. Although recipient withholdings/silences are generated by the speakers' initial assessments, those assessments are not, of course, designed to generate the sequence resulting in the speakers' backdowns. And whilst the speakers' backdowns display their recognition that the recipients disagree, we can only speculate that recipients hold off from responding (remain silent) in the first place in an unspoken effort to get their co-participants to modify their position, and thereby provide the opportunity, in a subsequent slot, for agreement. It seems very likely that recipients do so: based on what Heritage (1984:241) refers to as the symmetry between the procedures for the production of verbal conduct, and for its interpretation, recipients may withhold a response and hence 'produce' silences in order to have the speaker recognize their (implicit) disagreement. Recipients may thereby simultaneously orient to the *avoidance* of a projected action (i.e., their disagreement), and turn the sequence into one which will end instead in agreement. But the evidence for this orientation/management lies implicitly in the sequential pattern.

The points which emerge from this very preliminary consideration of three kinds of conversational sequences are, quite briefly, these. By no means are all sequential patterns or organizations evidence of interactive planning by participants. Whilst the orderliness of the pattern is produced in the first instance by participants, they may be acting in response to interactional contingencies, without any view to the overall organization of a sequence, or to any particular stage in it. What may be characteristic of sequences which appear to be the product of participants' interactive planning is that the sequential organization is sufficiently part of members' conscious linguistic/interactive repertoire that future moves in the sequence can be *projected*, or anticipated: and that such a projection can be exploited in order to pursue some interactional goal. (Though note that that goal may not necessarily spring from personal motivation or be strategically self-serving; it may be, as in withholding disagreement, a matter of social 'preference', 'face', or as Brown and Levinson have it 'politeness'.) By 'exploit', I mean that a current action/turn may be designed so as to avoid or to facilitate a future projected move in a recognizable sequential routine.

This introduces the possibility of speakers consciously exploiting routines, where the routines or patterns are sufficiently recognizable and predictable to participants for them quite explicitly to anticipate subsequent actions in a projected sequence. This brings us back to my earlier remarks concerning whether sequential patterns may become the overt objects of interactional mapping and planning, in the conscious attempt to achieve sequential goals. In this respect Heritage (1990/91) distinguishes oriented-to procedures which he terms strategy (cog), and procedures which are consciously employed, or strategy (cs). (In their consideration of intentionality and goals in conversation, Mandelbaum and Pomerantz (1991) make distinctions along similar lines; although their terminology differs from that of Heritage, many of the problems and themes being addressed in their paper are common to those in Heritage, and in this chapter.) The kinds of structural organizations which may 'fit' behaviour, for example the sequence illustrated in extract 1 above, are perhaps

'driven into the organism'. They are (or have become through experience) part of its 'software' or even its neurobiology. Thus strategy (cog) is a property predicated *of* an organism (or its program). It is not something available *to* the organism's (or the program's) unaided inspection. Thus it is relevant to distinguish between a strategy (cog) which *fits* behaviour and a strategy (cs) which *guides* behaviour. (Heritage 1990/91: 315.)

Comparing the pattern of speakers' modifications/backdowns in the face of recipients' withholdings in extracts 2 and 3 with the pre-requests in extract 4, one gets a sense of the fluctuating borderline to which Heritage refers between a strategy (cog) and a speaker employing a strategy (cs). The use of a withholding/silence in order to implicate (but not state) disagreement is oriented to a sequential procedure, the evidence for the consciously strategic use of which is only implicit (in a sequential pattern); by contrast, the conscious use of a sequential routine is quite manifest in extract 4, conspicuously so in the humorous treatment of the pre-sequence enquiry.

Some aspects of conversational strategy

'Avoidance' strategy

Few cases of the conscious exploitation of an anticipated or projected sequential routine will be as demonstrably clear as pre-requests. Most are likely to fluctuate around this borderline between (cog) and (cs) strategies, that is in the space between the second and third types of sequential pattern discussed above. I'd like to review some other patterns in which I think it can be demonstrated that, at the least, a move is made in an interactional sequence which exploits the anticipated development of the sequence. Whether such sequential routines can be consciously or mentally modelled by speakers, and hence whether a speaker is, on a given occasion, consciously exploiting a particular routine in making a particular move, may sometimes be less easily demonstrable – as will become evident, for good reason. Nevertheless, the following kinds of conversational patterns are among those which come closest, I think, to speakers exploiting what they anticipate will follow, in the sequence ahead, from making a given move in a current turn.

The first arises from the conversational routine of greetings exchanges. It involves an observation which Sacks made about telephone calls to a Suicide Prevention Centre, and which, as Schegloff (1992b: xvi) recalls, was a critical step in the development of what was to become conversation analysis (and it is the observation with which Sacks began his lectures about conversation analysis (see H. Sacks 1992, Vol. I, lecture 1)). Sacks noted that the emergency psychiatric hospital which operated the SPC line was concerned about the regularity with which people who called the centre would not give their names. And when Sacks looked to see 'where in the course of the conversation could you [*sic*] tell that somebody would not give their name?' (*ibid.*: 3), he noticed this:

Extract 5   (SPC)

(A is the SPC staff member answering calls, B is the caller.)

> A: This is Mr Smith may I help you?
> → B: I can't hear you.
> A: This is Mr <u>Smith</u>.
> B: Smith.

Sacks discussed this in the light of the procedure in greetings exchanges whereby the form of address which is adopted by the first speaker may be reciprocally adopted by next speaker. So that if the first speaker (the SPC staff member) identifies himself by name, so might the other (the caller[9]). Sacks observed about extract 5 and cases like it, that in the slot where a reciprocal identification by a caller would be conditionally relevant, the caller instead claims not to be able to hear. In reply to the caller's claimed trouble, 'I can't hear you', the staff member repeats what he said. In the sequence that therefore ensues – in which the staff member again gives his name; the caller repeats that name, to check that he has it right; the staff member confirms it and asks once more if he can help – the slot in which the caller's reciprocal self-identification would go never occurs. The caller has thereby managed to skip the move in which he might reciprocate with his name.

Extract 6   (SPC: from H. Sacks 1992, Vol.I: 7–8)

> A: . . my name is Smith and I'm with the Emergency Psychiatric Centre.
> → B: Your name is what?
> A: Smith.
> B: Smith.
> A: Yes.
> A: Can I help you?
> → B: I don't know hhheh I hope you can.

So there's a quite standard conversational routine, the procedure for greetings exchanges, which provides for a slot in which the caller should identify himself: it happens that for these callers (i.e., potential suicides) this slot is unwanted. The caller replaces that slot with an action (a claim not to be able to hear) which generates an extended sequence in which the slot in which he should make a return greeting with his name does not recur.

The question is, though, whether the caller really cannot hear, or whether he is using the claim not to hear as a strategy to avoid giving his name. Well, there is a glimmer of evidence in B's repeat after A has repeated his name. Certainly that's a regular thing to do after there's been a hitch; you ask them to repeat their name, they do so, you repeat it to check you have it right. But then there's the opportunity to latch onto your repeat the reciprocal self-introduction: that is, the turn can be managed in such a way that the opportunity to say who you are isn't lost – if you want to say who you are. For instance, compare B's repeat in extract 6 with the caller's (erroneous) repeat of the receptionist's name in extract 7.

Extract 7   (Minne: Cmas:X:1–2)

>   CALLER: Who am I talking with. =
>   WENDI: = .hhhh This is Wendi the receptionist?
>   →   CALLER: Linda the receptionist. Linda?hh This is =
>   = ((click click))
>   WENDI: Hello?

Evidently there is some difficulty about hearing in this extract (the caller hears 'Linda' instead of 'Wendi', for example). But notice that having repeated her name, the caller is then about to go on to self-identify with 'This is' before being cut off by some interference with the phone (the call ends after Wendi's 'Hello?'). So there is no difficulty in latching a self-identification onto a repeat if you want the other to know your name. This isn't proof that the caller in the SPC data is consciously using a repeat device as a strategy to avoid giving his name: but what happens, or does not happen, later in a sequence is perhaps relevant internal evidence for anticipatory planning. In this case the possibility is that he's projecting a (repair) sequence, the completion of which will be co-terminous with the end of the greetings exchanges; and hence the slot for his returning with his name will have been 'missed'.

Another case in which, again, a speaker avoids doing something in a sequential position where that action was relevant is illustrated in extract 8. This is from a call in which it is clear that on the coming weekend Charlie is going to drive down to Syracuse, and has arranged to give Ilene a ride. He's calling to tell her that, because the girl with whom he was intending to stay will be out of town, he is not going after all.

Extract 8   (Trip to Syracuse:1)

> CHARLIE: I spoke to the gi:r- I spoke tih Karen.
>   (0.4)
> CHARLIE: And u:m:: (.) it wz rea:lly ba:d because she decided of a:ll
>   weekends for this one tih go awa:y
>   (0.6)
> → ILENE: Wha:t?
>   (0.4)
> → CHARLIE: She decidih tih go away this weekend.
> ILENE: Yea:h,
> CHARLIE: .hhhh=
> ILENE: =.khh
>   [
> → CHARLIE: So tha::t yihknow I really don't have a place tuh
>   sta:y.
> ILENE: .hh Oh:::::.hh
> ILENE: .hhh So yih not g'nna go up this weeken'?
> CHARLIE: Nu::h I don't think so.

One can notice, first off, that it isn't Charlie who says that he's not going this weekend: the explicit version of the 'bad news' is articulated by Ilene ('.hhh So yih not g'nna go up this weeken'?'), much in line with Terasaki's observations about pre-announcements of bad news eliciting news deliveries from the erstwhile new recipient (Terasaki 1976; Schegloff 1988b). There is, of course, a similarity between this case and extract 4, insofar as the pre-request in extract 4 worked to elicit an offer, without Skip having formally to make the request: and here Charlie manages the sequence so as to avoid saying that he is not going, but instead to put Ilene in the position of figuring out and 'announcing' the bad news. The way the sequence runs off, Charlie is left just to confirm the bad news ('Nuh:: I don't think so.'). The speaker who initiated the sequence has managed it in such a way as to avoid doing an unwanted, dispreferred action, i.e., delivering bad news.

But a more intricate 'negotiation' can be discerned in this sequence, involving each of the participants avoiding making certain actions and thereby extending the projected sequence. I'll give only a skeletal account of this negotiation. Charlie's first version of the 'bad news' (in his first turn in the extract) is only that Karen will be away; he doesn't state the consequence this has for the arrangement he has with Ilene. In the next slot, Ilene might have given some form of acknowledgement of that upshot (e.g., along the lines of the disappointed 'Oh:::::.' she expresses later). Instead she makes the kind of claim not to have heard, or the repair/repeat device which Sacks noted the caller uses in extracts 5 and 6, when she asks 'Wha:t?'

```
CHARLIE:  And u:m:: (.) it wz rea:lly ba:d because she decided of a:ll
            weekends for this one tih go awa:y
          (0.6)
→  ILENE:   Wha:t?
          (0.4)
CHARLIE:  She decidih tih go away this weekend.
```

Charlie's partial repeat, 'She decidih tih go away this weekend', elects to
treat the problem only as one of hearing, and not that what he said needs
clarifying or elaborating (which might of course have put him in the
position of making explicit the consequence of Karen's being away, as in
'Karen decided to go away this weekend, so I'm not going up after all'). In
the next slot Ilene passes over yet another opportunity to acknowledge the
upshot of the news; she fills that slot with a continuer, 'Yea:h,', which
leaves Charlie back in the position of announcing his news:

```
CHARLIE:  She decidih tih go away this weekend.
→  ILENE:   Yea:h,
CHARLIE:  .hhhh =
ILENE:     = .khh
            [
CHARLIE:        So tha::t yihknow I really don't have a place tuh
            sta:y.
```

Charlie does now reveal a consequence of Karen's being away: but it's a
version in which the upshot for Ilene's ride still remains implicit, his not
having a place to stay being only another step towards the news that he's
not going. Charlie has thereby managed that slot to extend the sequence in
such a way that it's still left to Ilene, in her next slot, to state the upshot/
bad news.

In each slot after Charlie's first turn, some acknowledgement or explicit
formulation of the bad news was possibly relevant. Each of them,
however, manages their turns in those slots so as to avoid performing that
action; each turn is designed to project a sequence in which it is left to the
other, if they will, to state or to acknowledge the upshot for their trip.

'Facilitating' future sequential moves

The emphasis in the cases considered above has been on participants
avoiding performing some action in a slot in which that action might have
been relevant, and extending the sequence in order to provide a slot for
the co-participant to perform an equivalent action instead. I want to move
to consider sequences in which a speaker designs a current turn so as to
generate or facilitate a subsequent action in the sequence. The distinction
is sometimes more a matter of emphasis: cases in this set, though, don't
involve the degree of avoidance that was evident in extracts 5 to 8.

Perhaps the clearest instances of anticipatory planning are sequences in which, like the pre-requests discussed earlier, a speaker designs a turn which projects that, after recipient's response, another turn of a particular kind will be forthcoming. This is often the case in story telling, which can be initiated thus: A: 'Did I tell you about such-and-such?' B: 'No.' A: 'Well, [story].' A's first turn/enquiry is designed to project a subsequent telling, though that telling might be contingent upon the recipient's response. Two kinds of environments with which these projected action sequences are associated are what Schegloff has called 'preliminaries to preliminaries', and stories.

Schegloff (1980) observed that enquiries such as 'Do you mind if I ask you a question?' are, paradoxically, already questions; and that quite regularly what follows (i.e., after the recipient replies 'No, go ahead') is not a question, or at least not *the* question. This is one of the instances he cites.

Extract 9   (BC:12:18–19)

(A is the compère in a radio phone-in programme, B is the caller.)

→	B:	I like tuh ask you something.
	A:	Shoot.
	B:	Y'know I 'ad my license suspended fuh six munts,
	A:	Uh huh
	B:	Y'know for a reason which, I rathuh not, mention tuh you, in othuh words, – a serious reason,
→		en I like tuh know if I w'd talk to my senator,
→		or- somebuddy, could they help me get it back,

Schegloff (1980: 106) notes about this and similar instances that there is a kind of double displacement: 'Not only has the question that the speaker plans been "displaced" by his "projection" of its occurrence, but it is also not asked next.' Instead of the projected question, the thing that B would like to ask, B reports something (losing his driving licence): and only after that does he ask his question. Hence, B's initial turn projects an action after the next (i.e., a question, after a reporting). This is no place to review Schegloff's analysis of such 'pre-pre's' (but see Streeck, Chapter 4, this volume), except to highlight his point that 'They serve to exempt what directly follows them from being treated as "produced in its own right". They make room for, and mark, what follows them as "preliminary"' (1980: 116). What they are designed to achieve is the 'space' to give a report as a preliminary to something else, i.e., the enquiry – and thereby to restrict the recipient to *not* responding to the report as such, but to wait for the projected enquiry. Note that after the first stage of B's report in extract 9, A restricts himself to merely acknowledging it, and letting B continue.

Evidently, then, there is a symmetry between what the pre-pre is designed to achieve, and the recipient's understanding of that task; that is, his understanding that the subsequent action (the report) is *not* the one to deal with, but that instead he should respond to the action after that (the enquiry). The pre-pre is a shared intersubjective device for anticipatory planning. In the pre-request in extract 5 the evidence for the shared character of such a device was the humorous recognition by the recipient of what was anticipated: in extract 9, the evidence is that the recipient refrains from responding (other than with a continuer) until after the projected action. Either way, the co-participants' mutual orientation to projected action sequences is manifest in the recipients' behaviour, in a manner which connects closely with the issues Goody raises about the reciprocity of social relations in AIP.

Schegloff relates his analysis of 'preliminaries to preliminaries' to the other environment associated with projected action sequences, that of stories – and of course 'story prefaces'. These have been discussed extensively in the literature of conversation and discourse analysis, and are perhaps too familiar to need much elaboration here. Schegloff summarizes their employment thus:

The story preface is a device by which a prospective teller can display an intention to tell a story and yield a next turn to another, with the possible outcome that that other will reselect the prospective teller to talk again, that is to tell the story, in the course of which others will not treat each possible sentence/turn completion as a point at which possibly to take a next turn for themselves. (Schegloff 1980: 146.)

We might note here that in 'displaying an intention', the speaker does also intend to tell a story; so that the procedure, and the consciousness of the procedure's purpose, are indistinguishable.

I want to show just one example, in order to highlight the point concerning the shared orientation to projected action sequences: that is, whilst the prospective story teller initiates the projected sequence with a story preface, the recipient collaborates in the anticipatory planning by holding off until the projected action has been completed. This is thrown into relief by an instance where this goes awry.

Extract 10   (F:TC:1:1:18)

(The Warehouse is evidently a bar in which Shirley has a part-time job.)

> SHIRLEY: .hhh Listen, something very very: cute happened
> las' night at the Warehouse.
> (.)

GERI: What.
                  [
SHIRLEY: .hhhhhYih<u>KNOW</u> Cathy, (.) Larry Taylor's ex
             girlfriend,

                        [
GERI: <u>Y</u>eeah.
SHIRLEY: Okay. <u>C</u>athy came <u>i</u>n las'night.
             (1.0)
SHIRLEY: Whenever she comes in she always <u>w</u>ants me t'd<u>o</u>
             something for her.
GERI: <u>M</u>-hm,
SHIRLEY: Either <u>s</u>iddown'n ta:lk, what<u>e</u>ver. .hhhhh So she
             came in en she starts asking me if I'd seen <u>G</u>ary.
             <u>G</u>ary Klei:n, .hhhh I s'd <u>y</u>eh he's <u>here</u> t'night
             .hh she sz well would<u>ju g</u>o find him please'n tell
             him t'give me my ten d<u>o</u>llars thet he owes me,
→   GERI: <u>W</u>haddi<u>y</u>ou haftih get in on that for,
                                      [[
SHIRLEY: .hhhh   <u>W</u>ai:t. <u>I</u>
             started <u>l</u>au:ghing I l<u>o</u>oked at her en I said . . . .
             ((story continues))

It is fairly clear that Geri's 'contingent response' to the story telling, turns out to have been premature. Having restricted herself to responses which 'fit' the course of the projected sequence, Geri responds (in her arrowed turn) with the appropriate outrage to the report that Cathy asked Shirley to run an errand for her, thereby treating that as the 'something cute that happened at the Warehouse last night', and therefore the completion of the story projected in the preface. Now as it happens she's wrong, because that's only the beginning of the story. Shirley sanctions the premature response ('<u>W</u>ai:t.'), and does not respond in turn to Geri's outraged 'understanding' of the story. Instead she goes on to recount not only how she refused to get Cathy's money, but also a later incident in which Cathy was discovered to be drinking alcohol (underage), to which Shirley was deputed to put a stop. That's the *real* story, elaborately told over three and a half pages of transcript, during which Geri's responses are restricted once again to continuers.

Control

Thus story prefaces designedly 'control' a projected sequence (the story telling) in which the recipient's speaking role is restricted. But notice that this 'control' is only achieved through anticipatory planning on the part of both participants, recipient as well as story teller. Geri's premature incoming in extract 10 is not of course a deviant case (i.e., not an instance of non-collaboration, or evidence that story prefaces don't control the projected telling). She comes in with her appreciation or understanding of 'the story' at just the point where what has been told fits, and is a possible completion of, what the preface is designed to have her anticipate, the 'something cute that happened'. So the sequential control which is achieved through story prefaces is collaboratively managed. Again, to emphasize; the intentionality of sequential control is plainly an intersubjective, oriented-to property of story telling. For this reason, story prefaces, as with other kinds of prefatory actions (such as pre-sequences) are important evidence for AIP.

Finally, it may be worth noting in this context that moving onto or off topics of conversation may involve some degree of 'control' over the projected talk – and that this control can have a strategic character. This is perhaps evident in such instances as these, in which a speaker opens up a 'new' topic,[10] in a fashion which has the appearance of a stepwise connection with what was being talked about.

Extract 11   (NB:II:2:5)

(They have been talking about the assassination of Robert Kennedy a few days before, and to which Nancy refers when she says 'everybody is talking about it'.)

```
        NANCY:   Yeah it's been a rough week an everbuddy is (.) youknow
                 (0.2)
        EMMA:    Mmhm
                   [
        NANCY:     ta:lking about it en everbuddy: course I: don't
                 know whether it's that or just that we're js:t (.)
  →              completely bo:gging down at work,h .hhhhmh
                 (.)
  →     NANCY:   Er whatta WIH: WITH ME: with my finals?hhh
                   [
        EMMA:       Oh: well e v r y buddy's sa::d
        NANCY:   hhuh uh:::
                   [
  →     EMMA:               Oh ho:w'd you do with yer finals.
```

Extract 12   (NB:II:4:10)

(They have just been talking at length about an operation Emma has had on her toe, and whether they'll both go shopping.)

```
        EMMA:    A:nd uh I just am not gunnuh walk around a LOT
                 bec:u:z uh: Ah:::,hh (.) It's not worth it tuh be
```

```
                on my fee:t. Yih know
                                    [
NANCY:                              Ya:h, h ri:ght.
                (.)
NANCY:   Ah huh? .t.hhhhhh OH I WZ JUST OUT WA:SHING
         windo:ws: a:nd uh my mother ca:lled so I ca:me in
         I thought w'l while I'm here 'n I looked the
         clo:ck'n uz eleven thirty en I thought wul: (.)
         ther .hhh .hh ther uhm (,) surely they're UP  →
         yihknow I knew it wz kind'v a:sleep in da::y
                             [            [
EMMA:                        Y e s        Awee-
NANCY:   but uh: I didn't get home till (.) .hhh two last
  →      night I met a very: very n:i:ce gu:y.
```

In each case a new topic is opened, in extract 11 the university finals examinations which Nancy has taken, and in extract 12 the announcement that she met a man last night.[11] But in each case the new topic is not marked, disjunctively, as a new/next topic. It's led into in a stepwise fashion; and in extract 11 the speaker designs her talk to build the new topic out of what they had been talking about up to then. 'It's been a rough week' begins as a reference to the Kennedy assassination: then she speculates whether it's been rough because of the assassination, or because they're bogged down at work – or because of her finals. Thus a transition to the topic of her finals has been managed in a stepwise fashion through the reference to a 'rough week'. Additionally, Nancy manages that topic introduction in such a way that she can tell Emma about her finals *in response to* an enquiry by Emma ('Oh how:'d you do with yer finals'): that is, her 'listing' her finals as one of the things which has made it a 'rough week' elicits (and may have been designed to elicit) an enquiry from Emma.

Nancy's news about meeting a 'very very nice guy' in extract 11 is similarly built out of a stepwise connection, consisting of an account of how she came to call Emma (see Jefferson 1984: 195) – coming in to answer a call from her mother, noticing the time, figuring that they'd be up by now even though it's a 'sleep in day', through to 'didn't get home till two last night'. As in extract 11, then, the new topic is contrived out of other materials. The new topic is evidently one which the speaker really wants to talk about (in fact, in extract 11 the news about the man she met seems to have been the purpose behind suggesting a shopping trip/getting together). And in each case the stepwise move leads to a *pivotal* or bivalent segment, having the potential simultaneously to connect back and to introduce the new topic (I adopt this notion of pivotal utterances in stepwise topical transitions from Jefferson (1984)). So it's interesting that 'sleep in day' is selected as a way of describing the weekend (which is how, in overlap, Emma seems to be going to describe the day, but cuts off). It connects back to figuring that they would be up by now, and forward to 'late night' (i.e., late rising after a late night – even if the late rising is Emma's, and the late night was Nancy's). So too 'bogging down at work' connects back to why it's been a 'rough week' for everyone, and provides a warrant for introducing her finals (that being a form of work, and a form of labour which might be described as 'rough').

Parenthetically, it may be noticed that these pivotal segments, 'bogging down at work' and 'sleep in day' have an idiomatic quality. This may not be incidental to the use of idioms to 'legitimately' or accountably close down a prior topic (Drew and Holt 1988). That is, they may be being used here by a speaker who wants to close down one topic in order to open up something she's keen to talk about.

At any rate, in the light of what the speaker goes on to talk about, it looks as though the pivotal segments are designed to project a next and valued topic. But the speaker thereby contrives to manage the introduction of the new topic as a 'natural progression' out of a sequence of other materials. This looks very much like a strategy for disguising just how keen the speaker is to tell about it: to take a point from Sacks on invitations, managing the introduction of a topic in this way displays the topic as having been *occasioned by* other materials, and not as the reason for calling.

Discussion: sequential patterns and 'conscious' strategies?

There can be little doubt that whilst structures of sequences of turns/ actions are part of the cognitive processes through which the coherence of those sequences was produced in the first place in the course of interaction, the mental models of such structures may not be conscious, articulated resources. Sequential structures are some of the *procedures* whereby co-participants discover the meaning in, and goals behind, one another's utterances: that is, they are procedures which lie behind participants' analyses of meaning/action. The adjacent next turn is a basic structural position in interaction because it is there that participants' analyses or understandings of what they took the other to be meaning/ doing are displayed (understandings which may be ratified or repaired in the next turn after that, i.e., third turn (see Schegloff 1992a)). But although participants' analyses of one another's behaviour are certainly part of the 'conscious' level of conversation, the procedures which lie at the back of those analyses or understandings may not be.

Brown and Levinson's (1978: 90) caveat about their use of strategy arises, I think, from just that distinction between participants' analyses of one another's utterances, and the (cognitive) procedures which underlie their analyses. Participants' understandings of what the other means, or is up to, are indeed the conscious rational products of routines which themselves may not generally be subject to conscious modelling or deliberation. The social intelligibility and perceived rationality of talk-in-interaction is the product of the procedures – including sequential structures – which are part of the learned programmes which underlie social intelligence.

However, I have been reviewing some instances in which sequential routines are perhaps being employed strategically – in its sense of the conscious management of slots in a sequence whose organization can be anticipated by speakers. It may be worth highlighting some aspects of how I think this sense of conscious 'strategy' might be attributed to the kinds of cases I have described.

It should be stressed that none of the sequential devices considered above is intrinsically strategic. Sacks makes the following remark about the use of 'I can't hear you' in extracts 5 and 6 above:

a device like 'I can't hear you' – the repeat device, providing for a repetition of the thing that was first said, which is then repeated by the first person who said 'I can't hear you' – is not necessarily designed for skipping a move. It is not specific to providing a way of keeping in the conversation and behaving properly while not giving one's name. It can be used for other purposes and do other tasks, and it can be used with other items. That's why I talk about it as an 'occasional device'. (H. Sacks 1992: 7.)

Similarly 'what?', as in extract 8, pauses as in extracts 2 and 3, and enquiries like 'What are you doing?', such as that in extract 4, may all be used – indeed may generally be used – in other sequential environments or to manage sequential tasks quite different from the possibly strategic goals illustrated above. For example, just as someone may respond with 'What?' or 'I can't hear you' in circumstances where indeed they didn't hear what the other said, so also someone might enquire 'What are you doing?' just out of interest. It's not necessarily designedly a preliminary to something else, such as an invitation.[12]

Strategy in talk exploits the ordinary properties of ordinary sequential devices: thus the particular strategic work which a device may occasionally do is done at an *unofficial* level (on this, and many of the other issues being discussed here, see Mandelbaum and Pomerantz (1991)). The official business of 'I can't hear you' or 'What?' is to repair a problem to do with hearing (or possibly, in the latter case, understanding/clarification); and such objects are responded to by recipients in terms of their official business (for analyses of the 'official' and 'unofficial' work that the same object can do in conversation, see Pomerantz (1980) and Drew (1984)). The very matter of the talk being apparently organized in terms of the official business of some sequential objects has the consequence that its strategic but unofficial business may not show through on the surface of the conversation – indeed, it may be properly designed not to intrude or be recognized at that level (for the sakes of both participants). The ambiguity which results from an object's official and simultaneously possibly unofficial business is a resource whereby participants can (sometimes collaboratively) manage to disguise an object's strategic use. It is for this very reason that finding evidence in linguistic analysis for speakers' conscious strategies of anticipatory planning has proved so intractable. If it is to be hidden from co-participants, it may remain hidden from analysts.

Hence the rather special character of cases like extract 4, in which there is explicit acknowledgement by the participants that the enquiry was not 'innocent' but was leading up to something. Mostly, though, the analytic evidence that a turn has been designed to exploit other ('unofficial') properties and the anticipated sequential consequences of those properties is much less easy to discern. In the kinds of cases reviewed here, my best shot at what that evidence might be is that speakers exploit a sequential routine, in which the slot for a given action can be projected in the next turn, or the turn after that (i.e., the third turn). The anticipated slot in the sequence may be one which is valued/wanted, or unwanted/to be avoided. A current turn exploits such anticipated slots, by *initiating* the routine sequence which will hence generate the projected and valued slot.

Alternatively, in cases in which the projected slot is unwanted/to be avoided, there is evidence that the sequence is being 'misshaped', by being either *expanded* or *attenuated*. In expansions, the next turn is a slot in which the projected but unwanted action is relevant: the speaker avoids that action by instead filling that slot with an alternative action, the occurrence of which is occasioned by different and, thus far, unanticipated relevancies or contingencies. In this respect, troubles (in hearing etc.) are especially exploitable, because troubles are quite freely occurring in conversation; they may inhabit any turn-at-talk, and hence a 'next turn repair initiation' may always be mobilized in order to avoid doing something else (the unwanted action) in that turn.

But devices for avoiding relevant actions in the next slot are not restricted to repair devices. Extract 13 is an instance of something which may be quite frequently done: a speaker makes a sequential move which avoids an inauspicious environment, and instead delays a planned next move until a more auspicious environment can be produced. This extract illustrates just such an avoidance/delay: Emma's invitation to Nancy for lunch follows a pre-sequence enquiry 'What are you doing?' (not shown).

Extract 13 (NB:II:2:14)

> EMMA: Wanna come down'n av a bite'a l:unch with me:? =
> I got s'm bee:r en stu:ff,
> (0.2)

NANCY: Wul yer ril sweet hon:, uh::m
(0.9)
NANCY: l e t I: ha(v)
[
→ EMMA: or d'yuh'av sump'n else (t')
[
NANCY: No:, I haf to uh call Rol's
mother. .h I told'er I:'d ca:ll 'er this morning-I
gotta letter from 'er en (.) .hhhhh A:ndum
(1.0)
NANCY: p.So sh- in the letter she said if you can why (.)
yihknow call me Sa:turday mor:ning en I just
haven't hh.
EMMA: Mm hm
[
NANCY: .hh It's like takin' a beating. (.) mhh heh.
heh heh hh.
[
→ EMMA: Mm:: 'N yuh have'n heard a word huh.
((Nancy then reports and talk continues for some while
about her ex-husband's failure to get in touch with her or
any of the family.))

There are two positions in which Emma forestalls a rejection, or rejection implication. The first is when, after Nancy's appreciation and then evident hesitation, Emma anticipates the possibility of an upcoming rejection, and heads it off with 'or d'yuh 'av sump'n else' (it might do so only in the sense of now providing a slot for an account, in place of a slot in which Nancy might have been going to reject the invitation). The second occasion is her response to Nancy's account of what she has to do, and Nancy's complaint that 'It's like takin' a beating'. In that slot Emma might have displayed an understanding of the 'bad news' implication (as did Ilene in the previous extract) of the account for her lunch invitation, for example through a marker of disappointment. Instead Emma focuses on Nancy's ex-husband and what he's not doing – ''N yuh have'n heard a word huh.' – rather than on the call to her mother-in-law. Emma thereby avoids making explicit any upshot, for her invitation, of Nancy's having to make a call. In other words, by picking up on that particular implication of Nancy's account Emma manages to divert the talk away from the invitation (opening a 'new' topic, rather in the manner that Nancy did in extracts 11 and 12), until another and more auspicious opportunity arises to re-introduce her invitation – which she does several minutes later (for an analysis of which see Drew (1984)).

Sequence expansions therefore appear to be one means for avoiding unwanted actions. Sequence attentuations appear to be rather less common; indeed they might be restricted to sequential objects like pre-sequences, in which the pre-sequence enquiry or noticing is designed with an eye to the possibility that the recipient will make an offer, thus absolving the speaker from the necessity of having to make a request. Hence, the slot in which a request might have been made, after the recipient's response to the pre-request, is displaced by the recipient replying right away with an offer.[13] Of course such attenuations cannot be guaranteed; they rely on co-participants' collaboration, and that is not always forthcoming.

Sequence initiations, attentuations and expansions do not by themselves constitute evidence that speakers consciously anticipate some future move/action, and attempt to facilitate or avoid that projected move, depending on whether the action is valued or unwanted. The advantage of treating sequences and sequential slots/objects as *procedures* is that it avoids mentalistic attributions; and it avoids the seemingly intractable analytic task of deciding whether a speaker 'knows' that by doing something in this slot, they'll avoid having to do something else in a subsequent slot.

The disadvantage is that *any* sequential object can be regarded as a procedure: and so the distinction between kinds of sequences that I was trying to make at the outset of the chapter would count for nothing. All sequential patterns would be equivalent. Some routines are perhaps part of the vernacular: by contrast, the organizations of other sequences are not projectable by participants. So this disadvantage of referring only to 'procedures' folds into another, that that may fail to capture the projectable, anticipated moves which are contingent upon a current move. When, in designing a current turn, a speaker selects which activity shall go in that turn – in many of the cases reviewed above, departing from and expanding the 'standard' sequence – that selection must involve a degree of 'consciousness'. There seems no reason in principle to deny a commensurate degree of consciousness to constructing a current turn with an eye to a subsequent anticipated turn. Of course it's not the principle but the empirical substantiation of conscious strategy in some of the cases reviewed here, and in other interactional sequences, that causes us to vacillate between regarding them as empirical instances of procedural, programmable cognitive strategies, to the possibility that they are instances of speakers' conscious strategies in anticipating how to achieve certain outcomes in projected sequences. That empirical substantiation may involve the kinds of issues I have been discussing here concerning sequential initiation, attentuation and expansion.

Notes

1 This is close, I think, to Byrne and Whiten's middle level (level one) of 'intentional behaviour' in animals, which includes 'behaviour that is convincingly intentional, in the sense of goal directed, ... [although] the category is agnostic as to the animal's mental states ... [Hence] to qualify as tactical deception, an action must therefore indicate at least Level One evidence of intention to achieve a goal which can only be reached if an individual is deceived (*not* the same thing as "evidence of an intention to deceive")' (Byrne and Whiten 1991). The agnosticism of this category as regards the intentionality of action (for example, to deceive another) parallels that of 'oriented to procedures' in conversation analytic research. See for instance Heritage (1990/91).

2 Levinson (Chapter 11, this volume, n. 13) discusses just such a level of (self-)consciousness about the practice of handshaking during greetings and partings, in circumstances where interactants are from different cultural backgrounds. But such moments as he describes of indecision and misinterpretation are equally familiar in exchanges between people who share a common culture, but are not sure which of the candidate greetings routines they should adopt.

3 More complex sequential patterns are perhaps less likely to be consciously managed because knowledge about them may generally not be part of the vernacular. (For some observations on this, see Jefferson (1988a:439).)

4 Sequences in which there is a measure of control over the turn-after-next (i.e. the third turn) are more familiar in institutional settings; for instance in classroom interaction, participants' orientation to the 'correctness' (or otherwise) of answers generates sequences in which teachers respond to students' answers to their questions by evaluating those answers, in a third turn.

5 These findings are for a study of English (American and English) speakers. The anthropological literature, some of which is cited in Drew (1987), suggests that teasing in other societies generates different patterns, and that therefore such patterns are cultural forms. Esther Goody (personal communication) reports that in Gonja, teases *have* to be responded to in a joking fashion. I want to note, however, that the same might be said of teasing in English/ American culture: that is, there is a normative orientation to 'humour' as the proper response to teasing, even though on many or most occasions people who are teased 'fail' to respond as they should. So, for example, the laughter which regularly precedes the po-faced response, as here in Nancy's initial response in extract 1, is certainly evidence that participants orient to normative expectations, in advance of flouting them. Having not studied the details of the design of responses to teases in Gonja or in other cultures, I am not qualified to say whether anything similar happens (e.g., that the Gonja display an orientation to a proper joking response, whilst simultaneously defending themselves in a 'serious' fashion. But I am yet to be convinced that teasing and conventionalized normative responses to teasing are indeed a cultural form.

6 They are 'backward looking' in a less obvious sense, that of 'recasting' the character of the prior turns: so that the tease recasts the prior turn as having been exaggerated, and the po-faced response treats the 'joking' tease as having

had a serious import. Hence there is a retroactive quality to the manner in which turns in the sequence 're-interpret' prior turns, as discussed by Good in his contribution to this volume (Chapter 6).

7   Perhaps the clearest and most elaborate example of this kind of 'non-strategic' sequential pattern is the six-stage sequence which Jefferson describes for troubles telling in conversation (Jefferson 1988b). She refers to this pattern as a 'candidate sequence' because it is an artificial construction of a sequence which empirically never runs off in the precise order of the template she documents. The disorder is generated by the troubles-telling sequence being 'constantly encroached upon, and recurrently breached, by the pressure towards business as usual, to which talk about trouble seems irrevocably vulnerable, and to the concerns of which a "trouble" appears to be irremediably subordinate and accountable' (Jefferson 1988a: 440). Whilst progression through the troubles-telling sequence is therefore susceptible to participants' orientation to a quite general interactional principle (business as usual), that principle is embodied in the design of a given turn without being strategically mobilized with a view to (facilitating or avoiding) any actions later in the sequence.

8   In this respect it may be no accident that in their chapters in this volume both Streeck and Levinson also cite instances of pre-sequences in the context of the projectability associated with sequences.

9   This is illustrated in the greetings which precede the pre-request for a ride in extract 4 in a rather interesting way. The person who answers gives his name, rather formally; the caller then gives his name – but not before re-addressing, as it were, 'J.P. Blenkinsop' as 'Jim', for which an appropriate reciprocal diminutive, 'It's Skip', is used.

10   I am leaving aside for present an issue of considerable importance for AIP generally, and specifically for the possibility of the consciousness of AIP strategies; this is the matter of how some topics, especially sensitive ones, are initiated or introduced into the conversation. The recipient's design of topical initial utterances which include explicit reference to such matters as what has happened since we last spoke, or accounts of why one is calling or introducing this topic (on which, see especially Jefferson (1984)), might be analysed for evidence of a speaker's conscious planning of how to introduce the topic. Wootton (personal communication) suggests that offer sequences frequently involve some manifest planning on the part of the one making the offer, in the face of the delicacy of what is offered.

11   This is the man Nancy is describing in extract 1.

12   However, my guess is that the particular details of the design of 'What are you doing?' enquiries which are disinterestedly interested are probably different from the design of the 'same' enquiry when it's intended as a preliminary to something; and that from these design details, recipients have little difficulty in figuring out which sort of enquiry it is. Whether that's true of other devices such as 'I can't hear you' and other repairs we do not yet know.

13   Elsewhere I discussed a similar phenomenon in cases where, instead of inviting the recipient, the speaker uses a device, a form of 'reporting', which is designed to elicit a self-invitation by the recipient: similarly, reporting a difficulty may be designed to give the recipient the opportunity to offer assistance. (See Drew 1984.)

6 Where does foresight end and hindsight begin?

There is much to be said in favour of the idea that anticipation and the preemption and deception which it permits play an important role in the social life of both humans and a number of other primates. This idea has been developed anew, particularly for the human case, in a number of different disciplines for a variety of different reasons. Goody (this volume), points to a number of instances, and the list could be extened almost *ad nauseam*. It ranges from computer scientists proposing plan-construction algorithms and user-modelling procedures for natural lan-guage front-ends, to economists speculating on the actions of economic agents planning their moves in the market-place with respect to the actions of others. The scope and explanatory range of this idea in any of these fields has always been questionable. In economics, for example, the very different effects of ignorance, habit and culture on individual choice have often been far greater than those of individual ratiocination. Nevertheless, any area of human activity which involves actual or potential interaction with other humans (and that might mean all of human life) can be seen to have characteristics which reveal an anticipa-tion of how others will view and respond to one's actions.

If we restrict our consideration of anticipation to human conversations, many writers have proposed that they have a measure of foreseeability built in. For example, conversation analysts have argued that there are clear expectations as to what kinds of turn may follow other turns, as in adjacency pairs, and participants must mark utterances, which do not conform to the expected trajectory of the conversation in some way so that their marked or dispreferred status is signalled (see, for example, the discussion of their work in Levinson (1983), or the papers in Atkinson and Heritage (1986)). Alternatively, if one follows the line of most speech-act theorists, all human languages have a number of resources which enable a speaker to stake a claim for a particular future interpretation of what is being said at any one point. The essential difference between an utterance in which there is an explicit marker of illocutionary force, and one which might be characterized as an indirect speech act, is that, with the latter, the precise nature of the speaker's intent is more open to negotiation. For both traditions, and one does not need to be an adherent of either to appreciate this point, the speaker's interactional and linguistic resources are marshalled to make claims on the future and to achieve the kind of control which, as Goody (this volume) points out, is vital if anticipatory interactive planning (AIP, henceforth) is to be of value to the individual.

AIP clearly requires substantial intellectual resources, and it is not surprising that social life has been offered as an important part of the made environment which has been important in the evolution of primate intelligence. Much interest has been generated by the similarities between the human and non-human cases, but in considering the final steps in this evolution, it is important to understand the qualitative differences in social interaction which are made possible by the availability of human language. These will be crucial to an understanding of the role of culture in social life, the nature of human intelligence, and, conceivably, to an analysis of the evolution of language.

There are many differences between the human and other cases as the other contributors to this volume demonstrate, but I wish to focus on just one which I believe is amongst the most important, and possibly even the most important. This is the way in which human language transforms the nature of time in human social life. I will argue that it achieves this through the ways in which it permits description and redescription of past actions, a capacity which is bound up with the fact that it also permits actions which are open to many interpretations, and which can be revised in the course of production. Thus, retrospective re-appraisal becomes as important as prospective planning, foresight becomes focused on what hindsight can do. The properties of AIP and the actions to which it would lead are constrained by the prospect of this revision, and the cognitive resources required for successful performance become different and much greater. There are a number of reasons why I believe this to be so, but in this brief sketch, I will restrict myself to those which I take to be central to the argument, and briefly consider their implications.

The interactional arms race

Long range tactics

If the ability to understand enduring social relations, to predict with a fair degree of success what another individual will do and, as a result, to deceive, can provide a distinct reproductive advantage, then it seems reasonable to propose that the next level of anticipatory and interactive sophistication will lie in the ability to discover the deceiver or free-riding exploiter of these social contracts. An advantageous next development for the deceiver would then be to find some way of minimizing the negative consequences of a deceit being discovered. There is a greater potential for this when the original act in question is ambiguous, and that ambiguity can be addressed. As a result an individual could disclaim full responsibility for a deception, by characterizing it as a misunderstanding. This could minimize the harm which might follow from the truth being discovered, and maintain the individual's potential for future actions in that relationship.

The progression from simple referring expressions which stand for real world entities, as would seem to be the case, for example, with vervet monkey calls, to human language facilitates this process so that ambiguity and tentativeness become possible, as does subsequent denial. Take the case due to Seyfarth reported in Dennett's discussion of the 'intentional stance' (Dennett 1988:189). One vervet monkey, when involved in a skirmish between its own troop and another, issued the 'leopard call' which led both bands to take to the trees thereby creating a 'cease-fire' and apparently saving the day for its own troop which had been losing the fight. If a similar deception were used in an intra-group setting in an attempt to gain personal advantage, though, if discovered, the animal would presumably suffer. If, however, it could utter its cry in a way which indicated a possibility, not a certainty, of a leopard, that is, a measure of doubt, then if subsequently discovered to have misled other individuals, it could defend itself by elaborating an account of both its motives and the basis of its perception; it then has a basis for avoiding retribution. Such an indication of doubt might ultimately lead to the cry not being completely effective in causing all vervet monkeys in the vicinity to run for the trees, but the cost of scepticism on their part would be so high that it is unlikely that they would be. Therefore, any vervet monkey that could indicate an uncertainty about the truth-value of an assertion as to the presence of a leopard, and could subsequently exploit this indication as an excuse, would have made the next important step in the interactional arms race. It would also have uttered the first proto-question, and been the first to offer a pragmatic variation in meaning by linking the meaning of a sign to a property of its user. Esther Goody (1978a,b) has discussed the singular importance of questions in a way which is redolent of this speculation, and I will briefly return to this point later.

In the human case, deception and the breaking of promises, be they explicit or implicit, is much easier when the nature of the original contract, either implicit or explicit, is less than clear, because then it can be claimed that in fact no one is being deceived or dishonoured. A point which Brown and Levinson (1987) make so well in their analysis of face and politeness, and which Arundale (1993) has interestingly extended. Despite our usual perception, that what is said in a conversation is relatively clear, the basis of that clarity relies as much on an inarticulable set of background assumptions as it does on what is said. It is these which make it possible for ambiguity and uncertainty of meaning to be claimed at some future point in that conversation, or in a future engagement, and an alternative meaning attributed to what was said or done. The specific way in which this might be exploited has been considered by Weiser (1975), who described it as 'deliberate ambiguity', and is what Brown and Levinson (1987) refer to as an 'off-the-record' strategy.

At other times, of course, speakers seem to be forced to extremes of commitment to the words they have uttered. Sometimes, they are held to the very letter of what they said where that 'letter' is interpreted in a very specific way. Yet on other occasions they are allowed to disclaim responsibility for what was said. In a Humpty-Dumpty-like fashion they can proclaim themselves to be the masters of what their words meant, usually, via an argument that what was said did not reflect their true intentions because the context in which it was said was poorly understood, bizarre, or not the one which currently holds. Machiavelli was well aware of this when he observed that, 'A wise ruler cannot and should not keep his word when such an observance of faith would be to his disadvantage and when the reasons which made him promise are removed . . . Men are so simple-minded and so controlled by their present needs that one who deceives will always find another who will allow himself to be deceived.' (*The Prince*, ch. 18.) Each of these extremes is, nevertheless, dependent on the compliance of others, and it would be wrong to ignore the role of the relative power and positions of the speakers and hearers in determining which of these extremes is adopted. A point of which Machiavelli was very aware.

The idea that such uncertainty and under determination exist has been challenged by that part of the speech-act tradition which has followed from Searle's (1969) interpretation of Austin's (1962) original work. As most will know, Searle proposed that it was possible to specify the full set of conditions under which a particular speech act was felicitous. If the speaker knows that these conditions are satisfied, then the act is guaranteed to go through. The felicity conditions have been re-interpreted in a variety of ways, most interestingly, given the current topic, by workers in artificial intelligence (AI) who have seen them as akin to the steps in a plan-construction algorithm which can be used as the basis for the production and interpretation of utterances.

In attempting to fulfil Searle's ambition, workers in this tradition have come to realize that Austin's original characterization was correct, and that the task of specifying all that must hold for any particular speech act to be felicitous is never-ending. Essentially, Austin focused on the ways speech acts fail and are thus infelicitous, and recognized that these ways form an open-ended set. This focus undoubtedly reflected the legal aspect of Austin's philosophical background. Law-makers must rely on the judiciary to interpret their intention in making a statute, and then, through the application of that statute in ever new and unforeseen contexts, the courts provide an ever-growing corpus of cases which refine and redefine the meaning of that intention. This process is never-ending, as technological developments in areas to do with human life repeatedly demonstrate. The speech-act theorist and the speaker are in the same position as the law-maker and can never foresee all the contexts in which an utterance might be interpreted. Thus a specific interpretation can never be guaranteed, nor can the results which might follow from that interpretation. To guarantee an interpretation would require the individual to have a level of foresight which we do not seem to possess even at the level of the collected minds of the law-makers and the judiciary.

Medium-range tactics

In human conversation, the meaning of an utterance is not only revisable some time later, but is often revised at the time of production. As has often been observed, the individual speaker is not the sole arbiter of the meaning and significance of what he or she says. At the turn-by-turn level of organization, many have argued that what each speaker says offers, amongst many other things, a demonstration of his or her understanding of what the previous speaker has said. In so doing, the current speaker contributes to the definition of the meaning of what was said by that previous speaker. Consider an example taken from Heritage (1984): if, in response to 'Why don't you come and see me some time?' I reply 'I'd love to', then I have offered a reading of it as an invitation. If I reply, 'I'm sorry, but I just never get the time these days', I have offered a reading of it as a complaint. Now, the original speaker might not accept one interpretation if the other was intended, and he or she can seek to redefine the original utterance in his or her next turn, but if that is what happens the character of the exchange overall is necessarily altered. A misunderstood complaint which is explicitly repeated has a far greater interactional salience. Also, the point that each has taken a role in the definition of the meaning which is thereby negotiated is reinforced.

Short-range tactics

This process of negotiation which can occur in the production of a sequence of utterances suggests that the meanings derived are effectively a joint production. There are good reasons to believe that this process operates at the intra-utterance level too.

Necessarily, the content of an utterance is revealed gradually. Goodwin

(1979) has shown that speakers are sensitive to the reactions of others during their turn at talking, and that they may revise what is being said as a consequence of these reactions. He proposes that utterances are constructed interactively as joint accomplishments, and this view is also supported by work on within-turn self-initiated, self-accomplished repair (see Streeck, Chapter 4 and Drew, Chapter 5, this volume).[1] Also, it is not implausible to suggest that as an utterance is being produced, not only can it lead to recognizable reactions on the part of the hearer, but also a more complete recognition by the speaker of the significance of what is being said for that hearer. It is a common intuition that as soon as an utterance is said, it is much easier for the speaker to understand the hearer's likely reaction even if that reaction cannot be seen or heard. Both kinds of feedback could then lead the speaker to revise the plan for what is to be said next in the same utterance.

It is unclear how one could discern what limits there are on how often this revision process can happen, but if the work of Goodwin, Drew, Streeck and others is to be believed it can be rapid, and at any point, although as the work of G. Beattie (1983) illustrates, how often this will happen depends on the other cognitive and interactional demands the speaker is facing.

This potential for revision suggests that there is a progression through the production of an utterance in what is being anticipated. It also provides a basis for allowing the ambiguity, which is necessarily present in an incomplete utterance, to provide a test for the acceptability of what might be said. Thus, what is said towards the end of an utterance can revise what was said earlier so that the whole may end up as rather different to that which was initially projected by the speaker. A classic example of this is sentence-final negation in Japanese which permits the reversal of the truth value of an utterance with the final morpheme (R. Miller 1967).

Social life, chess and language

To understand fully the implications of the observations in the previous section, it is useful to consider the metaphor which underlies much of the thinking about non-human interaction, and the crucial feature of that metaphor which allows the division of time with respect to anticipation.

If it is being proposed that some agent is anticipating some future event, then for an adequate characterization of that anticipatory skill, it is necessary to define the period during which it is employed. This is a logical and theoretical necessity. An account of anticipatory planning must be based on what is known before the event, and this is temporally defined. The most important limit to this period is the latest point at which any anticipatory planning can be done, which is to say, just before the event or action in question occurs: a point in time which we might, for convenience's sake, refer to as the 'anticipation limit' (AL, henceforth). What, at one moment before the AL, is anticipation becomes reaction as the anticipated event or action occurs, the AL is passed, and different information becomes available. Subsequently, further (perhaps different) anticipatory planning will occur, but by definition it cannot be anticipating something which has already happened.

If we examine a game such as chess, the ALs are easy to define. They are the points at which each move is made. Before these points, each player speculates on what the likely intentions behind, and outcomes of his or her opponent's moves, the likely outcome of his or her own moves, and how his or her intentions might be perceived by his or her opponent. There is a period of reflection and planning, followed by a discrete and well-defined action, followed by a further period of reflection and planning as the opponent's next move is awaited. The actions, which are well-defined, chunk the interaction by specifying the beginning and end of every turn, and thereby the ALs. The time it takes to move a chess piece is seemingly irrelevant and can be ignored in the same way that the period of time for which a force is applied in an impact is ignored in classical physics.

Humphrey (1976) explicitly uses chess as the model for interaction, and in many respects this seems quite appropriate for the cases he discusses. It is tempting to think that the same structure is to be found in conversatons, and that each turn at speaking is similar to the sequence of plan and move in chess. Some psycholinguistic work has tried to exploit this metaphor, but the results of the related empirical work suggest that the proposed cognitive cycles are, at best, somewhat ephemeral (see G. Beattie (1983) for the best attempt). Such conceptualizations have been notoriously difficult to operationalize or support in any other way. Elsewhere (Good 1989), I have argued against the idea that conversations are made up of well-defined units that are like chess moves in their character, and the argument above that ambiguity, redescription, and joint production pervade every level of conversation renders the idea that an AL can be specified untenable.

As if this were not enough, the difficulty in defining an AL for a single turn is exacerbated when we contemplate the fact that many ambitions or goals in a conversation might be accomplished across a number of turns. For example, Brown and Levinson (1987) in their analysis of politeness propose that speakers take redressive action to ameliorate the face-threat offered by any utterance within that utterance. While this might be true in some instances, and is certainly a sensible simplifying move for their analysis, it is common to find that some kinds of redressive action are accomplished in more turns than the one which contains the specific face-threatening act. For example, if one is adopting a positive politeness strategy by using various markers of common group affiliation, such as a Basque speaker palatalizing his or her consonants (Corum 1975), it is singularly odd if the marker, in this case palatalization, is 'turned on' for just the utterance which contains the face-threatening act.

Implications

In the preceding paragraphs I have raised various points which, if fully supported, will require a different perspective on the nature of anticipation and forward planning when the individual is using a human language. The thesis I would propose is that given our imperfect knowledge of one another, the absence of a clear point at which anticipation may have a clear articulation, and the potential ambiguity of our actions which permits subsequent revision of their significance, the major concern in anticipating the social future is that the past may be re-interpreted. Therefore, the concern of the individual will be to constrain those future interpretations since no specific guarantee can ever be offered for the accomplishment of a specific reading. The best we can do is to take action to eliminate certain interpretations, and hope that the set of possible interpretations which remains provides sufficient scope for casting ourselves in a decent light in the future. The crucial thing for foresight then becomes the knowledge of what hindsight can do. This thesis has implications for our view of the role of culture, and the nature of the intelligence which we have as a result of our evolutionary history. I will conclude by speculating on these very briefly.

Culture, Machiavelli and Hume

The interpretation of past acts and the role of various actors in them is the stuff of courtroom disputes and deliberations. While barristers are adept at offering radical recastings of events so that their clients' or opponents' actions are seemingly transformed, there are constraints on what they can do. The same is true for all other speakers too. It is not the case that any behaviour or utterance can be taken to mean anything the barrister chooses. There is an accepted scheme of things, as in, for example, Burke's *Grammar of Motives*, within which the discussion of past action operates. A straightforward appeal to demonic possession as an account of a person's actions will not be accepted in the same way today as it was in sixteenth-century Europe. There is a culture of the courtroom which is, in many ways, a crystallization of the mores of the wider community, and which both facilitates and limits these re-interpretations. Similarly, the wider culture operates in everyday negotiations as to the significance of what is said and done. These constraints can also be seen as facilitators of everyday reasoning, and in many respects ease the cognitive burden which the individual in an uncertain ambiguous social world must shoulder.

The burden which is carried will almost certainly depend on the individual's ability to understand the interplay and coordination of one's own and others' actions. As Levinson (Chapter 11, this volume), rightly argues, Machiavellian competition is child's play compared to the Humean task which coordination produces. Again, the general expectations and representations of each other made available through our culture ease this task, but do not eliminate it.

Memory and self

To operate in this rather free-form ambiguous and ever-changing interactional environment obviously requires substantial cognitive skills, and it is tempting to think that, given my suggestion as to the role of hindsight, the nature and extent of the individual's memory will be crucial. There is much debate in the memory literature as to the nature and role of the different kinds of memory which have been proposed. Short-term stores of one sort or another, long-term memory, recall and recognition memory, and so forth, have all been examined and seen to have greater or lesser roles in language use. At the turn-by-turn level of revision and correction, a short-term store will be required, and this will arguably be different to that which is used directly in the production process. The speaker must orient to what he or she has said in the same way as the listener has if the need for repair is to be recognized, and this would seem to depend on the kind of memory which is tested in short-term memory tasks. The major problem when engaging in self-repair is to ensure that the target of the repair is recognized. The further away from the repair that the target is, the harder it is to ensure that the repair is linked to the repairable. Beyond a certain distance, this becomes a very chancy affair. It is tempting, therefore, to speculate that at least some characteristics of short-term memory have evolved because of the demands of coordination in utterance production and the limits on successful reference in accomplishing self-repair.

At a different level, a memory of self and the description of events in which one has been engaged, with self as the key reference point, becomes crucial for the language user in line with the position of the Symbolic Interactionists. The memory need not include specific detail, though, beyond the level which permits the elimination of those interpretations of self's performance which were not desired. The frame for this may well be culturally specific and will be both constraining and facilitating in the manner discussed in the previous section. It must include, however, memory for rudiments of the memories of self that others possess. Given the potential indeterminacy of any social action or utterance, the framework offered by others' memory of self is something which they must use to understand self's actions. The nature of their memories will be revealed to a greater or lesser extent by the character of their responsiveness in an interaction. Thus, the memory of self is as much a distributed model of self as a personal one, if we are concerned with how a memory of self determines and constrains our social performances.

The interactional moment

The process of coordination seems to both require and produce an extended sense of the conscious present. Since no single moment can be taken as an AL, the competent social performer must be able to preserve from decay the fleeting evidence of what self and other have done, in full, in case it is transformed by what is done next. The immediate past must be maintained as it if were happening just then, as there is inevitably a delay between self's own production and the other's reaction. Only then can the speaker fully exploit the cognitive resources of the other and the production be changed in an appropriate way. An awareness of how this interdependence might be further exploited by the other, and how the exchange and relationship might oscillate backwards and forwards between cooperation and competition, could be the basis of one account of self-consciousness.

Pragmatics and the evolution of language

As many studies of language-learning animals, be they pigeons, grey parrots, gorillas or pygmy chimpanzees, have shown, it is not hard to get an animal to pair a movement such as pecking at a disc or moving the hands with an object, or in response to another stimulus. Indeed, it would be very odd if this were not possible. Various claims have been made for certain primates as being able to use such pairings in a more sophisticated way partly as a function of their more sophisticated social lives, and consequently in a way which is more akin to human language. None of these cases, however, involves the animal in exploiting the relation between itself and the language being used to generate a variation in meaning. As was mentioned above, such a use, and thereby the introduction of pragmatic meaning, would produce a clear benefit in the interactional arms race. Discovered deceit would become less problematic for both the group and the individual in that it opens the possibility of less divisive outcomes in such cases. The simplest way in which pragmatic meaning could be introduced is by a query by self as to the truth of what self is indicating or asserting.

Endpoint

If the first part of this essay was speculative, the last part is wildly so. I hope, however, that this brief sketch is sufficient to move the role of hindsight to the forefront of everyone's mind so that we can give it the greater consideration which I believe it deserves in the anticipation of the interactional future.

Acknowledgements

My many thanks to Esther Goody for her encouragement, criticism, and endless patience. Thanks also to all the participants in the workshop from which this volume grew, for their comments on the original version of this chapter.

Note

1 There are, of course, some instances in a conversation where an action is dependent solely on the action of self like a movement in chess (see below). A real shibboleth is one such instance, as Jephthah the Gileadite realized to the cost of the Ephraimites. See Judges 12, 4–6.

PART III

Genres as tools that shape interaction

7 Politeness strategies and the attribution of intentions: the case of Tzeltal irony

In this chapter I want to take up the idea that human thinking is systematically biased in the direction of interactive thinking (E. Goody's anticipatory interactive planning, or AIP), that humans are peculiarly good at, and inordinately prone to, attributing intentions and goals to one another (as well as to non-humans), and that they routinely orient to presumptions about each other's intentions in what they say and do. I want to explore the implications of that idea for an understanding of politeness in interaction. I shall take as a starting point the Brown and Levinson model of politeness, which *assumes* interactive thinking, a notion implicit in the formulation of politeness as strategic orientation to face.

Brown and Levinson (1978, 1987) have proposed a model of politeness wherein human actors are endowed with two essential attributes: face and rationality. We claim that face consists of two specific kinds of wants: positive face (i.e., the desire to be approved of, admired, liked, validated), and negative face (the desire to be unimpeded in one's actions). The second ingredient in our model is rationality, the ability to reason from communicative goals to linguistic means that would achieve those goals. From these two assumptions – face and rationality – and the assumption that speakers universally *mutually know* that all speakers have these attributes, we developed a model of how speakers construct polite utterances in different contexts on the basis of assessments of three social factors: the relative power (P) of speaker and addressee, their social distance (D), and the intrinsic ranking (R) of the face-threateningness of an imposition. P, D and R are seen as abstract social dimensions indexing kinds of social relationship (P and D) and cultural values and definitions of impositions or threats to face (R). The claim, then is this: however culturally variable definitions of kinds of social relationship and kinds of face threat might be, underlying them are pan-cultural social dimensions (relative power, social distance, ranking of face-threateningness) which universally go into the reckoning – and the interpretation – of strategic language choice, and hence we derive the cross-cultural similarities in choice of linguistic realizations of politeness strategies that empirically seem to be in evidence. We then went on further, to claim that this model of politeness universals could be applied in particular cultural circumstances as an ethnographic tool for analysing the quality of social relationships.

In this Brown and Levinson framework, then, sociolinguistic variation (different kinds of language use in different situations) is portrayed as rationally tied – via demonstrable means–ends reasoning links – to the kinds of things people are trying to do when they speak, and cross-cultural parallels are viewed as attributable to the existence of similar rational processes underlying human interaction.

This model (and the Gricean model of communication which underlies it) makes very strong assumptions about humans' abilities to reason reflexively about each others' desires and intentions. To operate according to the model, speakers have to be able to modify the expression of their communicative intentions so as to take account of what they see as their interlocutor's views of what they might be taken to be wanting to communicate, including what impositions to face might be on the table, as well as his or her assessments of the speaker's and hearer's relative power and social distance. Correspondingly, interlocutors must be able to read such modifications as evidence that the speaker is inferring particular things about their own views, desires, and intentions in this context. An enormous amount of reasoning, therefore, would have to go into the construction of any utterance, and one might well be forgiven for thinking that human communication along these lines is simply impossible.

One way of finessing some of this reasoning might be by using conventionalized politeness strategies, where politeness meaning is conventionally attached to certain linguistic forms: for example, formulaic expressions like 'please' and 'thank you', or conventionally indirect speech acts like 'Could you pass the salt?' where the polite hesitancy of 'Could you?' cannot be read literally and therefore automatically conveys polite restraint. This is, I think, how the 'person on the street' tends to think about politeness, as inhering in particular linguistic forms.

And indeed, many interpreters of the Brown and Levinson model have fallen into the trap of thinking of linguistic realizations of politeness strategies as *necessarily* conveying the particular sort of politeness we associate them with, as if all politeness realizations were conventionalized, as if any instance of the use of an in-group address form or an exaggerated expression of interest were necessarily positively polite, for example.

What I want to demonstrate here is that not only is this clearly untrue – no necessary politeness associations attach to any linguistic form in situated discourse, or rather, whatever associations attach to a form out of context may be undone in its situated use. But further, conventionalization does not provide the easy solution to intention-attribution that it first appears to. Conventionalized politeness strategies still have to be interpreted in relation to presumed speaker intentions in context.

One of the ways this lesson was drummed home to me was in my confrontation with a conventionalized form of expression in Tzeltal, a Mayan language spoken in the peasant Indian community of Tenejapa, in southern Mexico, where my ethnographic fieldwork has been concentrated.[1] I have called the phenomenon 'Tzeltal irony', as it is basically a matter of uttering propositions which are in the context taken to convey the 'opposite' or the 'inverse' of what they literally appear to mean. Ironic assertions in Tzeltal most frequently appear phrased as hedged negative assertions usually preceded with *yu'*, 'because', such that uttering a proposition (P) in the form *yu' ma P-uk* ('because it is not, possibly, the case that P') conveys the emphatic assertion that 'P' *is* the case.[2] This form of expression is elaborated in Tzeltal to an extent that far exceeds the use of ironic expressions in, say, English or the other languages which have been used to elucidate the nature of irony. There is an enormous philosophical and linguistic literature on this topic; I do not address it here but rather try to disentangle the Tzeltal phenomenon as a thing *sui generis*.[3]

In the context of this book, there are two main reasons for taking an interest in this phenomenon:

First, because of the cognitive processes involved: the production and understanding of ironic utterances seems to require an enormous depth of reflexive reasoning, and a reliance on the firmness of mutual understanding between interlocutors, who must assume that they share mutual knowledge about what each other thinks each other thinks could/must be true. Just how is this mental acrobatics achieved?

Secondly, because of the ethnographic puzzle: in Tzeltal, ironies are used to construct social relationships of a particular kind. How and why is this done through conventionalized irony?

To elaborate: ironic expressions, and their close relative rhetorical questions, are a very pervasive and salient feature of Tzeltal speech in interaction. They are an important ingredient in the expression of positive politeness in this society, used for stressing agreement, sympathy, understanding and commiseration; they are therefore especially in evidence in women's speech. Both syntactically and functionally, Tzeltal ironies are very closely related to rhetorical questions, understatement, and negative assertions (presuming a positive response) – an intriguing class of utterance types that gives a distinctive flavour to Tzeltal interaction, all of which involve conveying the 'opposite' of the proposition expressed plus an attitude to it, and carrying the interactional pressure for the addressee to respond to this attitude.

They are therefore quintessential examples of 'inter-subjective perspective-setting and -taking' (Luckmann, Chapter 8, this volume), and merit our attention to the complex reasoning processes involved in the achievement of this.

In passing, I might add that Tzeltal ironic expressions lend themselves to a Sperber and Wilson (1982) type of treatment, which views irony (and more loosely ironical utterance types) as *echoic mention*. All these sorts of 'figures of speech' are seen as essentially 'echoing' or more loosely evoking a proposition which is placed in the context to be laughed at, scorned, or whatever, in order for an attitude to be conveyed towards it. Ironic utterances are like things in quotes, so for example if someone says 'Nice day, eh', in a context of a walk in the pouring rain and sleet, the false description evokes the image of the accurate description ('Rotten day, eh') as well as an image of who might have, or actually did, utter the hope/prediction/expectation that it would be a nice day, this person (or image) then being the imagined 'victim' or target of the ironic utterance. The Sperber and Wilson account doesn't claim that all this is the 'meaning' of the utterance, but rather a set of reasoning processes to get from what's said to what's intended to be conveyed.

In Tenejapa, ironies, rhetorical questions and understatements are an important ingredient in all sorts of evaluative discourse – gossip, complaint/commiseration sequences, verbal play (joking, mockery, banter) – as well as in other breaches of the 'quality maxim': verbal deceit, social lies (e.g., the token refusal of offers, pseudo agreement, and denying knowledge of answers to nosy questions). They add up to a peculiarly Tenejapan (and especially Tenejapan women's) way of speaking, conventionalized and elaborated in many domains, and tied to other aspects of Tenejapan social life – to non-committalness, fatalism, values about privacy, vulnerability to gossip, avoidance of open conflict, for example.[4]

Let's look, then, at the culturally standardized use of ironic expressions among Tzeltal-speaking Tenejapans.

Tzeltal ironic expression – some politeness strategies in use

An understanding of ironic expression in Tzeltal requires two things: (1) an analytical approach to irony within a universal framework – an analysis of the kinds of jobs irony can do in conversation, by virtue of its rationally based construction oriented to Grice's 'maxim of quality'. In Brown and Levinson (1987) we analyse irony as a politeness strategy which is an off record strategy in origin, but in context can be positively polite.[5] But ironic expression in Tzeltal is *conventionalized* off record, for very often no non-ironic reading is entertainable in the context, and therefore we also need (2) an understanding of normatively stabilized usages in Tzeltal, and of how such normative stabilizing affects what ironically phrased utterances can be taken to mean in different contexts.

I choose to develop such a complex example here because with it I can show how a given type of linguistic form can have multiple situated meanings and therefore multiple politeness (and impoliteness) functions; an ironically expressed utterance can, in context, convey any of the three types of politeness superstrategies: it can be (1) genuinely off record, ambiguous in the context as to whether an ironic reading is intended; it can be (2) negatively polite by virtue of being conventionally indirect, and (3) perhaps most characteristically, it can be positively polite, emphasizing common ground; it can also convey *im*politeness. But, though the interpretation changes with the context, the underlying strategic orientation to face concerns shows through across contexts. So in this society, in which I have described the women as prone to emphasizing positively polite expression amongst themselves (Brown 1979, 1980), I want to show what happens to women's affiliative speech style, and specifically what happens to the interpretation of potentially ironic expressions, when hostility, anger or mere suspicion characterizes their interaction.

First I'll briefly characterize the Tzeltal ironic formulations, and show how they work in ordinary cooperative speech. Then I'll illustrate their use in a Tenejapan courtroom confrontation, where they become sarcastic agreement used to emphasize *dis*agreement. And finally I'll illustrate the intricacies of ironic/rhetorical expressions in a more ambiguous case, where ironic expression hovers between affiliative and dissociative functions during the conversation.

Conventionalized Tzeltal ironic/rhetorical expression

There are three basic ways of constructing ironic/rhetorical utterances in Tzeltal, as summarized by the following formulae: (P represents the proposition as expressed in the surface structure; → is to be read as 'conversationally implicates', that is 'in the context conveys'):

Type 1: a hedged or questioned proposition, optionally introduced by 'because' (*yu'un*), optionally with the subjunctive -*uk*, and optionally with dubitative or emphatic particles which may force an ironic reading:

$(yu'un) + Q/\text{hedge} + P + (-uk) + (\text{emphatic particle(s)}) \rightarrow \text{'not P'}$

Type 2: a negative proposition, hedged or questioned, again optionally with -*uk* and dubitative or emphatic particles:

$(yu'un) + NEG + P + Q/\text{hedge} + (-uk) (\text{emphatic-particle(s)}) \rightarrow \text{'P'}$

Type 3: a WH-questioned proposition (who/why/when/where/what/ how), again optionally hedged and/or emphasized:

$WH-Q + P + (\text{hedge}) + (\text{emphatic particle(s)}) \rightarrow \text{'No one, no where, no way, for no reason, P'}$

My reason for treating ironies and rhetorical questions as essentially the same is that the basic mechanism of construction is the same for both, the only difference being that in ironies, the proposition (phrased as the 'opposite' of what the speaker intends to convey) is hedged with dubitative particles, while in rhetorical questions it is hedged with a question particle. In both cases emphatic particles and/or prosodics may (optionally) disambiguate the intended meaning.

Examples: the basic phenomenon[6]

Example 1.   Context: story about a girlfriend who hangs out with several different men; S is here emphasizing her own attitude to the risks of associating with her.

yu'un   niwan   ya   j-k'an   ya   j-ta   mul   ya   k-a'y
because   perhaps   ICP   I-want   ICP   I-find   crime   ICP   I-know/feel
Because perhaps I want to find trouble, I know.
((→'Of course I don't want to get into trouble!'))

Example 2.   Context: talk about a man who owes S money and won't pay it.

yu'   bal   jo'on   ay   ba   ya   j-ta   tak'in
because   Q   I   EXIST   where   ICP   I-find   money
Because is there anywhere I'll find money?
((→'Of course not!' (soliciting H's sympathy.)))

Example 3.   Context: S is commiserating about H's problems with her chickens, and offering sympathy.

ma   wan   tey-uk   nax   ay   ek
NEG   perhaps   there-SUBJ   just   EXIST   too
It might perhaps not be the case that (the weasels) just are there too.
(→'They certainly are there!'))

Example 4.   Context: following a humiliating request when a man has asked his younger sister to mend his son's schoolbook, thereby revealing a breach with his wife whose job it is; his mother sympathizes with his need.

bi_yu'un   nix ay   x-a'-na'   s-tz'isel   ek a
why   just EXIST   ASP-you-know   its-sewing   too
Just why would you know how to sew it?
((→'Of course you wouldn't!'))

It is important to note that utterances constructed according to these formulae are not *necessarily* ironic (though particle combinations – especially hedge + emphatic particle – may force an ironic reading, and so may prosodics, facial expressions, etc.). But they are contextually disambiguated, via the assumption of mutual knowledge of each other's beliefs, attitudes, values, and likely events. Further, when ironic they do not necessarily convey a barbed negative evaluation of some specific target; the proposition that is held up to scrutiny is not necessarily attributable to any particular person.

Sequencing in conversation

The archetypal use for Tzeltal irony and rhetorical questions is as positively polite emphasizing of held-in-common opinions, values, and understandings. This is displayed in the ways in which they are responded to in interaction. Sometimes the response continues in the ironic vein, sometimes it 'translates' the irony with a straight response.

Example 5.   Context: story about husbands working on coffee finca.

> A: ... mak ma wan xch' ajubotik ta stamel in ch'i
> ... perhaps it's not possibly that we get tired from bending over to pick (coffee, that has fallen to the ground) then! (($\rightarrow$sympathetic understanding: 'Of course, it's tiring!'))
>
> B: mak bi yu'uni ma xch'ajub
> Perhaps why don't (we) get tired. (($\rightarrow$'We sure do!'))
>
> A: yak mak
> Yes, perhaps. ((Agrees with implicature.))

Example 6.   Context: grown daughter just arrived back from several days' visit in town has been telling her mother what happened there. Her mother (A) reacts sympathetically to her tale of trials.

> A: yu' ma sakubenuk a jul ch'i
> Because not sort of pale, you arrived, to be sure! (($\rightarrow$'Gosh have you ever come home pale!' i.e., 'Poor you, what problems you've had!'))
>
> B: a sakub
> Oh (yes), pale. ((Straight reply, agrees with the implicature.))
>
> A: saktuntun nanix a kil
> Really pale, I see. ((Agrees with agreement.))
>
> B: ya'ben julel.
> Pale and thin (I've) come home. ((Agrees with agreement.))

Equally, ironies may be used to *elicit* sympathy:

Example 7.   Context: household visit; smalltalk about crops.

> P: jm. bi yilel? lek bal a laj ala ch'i yilel?
> Oh. How does it look? Is it (your chili) growing well? ((Straight question.))
>
> M: banti lek ya xch'i. mak yu' ma ja'uk kola' a ya'y xan, jich nix a taot xan ja'al ini.
> Where does it grow well. (($\rightarrow$'Nowhere; it's not growing well'.)) Perhaps because it's not the case that it's rotting again, thus it has just encountered this rain again. (($\rightarrow$'It *is* rotting, from the rain.'))

Example 7 also illustrates the fact that ironic utterances are not solely used to engender repeat cycles of agreement on mutually known facts; they are often used to *inform* on matters about which the addressee has no personal knowledge. However, in these cases the addressee has the option to respond without agreement – indeed, with doubt or outright denial of the conveyed proposition, thus conveying that the prior speaker's presumption of shared knowledge/attitudes was in this case unwarranted.

But when ironies are used to proffer an emphatic opinion, the response may continue in the same mode, so that the whole interchange is carried on in a non-literal mode (whilst appearing to be revelling in their agreement that 'P', they are really assuring each other on their agreement that 'not-P'). For example, in this exchange:

Example 8.   Context: girls gossiping about a newly married friend.

> A: ya wan xjalaj xkal
>   She perhaps will stay a long while, I say. ((→'Of course she won't stay long with her new husband.'))
> B: yu'wan ma ya sta o'tanil.
>   Because perhaps she won't get tired of him. ((→'Of course she will tire of him!'))

Here, by rephrasing A's ironic comment rather than merely repeating it, B demonstrates her understanding of A's ironic intention, and provides even stronger accord and agreement. This can presumably only be pulled off if they can with reason presume that they do in fact share similar presumptions about the likelihood of (in this case) the friend sticking to her new husband. (If in fact they didn't share the same views, the thing would proceed in a different direction, as each pulled the inferential structure in the direction of her own (incompatible) set of beliefs.) Similarly, in the following joking exchange, we find *ironic* irony, again requiring shared attitudes (in this case, to the undesirability of marrying a Ladinoized Indian and the probability of marrying a real Tenejapan) as a prerequisite to its successful achievement:

Example 9.   Joking exchange in context of gossip session about a woman who has been pursuing a married man; they've just agreed that it's better to go after unmarried men.

> ANT: ... ja' ya jk'an xbaon ek in ta lumi. ((laughing))   1
>   It's that I want to go to town, too. (Indirect reference to one of her unwanted suitors, who wears Ladino clothes, speaks Spanish and lives in town.)
>   ((→'I want to go to town to see this lovely boyfriend, ha ha.'))
> X: ((laughing)) solel ta lum ya'k'an ban.   2
>   Wow, to town you want to go!
> ANT: ja' ya jk'an ba jmulan ek in lumi, ja' eki sawuli.   3
>   It's that I want to go enjoy town, it's this Sawul-fellow (who tempts me there).
> X: yu'un nix wan ma ja'uk leke, joyob kaxlan ye tz'in.   4
>   Because perhaps it wouldn't just be good, he's completely Ladinoized.
>   ((→'That would be great, since he's Ladinoized.'))

ANT: joyob ye tz'in.   5
Completely, to be sure.

X: yu' wan indijena to yich'at yael ya'wa'y a tz'in ch'i.   6
Because perhaps an Indian will marry you you know then.
((→first-level implicature: 'Of course not; you'll marry a Ladino.'))
((→second-level implicature: joking; 'Of course we really know you'll
marry an Indian.'))

ANT: eh kaxlan ya xk'oon ta lum ya'wa'y tz'in ch'i.   7
Oh, as a Ladino I'll arrive in town you know then.
((→agreement with ironic reading; 'Not as an Indian's wife but as a
Ladino's wife will I appear in town.'))

X: k'unk'un ala bestido ya'wich'ix ala bechel ek a.   8
Gradually you'll wear Ladino clothes yourself too!

Here (lines 6–7) we have irony within irony: they both know perfectly well
that Ant has no intention of marrying a Ladino; this is a joking scenario in
ironic mode.[7]

Example 9 also illustrates the characteristic in-group Tenejapan response to teasing, which, apparently in contrast to English (see Drew 1987,
and Chapter 5, this volume) rather than being 'po-faced' (serious)
actually upgrades the tease as an elaborate self-tease, sequentially building up over several turns an increasingly ludicrous scenario in which
teaser and teasee collaborate. The initiators of such teases are designed to
provoke the sequence that follows, and this forward-looking joking is a
common form of verbal play among young Tenejapan women.

To sum up: perhaps the archetypal uses for the ironic forms of
expression we have been examining are in women's positive politeness
'grooming', relishing and elaborating their mutually shared views on an
issue. How they can so blithely assume that their views are mutually
shared (and despite the fact that they occasionally mistakenly make this
assumption) is a mystery; my data come largely from interactions between
people who know each other very well, and whether ironic expression
occurs freely between relative strangers I cannot say. I suspect that it
does, for just those sorts of attitudes that can be generally assumed to be
shared (attitudes to health, economic problems, ritual responsibilities, for
example).

This form of expression seems to be a highly conventionalized form of
feminine positive politeness in this society (see Brown 1979, ch. 4, for
more details). It takes perhaps its most extreme form in women's joking
scenarios like the one illustrated above, where they carry on in the ironic
mode as an activity in itself: a false picture of the world is elaborately
developed by speakers both uttering nothing but ironic utterances and
agreements (ironic or straight) with them. Who exactly the target is of
these 'false scenarios' – who might be being set up as the voice which is
being echoed in order to be mocked, in Sperber and Wilson's terms – is
not entirely clear. In many cases it seems to be something like the

personified voice of public opinion, or of malicious gossip – whoever might be likely to be making these patently false, and patently contra-normal female-role-expectations claims about the subject of the ironic assertions. Structurally what seems to be going on is that the girls play off their own (real) attitudes and fears against a personified voice of public opinion that is bad-mouthing them. This bad-mouthing can be straight, or it can be ironic itself, as we saw in example 9 where the girls were teasing one girl about marrying a Ladino. In that case, the apprehension about public opinion is that it will suggest that they, true Indian girls, will marry Ladinos and 'go over to the enemy' as it were. So representing that voice in an ironic manner, they say 'Oh yes, sure you're going to marry an Indian' conveying ironically the voice of public opinion's conviction 'I bet you're going to marry a Ladino.' It is against this puppet voice of public opinion that the jokes about sex role identity take their force.[8]

The same sort of process, the setting up of a 'voice of malicious gossip' against which communicative intent is to be read, seems to be involved in other characteristic forms of Tenejapan expression. It appears in Teneja-pans' self-mockery, as when they say, in effect: 'I'm stupid, lazy, useless, my clothes are full of holes, ...' This can be friendly joking; it can however take a more pointed turn, for example in teasing one's close household members about non-love and non-care (scenario: 'You (I) are poor and homeless, no parents, no food, will die of the cold and starvation, will be thrown to the dogs to eat, etc. etc.'). Such joking can carry heavy, non-affiliative implications, and the same format can be used as an indirect expression of anger.

Which leads us to our next set of examples: what happens to women's affiliative positively polite style in situations of open *conflict*?

Angry irony

Tenejapan women, of course, don't invariably engage in positively polite affiliative interactions. Conflict, overt anger and scolding, do occur, however normatively disapproved of, and it is instructive to look at ironic expressions in these sorts of contexts.

But first a few words about conflict in Tenejapa. Women in daily interaction tend to suppress conflict; it is veiled, even in private, and between non-intimate adult women openly angry confrontation rarely occurs. When one is angry, interaction with the provoker of one's anger is simply avoided, and gossip, mockery and backbiting against the object of one's anger are expressed to sympathetic intimates. Anger between women who are intimates is normally expressed through controlled 'leakage': silence, non-responsiveness or terse replies, and kinesic dis-tancing, which in contrast with normal relaxed behaviour may suggest anger.

There are however two types of contexts in which open conflict is not only tolerated but expected from women. One is in courtship, which traditionally is coloured by the girl's (apparent) outrage at being approached; the other is in court cases or more informal grievance hearings. In both of these contexts, ironic/rhetorical expressions abound. These, in such contexts of hostility or conflict, can be used to emphasize the attitude of hostility, as in this (reported) example of a girl's reaction to her unwanted suitor:

Example 10.

> ANT: ej yu' bal xbiket mach'a ya ya'yat mene' xkut.
> 'Oh, is it that the one who hears you is happy', I said.
> ((→'No, you sure don't make anyone happy, you creep.'))

In the next example, taken from a Tenejapan court case which was filmed and tape-recorded in 1980 by Stephen Levinson and myself, two women angrily confront one another in a public forum.

Example 11.   Context: P (plaintiff) is claiming that D (defendent) owes her various debts; D is denigrating the value of the goods she allegedly owes P for. Immediately preceding context: P has been listing her claims; J (judge) has just said 'wait a minute' and begun to write them down, one by one. (Underlined line numbers indicate ironic/rhetorical utterances)[9]

> J: te: um (1.5) tzekel tz'i   234
> (for the) skirt, then?
>
> P: jm (.) ox-chejp tz'in tzekele (1.5) cha'chejp chujkilal   235
> Hm, three hundred then for the skirt, two hundred for the belt. ((Making a claim for what D owes her for these items.))
>
> D: bi yu'un ma ja'uk tz'in mak yu' ma jo'winikuk (sti) =   <u>236</u>
> Why wasn't it then, perhaps it wasn't one hundred or so. ((→it was only worth 100 pesos (disputing P's claim in line 235).))
>
> = mak bit'il ta' ya stoytik yu' mak ja' te sle bi xan ae   <u>237</u>
> How is it that they overstate (the price of the belt) because perhaps it's that she (P) is looking for something more (from me)!
>
> (1)   238
> (..................)   239
> [   ]
>
> P: ya stak xa'leben (.)   240
> You can look for (it – a belt) for me,
>
> ya stak' xa'leben sjol teme jiche   241
> you can look for a replacement for it for me if that's how it is. ((→'If you think that was a cheap belt, get a better one!'))
> [   ]
>
> D: ja' yu' wan ja' tz'i batz'il stzotzil tz'i mak =   <u>242</u>
> It's that, perhaps it's that it's real wool then perhaps! ((→It wasn't of real wool; i.e., it was cheap!))

```
      = ma ja' (tay tz'in men)                                              243
      perhaps it's not (that)
                     [   ]
  P:                 manchuk a tz'in mak yu' ma toyoluk k'uxel tz'i =  244
                     So what about that then, perhaps it's not that it was
                     expensive then
                     ((→'It was expensive!'))
  D:  = toyol nanix stukel a tz'i bi mak                                    245
      Really expensive, (it is) itself then, perhaps eh?
      ((→sarcastic agreement: 'It was really cheap!'))
```

Now, as I develop in detail elsewhere (Brown 1990), not only in terms of how ironic expressions are used, but also in many other ways, the interactional conduct of a Tzeltal court case – a formal arena for face-to-face confrontation with the aim of settling disputes between people – is the *inverse* of interactional conduct in 'ordinary conversation' in Teneja-pan society. That is, ordinary conversational structures and interactional norms are systematically violated in a public display of indignation and anger. In this context, certain features – like irony – pervasive in women's speech in amicable conversation, features which are there used to convey positive affect, empathy, agreement, sympathetic understanding, are here used to convey the *opposite*: negative affect, hostility, contradiction.

In amicable interactions women's positively polite ironic phraseology assumes and stresses shared values and norms, mutual sympathy and understanding. In the courtroom confrontation this stance is evoked, but from a distance, ironically, in the sarcastic politeness of hostile pseudo-agreement. Presumably the courtroom frame, the mutual knowledge of licence for inverted conventions in this special context, as well as all the additional information about hostility (conveyed by kinesics and eye contact, intonation and gesture) makes it not only possible but inescap-able that the ironic utterances in this context must be interpreted as the opposite of what they would be interpreted as, were they to appear in a cooperative context. Certainly in the courtroom, the use of irony does not imply that the interactors know each other well, or share the same attitudes.

This suggests that in order to understand how even conventionalized ironic/rhetorical utterances are actually interpreted in speech, we need to look very closely at the uses of such forms of expression in different situations. One situation casts light on others, especially if one (like confrontation) is defined in opposition to the other (courteous interac-tion). The meaning-in-context of ironic expressions is clearly different in the two cases.

An ambiguous case

It will be instructive, therefore, to look at one more interaction, where what is going on is much more indeterminate. A woman (T) had come visiting to request an injection from one of the women (A) in the household who is authorized to give injections. A wasn't home, but T talked to A's sister X. Throughout the ten-minute encounter, the kinesics, gaze avoidance, smirking, general body orientation, and displacement activity combined to indicate acute discomfort and embarrassment on T's part, and awkwardness mixed with surreptitious enjoyment by X. The placement of ritual high pitch[10] and the sequencing of utterances shows where the awkwardness is focused, and it is instructive to look at the treatment of ironically phrased utterances in this context.[11] Example 12.   Context: T has been getting a series of injections from A, a local 'nurse'; she had come last night to get one but A had refused to give it. So T came again today, understanding that there might be reluctance on A's part to give her an injection. It emerges during this encounter that there *is* reluctance, due to gossip that A heard T said about her (A).

In this excerpt T is trying again; A isn't home but T has been invited by X to wait for A. After T and X chat about where A is, when she'll be back, health, weather and work, X mentions directly that A is angry. (Underlined line numbers indicate ironic/rhetorical utterances.)

x:	ay ja' chikan ya xlijkix sk'ajk'al ya'wil tz'ine mak	122
	It's apparent that she has begun to get angry, you see, perhaps.	
	[	
T:	eh yak ye in =	123
	eh, yes so it is	
x:	= yak =	124
	Yes.	
T:	= ma sk'an a xjulonix tal ye tz'in =	125
	She doesn't want to give me the injection.	
x:	= ej: lijkem laj sk'ajk'al	126
	Oh, she's gotten angry, (someone) says	
T:	jai: bi laj yu'uni	127
	What! Why (is she angry), does (someone) say?	
x:	ba xa'wili	<u>128</u>
	Who knows? ((Lit: Where do you see it? implies 'your guess is as good as mine'.))	
T:	yu' mati ay ya'yojben ka'yeje	129
	Perhaps she's heard something I said.	
x:	ay niwanix yu'un ay (.) k'anix ta yu' ay a ka'ye	130
	Perhaps that's it - I think I heard that that's it.	

At this point, despite her disclaimer ('Who knows?') and hedges ('I think', 'perhaps') it is clear that X has definite information about what someone

said T said about A; and T's belief that this is the case is made evident in
her replies and direct question to X in line 134:

T:	= ↑ binti laj xon ek tz'in	134
	So, what did (someone) say I said?	
	(0.5)	135
X:	↑ ma xkil (.) ay nax	136
	Who knows? ((Lit: I don't see)). It's just –	
	[	
	mach'a (.) mach'a xan ya'yej ek tz'in	137
	Who – who said it then?	
X:	↑ ma xkil me tz'in ma ba jojk'oyebe te banti ya'yoj a'yeje	138
	Who knows, I didn't ask her where she heard the gossip (about what you said about her).	
T:	jai:	139
	What?	
X:	ju'uj	140
	No (I didn't ask her).	
T:	ah solel ay wa'y ta ba'ay wejtem bi ka'yej	141
	Ah, just look where my words have become available! ((i.e., 'just look how what I said got spread around!'))	
X:	ay niwan ay in	142
	That's perhaps what happened.	

X's diplomatic denial of knowledge of the source of the gossip-mongering
prompts T's defence in line 141 ('just look how my words have been
spread around!') to which X's superficially agreeing reply ('That's
perhaps what happened') could be interpreted either as sympathetic
agreement or as sarcastic pseudo-agreement. She follows it up by quoting
T's alleged talk about A:

T:	mm: (1.0) mach'a me xkal	143
	Hm, who could it be (who told on me)?	
	((Lit: Who (is it) I say?))	
X:	[	
	kaxel =	144
	'Golly,	
	= ma'yuk ba'ay bak'en ya xba sjulon mene me xat (.)	145
	that one (A) certainly doesn't want to give me an injection,' if (that's what) you said,	
	mm bi'ora ay k'anbe spoxil mene bi'ora sjulon mene me xat,	146
	Mm, 'When is that one (A) going to get my medicine, when is she going to inject me?' if you said.	
	↑ bi laj bal ut'il	147
	What's the use of it? ((→No use, A implicated, in this reported conversation with X.))	

Here the direct quotes put the rhetorical question in the mouth of the
quoted speaker (A), and X thus remains uncommitted as to whether she
shares the attitude indicated (i.e., 'why bother to provide injections for
this woman who bad-mouths me to others?'). T responds with the

standard indication of non-hearing or non-comprehension, *jai?*, prompting X to expand on her claim:

> X: xi a ka'y ja' ya yali (.) peru ma ba la jojk'o mach'a yaloj   149
> I heard her say, so they say. But I didn't ask who said it.
> T: mach'a yaloj xkal =   150
> Who reported that, I wonder? ((→'No one knows.'))
> X: ju'u   151
> No. ((Replies to implicature: 'No, no one knows.'))

Having agreed (for current purposes, at least), that they don't know who the gossip-monger is, T goes on to deny her alleged words:

> T: ma'yuk to ba'ay ya xlok'on ta (.) a'yej a ka'y   153
> I didn't go around saying (those things) at all, I say!
> X: ma'yuk   154
> (You) didn't at all.
> T: ma'yuk, ma'yuk ba xlok'on ta julbal   155
> Not at all, not at all did I go out visiting ((→and gossiping)).
> X: ay (0.5) ay niwan ja' jich ya xlijk yala k'ajk'al yu'un ek tz'in 156
> It's, it's perhaps that that made her (A) get a bit angry then.
> T: ah: mak bi yu'uni lijk sk'ajk'al a ka'y tz'in   157
> Oh, why did she get angry then?
> ((→'How unfair, how could she?!'))
> X: bi yu'uni ya xlijk a'k'ajk'ali uta (tz'in)   158
> 'Why are you angry?' you should say to her (then).
> T: ya kalbe i mak   159
> Perhaps I'll say that to her.

They go on, shifting around the issue, T continuing to deny she said anything and to wonder who could have gossiped about her, X continuing to prick her, indirectly. The topic winds down, as follows:

> X: ya'wa'y (.) ya'k'anbe nix xan wokol (.)   233
> You see, you just ask her again to take the trouble (to inject you).
> T: ya ka'y   234
> I see.
> X: slajinbet ine yip xix jich a tz'i =   235
> She'll just finish you up (i.e., finish the series of injections).
> T: = yip =   236
> just (finish)
> X: = bi ja' to tz'in te ay ba'ay (.) yax- k'ejel xa'wakix a'ba ta julel
>   yu'un a tz'ine   237
> So how is it then, that there is somewhere else you can go to get injected
>   then ((→'Nowhere else can you go to get injections.'))
> T: [
>   ja' to xan =   238
>   There still is somewhere else
>   ((→'There sure isn't!'))
> = sok banti ya jta me ineksione =   239
> and where will I find an injection? ((→Nowhere!))
> = mak yu' ay jich (.) jtaoj ta jleel ek tz'in =   240

Perhaps that's how it is, I've found (another injection-giver) then
  ((→'I haven't.'))

= te manchuk ja'uk tz'in te (wa'y) bi jpasoj ch'e   241
so what if that's how it were then, (you see) what I'd have done (if there
  were an alternative to A as injection-giver).
  ((→ 'I couldn't do anything if A refused, as there's no alternative to her
  services.'))

X: ja' ya'wa'y   242
    That's so, you see

T: ja'   243
    It is.

X: ja'   244
    It is.

T: ja'   245
    It is.

    (1.0)   246

X: jich ya'wa'y tal (.) ya niwanix slajinbet tz'in,   247
    So you'll see, she'll perhaps finish you then,

    yu' bal kejchel ya xk'ot a'wu'un   248
    because is it that you'll be finished (with your series of injections)
      otherwise?
    ((→'Of course not, there's no one else to do it.'))

T: ba xa'wil   249
    Where, you see?
    ((→'Nowhere else (can I get injections!').))
    (The embarrassment more or less resolved, they go on talking of other
      things.)

In this example, then, the shared common ground on which ironic
expression normally relies is missing – X doesn't believe T didn't do this
gossiping about A. X's scepticism is made clear despite her denials (e.g.
lines 128, 138) and hedges (line 130), and her agreements with T's denials
(line 154). For example, the contradiction between line 154, where X
(superficially) agrees with T's denial of culpability to the accusation of
gossiping, and line 156, where X says that it's T's gossiping that made A
get angry, clearly indicates her actual belief.

Their relationship in this context is asymmetric, as T is a suppliant for
A's services and X is a mediator between the allegedly angry non-present
A and the suppliant T. In this context, T's rhetorical questions and ironic
utterances are essentially aimed at eliciting X's sympathetic understanding for her plight (needing A's injection-services, A reluctant to provide
them) (e.g. lines 125, 157, and 238–40). X's are more multi-functional, for
example denying knowledge and responsibility with the conventionalized
Tzeltal verbal equivalent to a hands-in-air gesture of hopeless fatalism (*ba
xa'wili* or *ma xkil* ('who knows', lines 128, 136, 138), followed by a patent
social lie ('I didn't ask her where she heard the gossip', line 138). Others
are potentially barbed, carrying a dual message as in lines 237 ('Is there
somewhere else you can go to get injections?' and 248 ('Will you finish
your injections otherwise?'), which can simultaneously be read as taunt-

ing or as sympathetic understanding for T's plight. And since T, in her response to X's potentially dual message, in line 238 takes up the second of those meanings, responding with an ironic agreement to the ironic implicature in X's line 237 (saying, in effect, 'I agree, there certainly *isn't* anywhere else I can go to get injected, oh poor me.'), she humbles herself by throwing herself in effect on X's (and thereby A's) mercy. As she solicits sympathy with piled-up ironies (lines 238–40), and accepts X's rubbing it in with agreements (lines 242, 244) and re-phrasings of T's dilemma (line 248), the uncomfortable ambiguity vanishes (T is humbled, X triumphant) and they can carry on conversing amicably.

This example shows that topic-summing-up with ironically phrased utterances does not necessarily display real common ground in the sense of shared attitudes. The agreement that there is nowhere else to go to finish her injections does not necessarily carry with it sincere humility on T's part, nor sincere sympathy on X's; the surface agreement simply provides a negotiated end to the topic.

Conclusion

The use of ironic expressions in Tzeltal is an elaborate and complex phenomenon, but I have used it to make a very simple point. One cannot mechanistically apply the Brown and Levinson model of politeness strategies to discourse data; particular linguistic realizations are not ever intrinsically positively or negatively polite, regardless of context. Politeness inheres not in forms, but in the attribution of polite intentions, and linguistic forms are only part of the evidence interlocutors use to assess utterances and infer polite intentions. So however many pleases, thank yous, bows and scrapes you may make, the polite attitude supposedly conveyed by them can be undermined, inverted, or cancelled by their interaction with other elements in the context, and interactors can't just sit back and let conventionalized expressions do their interpretive job for them. Rather, they must constantly work at inferring each other's intentions, including whether or not politeness is intended. This is especially obvious with irony, where they have to infer whether an utterance is ironically intended, whether it is ironic irony, who, if anyone, is the intended target or victim (obviously crucial to an interpretation of its politeness value), and who is the intended audience (in the court case, for example, the judge's role as arbitrator is crucial to the interpretation of the litigants' confrontational performance).

Successful irony thus relies completely on interlocutors' (and audiences') ability to decode mutual knowledge assumptions about what each thinks the other thinks must be true. The Tzeltal examples demonstrate that the reflexive reasoning involved must be at least four levels

Table 7.1. *Levels of reflexive reasoning*

Sincere assertion	I assert P I believe that you believe I believe P is true I hope therefore to get you to believe P is true
True deception	I assert not-P, though I believe P is true I hope you believe I believe P is not-true I therefore hope you'll believe P is not-true

Pseudo deception
(social lies)
	I assert P, though I believe not-P is true
	I believe you believe I believe P is not-true
	I believe you know (and believe I know) the customs concerning
	  constraints on revealing certain kinds of information
	I therefore don't expect you to believe P, but to desist from
	  pressing for this kind of information

Irony	I 'mention' P, hoping to evoke Q (which is systematically related to P) I want you not to think I believe that P is the case I believe you believe I believe that not-P is the case, and I believe you believe I believe *you* believe that not-P is the case I therefore hope you will respond to Q

Ironic irony	I 'mention' P, in the frame of non-serious joking
	I believe P is true, and I believe you believe P is true
	I believe you know this is non-serious talk, and therefore hope you
	  will within this joking frame take not-P to be true for current
	  purposes

deep. An informal Gricean account of these levels might go along the lines presented in Table 7.1.

There are of course many clues, in addition to Gricean flouts of sincerity, to prod the inferential process in a particular direction, restricting the range of possible meanings a speaker is, in the context, likely to be taken as intending, or hinting at his or her actual intentions. These include 'background knowledge' of the interlocutors' previous interactional history, their social roles and relationship, the nature of the speech event, and the immediately preceding discourse, insofar as it provides a record for current purposes of their respective beliefs. The characteristics of the ironically phrased utterance itself may also provide clues: non-verbal affective cues in the kinesics, facial expressions, and gestures accompanying the utterance; intonational and paralinguistic cues (timing, voice quality, stress).[12] In Tzeltal, especially important is the special set of emphatic and hedging particles which combined together force an ironic reading: an utterance along the lines of 'Perhaps it might be the case that P, to be sure!' can only be read as emphatically asserting not-P.

Furthermore, in Tzeltal the fact that irony is a conventionalized form for expressing sympathetic understanding affects the interpretive process, providing an extra layer as it were of possible embedding in the form of joking or of sarcastic irony-as-pseudo-agreement.

Nonetheless it is important that irony plays a role not only in well-defined interactions where a speaker's intent can in general be presumed to be either clearly sympathetic (as in positively polite 'grooming') or clearly hostile (as in confrontations). Irony in Tzeltal is exploitable as a resource for obscuring one's communicative intentions, muddying the waters so that interactors with potentially different goals can pursue them without flaunting their differences overtly. The indeterminacy of the relation between a speaker's expressed attitude and his or her real attitude may be put to the service of various devious interactional goals.

We might well ask: why in the world do Tenejapans bother to do all this? Why elaborate a form of discourse where you have to be constantly figuring out whether your interlocutor means what (s)he says, or the opposite, or the opposite of the opposite? Part of the answer might be that the very reliance of irony on mutually shared knowledge and values makes it a good test of whether in fact interlocutors do share knowledge and values, and thereby an excellent way of emphasizing and reinforcing claims to common ground. It is thereby an essential element in constructing the social relationship between the interlocutors, insofar as it succeeds in constructing the 'phatic communion' that inheres in demonstrations of mutual understanding. It is clear that in Tenejapa, for women at least, such interactions are an integral part of their social relations, they *must* have such conversations in order to consider themselves related to each other. That is perhaps the motivation behind positively polite uses of irony; then, given this resource, it is an obvious next step to its exploitation in order to sneer or insult.

I would suggest that there is a further reason why Tenejapan women, especially, make such elaborate verbal play with 'literally false' assertions, especially in relation to public opinion, and why they have elaborated their humour around the paradoxes which they pose. The ways in which women joke by claiming false things about themselves and each other – precisely those false things which in others' mouths would humiliate and destroy them (about their sexual exploits and desires, their failures as fulfillers of female roles, etc.) – is a way of neutralizing the destructive power of such falsehoods, just as joking about illness and death ('Maybe I'll be permanently lame from this sore on my leg; maybe I'll die from it.') is a way of undermining the poignancy of fears about incapacity and death that both men and women have in this society. Men, not nearly so vulnerable to the effects of gossip about their sexual – and sex role – misbehaviours, do not take the same lines in their solidarity-stressing joking. I think it is significant that men, to stress solidarity with each other, joke about what they do do, would do if they could, or have caught someone else doing; whereas women joke about doing what they wouldn't be caught dead doing and would be mortified and appalled if anyone seriously suggested that they would.

It seems probable that irony is a typical communicative strategy for certain kinds of social groups. Tenejapa, for example, is a 'gossip society', a small-scale face-to-face society where people are obsessed with what everyone is saying about others, and especially about themselves.[13] This may make it a good candidate for the sociolinguistic elaboration of ironic expression. I would also suggest that irony is a common strategy for the underdog, for persons in subordinate or vulnerable positions. Irony is a way of tacitly complaining about one's lot in life – of some of the consequences of one's underdog position – without actually upsetting the status quo. The complaint is off record (very much so in these ironic joking scenarios where interactors set up public opinion against themselves) and it essentially affirms the right of public opinion to maintain such an eagle eye on their behaviour. Indians have for 500 years been the underdogs in Mexican society, and women have been the underdogs within the Tenejapan community; this objective status contrasts with their strong sense of ethnic identity and community pride. As a technique for making play with the ambiguities of this contrast, irony seems ideally designed.

Finally, to return to the AIP model – Tzeltal irony provides a prime example of one way in which humans' highly developed intellectual machinery for inferring alter's intentions is put to the service of social relationships. Language allows us to make propositions, with which we can plan, discuss the future and non-present events, propositions which can be used non-seriously to joke, which can lie, or pretend (play-lie), and which can evoke mental models which are held up for affective comment (e.g., ridicule or contempt). The process of doing this successfully *is* to a large extent the social relationship of solidarity in Tenejapa, and this institutionalized socio-cultural strategy, in the form of a particular 'way of putting things', puts a characteristic stamp on Tenejapan social interaction.

Acknowledgements

This chapter amalgamates some points described in more detail in Brown (1990) with my analyses of Tzeltal irony first presented at seminars in Australia (Australian National University, 1982) and London (Sociolinguistics Symposium, 1989), as well as in Brown (1979: ch. 4). I am grateful to Stephen Levinson, Esther Goody, and John Haviland, and to the other participants in these seminars and the Workshop On the Implications of a Social Origin of Human Intelligence, for their helpful comments.

Notes

1 This fieldwork – over the past twenty years – has focused primarily on social interaction in Tenejapa, and a large corpus of tape-recorded and/or filmed

naturally occurring Tzeltal interaction has been built up, from which the data analysed here has been drawn. Tenejapa is a municipio in the Chiapas highlands, in a heavily populated rural area where there are many other communities of Tzeltal or Tzotzil speakers, each of which maintains a strong ethnic identity distinguishing it from the others and from the dominant Ladino (Mexican national) culture.

2 That is, where P can be expressed by any well-formed Tzeltal sentence, the position of the subjunctive suffix -uk (which conveys possibility-hedging) *mutatis mutandis*. The notion of 'opposite' is not quite accurate for the case, as Stephen Levinson has pointed out. Tzeltal irony is not just a matter of asserting P and conveying not-P, or vice versa, but rather something like the following: an assertion is made to the effect that one end of a scale is (possibly) the case, and in context this implicates the emphatic assertion that *the other end* of the scale is the case. Irony thus forces descriptions to polarized ends of a continuum of evaluation on some dimension (good/bad, desirable/undesirable, likely/unlikely, and so forth). I use 'opposite' as a shorthand for this flip between conveying the ends of an evaluative continuum.

3 For some discussions of irony in relation to the Gricean maxims, and in discourse contexts, see the references cited in Brown and Levinson (1987: 28).

4 Despite its omni-presence, ironical phrasing of utterances is not to my knowledge an 'emic' Tzeltal category. While Tenejapans explicitly distinguish two basic categories of speech, *poko-k'op* (traditional, ritual speech styles – in Stross's (1974) characterization 'elegant, stylized, serious, non-malicious speech') vs. *ach'k'op*, ('recent speech' including all forms of non-serious speech), and while they have lexical items denoting particular kinds of non-serious speech (e.g., *lotil*, 'lies'; *ixta-k'op*, 'joking'; *lo'il k'op*, 'carnival-style joking'; *tajimal k'op*, 'verbal games', *labanel*, 'mockery'), I don't know of any label specifically designating conventionalized Tzeltal irony.

5 In Brown and Levinson (1987) we make the following distinctions: *joking*, which as a positive politeness strategy stresses in-group relations and common ground, and can include non-serious insults; *mockery*, which when of someone other than the addressee can stress in-group solidarity; *teasing*, which can be joking or mockery even with the addressee as target, but playful; and *irony*, which is at root an off-record strategy but if on record in context can be positively polite solidarity stressing.

6 S stands for 'speaker' H for 'addressee'. The Tzeltal practical orthography has the following conventions (where they differ from the International Phonetic Alphabet): j represents /h/, ch represents /č/, x represents /ʃ/, tz represents /ts/ and ' represents either glottalization of the preceding consonant or, following a vowel, a glottal stop. Abbreviations for morpheme by morpheme glosses used in the text are as follows: ASP stands for neutral aspect, EMPH for emphatic particle, EXIST for the existential predicate, ICP incompletive aspect, NEG negative particle, Q question particle, SUBJ subjunctive.

7 Note that in line 6 of this example the trigger for irony is not a patent falsehood but a patent truth, which within the non-literal joking frame must then be reinterpreted. The levels of inference required may be diagrammed as follows:

lit: Because perhaps an Indian will marry you, you know.⎯⎯⎐ ⎤ ←
c.i.1: Of course no Indian will marry you; you'll marry a Ladino.⎽⎤ ⎥
But: Ha ha, we both know you'll certainly never marry a Ladino.← ⎦
Therefore c.i.2: You're joking; of course you'll marry an Indian!⎯⎯

8 Tenejapans distinguish 'real' lies (*lotil* – lies intended not to be seen through) from such joking lies, which are intended to reinforce solidarity. Akin to 'real' lies, perhaps, are those social lies which are non-joking but, though intended to conceal some fact, are so obviously false that there is no real deception. For example, in response to a 'nosy' question that one does not wish to answer (e.g., 'How much do you earn at that work?') a patently false answer is customary (e.g., 'I don't know, I can't count' or 'Two pesos per month'); this implies that the speaker has no intention of answering such uninvited questions. The effect of real lies, then is interactionally distancing, in contrast to the joking lies (or elaboration of non-truths) which reinforce mutual knowledge, mutual values, and friendship.

9 For conventions used in the transcription of this and the following example, see the 'Conventions used in transcripts' on p. x.

10 Very high or even falsetto pitch is used in Tzeltal to convey deference in ritual speech, greeting and farewell exchanges, and wherever formality is being emphasized. It tends to characterize the beginnings and endings of encounters in general, and often marks socially sensitive or potentially threatening utterances, as well as fatalistic resignation. It is marked in the transcription by an ↑ preceding the utterance.

11 This interaction took place in 1980 and was filmed by S. Levinson and myself. The soundtrack was transcribed with the assistance of one of the participants, X herself.

12 In his analysis of 'sarcasm as theater', Haiman (1990) has observed that a number of these cues appear to be cross-linguistically applicable. He mentions three kinds (1990: 181): 'a. formal indices of direct quotation or repetition . . .; b. incongruity between segmental and suprasegmental texts (incongruous suprasegmentals include the phonetic reflexes of sneers and laughter, deadpan monotone, caricatured exaggeration of the appropriate melody, and stylized or singsong intonation); c. hyper-formality (including both high register and the substitution of linguistic signs [like "ha, ha"] for paralinguistic symptoms [genuine laughter]).'

These 'stage separators' or mechanisms for indicating that what is acted out behind them is 'not serious' are *not* generally involved in routine Tzeltal ironies, though they (especially those under 'b') do mark as 'on stage' the joking sequences illustrated by example 9. Tzeltal speakers do not seem to find it necessary to heavily mark their non-straight utterances as non-straight; the inferential trigger is more likely to be simply a conflict between the expressed proposition and mutually assumed knowledge.

13 See for example Haviland's (1977) description of the neighbouring Tzotzil community of Zinacantan.

THOMAS LUCKMANN

8 Interaction planning and intersubjective adjustment of perspectives by communicative genres

The aim of this chapter is to show that communicative genres play a distinct and rather important role in the reciprocal, intersubjective setting of perspectives in human communicative social interaction. It will be useful first to establish the socio-cultural context within which communicative genres perform their function and to specify the levels of theory on which propositions about communicative genres in social interaction are to be placed.

It will eventually make sense to restrict the term *social interaction* to behaviour with which an individual organism which is phylogenetically equipped with consciousness in its 'biogram' associates a more or less definite meaning (a motive, a projected goal).[1] Here I first take the term to refer to any behaviour which is directed by one individual organism at other(s) of the same or a different species, and which has consequences for such behaviour of the other individual(s) as, in turn, is directed at the 'first' individual.[2]

Social interaction in the human species may be viewed in a comparative biological perspective and compared to social behaviour in species as closely related to ours as other apes and primates and as distantly as 'lower' mammals. It may be compared with respect to structural and functional analogies, and possible evolutionary connections may be considered. If ethological comparison navigates successfully between the Scylla of biological reductionism and the Charybdis of anthropomorphism, it may show suggestive similarities in the structures and functions of social interaction.[3] General features of human social interaction are also revealed by a philosophical approach. Phenomenological reduction strips away, layer after layer, the concrete socio-cultural, historical components of the processes of social interaction and shows their universal constituent elements.[4] Both approaches meet in the 'discovery' of the reciprocal attunement of social actors and of 'anticipatory interactive planning'.[5] Phenomenology can show this for the human, ethology for the human and for related species.

In the broadest sense of the term, all social interaction is communicative. Behaviour directed at others cannot help but convey something to others if they are in a position to observe that behaviour.[6] However, it makes sense to restrict the concept of communication to behaviour which expresses emotions, signals an incipient action or consists of 'abbreviated' gestures.[7] Even with this restriction, communicative interaction is found in many species, not only in those closely related to *Homo sapiens*.[8]

Human communicative social interaction shows the most elementary features of communicative interaction among apes. However, even in comparison to our closest relatives, the chimpanzees, there is a qualitative leap in several essential aspects of communicative interaction. This leap is attributable to the development of language as a referential, time- and space-transcending sign system.[9] With the emergence of language(s), a crucial step is taken which adds to the evolutionary level of causation obtaining on a time-scale measured in hundreds and thousands of generations, a historical, socio-cultural level of 'causation' measured in several dozens of generations – and less.

Even if the general formal structure of social interaction and communicative social interaction remains basically unchanged, or changes only slowly, the social, interactive and, most significantly, communicative construction of social reality (typical motives, typical goals, typical actors, and typical courses of action, typical explanations and interpretations, typical legitimations and delegitimations) provide historical patterns of meaning for the concrete contents of social interaction and communication. It should be noted that the distinction between formal structures and empirical (i.e., historical) contents is somewhat artificial. In human affairs, a historical level of 'causation', an evolutionary emergent, may interpenetrate with the phylogenic one.

It is evident that propositions about the function of communicative genres in communicative social interaction only apply to the concrete level of socio-historical processes and realities. On this level phylogeny, ontogeny and social construction seem to have merged indistinguishably.

The results of phenomenological analysis, of the search for universals in cross-cultural comparison, and of the simulation of 'social' processes on the basis of minimal 'logical' assumptions show a remarkable convergence regarding the elementary structure of human social and, more specifically, communicative interaction. It can, therefore, be assumed that anticipatory interactive orientations are one of the universal constituent elements of the latter. These anticipatory orientations sometimes take the form of conscious planning of future courses of action. In these, account is taken of potential, more or less likely courses of action and reaction by those individuals to whom the original project of action is directed. Such activities of consciousness will be involved when social interaction, and communicative interaction in particular, is uncertain and when it occurs in problematic situations. However, once plans with respect to certain courses of action directed to certain types of individuals prove reasonably satisfactory, they will routinely serve as plans for similar purposes under similar circumstances. The construction of plans, strategic calculation of possible reactions of others, complicated intersubjective adjustment of perspectives, and similar conscious activities which are characteristic of problematic situations are likely to recede into routines in unproblematic situations. That is not to say that social interaction becomes automatic. It may, however, become *more or less* routinized. Of course this applies to communicative interaction as well.

It is evident that routinization of social interaction may also be brought about intersubjectively, in overlapping stretches of social interaction.[10]

In the following I shall try to show that communicative genres perform an important function in many kinds of communicative interaction by serving as ready-made *plans* in at least partly routinized 'anticipatory communicative interaction *planning*'.

'Freedom' and 'constraint' in communicative social interaction

Communicative genres operate on a level *between* the socially constructed and transmitted codes of 'natural' languages and the reciprocal adjustment of perspectives, which is a presupposition for human communicative interaction.[11] They are a universal[12] formative element of human communication.

The relations between communicative codes as elements of social stocks of knowledge, social institutions as constitutive parts of social structures, and communicative acts as embodied components of ongoing human social life are complex, many-layered, and multi-directional. Conditions of social life, social codes of communication in general (and languages in particular) and concrete communicative acts influence and 'determine' each other. The lines of 'determination' criss-cross in social interactional space and time.

Human communicative acts are *pre*defined and thereby to a certain extent *pre*determined by an existing social code of communication. This holds both for the 'inner' core of that code, the phonological, morphological, semantic and syntactic structure of the language, as well as for its 'external' stratification in styles, registers, sociolects, and dialects. In addition, communicative acts are predefined and predetermined by explicit and implicit rules and regulations of the *use* of language, e.g., by forms of communicative etiquette. Furthermore, communicative acts are a form of social interaction and are therefore predefined and predetermined by non-communicative rules and regulations: by institutions, a set of social relations, a system of production and reproduction, in short, by a historical social structure.[13]

Languages originate, develop and change under varying social conditions. Social conditions determine the circumstances under which language is used in communicative acts. On the other hand, communicative acts – and, more generally, social interactions – are instrumental in changing social circumstances. They influence the development of the 'external' stratification of language; less directly and, ordinarily, also less swiftly, they influence the maintenance and the change of the elements in the 'inner' structure of language.

The social regulation of communication is an elementary prerequisite for the day-to-day working of any society. The flow of communication in institutional settings is channelled according to the functional requirements of the institution. The frequency and direction of communicative acts are subject to regulation. Special communicative networks may become established and segregated in order to prevent outside interference. There is, of course, considerable variation in the level of complexity and degree of specialization that characterize different institutions in the same society and the same kind of institutions in different societies.[14] The processes of sychronic and diachronic cross-influence between languages, social structures and communicative acts continue in history and result in new 'syntheses' in the real lives of real people.

Looking at the relation between society and language from the perspective of 'real people', we see that both the individual's initial access to the various means of communication and his subsequent actual use of them are socially determined. The child's chance of access to the repertoire of the means of social communication depends upon its specific location in a historical social structure. Socialization, by definition a communicative process, is determined by a given historical system of social inequality. In addition to the unequal distribution of goods, the structure of inequality consists of an uneven distribution of the social stock of knowledge and of unequal access to the means of social communication. In addition to its being a highly significant factor in socialization, the social structure regulates the actual *use* of the means of communication in concrete social interaction.[15] These means consist of language(s) as well as of the (generally) more loosely structured (and mostly also less strongly conventionalized) mimetic, gestural, postural, etc. expressive forms.

Social interactions in general, and communicative acts in particular, are only in part a matter of situation-bound intersubjective reciprocal attunement and interactive planning; a planning which originates in *subjective* projects of action and their step-by-step adjustment to the actions of others. But in part they *are* just that. The degree of interactional 'freedom' inherent in a situationally negotiated adjustment of perspectives varies historically from society to society, and it varies *within* a society in any given epoch from one social domain to another. Intersubjective adjustment of perspectives, anticipatory communicative interaction planning and socially constructed 'plans' in the form of communicative genres converge at the intersection of 'freedom' and 'constraint' in communicative interaction.

Interactive and socially pre-constructed solutions to communicative problems

The linguistic and institutional determinants of social communication operate simultaneously on the level of concrete communicative interaction. It is on this level that 'reciprocal perspective setting' and 'perspective taking'[16] must be accomplished by the persons engaging in social interaction. This intersubjective process involves situational adjustments of the basic principle of human social life, the principle of the reciprocity of perspectives.[17]

The adjustments may present practical problems. In clearly predefined situations, when the actors perform institutionally determined social roles, the adjustments may be accomplished quasi-automatically. All that is needed is the routine application of previously established, socially constructed and transmitted knowledge about typical settings, situations, social roles, and courses of action. At the other extreme one may imagine a situation in which neither background nor specific knowledge could be applied successfully. In such a situation almost everything that goes beyond the basic principle of the reciprocity of perspectives must be 'locally' negotiated after a trial-and-error exploration of the perspectives (previous knowledge, interests, etc.) which are brought into the situation by the participants. In fact, there will be only approximations of either extreme. Most cases will be characterized by a mixture of successful application of routine knowledge and situational exploration and negotiation.

Some, if not most of these adjustments concern specifically communicative aspects of interaction. They often become problematic. Specifically, communicative problems are normally solved in communicative 'repair procedures' for faulty 'recipient designs'.[18] All social communication is, of course, addressed to other persons, but there is a broad range of variation in the degree to which it is subject to intersubjective *pre*definition. The 'normal' mutual assumption of the participants – valid until evidence to the contrary appears – is that the social models for particular types of communicative acts available to one of them are also available to the other one. When such modelling is minimal, we may speak of 'spontaneous' communicative acts. On the other hand, when such modelling reaches a high degree of structural 'closure', and when it is associated with intersubjectively recognizable formal constraints, we are in the presence of communicative genres.

In 'spontaneous' communicative acts an individual does most of the selecting and constructing on his own, taking from the communicative code(s) available to him those elements which seem to fit his momentary communicative project, in calculated anticipation of typical interpretations by the addressee. When he follows a clearly defined communicative project he may do so with a high degree of awareness, selecting – and rejecting – minor and major components of his communicative act in turn-by-turn responses to the acts of the addressee. It is more likely, however, that at least some of the steps are routinized, that some of the parts are pre-assembled habitually.[19] Sentences are formed by taking those words and phrases from the semantic inventory of the speaker which seem appropriate to the purpose at hand, if they conform to the pragmatic principles of 'recipient design'. As utterances are built up, the internalized syntactic schemata are employed more or less automatically. In addition, the speaker will use stylistic devices and rhetorical stratagems, and he will obey – or break – the prevailing rules of communicative etiquette in relation to particular social types of addressees.

'Spontaneous' communicative acts are 'produced' by an individual from a mixture of explicit intention and habit in alignment with his communicative project and, occasionally, by following a superordinated interactional plan formulated in advance and geared into the intersubjectively constructed sequences of conversation. However, the parts of the communicative project are not assembled according to an intersubjectively recognizable overall model.[20]

Nevertheless, in many types of communicative situations individuals may draw upon pre-cut communicative patterns which seem to fit their communicative intentions, and which they use in order to carry out their communicative project – *if* they have grounds for assuming that the pattern is also known to the addressee. Such an assumption is based, generally, on the principle of the reciprocity of perspectives and, specifically, on the individual's knowledge of the general outlines of the social distribution of the elements contained in the social stock of knowledge. If one may say that the individual 'chooses' a genre according to his communicative project and the perceived requirements of the social situation, one may say correspondingly that once a genre is 'chosen', it is the model which 'chooses' the parts in executing the communicative project. Of course, the communicative realization of a genre may or may not 'fill' an entire communicative project. Whether it does depends on the *span* of the project and on the '*size*' of the genre involved.[21]

Although all communicative situations involve problems for the participants, some of these may be important, some less important, and others trivial. Some problems are new but many are familiar. Finding solutions to communicative problems may require much thought and effort, and, then again, solutions may merely involve the application of habitual procedures. The participants may solve their communicative problems 'spontaneously' or by using various minor or major communicative genres, and they may shift from one to the other in interactive turn-by-turn responses.[22]

Communicative genres may be 'functionally' defined as socially constructed models for the solution of communicative problems. It is plausible to assume that such solutions are constructed for recurrent problems and that, on the whole, they will be provided for relatively important problems of social communication.[23]

Communicative genres are part of the social stock of knowledge. Genre repertoires, along with all other components of social stocks of knowledge, differ from society to society; however, *some* repertoire of genres will be found in all societies. The social distribution of genre-related knowledge may be just as equal or unequal as that of any other part of the social stock of knowledge. An essential element of genre-related knowledge is knowledge about its appropriate use, including knowledge about alternative options and the degree of constraint for the employment of a particular genre in a particular situation. Evidently, this kind of knowledge goes far beyond the formal mastery of communicative codes, or for that matter, of competence with respect to the *internal* structure of genres. In other words, the use of genres is normally linked to clearly defined types of social situation. A given genre may never appear in one type of communicative situation, rarely in another, frequently in still another, and always in some. There may be situations in which an individual is *forced* to use a particular communicative genre, others in which he is merely *likely* to do so, and still others in which he will rigorously avoid its use. This is evidently of considerable significance for the role which genres play as ready-made 'plans' in relatively unproblematic communicative situations.

Social institutions and communicative genres

If social institutions are routinized, more or less obligatory solutions for *elementary* problems of social life, regulating functionally clearly definable kinds of social interaction (such as production, reproduction, the organization of power, etc.), communicative genres may be said to offer solutions for specifically *communicative* problems.

It hardly needs to be pointed out that it is often difficult to draw an exact line between the two kinds of problems. They are closely interwoven in human life. The elementary social problems are always also a matter *for*, and often even a matter *of*, communication. But these matters are first and last something other than communication: they are things to be done rather than things to be talked about.

There are many instances where social institutions and communicative genres intersect. This is the case wherever talking is a *constitutive* part of the resolution of elementary problems of social life. Of course, social communication itself is an elementary problem in human life – but it is a problem which in *human* societies underlies and overlies all other problems. It is not solvable by a specific set of institutions.

The elementary function of communicative genres in social life is to organize, routinize, and render (more or less) obligatory the solutions to recurrent communicative problems. The communicative problems for which such solutions are established and deposited in the social stock of knowledge tend to be those which touch upon the communicative aspects of those kinds of social interaction which are important for the maintenance of a given social order. Of course what is important differs from one kind of society to another, and different societies therefore do not have the same repertoire of communicative genres. The communicative genres of one epoch may dissolve into more 'spontaneous' communicative processes, while heretofore unbound communicative processes congeal into new genres within the history of one society. Nonetheless, because of the essential similarity of the human condition beneath the widest variety of ecological, socio-economic, technological, and cultural circumstances, cross-cultural and historical comparison shows that communicative genres are a universally important organizational principle of social communication and reveals, beyond that, certain similarities in their specific historical forms. Some genres, in somewhat variable forms, may be universal.

At any particular time in any particular society the repertoire of communicative genres constitutes the hard core of the communicative dimensions of social life. The patterning – with varying degrees of freedom and constraint – defines the situations in which a specific genre is to be employed, the 'external' (gender-, age-, kinship-, class-, etc.) status of those who are to be participants in the communicative process, and their 'internal' status (as speaker, listener, etc.). It preselects the linguistic (lexical, prosodic, etc.), paralinguistic, mimetic, gestural, etc. repertoires, co-determines the selection of topics and styles ('formal', 'informal', ironic,[24] etc.), and affects the management of turn-taking. Whenever genres are employed, communicative 'production' and 'reception', in their dialogical relationship, are thus not only constrained by the communicative codes and the general etiquette of communication but are also additionally pre-patterned by the genre model. The expectations of the participants are moulded by the knowledge that communicative processes with certain functions in certain situations will proceed in a certain manner. Genres are 'real' inasmuch as they are 'real' for the participants – that means, when knowledge pertaining to them is sedimented in the social stock of knowledge and has been transmitted to the actors on the social scene.[25] Knowledge of a genre need not be explicit 'theoretical' knowledge of rules; it suffices that one is acquainted with their practical operation.

Conclusion: genres as communicative plans

A recurrent, in fact, a universal communicative problem of varied severity which, in communicative processes, logically and temporally precedes all other potential problems is the 'reciprocal adjustment of perspectives'. It is the prototypical problem of 'anticipatory interactive planning'. It is a problem which does not normally become acute if clear indications of the perspectives and of the knowledge and interests brought into the situation are reliably available to the participants, or if the participants – or types of participants – are well known to one another as individuals or as social types from the same – or the same type of – communicative situation, where the perspectives have been adjusted beforehand, the 'planning' having been done in advance. Whatever else it may do for the solution of specifically communicative problems[26] – the use of genres in communicative interaction, combined with knowledge about the social distribution of genre-related knowledge, serves a double purpose with regard to the 'reciprocal adjustment of perspectives'. It provides easily recognizable indications for the initial mutual adoption of a communicative perspective for a definable kind of communicative interaction. And it helps to maintain the interlocking perspectives in its subsequent production and reception.

Communicative social interaction originates in action projects which are based on anticipations of the future actions of others – which, of course, are assumed to be based on corresponding typical anticipations. In everyday social practice, the infinite regress of these 'loops' is resolved by a variety of means, among which shared typifications (derived from the social stock of knowledge or built up in past social interactions[27]), institutions, and institutionally defined social roles are the most important ones. With respect to the communicative dimension of social interaction it is the communicative genres which play a particularly important role by providing 'communicative plans' for 'anticipatory communicative interaction planning'.

Notes

1 Whenever human social interaction is not systematically considered in a comparative biological frame but in a comparative historical, i.e., socio-cultural frame this is a useful restriction. It distinguishes motivated, goal-oriented action from 'mere' human behaviour and includes both overt action gearing into the world, which thus becomes observable by others, as well as 'thinking' as a covert form of action. For the sources of these distinctions, and for further analyses of the constitution of the meaning of action as motive and project, see Weber (1922: 1-16 [1968: 1–31]), Schutz (1932) and Schutz and Luckman (1989). For another approach, see Miller *et al.* 1960.

2 Analytically, social *inter*action should be distinguished from social action. The latter is one-sided, the former reciprocal.

3 See the contribution to this volume by Richard Byrne (Chapter 1). See also Byrne and Whiten (1991).

4 See Schutz and Luckmann (1989).

5 For a discussion of the concept see the Introduction to this volume by Esther Goody.

6 Presumably this is the meaning of the well-known sentence 'You cannot *not* communicate' (Beavin *et al.* 1969).

7 A term introduced by Mead (1967: 42–51 and 253–60).

8 Useful, although somewhat dated references to the relevant literature may be found in the subsections of Part I ('Phylogenetic and cultural ritualization') and Part III ('Ontogeny of primate behaviour') of von Cranach *et al.* (1979).

9 It seems reasonable to assume that – whatever the specific constellation of 'causes' and whichever time-scale is considered to have been obtained – the phylogeny of language presupposes a fairly complex *intersubjective* (i.e., involving a certain level of conscious, reciprocal orientation in the production and reception of communicative behaviour) level of communicative social interaction. At least in this instance there is a partial ontogenetic parallel: the emergence of 'dialogue' from the 'action dialogue' between mother and child, to borrow the terms from Bruner (1978). For a parallel phenomenological analysis of the constitution of language, see Luckmann 1983. For an attempt to simulate the generation of a 'stored system of signs' (with the assumption that an analogous procedure would yield an elementary grammar) from a mini-mum set of assumptions concerning the production and 'interpretation' of – potential – signs, see the contribution to this volume by Edwin Hutchins and Brian Hazlehurst (Chapter 2).

10 For a general discussion of routinization, institutionalization and the forma-tion of social stocks of knowledge, see Berger and Luckman (1966: 47–91). Cf. also Luckmann (1982). An account on the formation of kinship terminologies in the social stock of knowledge of gatherer-hunter societies, and some thoughts about their role in 'early anticipatory social interaction planning' is offered by Nurit Bird-David in this volume (Chapter 3).

11 Major parts of this and the next two sections are adapted from Luckmann (1992).

12 Universal in human societies – but not in every process of human communication. On this point I disagree with Bakhtin who maintains that *all* human speech is genre-bound: 'We speak only in definite speech genres, that is, all our utterances have definite and relatively stable typical *forms of construction of the whole*' (Bakhtin 1986: 78).

13 Social structure and communicative codes are neither god-given nor nature-given nor 'autopoetic' realities. Although they are objective components of human life, they originate in human activities. On the intersubjective constitution and social construction of language see Luckmann (1983).

14 The literature dealing with these matters is enormous and rapidly growing. My discussion of it in the 'Soziologie der Sprache' (Luckmann 1979) is already outdated.

15 The original impetus for, and the main contributions to, systematic research into 'language in use' have, of course, come from the ethnography of communication and related fields. For an early collection see Gumperz and Hymes (1964); see also Bauman and Sherzer (1974).

16 For a discussion of these concepts see Rommetveit (1990, 1992).

17 This was a key concept in Alfred Schutz's phenomenology of the social world. For a detailed presentation of the general thesis of the reciprocity of perspective see Schutz and Luckmann (1973, esp. pp. 59 ff.).

18 To expand the meaning of these terms beyond the very useful technical sense which they have in conversational analysis. For that, see Sacks *et al.* (1974), Sacks and Schegloff (1979), Schegloff *et al.* (1977).

19 For a detailed analysis of the structure of action, of projects, routinization, social interaction etc., see Schutz (1962); Schutz and Luckmann (1973: ch. 4) and Schutz and Luckmann (1989: ch. 5).

20 Different fields, among them especially the psychology of speech planning, discourse analysis, the 'new' rhetoric, and the ethnography of communication, have produced substantial bodies of literature on different aspects of these issues. In some fields there is a tendency to limit analysis to individual psychological perspectives. In others the problems are formulated in relation to *social* interaction. Occasionally the concept of 'genre' is used to good purpose. By way of illustration I mention a few examples: on rhetoric, Atkinson (1984); on communicative etiquette, Henn-Schmölders (1975) Laver (1981), and Brown and Levinson (1978); on speech planning, G. Beattie (1979) and the systematic analysis of Keenan (1977); on stylistic and rhetoric choice, Enkvist (1984); on individual 'assembly' despite the use of 'formulas', Coulmas (1981b).

21 With few exceptions the discussion of genre 'size' concerns literary genres. See, especially Jolles (1972), Jauss (1972), Nies (1978).

22 For a typology related to 'anticipatory interactive planning' in the context of turn construction see the contribution to this volume by Paul Drew (Chapter 5).

23 I have treated the function of genres more extensively in earlier papers (Luckman 1986, 1989).

24 On irony in social interaction see the contribution to this volume by Penelope Brown (Chapter 7). On formality, see Irvine (1974).

25 To paraphrase W.I. Thomas: 'When men define their situations as real they are real in their consequences' (Thomas 1960).

26 This will depend on the specific functions of the communicative interaction. An adequate identification of such functions presents serious difficulties. See, for example, Bascom (1954).

Theoretical speculation was rarely supported by detailed systematic investigation. In recent years, a close look was taken at the 'reconstructive' function in a research project (sponsored by the German Science Foundation in the Department of Sociology at the University of Constance) directed by Jörg R. Bergmann and myself. First results were published in a series of papers by Jörg Bergmann, Angela Keppler, Hubert Knoblauch, Bernd Ulmer, and myself. The joint publication of *Reconstructive Genres* will be published by de Gruyter, first in German (Berlin 1994), then in English (New York, probably 1994). For a full-fledged study of gossip see Bergmann (1993).

27 For a general consideration of the link between sedimentation of past experience and projects of action see Schutz (1962). Cf. also the contribution to this volume by David Good (Chapter 6).

PART IV

Expressions of a social bias in intelligence

9 Divination as dialogue: negotiation of meaning with random responses

In her introduction Goody proposes AIP as a set of fundamental assumptions pervasive in human society. In this chapter I shall examine some of the implications of AIP for the subject of divination.[1] Divination is an extremely widespread phenomenon which illustrates the 'dialogic template'. (It has also been used to illustrate communication without intention (Du Bois 1987).) The AIP template underlies the adjacency pair organization which structures conversation. To speak is to assume the possibility of a response. In particular, to question is to assume the possibility of an answer. Goody (Chapter 10, this volume) discusses prayers which may receive non-verbal replies, but from the point of view of the believer the prayers are answered.

Divination provides a means of asking questions. The questions are usually those which cannot be answered by other means available. Examples are questions such as 'Will my child recover from this illness?', 'Will there be an accident on the road if I travel tomorrow?', 'What is the cause of this misadventure?' and so on.

It is possible to do divination as a game, as a procedure without any cognitive or emotional load being carried. However, such cases (which occur both in Europe and elsewhere) are aberrant. They point to the usual perceived purpose of divination: to find answers to questions. Generally, divination is used as a means of resolving problems. Some corollaries of this will now be examined. If we view divination as the pursuit of answers to questions we can apply some of the insights of conversational analysis to understand the details of a divination session.

Divination must be recognized as being a means of obtaining true answers. Only if it is held to be a truth-telling exercise is it worth performing. Not that this rules out the possibility of cynical manipulation, but even that eventuality assumes the belief in the procedures of those being duped.

Most classifications of divination contrast divination by possession with technical divination. In divination by possession a spirit or other agency uses a human to communicate directly with people. Questions may be put and answers received. Sometimes speech may be uttered unprompted which must then be interpreted to find the answers to the problems at issue. On the other hand, technical divination is not, in general, concerned with the state of the diviner. True answers result from the correct performance of a set of procedures. Diviners are technicians. In my earlier work I have stressed that technical divination differs importantly from divination by possession since it alone allows for the possibility of 'faulty' or 'incorrect' practice. However, the presumption of AIP means that clients and practitioners view technical divination in the same light as possession, despite this difference.

The detailed case which follows considers contradiction management in Mambila 'spider' divination. Mambila ensure (by their own lights) the truth of their divination by regular inductive testing, and by requiring consistent answers to repeated questions.

Moreover, communicative constraints on the praxis of divination are found in the management of contradiction. If we apply the 'dialogic template' to the interaction between diviner[2] and divination (whatever type of divination is being used) then contradiction becomes an interesting test case. Contradiction may be a threat to the continuing dialogue. If it is perceived as such then Grice's cooperative maxim is no longer in play and the dialogue breaks down.

McHugh (1968) gives examples of experiments in which students were being counselled via an intercom, and receiving only yes/no answers to polar questions. When the students perceived (accurately) that the answers were in random sequence and were not 'generated as answers to their questions' they stopped in disgust. Garfinkel (1984) has discussed the same experiments and has analysed some of the reasons why the participants were so reluctant to recognize the randomness of the replies. The situation is directly analogous to Mambila divination as I show below. The point becomes critical when a contradiction occurs. When the same question first receives a 'yes' and then a 'no', a problem arises for the diviner as well as for us as analysts. Justification for this claim is that it is just where we as analysts perceive a problem that the line of questioning changes tack.

Although Goody has talked about a 'dialogue template', this should not be taken to imply a fixation on dyadic interaction.[3] Diviners divine to satisfy their peer group of fellow diviners as well as their clients. They must be judged to have really been possessed or to have performed the techniques correctly, or to have correctly interpreted the signs. Interpretation occurs both between divination and diviner as well as between diviner and client. My earlier discussion of classifications of divination sought to draw attention to the way in which the division of interpretative labour between these two affects the manner of divinatory practice (Zeitlyn 1987, 1990a: ch. 3).

Garfinkel's examination of 'Commonsense knowledge of social structures'

Garfinkel's paper presents an account of an experiment and an analysis of it, followed by his reflections on this analysis. The experiment involved American university students being counselled through an intercom. The students were told to pose questions in an either/or format. They received yes/no answers. The questions, and the students' 'reflections upon the answers they received', were tape-recorded. What the students were not told was that the yes/no responses were supplied in a predetermined random sequence. Each student received the same sequence of answers. Garfinkel quotes two sessions in full and then summarizes the results in a set of aphoristic comments.

I quote a short passage from the first case, in which a male Jewish student debates whether he should continue to date a non-Jew in the face of his family's displeasure.

SUBJECT: My question is, do you feel under the present circumstances [which he has just explained] that I should continue or stop dating the girl? Let me put that in a positive way. Do you feel that I should continue dating this girl?

EXPERIMENTER: My answer is no.

SUBJECT: No. Well that is kind of interesting. I kinda feel that there is really no great animosity between Dad and I but, well, perhaps he feels that greater dislike will grow out of this. I suppose or maybe it is easier for an outsider to see certain things that I am blind to at this moment. I would like to ask my second question now.

EXPERIMENTER: Okay.

SUBJECT: Do you feel that I should have a further discussion with Dad about this situation or not? Should I have further discussion with Dad over this subject about dating the Gentile girl?

EXPERIMENTER: My answer is yes.

This brief extract suffices to show how the subjects constructed for themselves a meaningful dialogue. The subject took the random responses of the experimenter as answers to the questions put and imputed an argument to the experimenter. Subjects behave *as if* they were negotiating meaning in the manner found in ordinary conversation.[4] However, in this experiment, just as in divination, the responses are *not* intentionally produced answers but are 'mere events'. It is this similarity which makes Garfinkel's discussion relevant to the analysis of divination. My concern is with the process of constructing an argument, or of imputing meanings.

Although few anthropologists would wish to use such cold-blooded 'experimental' methods of research, Garfinkel's techniques can help the analysis of the praxis of divination.[5] Eleven of his conclusions which are applicable to the analysis of divination are listed below (some are quotations, others have been rewritten in an attempt to render them more readily comprehensible).[6] The 'answerer' to whom I refer is not Garfinkel's counsellor but the divination.

After Garfinkel: eleven principles of divinatory interaction

(From Garfinkel 1984: 90–1, sections D and E)

1. Questions may be retrospectively redefined in the light of later answers.
2. 'The identical utterance is capable of answering several different questions simultaneously and of constituting an answer to a compound question that in terms of the strict logic of propositions does not permit either a yes or no or a single yes or no.'
3. One response can be understood to be answering several previous questions simultaneously.
4. 'Present answers provide answers to further questions that will never be asked.'
5. 'Where answers are unsatisfying or incomplete, the questioners are willing to wait for later answers in order to decide the sense of previous ones.'
6. Incompleteness is attributed by questioners to deficiencies in the method (of yes/no answers), or to incomplete comprehension on the part of the answerer (i.e. the divination) which can in turn be attributed to poor question-setting.
7. Reasons are assumed to exist for 'inappropriate' answers. Those reasons explain the answer which is given, and determine its sense.
8. 'When answers are incongruous or contradictory, subjects are able to continue by finding that the 'adviser' has learned more in the meantime, or that he has decided to change his mind, or that perhaps he is not sufficiently acquainted with the intricacies of the problem, or the fault was in the question so that another phrasing is necessary.' In other words, explanations or excuses can always be constructed *ad hoc*.
9. 'Incongruous answers are resolved by imputing knowledge and intent to the adviser.'
10. Contradictions force reinterpretation of the questions: further meanings to the questions are imputed which explain the answers, thus removing the contradiction.

11. Contradictory answers lead to a 'review of the possible intent of the answer so as to rid the answer of contradiction or meaninglessness, and to rid the answerer of untrustworthiness'.

Points 7–11 are particularly relevant to the analysis of contradiction in divination which follows.

Garfinkel also provides some maxims concerning the questioners' suspicions of the system.

12. The possibility of random answers may be considered by the subjects but is not tested. Suspicions are allayed if the answers 'make good sense'.
13. Suspicion turns the 'answers' into 'mere events' and there is then no point in continuing. Therefore,
14. Those who became suspicious are unwilling to continue.

During my fieldwork with Mambila in Cameroon, about which more below, I never encountered such express doubts about divination. I suggest that this is due to the intellectual protection given to the basic assumptions, a suggestion in accord with the argument presented by Evans-Pritchard (1937). These points are therefore complementary to Evans-Pritchard's twenty-two reasons why the Zande do not perceive the futility of their magic (1937:475–8). These are a catalogue of *ad hoc* hypotheses used to protect the validity of the central tenets, in this case that of divination itself, whereas the results of any individual divinatory session remain open to question. The creation and interpretation of a sequence of questions and answers is independent of any actions employed to protect divination, such as those listed by Evans-Pritchard. There is neither methodological nor logical contradiction between Evans-Pritchard's analysis, and that of Garfinkel.

Contradiction and re-interpretation

The second case used by Garfinkel to illustrate his argument includes an example of re-interpretation; remarkably, he does not comment upon this. The 'experimenter' (Garfinkel's term) should give yes/no answers to the questions put. A student of physics is considering whether to leave college or to change his subject. His first question is whether he should change subjects (answer: 'No'). Eight questions later he asks: 'Will I get a degree?' Answer: 'No'. I quote the questioner's response to this in full (Garfinkel 1984: 87):

STUDENT: According to that I won't get a degree.
                  What should I do?
                  Are you still there?
EXPERIMENTER: Yes, I am.

Consider the likely reactions of the subject if the experimenter had replied 'My answer is no'. It is clear that the experimenter has answered only the second of those two questions, and that he has stepped out of his 'experimental' framework. It is important to understand why the crisis of faith which occasioned this exchange occurred when it did. When the question 'Will I get a degree?' was answered in the negative the subject perceived the experimenter to be contradicting himself. By his negative answer, the experimenter was understood to be committing himself to the proposition

A: You will not get a degree in physics.

This was perceived to contradict an earlier answer wherein the experimenter was understood to commit himself to the proposition

B: You should not change your subject.

If one assumes that

C: If you will not get a degree in physics then you should change your subject,

then B entails

D: You will get a degree in physics [if you persevere].

But from above,

A: You will not get a degree in physics.

By asserting B, the subject is allowed (granted C) to infer D. But A and D are contradictories.

To invoke a Gricean relevance principle: if the questioner is not going to get a degree then it is irrelevant what subject he studies. The 'relevant' answer to the question 'Should I change my subject?' would be: 'You will not get a degree'. This would constitute a rejection of the question. However, the schema of the dialogue explicitly permitted only yes/no answers. In order to make sense of the answers received, the subject interpreted contradiction as a rejection of the question. This is a common conversational ploy. For example:

Shall we go to the pub?
Have you looked in your diary?

A question is rejected by answering it by another question. In order to do this the subject had to disregard the rules which had been presented. The fact that only yes/no answers to polar questions were possible was ignored, or perhaps subtly re-interpreted. The subject is now in the position of saying 'When I get answers like this they don't really mean yes and no, they mean something altogether more complicated . . .'

Conversational analysis encourages the detailed examination of the negotiation of meaning between speakers. Such negotiation is particularly apparent where misunderstanding or disagreement occurs. We can draw on the literature on 'repairs' for examples of the negotiation of meaning. A 'repair' occurs after normal turn-taking rules of dialogue breakdown. This is often caused by the speakers having different assessments of what is being said. Achieving sufficient consensus to continue the dialogue necessitates negotiation of meaning (see Levinson 1983: 16–19, 39–47; Schegloff *et al.* 1977). Conversational analysis can reveal instances in divinatory discourse where, in order to make sense of an utterance, context is strongly implicated.[7] It is clearly necessary to consider this context in order to understand the utterance. The perspective of the analysis is perforce widened to include not only divination but also the circumstances of the participants and the social structure within which the divination is practised.

An ethnomethodological focus on the negotiation of meaning between speakers is of more assistance than formal logic in understanding the manoeuvres adopted, for example, in response to contradiction. Formal logic identifies a contradiction but allows no other solution than the rejection of a premise. It cannot, however, suggest which premise is at fault. Ethnomethodology, on the other hand, identifies the redefinition of a premise as a constructive solution to the problems caused by contradiction. The empirical techniques of conversational analysis allow for the identification of the premise at issue, and for the study of the process of its redefinition. This seems more consistent with the questioners' responses as evidenced in the data.

In the cases of both divination and Garfinkel's experiment, analysis of the negotiation of meaning is facilitated since in both, one of the parties to the perceived conversation is not *in fact* negotiating. Paradoxically, divination can be seen to say so much precisely because it is mute.

Studying divination

Many reasons may be given to warrant the study of divination. I shall briefly present two of these, and go on to distinguish between two major classes of divination. A consideration of the limitations of classical sociological analysis of divinatory practice will serve as a prelude to my presentation of the Mambila material.

Evans-Pritchard sought to convince European readers that the Azande were rational to persist in their beliefs, and that their actions were therefore subject to rational explanation. In particular, he expressly addressed himself to 'political officers, doctors and missionaries in Zandeland, and later to Azande themselves'. Divination provided an excellent subject with which to challenge colonial prejudices. More recently, divination has featured as a leitmotif in the 'rationality debate'. Of its contributors however, only J. Beattie (1964, 1966 and 1967) and Horton (1967 and elsewhere) have published works about divination *per se*. Divination has figured so importantly because it is perceived as a paradigm for 'rationality in irrationality': that is, belief in divination is held to be irrational, but its practice is extremely rational according to the ethnographies. It therefore serves as an amenable synecdoche of religious belief and practice.

A second reason for studying divination is that it reveals the actors' understanding of their social structure. The process of posing the questions, by their phrasing, and by the range of possible solutions proposed, provides evidence about indigenous models of the world. Divination thus ranks alongside disputes as a social activity whose study can provide information about, and understanding of, much broader matters than the stated topic of analysis. Thus, although divination may occupy relatively little of the attention of a group, as with the Azande, it may provide a rewarding starting-point for a wider analysis.

Classes of divination

Many different classifications of different types of divination have been proposed. Some typologies cover more comprehensively than others the wide range of activities which may be glossed as divination. Whether they are sociologically revealing is another matter. Without entering into the arguments here I shall follow Cicero in making a distinction between 'artificial' and 'natural' divination (*De Div.* 1.vi.12). Later authors prefer the terms 'mechanical' and 'emotive' (see Devisch 1985; Vernant 1974; and Zeitlyn 1987 for further discussions.[8]

Natural, or emotive divination depends on the recognition of a direct relationship between the operator and some occult force or spirit, such that truth is achieved through contact with spirits or by exercise of 'intuition'. It typically involves some sort of 'possession' (this is further discussed in I.M. Lewis 1971).

By contrast, artificial divination aims to reveal truth through the performance of a variety of technical operations, all of which are mechanical in nature. The divination practices used by Mambila are exclusively of this kind, and are the subject of my discussion here.[9] Unlike emotive divination, technical divination appears to involve much clear ratiocination, and its results are open to question in quite different ways. Although practitioners of any type of divination can be accused of deceit and fraud, only technical divination can be performed 'incorrectly', thus allowing the possibility of mistaken practice. For in the case of emotive divination, the truth of the divinatory results is guaranteed by the possessed state of the diviner. Since possession is an unequivocal state, mistaken practice is impossible.[10] Any divinatory techniques associated with possession are employed simply as preliminaries necessary to attain this state; they are not means by which the results are obtained.

The factors which I examine in this chapter do not obtain in emotive forms of divination, although these clearly provide an alternative means of seeking truth. While focusing on ratiocination I do not intend to imply that technical divination is the sole means to the end of truth-seeking.[11] It should also be stressed that many kinds of 'technical' divination do not pose polar questions, and have answers in other than yes/no forms.

The incompleteness of sociological analysis

Sociological analyses of divination have treated divination as a procedure either for legitimating decisions (Park 1963) or for providing therapeutic benefit to the consultants (J. Beattie 1964). However their focus is on the social consequences of the use of divination rather than on the divination *per se*. They do not, therefore, consider the possibility, admitted only in technical divination, of mistaken practice. While such analyses may reveal important aspects of a divinatory system, the theoretical standpoint adopted allows for no detailed analysis of the praxis of consultation. Neither the interaction between diviner and client, nor the interaction between diviner and divination can be understood from this perspective. Conversational analysis, however, provides techniques to understand these interactions.

An analysis of this kind neither precludes nor invites functionalist arguments, rather it precedes and anticipates them. This is possible since the results of the analysis of divinatory practice may themselves be further analysed by conventional anthropological theories which have little or nothing to say about the details of divinatory practice. The results of our analysis of these details could be subjected to further interpretation in terms of any theory of society, for example, in a functionalist, a Marxist or a dramaturgical approach, for the analysis is independent of these types of theory. Thus, I regard as a neutral boon that which Gellner criticizes as sociological myopia in ethnomethodology (Gellner 1975).

Why study divination as situated dialogue?

Ethnomethodology provides productive techniques with which to study divination. Both the ratiocination involved in producing an answer and the contextualization of question and answer may be examined in the detail they deserve. Moreover, by analysing the process of divination we can avoid the reliance on abstract accounts which has previously limited descriptions, for example, of the Ifa divination practised by Nigerian Yoruba and neighbouring groups.[12] Garfinkel lists some of the ways by which (objectively random) utterances are endowed with meaning by listeners so as to construct a sensible dialogue. The study of divination reveals how a similar process occurs when the participants pose questions and receive answers. Such a procedure poses problems for conventional discussions of rationality. AIP strategies work for people. Diviners claim to have tested similar strategies with their divination systems. What grounds are there for analysts to call this irrational?

Ethnomethodology and Mambila divination

Divination systems allowing only yes/no answers involve similar processes of interpretation, particularly when the divination apparently contradicts itself. Following a summary introduction to Mambila society I shall illustrate this point with an account of Mambila spider divination (further details may be found in Zeitlyn 1993).

The Mambila lie on either side of the Nigeria/Cameroon border, the bulk of them living on the Mambila Plateau in Nigeria. A smaller number (c. 12,000) are to be found in Cameroon, especially at the foot of Mambila Plateau escarpment, on the Tikar Plain. My fieldwork was restricted to these latter groups, and in particular to the village of Somié. Somié had a population of approximately one thousand (based on the official 1986 tax census) at the time of fieldwork. Self-sufficient in food, the villagers have grown coffee as a cash crop since the early 1960s.

Cameroonian Mambila on the Tikar Plain have adopted the Tikar institution of the chiefship, yet their social structure otherwise closely resembles that described for the Nigerian village of Warwar given by Rehfisch (1972) based on fieldwork in 1953. Nigerian Mambila did not have the same type of institutionalized chiefship as is found in Cameroon. In Nigeria, villages were organized on gerontocratic principles, and largely lacked political offices. Most people in the villages are members of either the Catholic or Protestant church. However both men's and women's masquerades are still performed, and cases heard at the Chief's palace are regularly concluded with a ritual *sua*-oath.[13]

Most married men know how to divine, but have varying degrees of confidence in their own skills. Hence if a problem is serious, it is likely to be taken to one of the acknowledged experts. In the case considered below a man, named Wong, in his late thirties went, by arrangement, to divine with Bi, the head of Njerup hamlet, and an important elder. He is also well known as an accomplished diviner. In order to be confident of the results of divination Wong came to Bi in order to have Bi's sanction. Bi could correct any mistakes of interpretation, and thereby help ensure the accuracy of the results.

Mambila spider divination entails the posing of questions couched as binary alternatives, often requiring yes/no answers.

A hole in the ground inhabited by a spider is covered by an enclosure, usually an inverted pot. A stick and a stone are placed within this enclosure, near the entrance to the spider's hole. A set of marked leaves is placed over the entrance to the burrow. When questions are posed the pot is tapped; in response to the knocking the spider emerges from its hole. In doing so it disturbs the leaves. The resulting pattern of the leaves in relation to the stick and to the stone is interpreted as an answer to a question. Questions allow one of two responses, one is explicitly associated with the stick and the other with the stone.

Several different spiders may be consulted simultaneously. This enables a faster rate of questioning since some twenty minutes elapse before the diviner can check whether the spider has responded to a question. It also allows a consistency check to be made by asking the same question of different spiders. Diviners admit that ambiguous or unintelligible answers are possible, but few such instances were observed.

Table 9.1 shows the response to contradiction which arose during a six-hour divination session recorded in January 1987. The divination concerned a child (Wong's daughter) suffering from malaria. The main points at issue were whether the illness had been caused by witchcraft, and whether the taking of a *sua*-oath would be sufficient to protect the child from further attack. The table shows the questions addressed to two different spiders, and the answers received. In each case the alternative said by the diviners to have been chosen has been marked with asterisks. Forty-two questions were posed during the session; their order is indicated by the question numbers.

Responses to contradiction

Table 9.1 contains answers which directly contradict one another. The acceptance of direct contradiction is, according to the canons of traditional logic, a symptom of 'illogicality'.[14] Further comment is warranted.

The sequence starts with Question 33, which was addressed to Pot 1: will *sua* end the problem or not? A straightforward yes/no response was sought. Another pot (Pot 2) was asked a similar question (Q 34) before the response was obtained from Q 33. The response to Q 34 was taken to advocate the use of *sua*, as opposed to other sorts of treatments. This was immediately followed by Q 35 which repeated Q 33. The response to Q 35 was that *sua* would *not* end the problem. This contradicts Q 34. The

Table 9.1. *Divination questions*

Pot 1	Pot 2
Q 33: *sua* will end it vs. *sua will not end it*	Q 34: *sua will end it* vs. divine further/cut *kare*[1]
	Q 35: *sua* will end it vs. *sua will not end it*
	Q 36: male witch vs. *female witch*
Q 38: Something buried[2] vs. *sua will end it*	Q 37: *sua will end it* vs. witchcraft continues

Notes:
[1] The *kare* rite is sometimes referred to as a variety of *sua*. It is a domestic version of the *sua*-oath.
[2] 'Something buried' refers to some witchcraft treatment, which unless detected and removed would continue to act although its perpetrator might be caught by *sua*.

problem was then assumed to be one of witchcraft. In response to this, Q 36 sought to identify the sex of the witch. The divination was taken to have identified a female witch. The response to Q 36 was understood to be identical with an earlier diagnosis of 'problems among the women in Wong's house' (Q 26 and Q 29). There had in fact been a long-standing quarrel between Wong's wife and his classificatory sister about the usufruct of a field. Disputes over land tenure are typical of cases in which *sua*-oaths are taken. The parties to the dispute swear that, although they may be quarrelling, they bear no malice and will not seek to win their case through witchcraft, for example by causing illness among the children of the other litigant. The identification of the female witches as being those women embroiled in that dispute was assumed, and therefore not tested further by divination. This resolved the dilemma posed by the contradiction. Once the diviners are assured that the witchcraft referred to is only that connected with this quarrel, then *sua* becomes an appropriate and sufficient course of action. When that reassurance has been given they can return to the previous line of questioning. The earlier question was then repeated in a modified form: will *sua* end it, or is there other witchcraft to be dealt with, for example, in the form of buried treatments which remain active until discovered and destroyed (Q 37)? After putting this question, the response to Q 33 was sought by inspecting the pot. The answer found was '*sua* will not solve the problem'. This was immediately pursued in the light of the *question* which had just been put (Q 37), as to whether any witchcraft was to be dealt with. The diviners understood this to indicate that there might be further witchcraft. Hence Q 38 draws the distinction between buried witchcraft substances and the ending of the affair by *sua*. The responses to both Q 37 and Q 38 indicated that performance of the *sua* rite was the appropriate action to be taken. Thus a believable, because consistent, result was obtained.

The contradictory results preceding this were thenceforth ignored. They had, however, forced the diviners to examine the possibilities of more complicated problems. Once these possibilities had been eliminated the diviners could return to the main strand of the enquiry as if no contradiction had occurred.

We must take seriously the diviners' assumption that the sequence of questions is a dialogue between divination and diviner. Mambila diviners talk of asking (*bie*) questions of divination (*nggam*) as if it were a single entity. Looking at a result they say 'Divination says ...' (*Nggam je ...*). I was always given inductive and empirical justifications for the veracity of divination. Even formal initiation into the technique of spider divination contained no information about the origin of divinatory knowledge, nor was any account given of what divination was, or how it worked. The belief in the efficacy of the technique is held to be warranted by the success of the diviners.

If the process of divination is, in part, to be regarded as a dialogue between diviner and divination, then contradiction may be regarded as a rhetorical device used by the divination to make the diviner cast the net of his questions more widely. In the example illustrated, the divination has forced the diviners to consider the possibility, previously not addressed by them, that buried witchcraft substances may be responsible for the child's illness. Garfinkel's methods may be used to reveal the way in which diviners construct the dialogue. In essence: contradictions were understood as question-rejecting moves. They give pause for thought, and lead to changes in tack. If we return to Garfinkel's maxims listed above, numbers 7 to 11 may be summarized in a single maxim: 'The problem of contradiction may be defused by treating it as a rejection of the question.' Evidence for the validity of this position comes from our success at reconstructing the observed dialogue, which otherwise remains obscure.

It may be objected that the contradictions are only there from our analytical point of view. However, 'crises of faith' or 'changes in tack', or other breaks in the flow of dialogue, occur at or following the points where we identify a contradiction. This demonstrates that they are more than etic constructions. From an emic point of view no contradiction may be perceived, but it is clear that the actors have been given 'pause for thought'. I would suggest that since conversation assumes the absence of contradiction, speakers then strive to preserve the conversation by removing the contradictions.

A cynical account of this divination would be that since the performance of *sua* is the standard response to many problems, it is only to be expected that a *sua*-oath will be taken when there is concern about an illness. The process of divination would then be seen as an empty validating act whose outcome is known in advance. But in divination all the participants know the background and the likely results. Although I am sure that the participants would have admitted that *sua* was a likely result, I nonetheless reject such an approach. It allows no room for analysis of the actions and, most particularly, the ratiocination of the diviners is not considered. A similar objection applies to those analyses which see divination as a means of increasing psychological comfort by reducing stress (Park 1963). That the actors believe in what they are doing is clear from the attitudes expressed, and from the manner in which divination is practised. The analyst has a responsibility to be faithful to their beliefs.

Contradictions and inference merit consideration which is not possible with conventional sociological analysis. Both chains of reasoning and the consideration of hypothetical possibilities are involved, and these are capable of reconstruction, as I have attempted to show above. That some outcomes are highly probable may be regarded as a measure of the predictability of the world. The fact that time-worn techniques are repeated does not mean that they are not chosen with care and deliberation each time they are adopted.

Ethnomethodology and the techniques which have grown out of it, such as discourse or conversational analysis, provide means by which the care and deliberation exercised in making choices may be brought to light and analysed. The propositions by Shaw (1985), Parkin (1979) and Werbner (1989) that divination is best analysed as dialogue, can thus be realized.

Conclusion

I have been arguing that AIP forms part of the background to divinatory practice. It is found in the basic assumption that divination is a means to finding answers to questions. The management of contradiction exemplifies this. Contradictions are transformed out of court, and are taken to be allusions to unsuspected complexity. Diviners assume that divination produces contradiction in order to give subtle answers. The premise of dialogue is never threatened. A repair is performed by the diviner which makes the response (retrospectively) rational and informative. In divination (as elsewhere) we may find that we were asking the wrong questions. This chapter has been examining some of the means by which we come to such conclusions. Creative repairwork, redefining our own understanding of both the other party and ourselves is an essential part of AIP.

Acknowledgements

The initial research on which this study is based was funded by the ESRC (grant no. A00428424416) and by a scholarship from Trinity College, Cambridge. My research in Cameroon could not have been conducted without the research permits granted by His Excellency the Minister for Higher Education and Scientific Research (R.P. 13/85 and 62/86), and the help provided by his staff. This chapter was begun during the tenure of a Junior Research Fellowship at Wolfson College, Oxford and completed while holding a British Academy Research Fellowship. During this time I have been the holder of a short Junior Research Fellowship at Wadham College, Oxford followed by a Research Fellowship at Wolfson College, Oxford. I have also received assistance from the ESRC (grant no R000233311). I am very grateful for all the help I have received from these different sources.

Substantial portions of this chapter have already been published in D. Zeitlyn (1990) Professor Garfinkel visits the soothsayers. Ethnomethodology and Mambila divination. *Man* (n.s.) 25(4): 654–66. Permission to reprint these portions has been kindly given by the Royal Anthropological Institute.

Notes

Much of the data considered in this paper has also been published as Zeitlyn (1990b). Further consideration of related questions will be found in Zeitlyn (1993).

 1 AIP may also explain why gods behave like people. Horton has argued that gods, spirits, deities of all kinds have been ascribed human-like attributes so that we may interact with them. He argues (1982: 227–38, esp. 237–8) that in 'simple' technological societies human interaction is reliable and predictable in a way in which the 'physical world' is not. One then becomes a model for the other. In other words if AIP strategies work with gods then these gods must be like us in certain respects. Human-like gods may be approached to influence the world they control. The argument is safely circular: gods are like humans so they use AIP-based strategies. AIP-based strategies work for the gods so they must be like humans ... Horton's argument, however, rests on 'analogy' rather than AIP.

2 It applies in a non-controversial way to the subsequent discussion of dialogue between diviner and client.

3 As was recognized in the Garden of Eden myth the dyad is the minimum sized unit from which society may develop!

4 There is a telling similarity between this and the manner in which gamblers interact with croupiers and understand roulette as a game of skill rather than a game of chance (Oldman 1974).

5 This is quite apart from the suggestion that psychiatry and other therapies are the major type of divination used in America.

6 It would be interesting to attempt a sociological explanation of the opacity of the prose of those working in ethnomethodology. Sadly, this seems to have contributed to the sidelining of the approach, at least within British social anthropology. Nor has the prose style improved with the years. A recent paper by Garfinkel and some colleagues is a masterpiece of recondite impenetrability, a fact to which the comments made by Holton, who had the unenviable job of commenting on the paper when it was presented, mutely attest (Garfinkel *et al.* 1981; Holton 1981).

7 The process of such implicature was first outlined by Grice: superficially uncooperative utterances are taken to be relevant, meaningful contributions to a continuing conversation by making extra inferences. These presume that the basic principles of conversation (called Grice's maxims in the literature) hold at a deep level. There remains uncertainty as to the detailed workings of such 'implicatures' (see the discussion in Levinson 1983: ch. 3). Sperber and Wilson (1986) have produced a general theory of relevance to account for such implicatures. This remains controversial (see Sanders 1988; Levinson 1989).

8 Confusion may be caused by inconsistencies of usage between different authors. Evans-Pritchard (1937: 10–11) contrasts oracles with divination in order to express the distinction made here between mechanical (or technical) divination and emotive divination.

9 An anti-witchcraft cult called 'Makka' existed around the time of the Second World War. Some practitioners of 'Makka' appear to have been possessed when detecting witches, although others relied on the administration of ordeals.

10 A Sudanese counter-example has been pointed out to me in which possession at the wrong time of day leads to wrong predictions which can be attributed to a mistake about the time. Nevertheless, I believe that the broad contrast drawn here is helpful in the analysis and comparison of different divinatory systems.

11 While focusing on ratiocination I do not intend to imply that mechanical divination is the sole means to the end of truth-seeking (Esther Goody, personal communication). I should also stress that there are many kinds of mechanical divination which do not pose polar questions, and which have answers in other than yes/no forms.

12 I know of no work on Ifa or on Ifa-type divinations which devotes much attention to the details of praxis. Maupoil (1943) concentrates on the mathematics, Bascom (1969) on the verses. Only de Surgy (1981) includes some case material, albeit principally as an introduction to the sacrificial sequences which follow. It is surely the case that sufficient is now known about both the

ese verses and the cult of Ifa. But what actually happens, the way in which the documented theory is put into practice, remains unstudied.

13 *Sua* names a variety of ritual oaths, often accompanied by the ritual killing of a chicken as well as some masquerades. It is the nexus of Mambila religion, and has been extensively analysed in Zeitlyn (1990a). It is sufficient here to note that it is both an oath which binds the oath-takers not to cause illness, and a death threat to any other persons seeking to do evil.

14 Possible responses are discussed in Zeitlyn (1990b: 665).

10 Social intelligence and prayer as dialogue

Homo sapiens is the clever hominid: primate social intelligence plus language

This chapter is part of a long-term project for the teasing out of implications of a social origin of human intelligence – for of course our species is distinguished as *Homo sapiens sapiens* – the intelligent hominid. Recent ethological research argues convincingly that primates are on many measures highly intelligent, and that this can best be explained as a product of social interdependence. Higher primate species appear to have a progressively greater capacity to cognitively model responses of others. For convenience this modelling of alternative contingent responses to others' actions can be termed *anticipatory interactive planning* (AIP). It is also argued in the Introduction that human intelligence was intimately linked to the emergence of language, which fundamentally changed the ways in which primates managed social interdependence.

Spoken language offers ways of influencing others' behaviour. It permits more elaborate negotiation of social interactions, the negotiation of *joint* AIP strategies. It becomes possible to seek cooperation with one's own goals through the exchange of information ('there are more nuts over there under the big tree'); and to manipulate relationships themselves through asking, pleading, begging, pretending, threatening, insisting, promising. Spoken language became, as it continues to be, central to our human AIP modelling. As speech presumes an exchange of messages, this makes *dialogue*, literally 'speaking alternately', a fundamental form in hominid sociality. The importance of an exchange of messages for the emergence of a lexicon, i.e. shared meanings, is modelled by Hutchins and Hazlehurst in Chapter 2.

Particularly significant here is Vygotsky's argument that conscious thought is internalized speech (1962). He showed experimentally that young children speak aloud to themselves the reasoning accompanying complex actions; the more difficulty encountered in the action, the more elaborated the spoken accompaniment. This speaking-out of action plans appears to be a regular preliminary to the internal conscious planning of older children and adults. Vygotsky's account of learning emphasizes that the roles of both novice and expert are internalized; in the case of speech it would be the dialogue template that is internalized by each child.

The symbolic power of language multiplied the levels of complexity in the mental representations necessary for AIP strategies, particularly through the capacity for naming, leading to classification. To this is linked the ability to represent, to ourselves and to others, *accounts* of how the world is – of what is happening, has happened, will happen, should happen – leading to cultural accounts of how to understand, how to behave and what to teach. Such accounts create a new kind of reality for past and future time, for intention, obligation, and causality, and for representations of dreams, the dead and spiritual forces. They come to have a separate identity as beliefs, myths and religions (see Rappaport 1988; Goodenough 1990).

The ethnomethodological term 'accountability' refers to the fact that orderly social relations demand that we are *accountable* to one another for our actions, that is, where actions differ from what we expect (often what we feel is our right), they have to be capable of explanation, of repair, and of negotiation (see especially Heritage 1984). This is possible in an entirely new way through the medium of language, and several chapters in this volume explore in detail ways in which accountability occurs in the course of conversation. *Accounts* of 'how the world is' set the conditions for the *accountability* of our actions. In a sense prayer, the subject of this chapter, can be seen as an attempt to engage powerful non-human forces in accountability.

Prayer as dialogue

Some of the puzzles about prayer can be illuminated by seeing it as the use of social intelligence. For social intelligence seeks to reach goals and solve problems by modelling the ways in which our actions are contingent on others' responses. This creates a premise that problems will be resolved by modelling and managing others' reactions to our own actions. One might call this a *dyadic premise*. Social intelligence means that problem-solving schemata have a slot for modelling the responses of a social Other.

The premise itself is invisible in ordinary social life where problem-solving concerns real people. The social Other slot is occupied by grandma, or the milkman, or 'the government'. Occasionally the premise of a social Other is revealed where an individual is relating to the non-social world.[1] The dyadic premise is so deeply embedded in human schemata that we find it difficult to tackle problems such as illness without positing an Other.

On another level, major problems – illness, death, famine, earthquakes – force individuals, and communities, to recognize our powerlessness; just as important, they make us afraid. At the same time these experiences lead people to wonder and feel awe. But as socially intelligent creatures, with the capacity to construct concepts around experience, and to conceptualize cause and effect, we try to construct an account of what is happening, and to explain why it is happening to us. Who/what is this power? Why this injury to *me*? I suggest that it is because of the dyadic premise of social intelligence that we find explanations based on chance difficult to accept. We cannot easily incorporate chance occurrences into an AIP model. Instead, as socially intelligent creatures possessing, through language, the capacity to name feelings and ideas, when we try to model strategies for solving grave problems we construct ancestral spirits, ghosts, and gods to fill the 'social Other' slot.

The particularly human form of pursuing AIP strategies (though obviously not the only one) is through *talk*. Thus 'dialogue' with the social Other slot becomes prayer when we believe that the Other is a powerful spiritual being.

The problem of evidence

A major problem for the project of looking at the implications of a social intelligence concerns the possible nature of evidence. This chapter offers one approach by proposing that prayer may be seen as an expression of the dyadic premise, and trying to understand the dynamic of prayer in a few, particularly well-documented societies. What follows is not an exhaustive study of prayer; certainly not from a theological perspective. Even treating a few ethnographies in adequate detail would result in a book rather than a chapter, so the examples used here are necessarily abbreviated.

It seems that there are two stages, two processes, involved in the emergence of prayer as an institutional form in a given religious community.

First, and necessarily prior, is the process in individual social cognition of seeking to reach goals by negotiation with social Others. The evidence that prayer involves social cognition would lie in its use in negotiating goals with objectifications of power, misfortune and benevolence.

The second process is socio-cultural; it concerns the construction of accounts that explain to us how the world is as it is. When things happen to us, we explain them in terms required by our AIP contingency models. Religious beliefs can be seen as one of the forms taken by the stories we construct to explain things we don't understand – about the universe, about morality, about misfortune. These stories are also a way of helping ourselves predict the actions of others, which we must do for AIP modelling. Evidence for the influence of social cognition in religious beliefs and institutions would lie in their incorporation of objectified Others and in the elaboration of cultural processes both for negotiation and for the control of negotiation.

The nature of the Other to whom prayer is addressed varies widely from one society to another. But in every society we examine there is some form of prayer, of using spoken language to 'make an earnest request or petition; to make entreaty or supplication; to ask earnestly, humbly, or supplicatingly, to beseech' a powerful force or being. The 'solemn and humble request to God, or an object of worship', is 'usually expressed in words' (as defined by the Oxford English Dictionary). In this sense, prayer embodies the dialogue mode of negotiating with another; it fits the dialogue template.

As anthropologists our 'laboratory' is ethnographic descriptions of prayer set in their normal daily context, and these can contribute to an understanding of the *process* involved when individuals use prayer to solve problems. If these processes are at least congruent with an AIP model of social cognition in the ways outlined above, then they provide one sort of evidence for intelligence as social.

Prayer as dialogue in preliterate societies

Ancestors in Ashanti

The clearest case for prayer as dialogue can probably be made for ancestor worship since known dead individuals may be addressed. This can be particularly obvious at the time of a funeral, and in turn makes evident the extension to those longer dead, the ancestors. Among the Ashanti of West Africa, just before the body was carried out for burial, one of the family members came forward and addressed it:

> Today you go
> We have fired guns
> We have killed sheep
> We have brought cloths
> We have made a fine funeral
> Do not let anyone fall ill
> Let us get money to pay for the expenses we have made
> Let all the mourners have strength
> Life to the chief
> Let him beget children
> Let all be fertile.

Then en route to the graveyard the head of the matrilineage touched the coffin with branches, saying:

Kwame [name] I separate your soul from us. (Rattray 1927: 159–60.)

When an elder of the matrilineage dies, his or her personal stool is consecrated with sacrificial blood and wine and placed in the shrine room of the lineage. Every forty days there is a lineage ceremony at which libations are poured to these ancestral stools; at this time the ancestors are told of lineage affairs and asked to bring peace, health and fertility to lineage members.

Here we can see the continuity between conversation with a close kinsman, and the attempt to conduct a dialogue with him after his death. The dead person is asked not to harm those left behind, and to help them – to be fertile, not to become ill, and to get money. The elders whose stools are prayed to in the shrine house are those who controlled the affairs of the lineage when alive. All important affairs are still brought to them as ancestors at the forty-day *adua* ceremonies. In this way they remain in intimate contact with their descendants. And indeed dreams of the dead are taken as evidence of their continuing involvement (see Humphrey 1986).

We could stop here, claiming that prayers are effective because for believers they are dialogues with 'real' superior beings who actually have the power to aid the supplicant. Ashanti prayers are entirely consistent with the stories Ashanti tell themselves about the role of ancestors in the causes and remedies of blessing and misfortune.

Prayer: dialogue in performative ritual

Ancestor worship offers the strongest possible case for the dialogue of prayer as a straight extension of relations with the living to the realm of the supernatural. What of other forms of religion? The problem of the efficacy of prayer is similar to the problem of the efficacy of ritual. Anthropologists have often asked 'Why are rituals so central to religious practice when "objectively" they cannot have the effects they are supposed to produce?' It seems obvious that most 'magical spells' cannot cure illness, ensure rich harvests or success in war. Yet their use has probably been universal in preliterate societies (and might well prove to be more widespread in our own than we think). Tambiah (1970, 1985) has approached this problem through the idea of 'performative force' as used by Austin and his followers in sociolinguistics (see also Finnegan 1969). Ritual has its efficacy *in* and *through* its performance. One way that this works is that *words* in ritual are often used with *performative* force in Austin's sense. Speaking them is held to cause the action they refer to. For instance, cultural and ritual conventions ensure that verbs like 'swell, grow, be fertile' are understood as commands that bring about their object. There are much more complicated recursive patterns, like the rubbing of leaves of a prolific species onto seeds while commanding them

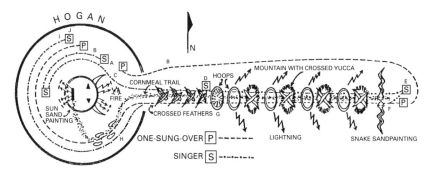

Figure 10.1 Diagram of hoop ceremonial process. (*Source*: Gill 1981.)

to germinate. There are direct parallels to this metaphoric use of performatives in prayer.

Tambiah also holds that the performance of rituals has itself a special sort of efficacy; the activity of ritual can be seen as directly parallel to the performative force of words. Verbal and ritual performative force have an interwoven dynamic.

Navajo prayers as both dialogue and performative ritual

Navajo prayers are not to ancestors but to the Holy People, those who emerged from the lower worlds and created humans. Why do these prayers 'work'? Navajo spoken prayers are part of what Gill (1981) calls 'prayer acts' – rituals which summon one of the ancestral Holy People into the presence of the person or community being prayed for, and which symbolically act out the assistance required. The pragmatic force of these prayers comes from the myths of Navajo cosmology familiar to everyone. Praying calls up Holy People from their other worlds and tells them what is needed, and through prayers, the desired changes are 'created' – much as the Holy People once created the Navajo culture and people. All these worlds continue to exist and interact.

In the *Ch'eehoyateeh* prayer act the hoop ceremonial takes the singer on a journey to find the life form of an ill person which has been stolen by Holy People; the singer returns and restores it to the one-sung-over. The ceremony is a complex composition of ritual acts, ritual objects, and ritual speech acts (prayers). A *Ch'eehoyateeh* prayer is intoned inside the ceremonial hogan each day at the conclusion of the rite. The singer sits in front of the one-sung-over and recites the prayer; the one-sung-over repeats each verse in turn. 'The prayer describes the journey of Talking God over the obstacles which guard the home of the ugly one [one of the Holy People] as he moves to rescue the life form of the one suffering from its captivity there. The return journey is directed to the home of the one suffering. Its conclusion will result in a return to health and blessing' (Gill 1981: 147).

The prayer journey is parallel to the journey performed by the singer, who inside the ceremonial hogan moves over feathers, through hoops, over 'mountains' and finally over the snakes to reach the one-sung-over. 'The hoops ... may represent the levels of the lower worlds through which the prayer "talks" the one praying. This interpretation ... suggests that the transformation enacted in a hoop prayer ceremony is modeled upon the emergence paradigm of the transformations which were experienced in sacred history as the way was made to the earth surface' (*Ibid.*: 150; see Figure 10.1).

'The other primary ritual object [beside the hoops] is the talking prayerstick bundle. The talking prayersticks provide the power of movement in the prayers bridging the gap between the earth surface and other worlds. Without the talking prayersticks the singer could not pass through the hoops to rescue the one-sung-over, nor could the one-sung-over pass back through the hoops to be retransformed' (*ibid.*: 150-1).

The dialogue form of Navajo prayer is particularly clear in the *ha'ayateeh* Liberation prayer. The singer describes the journey of Monster Slayer, 'armed with his dark staff and lightnings and carrying his rock crystal and talking prayersticks, as he searches through mountains, clouds, mists, mosses, and waters for the means of health which had been abducted and is being detained in the home of the ghosts in the lower worlds' (*ibid.*: 143). When he returns to the earth's surface Talking God reaches the home of the lost one; 'Upon reaching the most interior, and thus the safest, place in the home, Talking God reunites the lost one with the things with which he had been formerly associated.' Then Talking God bestows blessings on the restored person through identification with him. The prayer concludes by announcing a state of blessing (*ibid.*: 143-4).

The prayer chants of the ceremonies can be seen as successive dialogues:

1. Singer recites prayer addressed to one of Holy People
    = dialogue between singer and Holy Person.
2. Singer places supplicant in role of addressee
    = singer is praying on behalf of supplicant, to Holy Person.

The dialogue form is particularly clear in the Blessing prayer act for an expectant mother. First the Singer speaks on behalf of the Holy Person to supplicant:

> From the heart of Earth, by means of yellow pollen blessing is extended.
> From the heart of Sky, by means of blue pollen blessing is extended.

To which the expectant mother (echoing the singer) replies:

> On top of pollen floor may I there in blessing give birth!
> On top of a floor of fabrics may I there in blessing give birth!
> . . .
> May I give birth to Pollen Boy, may I give birth to Corn Beetle Boy, may
>   I give birth to Long Life Boy, may I give birth to Happiness Boy!
> With long life happiness surrounding me may I in blessing give birth!
> May I quickly give birth! [etc. etc.]

(Ibid.: 69–70.)

This sequence sets up a complex discourse with the prayer containing 'parts' for the supplicant and then the Holy Person. Both 'parts' are recited first by the singer and then, verbatim after him, by the supplicant. First the singer takes both parts, then the supplicant himself/herself takes both parts. In this process there is a clear identification between the two main participants, the supplicant, and the Holy Person. The singer never establishes an independent identity, but acts to blur the boundaries between the two.

While Navajo prayer acts elegantly illustrate the processes of performative ritual, they clearly take their meaning – and thus their performative force – from prayer in dialogue form.

Dinka prayers: priest and congregation

Prayers accompanying sacrificial ritual among the pastoral Dinka of the Sudan are described by Lienhardt (1961) as 'essentially public forms'. They are spoken by men of certain agnatic groups who, by virtue of inherited powers, are known as Masters of the Fishing Spears. The prayers are more or less efficacious depending on their ability to speak with 'bite' – forcefully, efficaciously, truly. They speak the truth in two senses; they do not speak falsehood, and that which they say comes true. Lienhardt uses the term proleptic: 'the representation or taking something future as already done'. The prayer of a powerful Master is a performative speech act in that it causes to be true what is spoken.[2] Lienhardt says that in the prayers the subjective experience of sufferers (from illness, sterility, guilt) is objectified – represented as external. The Master then addresses this objectified power in prayer and, by speech-which-becomes-truth, forces it to leave the human victim and to go away, with the life-breath of the sacrificial animal, to 'the land of those with lower incisors [i.e. the land of the dead]' (see especially Lienhardt 1961: ch. 6).

The prayer speech act is given greater force by the symbolic nature of the sacrificial ritual, and by the echoing of the key phrases by the audience as a choral response. It is given force in a further sense when deities show their presence and willingness to help by possessing the men of the Master's lineage. Lienhardt's discussion of who is being addressed in such prayers and invocations is subtle and persuasive. Briefly, the Master addresses the Power, a deity or perhaps a witch, who represents the affliction the sacrifice is intended to treat; but he addresses also the sacrificial ox, affirming an identification between sacrificial victim and sufferer and between victim and Power causing the affliction. Many things are happening in these rituals. The prayers objectify the source of the suffering, and separate this from the sufferer himself; they then describe what will happen to the Power causing the suffering – and as the words are spoken by the Master whose words become/contain truth, the repairing events will indeed happen. Through many prayers and invocations directed at the sacrificial animal, and echoed by the congregation, the suffering is transformed into an emblem of the sufferer and his agnatic group, and control and departure of the threatening Power is proclaimed and enacted. The congregation participates with increasing intensity in the whole process, verbal, rhythmic and constraining, and thus comes to share in the experience of transformation achieved by the prayers and sacrifice.

The Dinka provide a critical instance of an unwritten religion in which prayers are initiated and led by a priest on behalf of a supplicant, and reinforced by their repetition by the congregation. This pattern is strikingly similar to that found in the 'religions of the book', where the priesthood assumes a central mediating role between the individual and his god. Lienhardt describes the Masters as holding a role at once religious and political, and stresses their importance in warfare. Much the same could be said for the archbishops and popes of medieval Catholicism, the elders of the early Protestant churches, the founders of Islam, as well as contemporary ayatollahs.

The nature of the powers addressed in the prayers of Ashanti, Navajo and Dinka varies, but in each case they are believed to 'hear' the prayers, and to respond with actions which affect living people. In the prayer ceremonies of the Navajo the words and actions of the ritual enact not only the seeking of assistance from the Holy People, but also their intervention. In Dinka sacrificial ceremonies there is an added element of constraint. The power of the Master of the Fishing Spear to 'speak truth' forces the compliance of the Powers. The constraint arises through the power of the prayers of the Master. But the power is also in the words as part of a ritual speech act. Lienhardt notes the similarity between such prayers and the exhorting of men about to go into battle to fight bravely, as well as to the cursing of an enemy.

Monotheistic religions – does dialogue become monologue?

The several monotheistic religions originating in the Middle East shared a striking difference from these religions of multiple powers; they all insisted that prayer was the daily duty of every individual. This is basic in early Zoroastrian religion, in Judaism, in Christianity and in Islam. Of course priests become central for religious institutional structures (often linked to states), and to the welfare of believers. But the priest cannot fulfil the duty of daily prayer which falls on each individual.

With this individual duty to pray, a reflexive element appears in the relationship of the individual to the High God: God demands not only certain words and actions from the devotee, but he makes demands concerning his mental attitude as well. The prophet Zoroaster required that his followers love the god of light and the right – Ahura Mazda – and hate and renounce the god of darkness. Good and evil were here cast as perpetual opponents, battling in the world of the gods, but also in men's actions and in their hearts. The individual could determine his own ultimate fate by following the ways of good and renouncing evil (Boyce 1979; Moulton 1913). The Jew is warned not to pray unless he can attain *kavanah*, – a sense of standing in the presence of God, and the intention to fulfill one of His commandments (Donin 1980). Christians are enjoined to love Jesus, just as they are promised that Jesus and God love them; and they are exhorted to do the will of God – 'Thy will be done'. Immanuel Kant[3] wrote that '*Praying*, thought of as an *inner formal* service of God . . . is a superstitious illusion . . . for it is no more than a *stated wish* directed to a Being who needs no such information . . . hence God is not really served. A heart-felt wish to be well-pleasing to God in our every act and abstention . . . is the *spirit of prayer*' (1934: 182–3, italics in original). The core of the Quaker faith is the conviction that God speaks to us in our hearts, but He can only do this if we have the correct attitude. The quiet of the Quaker meeting is necessary so that God's words may be heard in each heart. Both the impulse to speak out in meeting, and the very words themselves are given by God (Bauman 1983: 121ff.).

One of the classic debates in western theology concerns whether prayer is a dialogue or a monologue. Is prayer simply the individual talking to himself? Clearly for the Ashanti their ancestors are real – have they not known them in life? But what about prayer in monotheistic religions? Alhonsaari (1973) says, of Christian prayer, that this is not a monologue because the one who prays *believes* he is really addressing the Lord. But for those who do not share this belief, prayer is a 'false' dialogue; the person thinks he is addressing a superior bring, but there is no one there. A better stance would be that this is an intended dialogue; but surely still a dialogue.

Kant on the other hand argues that we are really confronting our own consciences when we pray.[4] It is a monologue – or at best a dialogue with ourselves. This corresponds to Lienhardt's framework in which the powers addressed by the Master of the Fishing Spears are images, representations, of our own feelings. But the monotheistic religions have required individuals themselves to address these (culturally provided) representations. And, further, they have laid great stress on the sincerity with which this is done. So, by an ironic twist, the daily individual prayers of monotheism, instead of externalizing passions and conflict, have again brought the attempt to deal with them inside our own heads.[5] It is true that these sufferings may be labelled as external acts – sins; however a new source of suffering is added, that of wrong belief, wrong attitude, lack of faith. At its most extreme the goal of prayer also lies in the realm of representation of subjective feeling. St Theresa of the Little Way resolved her conflicts about a Christ who allowed her to suffer by no longer seeking relief, only the assurance of His love. Her way of achieving this love was through prayer which allowed her to construct an intensely personal relationship with Jesus. Thus even where prayer is an internal 'monologue' about subjective experience, it may be explicitly directed to external powers.

Buddhism: prayer without a god?

Buddhism is identified with meditation, 'the exercise of the mind in religious contemplation' rather than prayer. Indeed Anesaki (1980 [1918]: 166) claims that since Buddhism teaches that there is no personal creator or ruler of the world, and since perfection of religious and moral ideals rests solely with one's own self-perfection, 'in the Buddhist religion there is no room for prayer, in the sense of a petition or solicitation addressed to a god'. The Buddha carefully guarded against the use of prayer (*mantra*) addressed to a god for the purpose of securing a certain benefit through his special favour. However as Buddhism later developed, particularly in the Mahāyāna form, prayer became important. The novice took solemn vows (*pranidhāna*) to one of the manifestations of Buddha to commit himself to the search for enlightenment. These vows were believed to be answered by the Buddha with an assurance (*vyākarana*) that ultimately his efforts would succeed: 'this ... *vyākarana* is the necessary counterpart of the vow' (*ibid.*: 167). Anesaki considers that 'many of these vows were in reality prayers, addressed to the Buddha, as well as to the universal truths revealed by him' (*ibid.*: 166). This pattern of vow and assurance clearly fits the model of a dialogue between believer and superior being. In one account of Buddha's early training his own prayer is rendered as:

> Indeed let it be so, that I could be born as one who,
> having overcome the world,
> would work in the world for the benefit
> of the world and should live for the weal
> of this world ... [etc.]

Dīpaṅkara reassures him:

> Thou shalt at a certain future time become a Buddha,
>   being born as a son to the Sakya clan, and work
>   for the benefit of men and gods.
>   (*Mahāvastu* i:3; *ibid.*: 167.)

In Mahayana Buddhism all Buddhists are considered to be earnestly seeking enlightenment, and thus to be *bodhisattvas*. 'Thus every prayer addressed to Buddha is at the same time a vow ... vows are taken by a Buddhist, and assurance given by a Buddha.' One of the most frequently recited prayers is a verse from the *Lotus of Truth*:

> Let these merits (now performed) universally pervade all,
> And let us, together with them, soon realise the life of
> Buddhahood.
> (*Lotus of the True Law (Saddharmapuṇḍarīka)*; *ibid.*: 168.)

The most extreme realization of prayer in Mahāyāna Buddhism may be seen in the transformation of the *Lotus of Truth* into a schematic visual representation which itself became the object of prayer for the followers of Nichiren (AD 1222–82).

Prayer is of central importance in Thai Tharavada Buddhism, both in the life of the monasteries, and for the community. In his detailed study of the Tharavada practice in northeast Thailand, Tambiah found that through their withdrawal from secular life and their attempt to realize the mastery of those things which chain them to earthly existence, the Buddhist monks are believed to have great sacred power. They use this to recite the words of the scriptures to do religious 'work' on behalf of the villagers – to bury the dead, ensure the round of the seasons, and create merit for future rebirth. The compact with the villagers is 'We will feed you, but you must pray for us'. The monks' prayers are on each occasion formally 'invited' by the lay leader of the village congregation, and after monks receive food, there is a formal response; that is, there is a dialogue form between the congregation and monks' prayers, as well as between the monks and Buddha (Tambiah 1970: 133–4).

Prayer and meditation

But in Buddhism it is meditation, not prayer, that is central to practice and theology. The difference between the two would seem to be that between 'contemplation of religious ideas' and 'addressing a superior being, usually through speech'. In meditation the focus is on emptying the mind of all but the chosen thought in its most abstract sense. There is no Other, and no dialogue. Anesaki (writing well before the medical use of tranquillizers) says that meditation is intended to tranquillize the mind:

That disciple should concentrate (*paṇidahitabbam*) his mind on a certain thing (*attha*) as the condition of tranquilizing; when the mind is concentrated upon that tranquilizing condition, cheer arises and from cheer, joy arises.

(*Samyutta* xvii (10); Anesaki 1980 [1918]: 166.)

This 'tranquillizing function' of meditation is important in the relationship between prayer and anticipatory interactive planning, discussed below. But despite the theological interdiction on prayer, at the everyday level Buddhism has often 're-invented' prayer – presumably because the functions it fulfils for the individual are important ones.

Animism: an early false belief, or a basic paradigm?

Writing in 1871, Tylor (1958) proposed the term *animism* for the 'deep lying doctrine of spiritual beings' which he saw as the minimum definition of religion, and which he attributed to the transformation of images of the dead in dreams. Marett's *animatism*, 'a thing, situation, or state of affairs that is enlivened or animated, but not in any individual, soul-like manner' partly corresponds to notions of the Navajo kind (1909). Using a Darwinian evolutionary model, these writers considered primitive religion to be an early stage, later superseded by more 'developed' religions until the last 'high' form of monotheism was finally attained. But theologians as recent as Martin Buber (1970) have seen that even in this 'final' stage we seek to have 'I–Thou' relations with inanimate objects in nature. And Elaine Scarry (personal communication) finds that even in twentieth-century litigation there is a tendency to treat objects – for instance a ship – as morally guilty. Sophisticated western humans still tend to attribute intentional actions to things with which we are interdependent. We are no more ready to leave all to chance than earlier peoples.

Conclusions

Let me return to the suggestion that there are two processes involved in the emergence of prayer as a religious form, first in individual social cognition, and then in the socio-cultural construction of accounts of the world.

It has been argued that *Homo sapiens*' use of spoken language fundamentally altered the modelling of actions through anticipatory interactive planning. If this has resulted in the dialogue template as a constant feature of individual social cognition, then we would expect to find it expressed in all human societies; prayer may be such an expression. But as human societies vary hugely in their social structures and cultural forms, so we would expect to find they have constructed different cultural *accounts*, different stories, to explain to themselves this universally human experience of seeking assistance in crisis by 'speaking' to a powerful Other. We can, and should, ask under what conditions different sorts of accounts tend to appear. But in looking for the factors leading to particular kinds of accounts we need not assume any particular evolutionary sequence, only that certain forms of society in their historical contexts tend to form certain kinds of representations of non-human powers.

Here it is useful to recall the Buddhist emphasis on meditation as a way of achieving tranquillity of mind through the focusing of attention. For Buddhists this may serve as an experiential model of the desired state of 'nothingness' in which the individual merges for ever with the universe. In terms of a human capacity for modelling problem solutions as contingent responses to others' actions, deep meditation on 'the absolute' may finally succeed in eliminating the Other. While a central tenet of Buddhist thought holds that all external experience is ultimately meaningless, it is also insisted that this cannot be truly understood intellectually, but is realized through mental exercises such as meditation. In our own terms the mental modelling of AIP strategies is a necessary *prerequisite to action*. Once represented mentally, these strategies must be negotiated with the social Others they represent. But in meditation, mental modelling is directed not to action, but to its absence. The goal ceases to be effective management of relations with others, and the significance, indeed the validity, of interdependence with others is denied. For a species in which thought entails plans for contingent action, this is a profound change. Perhaps the peace which rewards truly effective meditation comes from disengaging from the constant challenge of social intelligence.

Prayer, on the other hand, can be seen as an attempt to negotiate goals with powerful beings in the Other slot. If this *is* part of what is happening in prayer, then it suggests that the model of individual cognitive processes as fundamentally social can help to account for this very pervasive dynamic in individual behaviour, a dynamic so powerful that it has shaped, and in the case of Buddhism, reshaped, the major world religions.

Acknowledgements

This paper was written while the author was a Fellow at the Wissenschaftskolleg zu Berlin in 1989–90. Without freedom from teaching through the generous Fellowship it would not have been possible to consider, even in this partial way, the vast amount of material on this subject.

Notes

1 Johnson-Laird and his colleagues studied mental models where even university students find difficulty with abstract syllogisms although they can solve exactly comparable problems phrased in terms of actual people and situations (Johnson-Laird and Wason 1977b; Johnson-Laird 1983). Elaine Scarry comments that there have been legal cases in which a ship is treated as though it had acted intentionally like a person (personal communication).
2 It is unlikely that Lienhardt could have read Austin at the time this study was written. Had he done so the appropriateness of Austin's idea of performative force for Dinka prayers would surely have struck him.
3 The full title of Kant's book is *Religion Within the Limits of Reason Alone*'!
4 The psychoanalytic view would insist that the conscience with which we wrestle in prayer is an internalization of morality based on our parents' authority. If indeed we are conducting a perpetual dialogue as though still children with all-powerful parents, this is perhaps closest to the Ashanti continuing dialogue with ancestors.
5 The several monotheistic religions lay different stress on guilt and sin. And of course individuals vary greatly in their concern with both. But anxious concern with the sincerity of feelings and intentions towards a deity would seem to be associated with monotheism.

STEPHEN C. LEVINSON

11   Interactional biases in human thinking

The human mind is something of an embarassment to certain disciplines, notably economics, decision theory and others that have found the model of the rational consumer to be a powerful one.   (Schelling 1988: 353.)

Background

This chapter sets out to weave an improbable web through such topics as animism, common tendencies in the purchase of soap powder, extra-terrestrial lifeforms, the phrase 'the whatdoyoucallit', and the theory of communication. The thread, if it doesn't break, is the theme of a systematic bias in human thinking, in the direction of interactive thinking (E. Goody's *anticipatory interactive planning* or AIP). Because the argument is somewhat indirect, let me state the thesis right here in the beginning in semi-syllogistic form:

1.   Communication is *logically* impossible
2.   Nevertheless we humans can communicate
3.   Therefore, we must use *non-logical* heuristics and a special form of reasoning to bridge the gap
4.   For communication to work routinely, these heuristics must be dominant in our thinking all the time
5.   Therefore, these heuristics spill over to bias our thinking in non-communication domains.

   As in the famous conclusion to Wittgenstein's *Tractatus*, where we are advised not to think that which cannot be thought, so there is a certain paradox in thinking about biases in human thinking. (You can climb outside human thought, Wittgenstein hinted, just so long as you throw the ladder away and climb quickly back in.) We can only do so with real confidence, perhaps, where we can discern an indubitably correct way of thinking, guaranteed by the laws of mathematics or logic, from which human thinking tends to deviate. One such area is human judgement about uncertain events, and it is here that there has grown, largely

through the efforts of Tversky and Kahneman, a rich literature on biases
in human thinking. I am a complete novice in this field, but I can't help
considering that it might offer rich pickings for those who discern an
underlying human preoccupation with social interaction as the evolutionary source of human intelligence. This then is an entirely exploratory
foray out of the theory of communication into a neighbouring field. I am
not optimistic that it will be well received in that neighbouring field, but
interdisciplinary activity has always been a risky enterprise.

I   Interactional intelligence, coordination and communication

Interactional intelligence[1]

In an engaging book (*Frames of Mind*, 1985), Howard Gardner argued
forcefully for the diversity of kinds of human intelligence, using a range of
evidence from psychological theory, neurology, case studies of cultural,
personal hyperachievements, so-called 'idiot savants', and so on.
Amongst the specialized, compartmentalized intelligences, he listed
linguistic, musical, logico-mathematical, spatial, kinaesthetic and
personal intelligences. Within the latter, he includes what I would choose
to isolate as *interactional intelligence*, and he lists as evidence for such a
specialized skill the special role of the frontal lobes of the human brain.
Persons with frontal lobe damage of various kinds exhibit different but
related inabilities: 'No longer does the individual express his earlier sense
of purpose, motivation, goals, and desire for contact with others; the
individual's reaction to others has been profoundly altered, and his own
sense of self seems to have been suspended' (1985: 262). Conversely,
patients with massive brain damage to other areas who retain fully
functional frontal lobes – like Luria's 'man with the shattered world' –
retain the capacity to plan actions and to relate to others to a surprising
degree. Similarly, one can point to autistic (and perhaps schizophrenic)
patients, who often show signs of unimpaired reasoning ability, but who
cannot relate to others; and conversely to reasoning-impaired individuals
(like those with Down's syndrome or Alzheimer's) who seem to retain
great interpersonal skills.

Making due allowance for the lay misuse of neurological and patholo-
gical data, there is here the same kind of range of suggestive evidence for a
specific interactional intelligence as there is for other specialized human
skills. One should add to this further evidence from the cross-cultural
study of interaction: although still in its infancy, and still largely unpublished, such work would seem to establish that there are striking universals in interactional organization, facts compatible with a theory of the
biological basis for interactional skills. Studies with infants strongly

suggest such an innate basis under rapid maturation: newborn infants are subtly adaptive to the caretaker's presence and handling, and by two months the child already displays 'a rich repertoire of expressive behaviours ... combined with ready orientation of the gaze to or away from the mother's face and immediate response to her signs of interest and her talking' (Trevarthen 1979b: 541). That biological basis for interactive skills is further attested to by a wide range of facts about human perception, for example our hearing is acute precisely in the range of wavelengths where speech is broadcast (rather than being specialized like, say, the owl's auditory system, to the noises of prey).[2] Similarly, there is considerable evidence for a specifically human neurological specialization for face recognition, implying the fundamental importance of human face-to-face interaction in human phylogeny.[3] And of course all the physiological, neurological and ontogenetic foundations for language point in the same direction.

The theory of multiple intelligences should not, though, be equated with the modular theory of mind à la Fodor (1983); the latter is a particular theory about how specific specialized skills or 'modules' fit together with general thought processes to form a computational whole. The Fodorean requirements for modularity seem altogether too strong to be correct even for linguistic ability taken as a whole (although they plausibly hold for specialist subsystems, like segment recognition), because language understanding necessarily involves general thought processes. In the same way, interactional intelligence (for reasons that will become clear) would have to involve central processing and could not therefore be remotely 'modular' in the Fodorean sense. Nevertheless the skills that jointly make up interactional intelligence seem to be connected intimately enough to make up a package of abilities that can suffer simultaneous neurological impairment.

In this chapter, I shall assume that there is such a form of intellect as an interactional intelligence, and my central concern is whether we can detect a systematic bias in human thinking in other domains which might be attributed to the centrality of interactional intelligence in our intellectual makeup. In order to explore this bias (if such it is), we will need to have some characterization of the central properties of interactional intelligence, which I will attempt to provide.[4]

Anecdotal evidence in favour of an interactional bias in human thinking

Those who would like to replace *Homo ludens*, *Homo hierarchicus* and other such creatures and caricatures with *Homo interactans* (not a possible Latin formation unfortunately,[5] but much more plausible) can find much anecdotal evidence for such a chap. One of the things that struck Victorian observers (like Fraser and Levy-Bruhl) of 'primitive' peoples was that their world is apparently pervaded by mystic forces in para-human form. Natural causes are mere means subtly utilized by witches, sorcerers, spirits, gods and demons. It is as if the perceptible natural world were a stage set, manipulated by supernatural agents always in interaction with man. Although later ethnographic research (as with Evans-Pritchard's (1937) classic work on Azande witchcraft) has shown us how systems of witchcraft and sorcery have an irrefutable internal reason, make sense in a world imbued with the primacy of social relationships, and so on, it has not thereby made the central problem of such intellectual genera disappear – namely, why we as a species seem predisposed to such intellectual systems, even when they are not socially reinforced or are contrary to our own ideas about real knowledge (as with the astrological systems of early modern astronomers like Tycho Brahe or even Newton[6]). That natural science and magical systems have not only coexisted but often mutually reinforced one another is now a commonplace of the history of science (see, e.g., Lloyd 1979). Scientists often operate (like Watson and Crick) as if nature were a book to be read, a message to be decoded, a syntax to be parsed, a mode of thought that harmlessly enough might be held to presuppose a writer, a coder, a puzzle-setter rigging things behind the perceptible veil.

If scientists are sometimes covert magicians and animists, so of course are children. Piaget (1929) found that children imbue some inanimate objects with intentions, feelings and knowledge, and although later work by Trevarthen and others has shown that very young infants distinguish interactional partners from other kinds of objects for purposes of communication, yet there seems to be a residual blurring of the distinction in the belief world of the child (Gelman and Spelke 1981: 56). One is reminded too of Vygotsky's views about 'inner speech', and indeed the role that an imaginary interlocutor plays in adult thinking.[7]

Other areas where animistic and interactional thinking abound are not hard to find. Consider for example Kahneman and Tversky's finding that experimental subjects treat random processes as if the processes themselves are acting to achieve their own randomness: 'Idioms such as "errors cancel themselves out" reflect the image of an active self-correcting process. Some familiar processes in nature obey such laws ... The laws of chance, in contrast, do not work that way' (Kahneman et al. 1982: 24). Economists are often puzzled by the odd purchasing behaviour of consumers – why do they often just buy the most expensive soap-powder? My strategy is to buy the cheapest; my wife's to buy the most expensive. I operate with a vision of some mean, cheating fellow filling different cartons all with the same rotten stuff; she operates with the vision of the old-fashioned but always reliable and trustworthy owner of the corner-store, whose goods are always more expensive but worth it. The moral is that it's hard to dehumanize even soap-powder. In 1959 astronomical observers started picking up patterned radio signals from outer space. Someone had the idea that extraterrestrial intelligence was trying to contact us: suddenly the signals were being scrutinized in a quite different way, no longer as 'natural signs' of distant physical events, but as 'signals' coded in such a way that any intelligent receiver should be able to decode them.

Presuming an interactor in the inanimate world is one kind of striking conceptual 'error' in human thought; another, less obvious, is the tendency to think of social agglomerations as human actors: we talk happily of what Russia intends in the Baltic, how it will react to NATO, or respond to Islamic fundamentalism. Diplomatic protocol is based on the same principles as interactional politeness (Brown and Levinson 1987); game theory is applied equally to the moves of military or economic conglomerates as to the moves of individual players of parlour games; historians talk in terms of the will of nations. In fact, of course, human agglomerations are propelled through history largely by forces beyond their control: the Russian dismantling of the Iron Curtain may have been no more intentional than an earthquake. Such animistic thinking can have pernicious consequences: we may detect threats where none exists, interpret delayed responses as reluctant or hesitant in character, and find strategic intentions attributed to our non-intentional collective 'actions'.

And so on. There is room enough in the natural history of human belief systems for much speculation about a bias towards the assumption of a world constructed out of human interaction with human and super-human agents. But we seek for some less Victorian level of speculation.

Properties of an interactional intelligence

Human interaction is clearly characterized by an inordinate concern with the implications that an actor's actions have for other actors' expectations, emotions, self-esteem, social status – in short it takes place within a highly structured and often restrictive set of social relationships which permeate the most intricate details of interactional patterning. Nevertheless I want to abstract away from that social matrix, to ask about the underlying *conceptual abilities* that make social interaction possible.[8]

The properties exhibited by human interactants are (from an ethological perspective at least) extraordinary in a number of ways – exactitude of timing, complexity of response, layeredness of meaning, and so on.[9] It is obvious enough that interactional capacity relies on a number of core abilities: the ability to make models of the other, to 'read' the intentions behind actions, to make rapid interactional moves in an ongoing sequence of actions structured at many levels. But what I think perhaps has not been appreciated is the *computational complexity*, indeed *intractability*, of some of these processes, which is what I want to highlight here.

The computational feat is well illustrated by the ability of humans to defy the laws of chance: to coordinate mutual actions even when unable to communicate with one another.

Schelling, in the *Strategy of Conflict*, reports on some informal experiments that showed that, roughly nine times out of ten, subjects can coordinate plans without communication (1960: 54ff.). Subjects were given a joint goal, but then had to independently work out which means the others would use to solve it, and to choose just that same means. The kinds of problems solved were (a) to think of the same number, the higher the number the higher the reward; or (b) go somewhere determinate in a city to which the other party will also go simply by knowing that each is trying to select the same location and the same time for a meeting (*ibid.*). Subjects coordinated on the number one million, or on the information booth in Grand Central Station. As Schelling remarked, 'the chances [of a successful coordinated solution] are ever so much better than the bare logic of abstract random possibilities would suggest' (p. 57). The joint goal can require different actions from each party, as when during a telephone conversation the line is cut, and each party must independently but jointly decide who will put the receiver down to enable a reconnection. How coordination is achieved so reliably against such overwhelming odds remains I think a mystery; but both Schelling and later commentators have pointed out that it must have something to do with (a) the provision by the situation of a unique determinate clue, around which coordination can be achieved; and (b) some powerful property of the reflexive reasoning that inevitably comes into play: each must do what the other thinks that the other is likely to do. The two factors together, mutual salience and mutual computation of mutual salience, seem to be sufficient to turn a mere lottery into a near certainty.

Schelling (and later commentators like Schiffer 1972) was keen to point out that the computational problem posed by coordination is really very different from the formal properties exhibited by agonistic interaction, as explored in the mathematical theory of games (Luce and Raiffa 1957). In a zero-sum game (game of pure conflict), you can lay out the action–reaction sequences 'in extensive form' as a game tree or directed graph and calculate the relative utilities in advance of play. In contrast, in a cooperative game of pure coordination, each option of each player yields zero payoff unless it is matched by the coordinating option of the other player.[10] Both win if and only if each does what the other expects each to do; otherwise, both lose. In a zero-sum game, one's own preferences are clear in advance; in a coordination game, it doesn't much matter which action is taken as long as it matches the other's expectation. Zero-sum games can be reduced to relatively simple mathematics; but nobody knows if a mathematics for coordination games could even be formulated. Thus, calculating optimal behaviour in agonistic interaction is a far simpler computational problem than calculating coordination: strictly speaking, *Machiavellian intelligence* is child's play, a lower-order computational ability; *Humeian intelligence* (coordination through implicit contract) is the adult stuff.[11]

Curiously, though more than thirty years have elapsed since Schelling's work, there has been little empirical exploration of this striking kind of human ability to coordinate action through apparent 'mind-reading'. About the same time that Schelling was exploring these problems, Grice (1957) was devising his theory of (so-called) meaning, which is in fact a theory of communication which relies on intention-attribution. Although the theory has been around for thirty years, was subjected to thorough philosophical scrutiny twenty years ago, and continues to play an important role in theoretical work on communication, its relevance to empirical work has not generally been appreciated: it has appeared too complex, too intentional, too armchair philosophical to form a theoretical base for practical work. Recently, though, there has been a swing towards exploring its practical consequences in subjects as diverse as ethology (see, e.g., suggestions in Dennett 1988) and artificial intelligence (Perrault 1987; Cohen *et al.* 1990), not to mention linguistic pragmatics (Levinson 1983; Sperber and Wilson 1986) and the psychology of language (Clark 1992). But above all, it has stood the test of time, and remains a theory without a systematic rival of any consequence (see Avramides 1989 for recent commentary). The central idea is that communication is achieved when a recipient recognizes the special kind of intention with which a communicative act is produced. In one of many formulations it runs as follows:

Grice's theory of 'meaning':

> S means p by x if:
> S utters x
> (a) intending to get H to think p
> (b) intending H to recognize (a)
> (c) intending (b) to be the reason for (a).

The point of the theory is that a communicative action is distinguished by its associated complex intention, which specifies that the 'signal' is a chunk of behaviour emitted solely (or at least largely) with the intention of having its background intention recognized. (In contrast, many of our behaviours have an instrumental intentional background, where intention-recognition plays no part, as when I reach out to grasp a glass of water.)

Grice's theory of communication needs to be placed in the context of a general 'intentionalism', the view that any kind of interaction involves an attribution of meaning or intention to the other; it is discerning a chunk of behaviour as an action, that is, as a bundle of linked intention and behaviour, that is the prerequisite to response. The response in turn relies on the other's ability to read the intention or meaning from the behaviour. Of course there is usually a variety of ancillary information available to aid and abet this intention-attribution – preeminent sources being perhaps social roles which act to stereotype intentions (as E. Goody (1978a and this volume) suggests) and sequential patterns in interaction (see below). But producing behaviour in such a way that its intentional background is perspicuous requires a model of the other's ability to so recognize a behaviour 'x' as an expression of intention 'p'. Thus we enter the peculiar mirror world of reflexive intentions, now happily occupied by philosophers, computational logicians, theoretical psychologists and others. What distinguishes a Gricean reflexive intention from other kinds of complex reflexive intention is that the communicator's goal or intention is achieved simply by being perceived: recognition exhausts or realizes the intention.

There have been various attempts to marry Schelling's observations with Grice's, mainly with the aim of giving a philosophical account of how linguistic conventions may arise (and thus provocatively raising the possibility of reducing the concept of meaning entirely to psychological concepts (see, e.g., D. Lewis 1969; Schiffer 1972; Avramides 1989)). But there is a more direct and interesting application of Schelling's ideas to Grice's (Levinson 1985). For the obvious problem raised by Grice's theory is: how on earth are communicative intentions recognized? The traditional answer is: by means of a linguistic code (see Ziff 1971 on Grice). But this turns out to be no explanation even for linguistic communication, as is explained in the next section, and certainly not for non-conventional, non-linguistic communication. The fact of the matter is that we can communicate with 'nonce' signals (Clark 1992: ch. 10). An alternative answer suggested by Schelling's problems is that we can choose a behavioural token that is mutually computable as having been issued with a specific communicative intention, using the same techniques that allow us to coordinate on a unique solution to one of his coordination problems.

Assuming temporarily that some such picture is correct, let us take stock of the computational consequences so far. We are already in deep water:

1. Propositional attitudes

Obviously, computations about other's intentions presuppose computations over propositions embedded under propositional attitudes. As is well known, these are 'opaque contexts', contexts where Leibniz's law of the substitution of referring terms *salva veritate*, fails: we cannot assume from the assertion that *Esther believes the Chancellor of Cambridge University should be sacked* that she also believes that the Duke of Edinburgh should be sacked (she may think him competent, believe his title to be inalienable and certainly not realize he's the Chancellor). This well-known little conundrum is of course just the logical consequence of computations over other people's belief worlds (see, e.g., Fauconnier 1985), but it obviously raises difficult computational problems. There are a number of persistent logical paradoxes, like the Cretan Liar, which also plausibly have their roots here.[12]

2. Mutual belief and infinite regress

As mentioned, the Schelling problems seem to require that A and B, in order to coordinate, come to believe that some salient action is *mutually believed* to be the coordination point. But the notion of mutual belief seems to offer infinite regress: A must believe that B believes that A believes ... *ad infinitum* ... that p. This has attracted much attention, with philosophers (D. Lewis 1969; Schiffer 1972; Harman 1974; Avramides 1989), psychologists (Clark and Marshall 1981; Clark and Carlson 1982) and artificial intelligence (AI) workers (see, e.g., Allen 1983: 149) competing with different accounts each purporting to show how the regression can be circumvented. Nevertheless the threat of infinite regress has not endeared the idea of mutual knowledge to those interested in plausible models of psychological process. But the point of the Schelling experiments is that they demonstrate that people can indeed handle just this kind of reflexive reasoning.

3. Gricean reflexive intentions and infinite regress

As was early pointed out by Strawson, Grice's analysis alone might prove insufficient: one can produce counter-examples which satisfy the conditions but which intuitively are not cases of communication. These are cases where there is some higher intention of communicator S, not available to recipient H, and there is thus a discrepancy between the intention H is meant to discern and that which S actually has. This then threatens an infinite regress of conditions, with S intending that H should recognize that S intends that H should recognize ... and so on.

Various proposals have been made to overcome this potential infinite regress. One is to ensure that all intentions are out in the open, as it were, if the behaviour is to count as genuinely communicative – Schiffer proposing for example that there be a condition of *mutual knowledge* that S has uttered x with all the necessary intentions. But the notion of mutual knowledge must itself be cashed out as an infinite regress of the form 'S knows that H knows that S knows . . .', as we've just seen. Other solutions involve self-reflexive intentions (Harman 1974; see discussion in Avramides 1989: 58–9), or default inference rules relating *communicating p* to *believing that p* (Perrault 1988: 13).[13]

4. *Mutual salience*

We need not only a notion of salience, but a notion of 'natural salience', such that I can be sure, for an indefinite range of phenomena or scenarios, that what is salient for me is salient for you. This turns out to be crucial in ways I shall make clear (see also Schiffer 1972; for a variant suggestion see Sperber and Wilson 1986).

5. *Logic of action*

Clearly we need to compute the intentions that lie behind behaviours, if any kind of coordination is going to be achieved. That would seem to presuppose an understanding of the derivation of action from intention in our own planning and acting: one has to choose the means that will most effectively achieve the desired ends, while balancing incommensurable goals. As Aristotle argued, the logic of action is a distinct species of non-monotonic (defeasible) reasoning, a *practical reasoning* (PR) as it has been dubbed by philosophers. Von Wright (1971), Ross, Casteneda, Rescher and others have explored such systems, but there is still much to recommend the outlines of an Aristotelian system provided by Kenny (1966), which was developed into a formal system by Atlas and Levinson (1973) which we may call 'Kenny Logic' (see introduction in Brown and Levinson 1978: 69–70, 92–6). Kenny Logic has many interesting properties, like the fact that the deductive fallacy of 'affirming the consequent' is valid in this system, or the fact that if 'p' deductively implies 'q', then if an agent desires 'q' he'll desire 'p' (i.e., the logic of practical reasoning looks like 'backwards' logical implication, a fact that shows up in AI planning programs like Allen's – see the 'nested planning rule' in Allen (1983: 124)). But the relevant properties here are that Kenny Logic inferences are both *ampliative* and *defeasible*. They are ampliative because one may reason from a goal to a means that is more specific than is required to achieve the goal ('I'm thirsty and would rather not be so; here's a Coke; if I drink this Coke, I won't be thirsty; ergo I'll drink this Coke.'). They are defeasible because any valid inference from goal G1 to the desirability of action A1 will be abandoned if there is a conflicting goal G2 ('Coke is bad for my diet.'), from which the desirability of the negation of A1 can be derived. Such a logic of action must also explain how goals can be ranked, and means of achieving them differentially weighted, in such a way that the action performed may depend on the 'cost' of the means of achieving it.[14]

A logic of action is going to be a complex thing. However, all this turns out to be the least of the computational problems. Despite all the philosophical, logical and artificial intelligence work that lies behind all these ideas, there as been a fatal neglect of one problem. The Schelling-cum-Grice model of coordination and communication relies on *the recognition of intentions*: that is, the need to compute not only from intention to action (as in a logic of action or planning) but also in reverse as it were, from behaviour to the intention that lies behind it. It may seem that if we already have an account, in terms of a logic of practical reasoning, linking utterances or other actions with the goals that lie behind them, then all we now need to do is run the reasoning backwards, from the utterances or actions to the goals. Even logicians who should know a lot better talk as if intention-recognition is merely a matter of practical inference 'turned upside down' (as Von Wright (1971: 96) puts it in an uncharacteristic moment of incautiousness).

However, there is an overwhelming problem in equating understanding with 'upside down' practical inference, namely the very great difference between an actor-based account of actions (in terms of plans, goals and intentions) and an interpreter-based account (in terms of heuristics of various kinds). For the nature of logical inference in general, and practical reasoning in particular, is that *there can be no determinate way of inferring premises from conclusions*. Inferences are asymmetrical things. If I conclude from 'p and q' that 'p', you cannot, given the conclusion alone, know whether the premise was 'p and q', 'p and r', 'p and r and s', or 'q and (q p)', etc.: there are literally an infinite number of premises that would yield the appropriate conclusion. Simple though the point is, it establishes a fundamental asymmetry between actor-based accounts and interpreter-based accounts, between acting and understanding others' actions. There simply cannot be any computational solution to this problem, as so far described. The problem is intractable![15] Because the point is important let me put it in a more concrete way. Suppose I see you raise your arm outstretched in front of you: your doing this might be compatible, let us say, given the environmental possibilities, with the following intentions – waving off a fly, reaching for a glass, greeting an acquaintance, stretching, etc.[16] Even this set of descriptions is to 'cook the books': instead of 'reaching for a glass' why not go down a stage in specificity to 'extending an arm' or upwards to 'having a drink'? What we take to be a natural level of action description is anything but given (as philosophers from Anscombe to Davidson have been keen to point out). But then how do we decide what the hell you are doing, and what we should do in response (raise our hands too, do 'civil inattention', or

whatever is appropriate), all in the twinkling of an eye (say, 100 milliseconds)?[17] Going 'backwards' from the behaviour to the intention, at
some appropriate level of specificity, is an absolute inferential miracle.[18]

Language, communication and interactional intelligence

It is easy to imagine that the main role of language in the evolution of
interactional intelligence is as an independent channel of information
about others' plans and desires, which then makes coordinated interaction possible. That threatens to miss the point – *language didn't make
interactional intelligence possible, it is interactional intelligence that made
language possible as a means of communication.*[19]

Non-linguists may require a word of explanation. The model we used
to have, both lay and expert (from Saussure to Shannon and Weaver), of
the way that language works in communication goes something like this:
we have a thought, we encode it in an expression, emit the encoded signal,
the recipient decodes it at the other end, and thus recovers the identical
thought. A moment's reflection will reveal that this picture is absurd.
Consider the 'thing-a-me-jigg' phenomenon:

> A: Where the hell's the whatdjacallit?
> B: Behind the desk.

Just as in a crossword puzzle, the filled blank, *the whatdjacallit*,
advertises itself to the recipient as a puzzle the recipient can solve. This
works. In fact it works all the time – we don't say exactly what we mean.
We don't have to and anyway we couldn't. For example, consider the
relation *at* in

> 'The car is at the door.'

> 'The man is at the door.'

> 'He's at his desk/at University/at work/at lunch/at the telephone.'

There is no unified concept '*at*', except in some highly abstract way: we
figure out the relation by thinking about the objects related and their
stereotypical dispositions. Everything is amplified and specified through
a complex mode of interactional reasoning.

The consequences of this kind of observation are rather far-reaching.
Linguistic competence is not *sui generis* (at least not *this* part of it); it is not
'encapsulated' in Fodor's (1983) sense of a specialized, closed-off, module
of mental processing. Semantic representations, or at least interpreted
semantic representations, can't be the 'language of thought' – we think
specifically, we talk generally.[20] I can't say what I mean in some absolute
sense: I have to take into account what you will think I mean by it. One
can't *encode* a proposition; all one can do is sketch the outlines, hoping the

recipient will know how to turn the sketch into something more precise (if something more precise was intended). The slow realization of all this (Atlas 1989; Clark 1992; Levinson, in press; Sperber and Wilson 1986) portends a sea-change in the theory of language: linguistic mechanisms are deeply interpenetrated by interactive thinking.[21]

But if we can't say what we mean, how do we understand one another? When I say 'The coffee is in the cup', I don't have the same kind of IN-ness in mind as when I say 'The pencil is in the cup'. And when I said 'The coffee is in the cup', how come you didn't wonder: 'Does he mean the cup is full of beans, or granulated coffee, or the liquid stuff essential to academic life?' Nor for one moment, upon hearing 'The pencil is in the cup', are you likely to think of granulated pencils. Nor are you likely to worry that the pencil is more than half out of the cup, although on just those grounds we might expect a quarrel about the truth of 'The arrow is in the bull's eye'.

It is trying to understand mutual comprehension, given the paucity and generality of coded linguistic content that now preoccupies theoretical linguistic pragmatics (cf. Atlas 1989; Horn 1989; Sperber and Wilson 1986; Levinson 1989). We have made some progress in the last twenty years or so, by identifying heuristics that guide the reasoning process. I believe that the two cardinal achievements have been to identify two rather different kinds of heuristics. The one kind is a set of heuristics based on utterance-type, that is to say that the 'way of putting things' suggests a specific direction of interpretation. The other kind is provided by the intricate sequential expectations that are triggered by utterance and response in conversation.

To take these briefly in turn, the first kind of heuristic, which has been developed from seminal ideas of Paul Grice, in turn has a number of sub-types. These play off each other. For example, there seems to be an utterance-type heuristic that runs: 'normal expression indicates stereo-typical relation'.[22] Consider expressions of the form X is at Y: when we say 'There's a man at the door', we have in mind a relation of proximity such that the man can reach the door-bell, say, and is facing it in expectation. But when we say 'Your taxi is at the door' it may be twenty feet away and its front not oriented to the front of the door. If your taxi was to nose its way in, the non-stereotypical event would warrant a non-normal description; while if the man waited twenty feet in front of the door, we might prefer another description, say, 'The man is standing some distance in front of the door'. That seems to be based on another heuristic: 'abnormal relation warrants abnormal/marked description'. The two heuristics together explain why 'It's possible to climb that mountain' and 'It's not impossible to climb that mountain' don't mean the same thing. A third heuristic runs: 'If an informationally richer description applies, use it'. It's this that is responsible for the inference from 'Some of the Fellows of the College are lazy' to 'Not all of the Fellows of the College are lazy' – if you meant the stronger statement ('All of them are lazy') you should have used it.

In what follows I shall rely heavily on the importance of the inference to the stereotype. It's this that is responsible for such inferences as: 'The pencil is in the cup', suggesting 'The standard-type pencil (as opposed to, e.g., a propelling pencil or one with red lead) is projecting out of, but is supported by, the inside walls of the cup'. As we saw, we come to rather different conclusions from, 'The coffee is in the cup' (liquid rather than beans, fully within rather than projecting, etc.), or from, 'The key is in the lock' (projecting horizontally, not vertically). Some linguists will protest that these inferences are not pragmatic in nature but rather attributable to so-called *prototype semantics*. This I believe to be a rampant conceptual error, but regardless of that, it really makes little gross difference to the dimensions of the inferential problem: the particular relation intended by *in* for example still has to be inferred by reference to the things related.

The combination of these preferred interpretations of utterance-types can yield far-reaching enrichments of coded information. From 'Some of the nurses are not incompetent', one may infer that all the nurses are female (inference to stereotype), that not all of them are competent (informative strength), and that the remainder do not fully deserve the attribution of competence (marked description – the use of double negation). Or from 'If you wash the dishes, I'll give you 10 Deutsch marks' one may infer that if you don't, I won't (inference similar to inference to stereotype), that in any case I won't give you more than 10 DM (informational strength), etc. But I refer the reader to Horn (1989), Levinson (1983: ch. 3, 1987a, b) and Atlas (1989) for details. The point to grasp here is that *without* such inferential enrichments, what we say would tend towards the vacuous: not only do we talk generally, tautologically and elliptically (as in 'I'll be there in a while', 'If you manage, you manage', 'Could you please . . .?'), but also, as illustrated with the example of the relation *at*, even when we try to be precise we necessarily trade on suppositions our interlocutors must make.

The second kind of inferential enrichment that seems to me critical in language understanding is based upon the fact that, in the conversational mode that is the prototypical form of all languages use, speakers alternate, handing over to another party for response at the end of relatively short turns at speaking. And there's an expectation that responses are generally tied in close ways to what has gone before. As Sacks and Schegloff pointed out twenty years ago,[23] this makes it likely that if B responds to A in such a way that it is clear that B misconstrued what A said, there's a good opportunity provided in the third turn for A to correct, clarify or elaborate. Thus recipients can be nudged along into what at least passes for understanding.

Take for example the following:

1. *From Terasaki (1976: 45)*

> M: ... Do you know who's going to that meeting?
> K: Who?
> M: I don't know!
> K: o::h prob'ly Mr Murphy and Dad said prob'ly Mrs Timpte ...

Here M asks a question of K; but K responds with a question ('Who?'). It is clear that K takes M's first utterance to be a prelude to an announcement, as in the canonical example that follows:

2. *From Terasaki (1976: 53)*

> D: Y'wanna know <u>who</u> I got stoned with a few w(hh)weeks ago?
> R: Who.
> D: Mary Carter and her boy(hh) frie(hhh)nd.

There are systematic reasons why M's utterance in example 1 might be heard as the same kind of prelude or 'pre-announcement' as D's first utterance in example 2. But in any case, K got it wrong: M's utterance was not an offer to tell, conditional on K's not knowing the facts, but just a question as made clear in M's second, corrective, turn.

The power of such a system of feedback is well illustrated by the game of twenty questions: it's generally possible in just twenty question–answer pairs to guess what the other is secretly thinking of despite the fact that it might be anything under the sun.[24] In addition to such general corrective potentialities, we should add a large number of very detailed expectations about how particular sequences may run (like: question followed by answer, request followed by compliance followed by thanks, and so on). For a two-turn sequence A–B (like question–answer or offer–acceptance), each turn usually has rather restrictive specifications on form and content: the first turn because otherwise it will fail to be recognized as kicking off such a sequence, and the second because the first has been designed specifically to elicit it.

These sequential clues and constraints help to explain the rather astounding guesses that can be found in recorded conversations. In example 2 above, we saw an example of a sequential pattern that runs:[25]

> A: Pre-announcement (request, offer, etc.)
>   ((a turn that pre-figures what will come in third turn, conditional
>   on B's signal to proceed))

B: Go-ahead
A: Announcement (request, offer, etc.)
B: Appreciation (acceptance, declination, etc.)

Mutual orientation to such patterns then helps to explain how a recipient can guess not only that something else is coming up, but that what will come is of a particular sort:

3.   *Tape 170*

E: Hello I was wondering whether you were intending to go to
     Swanson's talk this afternoon
M: Not today I'm afraid I can't really make this one
E: Oh okay
M: You wanted someone to record it didn't you heh
E: Yeah heheh
M: Heheh no I'm sorry about that . . .

4.   *From Terasaki (1976: 29)*

D: I-I-I- had something terrible t' tell you
     so uh
          [
R: How terrible is it?
D: Uh, th- as worse it could be
     (0.8)
R: W- y'mean Edna?
D: Uh yah
R: Whad she do, die?
D: Mm:mh

5.   *From Terasaki (1976: 28)*

D: Didju hear the terrible news?
R: No. What?
D: Y'know your Grandpa Bill's brother Dan?
R: He died?
D: Yeah

Less dramatically, but more importantly and perennially, these sequential constraints help to explain how the often near-vacuous nature of what is actually 'coded' in conversation can carry so much meaning. In the following extract, for example, co-members of a band are haggling about how much they ought to practise together, and something as vacuous as 'Yeah I know but I mean' can serve to suggest that R's excuses for avoiding the next session really are not good enough:

6. *Tape 'Vicar' 144*

> C: Yeah but I mean we'll be working all night
> (1.0)
> R: Uh [hh (I see)
> C: er (   )(.) quite late
> Well I mean it'- it's up to you I suppose
> [
> R: yeah
> R: But I mean I've got the exam tomorrow so I can't
> [
> C: I mean I've
> C: Yeah I know but I mean
> (1.5)
> R: Yeah alright yes =
> C: = You understand what I mean
> R: Yeah, do you want me to bring my guitar or not =
> C: = Yeah

The limiting case is provided by the absence of speech altogether, which can alone be sufficient to engender detailed inferences, as in the following example where the speaker takes the absence of response to signify a clear negative answer:

7. *Tape: 'Oscillomink'*

> C: So: u::m (0.2) I was wondering would you be in your office (0.63)
> on Monday (0.42)
> by any cha:nce?
> (1.86)
> probably not

This example illustrates another important feature of conversational organization, namely that it has very precise temporal characteristics. Here, C has produced a pre-request in the form of a question, and here, as generally in English conversation, a pause of over half a second after such a question may be taken to indicate that the desired response cannot be easily produced. Due to such temporal characteristics, quite minute pauses can be most symbolic.

How does all this work? In the case of the utterance-type heuristics, it only works because speaker and recipient(s) agree that, other things being equal, there is a normal way to say things. That being so, a normal description can be taken to implicate that all the normal conditions apply, in all their empirical specificity: if I say 'John drove off, but he'd forgotten to loosen the hand brake', you envision a motor car and all the mechanical consequences that such a failure of action would entail in such a mechanism. You know that I know that you will so imagine; you can therefore take me to be intending that you so imagine; and I can rely on you so imagining. You would be amazed if it later transpired that John drove off in a coach and four, or even a tractor! The same goes for the conversational sequences: you know that I know that you know that I expect an answer to my question within, say, 500 milliseconds; when you don't provide it, you know that I know that you have a problem – say, the desired answer can't be produced. Knowing that, I know from your silence that the answer is 'no', also of course that you are reluctant to give it, as you know that I know you should be ...

These examples, informally sketched, will suffice, I hope, to indicate the peculiar inferential richness that can be extracted by the combination of reflexive intentional reasoning and a handful of detailed mutual expectations. Conversational inferences have a number of very special properties: they are speedy, they are non-monotonic (the same premises can give different conclusions in different contexts), they are ampliative (you get more information out than went in) and they are subjectively *determinate*. The last point is important: when John says 'I'd like some water' we don't come away with a feeling that there's a 65 per cent probability that he had a glass of drinking water in mind, and a 35 per cent chance he was praying for rain; we come to a definite conclusion, which may of course turn out to be wrong (but then he'll tell us).[26]

In all this, conversational inferences are different from logical or monotonic inferences on the one hand, and inductive ones on the other. Inferring what is meant in conversation is much more like solving a slot in a crossword puzzle: such inferences have the rather special property of having been *designed* to be solved and the clues have been designed to be just sufficient to yield such a determinate solution. We might dub this central feature of language understanding the *whatdoyoucallit* property of language, in honour of the magical efficacy of that phrase.

Let me sum up these remarks about language so far. Linguistic communication is fundamentally parasitic on the kind of reasoning about others' intentions that Schelling and Grice have drawn attention to: no-one says what they mean, and indeed they couldn't – the specificity and detail of ordinary communicated contents lies beyond the capabilities of the linguistic channel: speech is a much too slow and semantically undifferentiated medium to fill that role alone. But the study of linguistic pragmatics reveals that there are detailed ways in which such specific content can be suggested – by relying on some simple heuristics about the 'normal way of putting things' on the one hand, and the feedback potential and sequential constraints of conversational exchange on the other. The astounding speed of conversational inference is something that should also be noted; these are inferences clearly made well before responses can be composed, yet responses are, at least a third of the time, separated by less than 200 milliseconds, and on-line testing shows pragmatic inferences already well under way immediately after the relevant word or expression.[27]

Conclusion to section I

We are now in a position to try and unravel the mystery. Recollect we concluded that the computational problem posed by Gricean communication or Schelling games looks simply intractable, largely because a system of inference from intention to behaviour tells us nothing about how to compute the reverse inference from behaviour to intent. And yet we routinely manage these things. The pragmatic heuristics may give us the clue to a solution. The inference to communicative intention from overt behaviour is so constrained by these heuristics or expectations that it is possible to select a unique path from within the interminable possible teleological explanations for the behaviour.

For example, if you know that I know that you know that, for principled and general reasons, a pause after a question seeking a 'yes'-answer will suggest a reluctance to provide it, then you know that your pause will lead me to think that you intended that I think that the answer is 'no'. Both knowing this, we both know that if you don't do something to correct the impression, then I'll feel sure that you wanted me so to think. Thus even the absence of a behaviour may be sufficient to yield the determinate attribution of an intention.

Or, you say: 'Put some bread and butter on the plates'. What do you intend? The stereotypical dispositions of course – not, for instance, a well-buttered plate, or bread on half the plates and butter on the other half. Even if there are only two plates, you're likely (in England anyway) to end up with buttered bread, not a plate of bread and a plate of butter. I don't need to ask you what you intended; I know that you know that we'll both be oriented to the heuristic authorizing inferences to the stereotype; so both you and I know that if you want something other than the usual, you'll have to make warning noises. You haven't; so the probability that what you wanted was buttered bread is now, for all current purposes, a dead certainty.[28]

How might this generalize from linguistic interaction to other forms of social interaction? In all cases, intention-attribution will be crucial, and the actual chunk of behaviour will be insufficient evidence alone for the attribution of an intent. We can carry out mental simulations: I can ask myself 'What would I be intending in these circumstance were I not me but him?' But that won't necessarily help me decide whether the outstretched arm is a greeting or a reach for the drink or the beginning of a swipe at a fly; there are too many possibilities, too unconstrained a mental life in the other. What we need, just like the linguistic cases, is some basis for default presumptions – it really doesn't matter whether these are wrong or right, arbitrary or well motivated, etc., because once the expectations are in place you will know that I will know that you will think that I will use them to attribute an intention to your action, and then you can go about encouraging or discouraging that presumption (by modulating the behavioural manifestation).

It is in this context that Esther Goody's suggestion that social roles may play a special role in interactional coordination is, I think, important (see also Schelling 1960: 92). The point is made rather well by an artificial intelligence program designed by Allen (1983), one of the first to draw attention to the need for intention-attribution in the design of intelligent responses. The problem was to program an artificial railway-station information clerk. People might come to 'him' with questions like 'When does the train to Windsor leave?' or just 'The train to Windsor?' He ought to answer '11.15 at platform 5': that is, he ought to reconstruct the intentions behind the often elliptical question, e.g. that the traveller intends to find the train to catch, and then provide all the information relevant to that goal. How did Allen solve our intractable intention-attribution problem? Just by presuming that clients would come to the clerk presuming that his role was to answer travel questions, and they'd come with just two of their own goals in mind – catching a train or meeting one. Thus, by guessing the goals in advance, the program could simulate the plan-generation that might have led the client to say what he did, see if he could find an intention chain that culminated in that observable output, and then assume the client had those nested goals which the simulation used to arrive at the output (the client's question). In short, a presumption of the rights and duties of each party to the transaction made it possible to run the practical reasoning forwards, instead of in the impossible direction, backwards.

In the same sort of way, social roles may play a crucial role in ascribing intentions to our co-interactants. Often they won't have the intentions so ascribed – but that doesn't matter: by setting up the expectational background, interactants will know equally that they will have to do something rather special to escape it.

It is tempting, and not altogether implausible, to go the whole hog: what else is Culture, one might ask, other than a set of heuristics for intention-attribution? That clearly encompasses language usage, social roles (as just argued), and a host of heuristics for the interpretation of mundane and artistic productions. And why else do we feel so at sea in an alien culture? We may understand the coded content of verbal interaction and fail to understand the import, observe behaviour but fail to comprehend its wellsprings, see mumbo-jumbo where we know there must be sense, and so on. Any facile definition of 'Culture' with a capital C deserves, no doubt, a certain modicum of derision, but I can think of definitions deserving louder hoots.

To sum up: human interaction, and thus communication, depends on intention-ascription. Achieving this is a computational miracle: inference must be made way beyond the available data. It is an *abductive* process of hypothesis formation, yet it appears subjectively as fast and certain – the inferences seem determinate, though we are happy to revise them when forced to do so. The extraordinary thing is that it seems, for all practical purposes, to work most of the time.

The question is: how? The best answer that we seem to be able to give at the moment is to take the Schelling games as model: there is an extraordinary shift in our thinking when we start to act intending that our actions should be coordinated with – then we have to design our actions so that they are self-evidently perspicuous. The crucial ingredients are (1) computations over reflexive intentions and mutual beliefs, and (2) the ability to settle on identical heuristics, mutually shared, which will yield default presumptions of intent. Without the heuristics, such coordination would not be possible: we have to agree in advance, as it were, what the salient features of the situation are, what any 'reasonable man' would think such a behaviour betokened, what one would 'normally' mean by saying 'He's at the door', and so on.

This kind of thinking turns mere probabilities into near certainties. Example: I try to guess your social security number (chances near to zero). I try to guess the seven-figure number that you have secretly chosen in the hope that I can guess it (chances over 0.9).[29] We can beat the odds. Otherwise humans couldn't coordinate in interaction. But it only works because we think there is a determinate solution, which we only have to find, like in a crossword puzzle.

That is the peculiar kind of thinking intrinsic to interactional intelligence. If interactional intelligence was the root of human intelligence in general, which is the idea we are exploring, then we would expect to find 'spill-over' effects in other task domains. For example, when thinking about (non-human) 'nature', we might expect to find 'nature' treated as a crossword puzzle, designed (by super-human agency perhaps) to be decoded and understood. And when humans come to think about chance, they should fail rather miserably to come to grips with the absence of non-deterministic solutions, with the fact that apparent patterns are in fact random assemblages, that a chance exemplar is not custom-made to be an exemplar, that a sample could be unrepresentative, etc. It seems that there is in fact rather a lot of evidence from cognitive psychology in that direction, which I now review.

II   Biases in human thinking: psychological studies

'Judgement under uncertainty': Tversky and Kahneman

Tversky and Kahneman (1977; Kahneman *et al.* 1982) conducted a series of now classic experiments on judgement under uncertainty – in effect intuitive responses to probabilistic problems. They found that despite the overwhelming everyday evidence to support basic principles of probability, people tend to follow other principles that yield incorrect conclusions. For example, everyday reasoning seems to ignore (or only partially take into account) the following basic statistical principles: (1) the prior probability of outcomes, (2) the confidence attached to large samples, (3) the potential independence of properties, (4) the possible chance occurrence of an expected outcome, (5) regression towards the mean, and so on.

More concretely, the following examples may give a clearer idea of the kind of errors systematically repeated:

1. Neglect of prior probability

If subjects are told, e.g., that X is meek, shy and very tidy, they'll guess X to be a librarian rather than a farmer even when told that there are twenty times as many farmers as librarians.

2. Neglect of sample size

If subjects are asked what is the better evidence that an urn contains $\frac{2}{3}$ red balls and $\frac{1}{3}$ white balls: (a) a sample of 4 red and 1 white or (b) a sample of 12 red and 8 white, they favour the smaller sample with the stronger proportion (even though the odds are half as good).

3. Gambler's fallacy

Given a sequence of 'heads-heads-heads-heads' even professional gamblers often presume a 'tails' must now be almost certain (the 'gambler's fallacy' (Tversky and Kahneman 1977: 330)).

4. Neglect of regression towards the mean

Trainers of airplane pilots come repeatedly to the conclusion that punishing bad landings has a much more powerful effect than rewarding good ones – failing to take into account that by natural regression the chances are that a really good landing will be followed by a worse one, and a terrible one by a better one (Tversky and Kahneman 1977: 332;

Kahneman *et al.* 1982: 67–8). It seems not to have been noted by sociologists that this simple failure of statistical reasoning might be responsible for the vast asymmetry in the size of our penal codes compared to our system of honours!

Kahneman and Tversky attribute the majority of these 'mistakes' to a systematic bias to 'representativeness', i.e., 'a representative sample is one in which the essential characteristics of the parent population are represented not only globally in the entire sample, but also locally in each of its parts' (Kahneman *et al.* 1982: 36). This mistaken assumption of a representative sample explains the neglect of sample size in everyday reasoning: a small hospital's obstetrics ward is felt to reflect the sex ratio of newborns just as accurately as a large one. It also explains the ignoring of base-rate probabilities: if asked what is the probability of Mr X being a librarian, when X has all the stereotypical properties of librarians, then the fact that X is a typical representative candidate overwhelms thoughts about the rarity of librarians in the population at large.

Representativeness seems also to offer an explanation for the consistent and rather astounding tendency for people to ignore the most basic law of probability, Bayesian conjunction, whereby the probability of a joint event of greater specificity cannot be more than the probability of one of them alone. Thus the probability of John being both an accountant and a jazz player cannot be more than the probability of John being a jazz player – but subjects told that John is a compulsive person with mathematical skills and no interest in the humanities, feel the conjunction is more probable (which at least includes the representative profession) than the single attribute of being a jazz player (which alone seems unrepresentative (*ibid.*: 92ff., 496)). Representatives may also explain the gambler's fallacy: the feeling that having lost three times in a row, one is bound to win next time – the feeling being based on the expectation that a short run of dice should exhibit the same randomness of pattern found in a much longer run.

In short, single facts or small samples overdetermine conclusions because they are not considered in the larger picture of likely distribution. Instead, the subject's focus is on typicality, even though typicality and probability can obviously part company dramatically (e.g., an adult male weight of 157.85lb is highly typical, but less likely than a rough untypical weight of around 135lb (*ibid.*: 89)). These mistakes are intriguing because, not only do they fool the statistically naive, but also (sometimes only in less transparent examples) dedicated statisticians. It seems therefore that 'the bias cannot be unlearned', 'since related biases, such as the gambler's fallacy, survive considerable contradictory evidence' (*ibid.*: 30).

Kahneman and Tversky detect other, partially related biases. For example, there is a tendency to presume *causal relations*, and to find it easier to infer effects from causes than causes from effects (*ibid.*: 118). There is also a strong bias to what the authors call *availability* (Tversky and Kahneman 1977: 333ff.), i.e., to salience or ease of recall, so that if it is easy to think of instances, then the event type may be thought to be frequent. For example, people overestimate the number of words beginning with R over the number with R in third place, because it is relatively much easier to retrieve words beginning with a letter than having such a letter in third position (Kahneman *et al.* 1982: 166). And quickly made associations are often presumed to be accurate correlations, despite evidence to the contrary: if recurrent correlation is one source of mental association, it is nevertheless of course illegitimate to assume that all associations are based on correlations (Tversky and Kahneman 1977: 335). Availability is thus a matter of *focus*; people overestimate the importance of what is in focus and underestimate what is out of focus: preoccupied with winning the lottery or with the thought of an aircrash, they overestimate the probabilities of both. One aspect of this directly relevant to agonistic interaction is the tendency to underestimate the opponent (Kahneman *et al.* 1982: 177).

Kahneman and Tversky conclude: 'In his evaluation of evidence, man is apparently not a conservative Bayesian: he is not Bayesian at all' (*ibid.*: 46). If this is correct, one must wonder why; after all, we live in a world dominated by chance events. It is self-evident that in the period in which our genetic makeup was laid down the dependence on chance, uncertain events, from the success of the hunt or harvest to the health of the chief or leader, must have been much greater than in the cybernetically controlled western world of today. How could we afford mental biases in such non-adaptive directions?

Kahneman and Tversky themselves offer no speculations, but they do offer us some tantalizing clues as to how their observations might tie into the biases or tendencies that are prerequisites for human communication – the overdeterministic mode of thought typical of, and necessary for, interactional coordination. They too notice the 'illusion of validity', 'the unwarranted confidence' which 'persists even when the judge is aware of the factors that limit the accuracy of his predictions' (Tversky and Kahneman 1977: 331). One such connecting clue is the obvious relation between their notion of representativeness and the notion of prototypicality (Kahneman *et al.* 1982: 86–9), as that latter notion has been explored in linguistic categorization. A representative individual would indeed be a prototypical one, and thus a special case of a representative sample, which should represent in microcosm the population as a whole, and thus also mirror its variability.

If the reliance on representativeness leads to systematic errors, why do people use this relation as a basis for prediction and judgement? ... Modern research on categorization (Mervis and Rosch 1981; Rosch 1978) suggests that conceptual knowledge is often organized and processed in terms of prototypes or representative examples. Consequently we find it easier to evaluate the representativeness of an instance to a class than to assess its conditional probability. (Kahneman *et al.* 1982: 89.)

Our earlier suggestion, recollect, was that prototypicality or stereotypicality plays an essential role in communication and action coordination by providing a salient coordination point to which parties to interaction can each be sure the other will attend. Hence I can assume that you will understand what 'The pencil is IN the cup' would stereotypically suggest – if it lies in the bottom in broken pieces, I'd better tell you so. Likewise, if you move aside at the door, deference may be presumed as the motive rather than, say, fear. Stereotypicality provides the heuristic for a solution to the intention-attribution problem: each can assume that the other will use this heuristic and will therefore act accordingly, thus giving a deterministic solution to an otherwise impossible problem.

Other clues for connecting Kahneman and Tversky's observations to interactional intelligence may be found in their remarks about intuitive patterns of randomness, salience ('availability'), causality, sequentiality and so on. First, people find it unintuitive that short highly patterned sequences could be random. For example (where H = heads, T = tails), that HHH could be random, let alone HTHTHT or HHHTTT is counter-intuitive (Kahneman *et al.* 1982: 37). For even randomness is expected to be 'representative', i.e., exhibited over short stretches as an unpatterned sequence, for which one could write, for example, no little generative grammar. The corollary is: we see design in randomness, think we can detect signals from outer space in stellar X-rays, suspect some doodles on archaeological artefacts to constitute an undiscovered code, detect hidden structures in Amazonian myths. If we are attuned to think that way, then that is perhaps further evidence for the biases of interactional intelligence: in the interactional arena, we must take all behaviour to be specifically designed to reveal its intentional source. Second, people seem to favour higher probabilities where a causal or teleological connection can be posited, which is as might be expected from an interest in the wellsprings of action (*ibid.*: ch. 8); and they attribute quasi-intentionality to random processes when they act as if such processes were self-correcting (*ibid.*: 24). Further, they believe that they can somehow exercise control over chance, as we can over our fellows, as when they prefer a lottery ticket they have selected over one given out (*ibid.*: 236). Third, salience or mental 'availability', which Kahneman and Tversky construe as a separate bias, plays a special role in the solution to Schelling games and communicational coordination: when we manage to meet again in a foreign city after getting accidentally separated, we do so by each thinking where the other will go, mutually deciding that a particular location (e.g., the café we were last together in) will be to each of us the most salient meeting place. Finally, when we find significance in the pattern of coin tosses THTH or think that after TTT we must have an H, we exhibit a sheer preoccupation with sequential pattern, where sequential patterning was one of the essential heuristics that we listed as making communication possible.

Consider again our treatment of communication as a 'crossword puzzle': there are multiple constraints on the 'slot' in which a communicative action is fitted, and the communicative act itself is only a clue to its proper interpretation. But it is a determinative clue: once you have it, you have it – you don't generally have it to 65 per cent certainty or the like; for it's taken to have been designed to yield a single, determinate interpretation. It's also taken to have sequential implications of a determinative sort – other communicative acts should now be opened up. The kind of thinking required in communication is a mental search for a salient – for example, stereotypical – interpretation, the psychological prominence of which is the best guarantee that this interpretation is indeed the mutually intended one. All the biases that Kahneman and Tversky list:

1. determinism, overconfidence, representativeness;
2. prototypicality;
3. sequentiality;
4. the ascription of teleology (e.g., in the belief in self-correcting random sequences),

would seem to be relatable to a communicational mode of thought – on this hypothesis they would be the side-effects of an interactional intelligence.

Of course one radical possibility is that Kahneman and Tversky's results are entirely a byproduct of the communicational context in which the experiments were carried out. Instead of focusing on the tasks as real-world problems, perhaps the subjects see the experimental tasks as communicative crossword puzzles: the experimenter has given clues as to what he wants – the subject must guess the desired outcome which has been designed to be guessed, like a problem in the classroom. Recently Kahneman and Tversky (postscript to Kahneman et al. 1982: 502) themselves have come to see that Gricean implicatures may play a role in their results through biasing the experimental description. However, they continue to underestimate that possibility severely. For example, they fail to note (ibid.: 497–8) that the famous Wason four card problem[30] is entirely explained by what linguists call 'conditional perfection', the Gricean conversational implicature from 'If' to 'If and only if'.[31]

8. Wason four card problem

Instruction: Given the rule 'If a card has a vowel on one side, it has an even number on the other', which of the following cards should you turn over to test whether it is correct: A, B, 4, 7?
Correct Answer: A and 7. (Since the rules states 'If it's an A, it's even', or symbolically: 'A = even' which implies by *modus tollens* 'not-even = not-A'.)
Predominant answers: A and 4.
Gricean explanation: 'A = even' implicates 'A = even', thus 'even = A' (i.e. saying 'If it's an A it's even' implicates 'If and only if it's an A, it's even', from which it follows 'If it's even it's an A'.)

Similarly, there may be implicatural reasons for the failure to operate the Bayesian conjunction rule (that the probability of A and B cannot exceed either the probability of A or the probability of B). Consider the following task:

9. Written background detail (Kahneman et al. 1982: 496)

Linda is 31, single, outspoken and very bright. She majored in Philosophy. As a student, she was deeply concerned with issues of discrimination and social justice, and also participated in anti-nuclear demonstrations.
Instruction: Which is more likely:

    A: Linda is a bank teller;
    B: Linda is a bank teller who is active in the feminist movement?

Correct answer: A
Predominant answers: B
The Gricean explanation here would rely on the presumption of a cooperative experimenter, who has produced (just as is always expected in conversation) only the relevant facts in the background description. But if judgement A is correct, then the facts must be irrelevant; since *ex hypothesi* the facts *are* relevant, A cannot be correct, so the only given alternative (B) must be right.

However, in addition to neglecting the possibility of a Gricean explanation of their alleged biases in thinking, Kahneman and Tversky have also failed to note the formal similarity between the basis of Gricean implicatures and some of their biases – those that we have noted under the rubrics of salience (availability), prototypicality, representativeness, etc. There are thus two possibilities: the entire Kahneman and Tversky research programme is vitiated by the failure to consider the biases introduced by Gricean heuristics due to the verbal nature of the task-setting, or there is a real non-communicative bias in thinking, but one which mimics Gricean patterns because communicative heuristics inhabit, as it were, the deeper reaches of our minds. Given the breadth of experimental data, and the fact that at least some of the findings do not allow Gricean explanations directly, the second possibility seems the more likely interpretation of the facts.

Dörner's planning and decision-making with complex systems

Kahneman and Tversky's tasks are presented verbally, thus opening them up to a critique in terms of communicative bias rather than cognitive bias. They also perhaps suffer from a parlour-game quality that may introduce Schelling's game coordination reasoning irrelevant to the design of the tasks. But there are other lines of psychological research that tend in the same direction. We turn now to just one further example.

Dörner (1990) has been exploring how subjects try to cope with complex, dynamic systems, often with hidden interconnected variables, delayed responses, patterns not available on short-term inspection, etc. Such systems, he argues, form an important part of the human decision-making environment, with good examples being agricultural and ecological systems, politico-economic systems, industrial plants, and so on.

The kind of problems posed by Dörner's simulations seem typical both of complex natural systems (like ecologies, predator–prey relationships) and complex artificial systems (like economies, polities, armies, industrial plant and other cybernetic machines). Yet our failures to understand quite simple indirect causations can have quite dramatic consequences (as with the Chernobyl accident, where increasing the flow of cooling water indirectly caused the removal of graphite moderators (Reason 1987)). Just as Kahneman and Tversky's results show a failure to understand the most elementary aspects of our largely random world, it is again rather striking that humans seem ill-adapted to coping with such complex systems, the manipulation of which might have been expected to have co-evolved with human intelligence. Surely, one might argue, a hunting-gathering prehistory might have led us to have intellectual mastery over predator–prey and other ecological systems, whereas in fact, of course, our understanding here has proved lamentable. Indeed, we carry one prototypical complex system permanently around with ourselves, namely our bodies, and yet it is notable how little we naively understand the complex system in which we are thus imprisoned – for example, how is it possible that the relation between sepsis and lack of cleanliness had to await discovery in nineteenth-century Europe?[32]

In Dörner's paradigm of research, unlike the Kahneman and Tversky one, there is often no mathematical or other precise way to measure optimal behaviour – in even a simple ecological system the variables are too many and their interaction too complex. Instead, one can measure the relative success or failure of individuals against the performance of their peers, in computer simulations of the relevant domains.

What Dörner has found is that when performance is bad, this is attributable to a number of recurrent 'errors', for example:

1. Failure to cope with delayed responses or long-term time series: e.g., failure to regulate a thermostat with a time-delayed, damped oscillation pattern (1990: 20). Subjects had a great tendency to react to the immediate state of the system, without taking into account underlying trends.

2. There was a tendency to interdigitate action and analysis, instead of doing prolonged analysis first.

3. There was a tendency to not look back and check the current consequences of past actions or guide them further.

4. While subjects often focus too hard on a salient problem, thus neglecting parallel problems and side-effects of the focal problem, they nevertheless jump from problem to problem, often without seeing the problem through to the end.

5. As subjects fail to control a complex system, they often take increasingly ill-adaptive measures – they seek for continued confirmation of failing hypotheses, become entrenched in their thinking and less observant of changes in the system.

Dörner attributes many of these 'failures' to a relatively small number of mental tendencies (1990). First, there are apparently irrational[33] or emotive factors, which he believes can be attributed largely to the desire to 'guard one's feeling of competence', especially by avoiding retrospective examinations of failures. Hence one finds, especially as the loss of control over a system builds up, a failure to check consequences of past actions, a 'dogmatic entrenchment' of failed hypotheses, a fleeting attention paid to one problem after another – a kind of mental 'panic' accompanied by behavioural rigidity, all a kind of escape behaviour, as subjects avoid facing up to the facts of loss of control of the system.

A second major source of failure he ascribes to sheer overburdening of mental processing. Hence subjects tend to seek single central explanations, or to judge a single variable to be the one determinative factor ('central reduction' (1987: 21)); and they fail to pursue consolidated prior information gathering.

A third factor may be the sheer inability to perceive patterns distributed over time because of *forgetting*; hence the failure to perceive time series, exponential growth patterns, etc.[34] A final factor Dörner isolates is overemphasis on the current problem, with consequent neglect of side-effects and long-term effects, which he attributes to an attentional mechanism.

Dörner's explanations of the human failure to come to terms with complex systems can be pushed one stage further by asking why the 'errors' of thinking that he detects should be there in the first place. By innuendo, like Kahneman and Tversky, these mental failings are held up as natural deficiencies, as it were, for which no explanation is required. Thus 'human beings are "creatures of space" not "creatures of time"' and hence they fail to 'see' time-series or exponential growth patterns (1987: 22). The overall explanation is given in terms of a mixture of processing deficiencies and irrational self-deception.

Instead, accepting Dörner's analysis for a moment, one might try to find an explanation of the failings in our hypothesized interactional intelligence. One of his factors, the protection of one's feelings of competence, is easy enough to relate to interactional concerns. Self-esteem is not generally won or lost by encounters with 'nature', but rather by encounters with the fellow members of our species. We care about admitting mistakes to ourselves because we care about admitting them to others.[35] Thus if the 'irrational' factors involved in poor performance in struggles with complex systems can be rightly attributed to this preservation of the self from its failures, then these would seem to be deeply tied into factors at the heart of social interaction (although not the ones we focused on in section 1).

The other key factors, the processing deficiencies, have certain striking similarities with the Kahneman and Tversky findings. Kahneman and Tversky's 'representativeness' carries with it a tendency to ignore the larger distributional pattern, and to focus on local patterns as if they were truly representative of the larger picture. Dörner's findings about restricted information-collection, restricted planning and the entrenchment of old hypotheses closely echo the Kahneman and Tversky findings, including that same insistent confidence in transparently erroneous inferences. For example, Dörner has found subjects to become totally preoccupied with the most salient problem, just as Kahneman and Tversky found naive thinking about uncertainty to be partially determined by 'availability' – i.e., salience, recoverability and focus. The same remarks about a possible source for such a focus in interactional intelligence carry over to Dörner's work: intention-recovery relies on coordination on a solution to the interactional 'crossword puzzle' – there must be a mutual focus on a single interpretation, and so the interactant must be forever seeking the single, determinative key to the intention-recovery problem. To this we can therefore assimilate also the tendency to seek just one single all-explaining factor, the critical variable on which the whole complex system is thought to hang. Interaction requires single-solution thinking; complex systems require multiple-solution thinking – but humans are only good at the former.

Recollect that we suggested that there are two critical kinds of heuristics that make intention-recovery possible. One is the kind that yields a default interpretation for an action – the kind exemplified in verbal interaction by heuristics that legitimize the assumption of stereotypical attributes, and so on. The other is the kind based on sequential information. This latter kind shows up in the Kahneman and Tversky material as a presumption of the highly structured nature of any short sequence – thus accounting for the gambler's error, and the converse effect of the refusal to consider a patterned sequence as possibly random. Interaction sequences display certain clear properties:

1. The last action in an action chain is usually the focus of response (but not always, e.g. after an embedded 'insertion sequence').
2. Human interaction sequences which form canonical linear structures are usually rather short – for example a pre-sequence of four turns is relatively long (as in A: 'Doing anything tonight?', B: 'No, why?', A: 'How about having a meal together?', B: 'Great idea'.).
3. Interaction sequences are generally single-stranded – that is, one doesn't run two or more equally prominent chains of interaction simultaneously (there are of course exceptions, as with stockbrokers simultaneously dealing on phone and floor, etc.).
4. Interaction chains are characterized by rapid turn-taking, with short (average 400 millisecond) intervals between them.[36]

In Dörner's material one can find perhaps echoes of each of these expectations. The echo of property (1) is the tendency to focus on just the matter in hand, while being prepared to rapidly switch to other concerns. Echoes of property (2) would be the failure to discern much longer time series – the action–reaction style of human interaction ill prepares us for a complex system that reacts suddenly and catastrophically after a long time delay (as when an environment suddenly degrades, or when our bodies react to an earlier ingestion or infection). It also ill prepares us for reactions with relatively small time delays, but just sufficient to be beyond the normal action–reaction time span, as the subjects found in their unsuccessful attempts to control a simple time-delayed thermostat.[37] Echoes of property (3) (single-stranded interaction chains) are Dörner's observations about the single-strandedness of thinking, the preoccupation with only one causal chain at a time. Echoes of property (4) can perhaps be found not only in the temporal properties of the human attention span, but also in the tendency, for example, to collect minimal information, then act, collect, act and so on, hoping to learn from interdigitated action–reaction rather than exhaustive prior analysis. Given the possibilities of interactional feedback, that is the right way to operate in the interactional domain.

Dörner's work, unlike Kahneman and Tversky's, is concerned with human abilities to cope with dynamic systems as they react over time – it thus serves to bring out some of the possible biases in temporal thinking that are not illuminated by the Kahneman and Tversky paradigm. It provides therefore a different kind of ammunition for the protagonists of the primacy of interactional intelligence. Those protagonists would be in trouble if Dörner's findings had indicated that people are good, say, at dealing with time-delayed reactions; or find long-term oscillations easy to discern; or can easily cope with multiple strands of sequential events. But Dörner's findings are all comfortably in the right direction – towards the conclusion that humans are good at dealing with single-stranded teleological or causal chains, with immediate action–reaction expectations which require immediate attention or allow only a small 'push-down stack', four or five 'plates' deep.

Kahneman and Tversky's results are vulnerable to the charge that all the observed biases are introduced by the linguistic communication that sets the task for subjects. Dörner's non-verbal tasks where the subject wrestles with a computer simulation escape that charge. However, they are arguably vulnerable to a parallel charge in just the area of most interest, the temporal characteristics of human behaviour: perhaps in setting up the computer simulations we have unwittingly introduced properties of human–human interaction into the design of human–computer interaction. For example, a keyboard or other input device will typically control only one variable at a time, nor are commands normally set to act at remote time intervals or at fixed delays to govern future states. To introduce such a system of relations between human and machine would be 'un-natural' – the very structure of the machines and programs we make for humans to interact with reflects (often to the rather lowly limitations of the engineer's imagination) the temporal properties that we, as humans, find it comfortable to work with. Thus the very set of biases we seek to illuminate in an objective way by setting subjects tasks that have intrinsically good solutions, may in fact have been built into the structure of the tasks themselves.

Conclusions

I have argued that intersubjectivity requires peculiar computational properties, which may then bias many aspects of human thinking. On the one hand, one finds the presumption of deterministic solutions, what one may call the 'crossword puzzle effect' (problems are treated as if they were *designed* to be solved): hence the presumption that patterns can't be random, exemplars are prototypical, samples are 'representative' and conclusions can be certain. On the other hand, one finds some evidence that attention and memory are geared to interaction tempo: humans presume single-stranded causal chains, respond (usually) to the immediately previous event, expect brief action-response intervals and very short sequential patterns.

The first group of biases can be plausibly related to the necessity of having mutual orientation to the kind of heuristics we discussed as essential to language-understanding, e.g., the kind that gives us the strong readings of a preposition like *at*, according to the *relata*. The second group of biases, of attention and memory, may be related to the sequential heuristics for the attribution of intent in interaction – when talking, we are mutually oriented to the potential for immediate correction, and to canonical sequences of certain kinds.

Without such an explanation, the kind of biases noted by Kahneman and Tversky on the one hand, and Dörner on the other, would be puzzling indeed from an evolutionary perspective. The ability to make objective estimates of probability would offer immediate adaptive advantage, e.g., to a hunter faced with a decision to go after one kind of game or another.[38] Likewise the ability to comprehend complex systems, whether natural (like our own bodies, or the ecologies we live in) or socio-political, ought to offer significant adaptive advantages. It seems reasonable to suppose that, instead, there must be some greater adaptive advantage to thinking in the ways we actually do, and my suggestion is that these biases are essential ingredients for intersubjective reasoning. The corollary would be that the main evolutionary pressures on our species have been intra-specific. That accords with at least the views collected in Byrne and Whiten (1988), who have urged us to substitute a 'Lord of the Flies' scenario for a 'Robinson Crusoe' scenario for human adaptation. To that view, the speculations in this chapter add, hopefully, a corrective: it is cooperative, mutual intersubjectivity that is the computationally complex task that we seem especially adapted to. Machiavellian intelligence merely exploits this underlying Humeian intelligence that makes intersubjectivity possible. One needs too to stress that it is this cooperative intersubjective background that makes language interpretation possible (as shown by the need for all those heuristics) – not, as non-semanticists may assume, language which makes intersubjectivity possible (although it obviously vastly increases its scope).

In this chapter, I have stressed two pervading characteristics of human thought – attribution of intentionality and overdeterminism – which may be directly related to interactional intelligence. For without that overdeterminism, we would never have the heuristics that make it possible to ascribe intentions to human behaviour. As Peirce and many more recent writers have been keen to emphasize, deduction and induction are relatively trivial human skills, of no great computational complexity; it is abduction or theory construction which is the outstanding characteristic of human intelligence.[39] Abduction is the leap of faith from data to the theory that explains it, just like the leap of imagination from observed behaviour to others' intentions. While most explicit human theories or abductions are wrong, our implicit ones about interactional others are mostly good enough for current purposes. Both, though, come with that striking element of overconfidence, overdeterminism (even when we know, as in the case of scientific theories, that the half-life of the theory is only a year or two). Which allows me to end on a paradox: were we to feel any confidence that the roots of abductive ability (and it's peculiar phenomenology of certainty) lay indeed in interactional intelligence, and thus any confidence at all in the thesis of this chapter, then we could ascribe that feeling entirely to the overdeterminism of interactional intelligence itself.

Acknowledgements

This chapter owes much to Esther Goody, who provided the stimulus to crystallize these thoughts. My second important debt is to London Transport, since some of the ideas here transcribed arose out of a long conversation with Dietrich Dörner while perforce walking the streets of London to and from meetings of the Royal Society during the transport strike, June 1989 (see Dörner 1990). Other ideas in this paper were first tried out at a meeting of the British Psychological Association (Levinson 1985), and I thank various commentators there, especially David Good, L. Jonathan Cohen and Phil Johnson-Laird. I have had helpful comments on this chapter from Penny Brown, Dietrich Dörner, Esther Goody, and Alex Wearing, for which I am most grateful. Much further back, Esther Goody (1978a) first pointed out to me (and us anthropologists generally I suspect) the relevance of the study of social interaction for theories about the evolution of human intelligence.

Notes

1 I see the notion of *interactional intelligence* contrasting in specifity with other related notions. *Social intelligence* (or *social cognition*), as used for example in Flavell and Ross (1981), is an altogether broader conception, including the apprehension of morality, dominance, friendship and appropriate social role and affect. The *Machiavellian intelligence* of Byrne and Whiten (1988) is also wider, encompassing social knowledge, problem-solving in a world of flexible and fickle social relations, and so on (pp. 50ff.). By *interactional intelligence*, I have in mind just and only the core ability to attribute intention to other

agent's actions, communicative or otherwise, and to respond appropriately in interdigitated sequences of actions; and I want to emphasize particularly the computational intractability of intention-attribution. I take this ability to be the bedrock feature of all the other, wider concepts, as recognized clearly in Esther Goody's term *anticipatory interactive planning* (AIP), which differs from my notion, I think, only in breadth and emphasis. All of these modified uses of the term *intelligence*, Alex Wearing points out to me, refer to a faculty or ability, and not the inherently comparative notion that the unadorned noun refers to.

2 For the prey orientation of the owl auditory system, see Schöne (1984: 212). For the matching of speech signal and auditory system in humans see, e.g., Lafon (1968: 81, fig. 2). However, in the human case there is more than mere matching of frequency and amplitude between speech signal and auditory discrimination; there is also a special kind of neural processing that clocks in when speech sounds are heard (Lieberman and Blumstein 1988: 148ff.). There are also fairly clear patterns of matching between properties of speech and properties of short-term memory (see note 37). Unfortunately, there is no one locus where all these sorts of facts are laid out for non-specialists, although they are essential background to speculations about the evolution of language.

3 See, e.g., Kolb and Whishaw 1990: 237–41; for a wider-ranging popular account see Landau 1989.

4 If there is such an assemblage of abilities that we can call interactional intelligence, why has it been so neglected in the wide range of disciplines (from anthropology to neurology) that might have studied it? Presumably, partly because of the tendency to take for granted what humans are naturally good at. We do not cherish bipedalism in the same way that we celebrate our ability to do calculus. The corollary is that we value that which we are not very good at: dancing *au point*, calculating decontextualized syllogisms, democracy, etc. But there may be another reason for the neglect of the study of interaction, namely inhibition or repression. It is not only that (as every transcriber of a conversation knows) friendly interaction is, on minute inspection, replete with nasty little jabs. It's also that certain human skills only run fluidly out of conscious awareness. Just as it is awfully hard to drive when taking a driving test, walk in a straight line when arraigned on suspicion of drunken driving, or appreciate a symphony when trying too hard to appreciate it, so self-conscious interactants generally do themselves a disservice (see, e.g., Field 1955 [1934]). If so, the repressive mechanism that aids our daily interaction may be responsible for making us equally reluctant to look at it scientifically. (On the role of inhibition in controlling, e.g., our perceptual world of smells, see O. Sacks (1985: 151).)

5 Dietrich Dörner suggests *Homo interagens*.

6 J.Z. Young (1951: 3) reporting Lord Keynes's comments on looking through Newton's alchemical papers: 'Newton was not so much one of the first men of the age of reason as the last of the magicians. He seems to have thought of the universe as a riddle posed by God, which could be solved if one looked hard enough for the clues. Some of the clues were to be found in nature, others had been revealed in sacred and occult writings.'

 7 On speech to the self, see Goffman (1978) and Levinson (1988).

 8 However, I return briefly to one social aspect in the review of Dörner's work below.

 9 See, e.g., Goffman 1981; Levinson 1983: ch. 6; Clark 1992.

10 Humphrey's (1976: 19) seminal paper on the social function of the intellect uses the zero-sum game as a model of the computational demands of social life which 'asks for a level of intelligence ... unparalleled in any other sphere of living'. My point is that zero-sum games *merely* require decision trees for different contingencies; coordination games require deep reflexive thinking about other minds, and constitute a much more demanding intellectual task. In Schelling's (1960: 96) words: 'In the pure coordination game, the player's objective is to make contact with the other player through some imaginative process of introspection, of searching for shared clues; in the minimax strategy of a zero-sum game ... one's whole objective is to avoid any meeting of minds.'

11 Hence a superficial objection to the terminology of Byrne and Whiten (1988). Actually of course what they intend is a Machiavellian intelligence superimposed on a Humeian one, i.e., the potential for an agonistic exploitation of a supposedly cooperative understanding (cf. their quote (p. vi) from Machiavelli: 'For a prince, then, it is not necessary to have all the [virtuous] qualities, but it is very necessary to appear to have them.'). Nevertheless, one can't help feeling that their ethology is pervaded by the very agonistic bias (vicious struggle for survival of the fittest) that underlies the very Robinson Crusoe model (man's mind against 'nature') which they are complaining about. We all know cooperation is harder than conflict; it is not so obvious that one reason is that it's computationally harder too. (By the way, the reference to Hume is to *A Treatise of Human Nature* (III, ii.2.) where reflexive reasoning about the benefits of mutual cooperation is supposed to underlie our tacit acceptance of conventions (see Schiffer 1972: 137ff.).

12 'One of themselves, even a prophet of their own, said, the Cretans are always liars' (St Paul's epistle to Titus 1, 12). If the Cretan prophet speaks truly, then what he says is false; if he speaks falsely, then what he says would truly characterize him, but must nevertheless be false. The quotational aspects of the paradox are usually abstracted away from in philosophical discussion.

13 Do humans really go through all this reasoning about what each thinks the other thinks, and if so to what depth? The answers seem to be 'yes' and 'indefinitely deep' respectively, as is most clearly revealed where asymmetrical beliefs at a deep level are the name of the game, as in military strategy, paranoia, fraud and the like. Consider the beginnings of recorded western military strategy: e.g., Hannibal beat Scipio at the battle of Trebbia by making his centre only look like the normal thick phalanx, drawing the troops onto the wings, so the centre would collapse and the wings wrap round. Next time round the Romans might expect the same strategy, so this time Hannibal might stack the centre for a central concentrated punch: Hannibal's thinking that Scipio's thinking that Hannibal is thinking that Scipio will suspect a weak centre; Hannibal's hoping that Scipio will think all that but *not also* that Hannibal thinks Scipio will therefore weaken his centre to reinforce the wings making the centre an obvious target. However, suppose Scipio (or his

successors) figure all that out – then they will thicken up the centre. Best then to repeat the Trebbia formation, but to bow the centre out so that it *really* looks packed, but in fact is a hollow crescent, designed to crumble. So Hannibal thought and won the battle of Cannae by another pincer movement from the flanks (Connolly 1978). If early classical military strategy went that deep, how deep was the reflexive thinking that, e.g., Kennedy and Krushchev got into over the Berlin wall/Cuban-missile crisis of 1961–2 (Gelb 1986)? For depth in cooperative reflexive reasoning, consider, e.g., irony and double irony (see Penelope Brown's contribution to this volume (Chapter 7)).

14 See Cohen *et al.* (1990) for some recent ideas here.

15 This has not of course prevented computational attempts to circumvent the problem (see, e.g., Allen 1983; Perrault, 1987; Pollack 1986a, b; and papers (especially by Kautz and Pollack) in Cohen *et al.* 1990.)

16 Lest this seem too academic a possibility, an anecdote: the Germans are great hand-shakers; when we were living in Berlin, our Hausmeister, for example, descended on one, regardless of one's current preoccupations, to grasp the hand on first and last sighting of the day. But Germans more used to casual Anglo-Saxon ways curb the custom. Puzzled at first, I found myself inspecting every hand-jerk during greeting/parting moments as a possible candidate for a proferred hand, only to find it turn, more often than not, into a buttoning of the coat or a struggle with a sleeve!

17 Since conversational response can routinely fall within 200 milliseconds of the prior utterance, if one modestly ascribes half of that delay to planning of the response, then that leaves only the other half for comprehension, including intention- or plan-recognition, of the prior utterance.

18 One is struck too by how our abilities here are not greatly helped by ratiocinative leisure. For example, historians make a modest, and lawyers an immodest, living out of pondering on, and quarrelling about, intention-attribution.

19 In papers circulated prior to the conference behind this volume, Esther Goody argues that, although primate interactive intelligence presumably preceded the origins of language, it is language that has projected us beyond our primate counterparts by allowing the management and codification of social interaction. If one thinks about linguistic ability as a relatively encapsulated human skill, then its acquisition might be an explanation for our zoom into a sapient state. But if, as this section sketches, linguistic ability is *necessarily and essentially parasitic on highly evolved interactive reasoning*, then language is not the evolutionary rocket fuel; it's the rocket (see here Sperber and Wilson 1986). One must then accept a synergistic explanation: higher levels of AIP make higher levels of communication possible, but equally vice versa.

20 If 'the language of thought' is rather independent of 'the language of communication', then I don't see the latter playing the crucial role in internal representation of AIP that E. Goody hypothesizes. Alex Wearing points out to me that the phenomenon of 'gist memory' might argue against my aphorism – thoughts bleached by time may not be so specific. But, at least when we communicate about our immediate environs the aphorism would seem to hold good.

21 Those who follow Chomsky in thinking of a core linguistic ability as a highly specialized, innate mental module, must now exclude semantics from that domain. But many of us think that central aspects of syntax too show the stigmata of interactive reasoning (see Levinson 1987b, 1991).

22 In what follows I simplify drastically from a complex, intricate, clockwork series of mechanisms (see Levinsom 1983: ch. 3; 1987b; 1991; forthcoming). For an alternative version, see Horn 1989.

23 See, e.g., Sacks *et al.* 1974; for further references see Levinson 1983: ch. 6.

24 This trick, though, may rely on something beyond the simple mathematics of set partition, e.g., the idea of the uniquely salient solution that lies behind Schelling's games of coordination.

25 It was striking that in the conference at which this paper was delivered, Drew, Streeck and myself all produced pre-sequences as prototypical examples of interactive planning. It then struck us that such four-turn ('pre-sequence') sequences are perhaps the longest canonical sequences observable in normal conversation, barring the 'rituals' of greeting and parting. This is surely striking, especially when one considers that in situations of asymmetric power and authority (of a kind frequent enough in human societies) one might expect 'superiors' to be able to impose their multi-staged 'plans' on 'inferiors'. (Indeed, such three- or four- stage planning hardly counts as a major intellectual achievement for *Homo sapiens* – Haimoff (n.d.) arguing that gibbon calls exhibit pre-sequential structure.) Instead of forward imposition of structure, what one finds in conversation is a *robust contingency*: no-one, almost regardless of status or rank, seems able to guarantee what will happen beyond the turn after next! I think a good case could be made that such turn-by-turn contingency argues for a fundamentally egalitarian state in the Garden of Eden: we are as a species adjusted to adjusting to others.

26 There is now a burgeoning literature on non-monotonic reasoning systems (see, e.g., Ginsberg 1987). But rather than viewing these developments as technical solutions to how conversational (and more generally interactional) inference might work, I view them more sceptically as systems that ape the results of inference under mutually assumed heuristics (see next section, and Levinson forthcoming: ch. 1). In short, conversational inference is the *Ur* form of default reasoning; default reasoning is not some peculiar unmotivated property of the human mind to be copied slavishly on machine models of intelligence – default reasoning is a mode of thinking that arises as a necessary solution to interactional coordination. It may then spill over to other domains of reasoning – that's the thesis of this chapter – but it is primarily motivated by the need to find a solution to intention-attribution.

27 See, e.g., Marslen-Wilson *et al.* 1982; or Tyler 1992.

28 Of course, we can enjoy the jokey qualities of such examples. But specialists in computational language understanding don't; they are plagued by just those 'silly' misconstruals we enjoy. They have no computationally tractable system of heuristics under reflexive intentional reasoning to rid themselves of these (to us) 'obvious' misconstruals. A machine can have a database full of semantic knowledge, and may be replete with knowledge about probable relations between things in the world, and still fail to find the 'obvious'. See, e.g., Herskovits (1986) on spatial relations like *at* and *in*.

29 Another example: 'I've lost my senile grandmother in the department store; I've got to think what she'll do, expecting her to wander blissfully on.' (Chances for a quick meeting: slim.) Versus: 'I've lost my wife in the department store: she'll be thinking where I'll be thinking she'll go.' (Chances for a quick meeting: good.)

30 See Johnson-Laird and Watson 1977a: ch. 9.

31 'Conditional perfection' was so christened by Geiss and Zwicky (1971). The inference is often subjectively very strong, as from 'If you pay me $5, I'll mow the lawn' to 'If you don't pay me $5, I won't mow the lawn'. In the Atlas–Levinson (1981) scheme of pragmatic inferences this is a generalized conversational implicature, attributable to the Principle of Informativeness, or Grice's second Maxim of Quantity.

32 Ethnomedicine might provide a rich area for the comparison of cultural modes of dealing with complex systems, the essential cross-cultural similarity of the body providing a natural control, as it were.

33 Dörner points out that such behaviour may be perfectly rational in the sense that there is a rational means–end relation; it is the apparent over-evaluation of the goal that inclines us to view such behaviour with analytic pity. But compare the importance attached to the preservation of 'face' in interaction (Brown and Levinson 1987).

34 Forgetting, on Dörner's analysis, is not (or not only) mere mechanical failure, as it were, but also the side-effect of abstraction, or pattern-determining processes (shades of Galton).

35 Brown and Levinson (1987) argue that the protection of a notion of self-esteem and the projection of esteem for alter, motivate much of the detailed patterning of social interaction. Thus we can ground in interaction Dörner's observation that 'In a certain sense, maintaining a positive self-image is the requirement for acting at all' (Dörner 1987: 36).

36 See Ervin-Tripp (1979), and references cited there, for temporal properties of turn-taking.

37 One might speculate, indeed, that the temporal characteristics of short-term memory have evolved just to cope with the short spans posed by the action–reaction interval, on the one hand, and the maximal conversational sequential pattern, on the other. There is, for example, a striking parallel between the maximum capacity of the short-lived buffer known as 'echoic memory' and MLU (or mean length of utterance in conversation). Or, as Alex Wearing has put it to me, the properties of short-term memory and limited information-processing capacity (which together necessitate frequent feedback) show how *Homo sapiens* is virtually hard-wired for high-frequency conversational turn-taking.

38 Such ratiocination is ethnographically real, as we experienced when working with Aboriginal people in Cape York, still much concerned with the success of the hunt or fishing expedition. It is not straightforward to work out the probabilities of whether the mullet will be running at Aylem beach and whether the water will be clear enough to spear such fish under conditions only half predictable from the base camp, or whether it might be better to head for more dependable but less rewarding line fishing off a mangrove swamp. That's the stuff and excitement of the hunter's life.

39 This is, of course, not the view of Piaget, who viewed the logico-mathematical as the apical intelligence, but it must now be a commonplace in the cognitive sciences. Computationally, bipedal locomotion is vastly more complex than calculus. What we can do 'without thinking' we devalue as not real thinking; hence our disregard for interactional intelligence. Curiously, though, some logico-mathematical tasks of the highest order are performed by 'idiot savants' who typically exhibit low IQs and gross interactional inabilities or autism (see O. Sacks 1985: ch. 23; and more scientifically, Howe 1989). They can calculate twelve-figure primes 'without thinking', a task for which there is no known algorithm.

12 Stories in the social and mental life of people

In this chapter I want to discuss what has been called the 'narrative mode of understanding' (Bruner 1986), the ability to create, narrate, and comprehend stories. This ability enables us, I suggest, to grasp a flow of social events and to convey that grasp to others. To share stories in this way is a particularly powerful form of interactive planning: for in fashioning an account of what has been happening and what is happening, we lay down the background against which future mutual action may sensibly unfold. Stories, moreover, have the capacity to frame a markedly intricate and elaborate flow of social events, indeed just the sort of flow that seems even more characteristic of human than of other social primate societies (Byrne and Whiten 1988; Whiten 1991; Carrithers 1991a, 1992). We understand our social world by means of stories, and we use those stories to create distinctively human society.

The general idea

As I understand it, narrative thinking differs from, but complements, the other means of interactive planning discussed in this volume. This is partly a matter of scale. Conversation and discourse analysis (Streeck, Drew, Brown, this volume) work usually on two interlocutors interacting for perhaps no more than a few seconds or minutes. On the other hand, narrative thought may easily comprehend more – sometimes many more – than two people and may cover days, years, or even a lifetime and beyond. Moreover, the narrative thought transmitted in a story may depend on a communicative genre (Luckmann, Chapter 8, this volume), and may even be partly determined by the conventions of a genre. But stories may also have an originality, that is, an appositeness to a particular unique flow of action, which is not wholly comprehended within the convention alone. Moreover, I hope to make clear that narrative thought can be evidenced and conveyed in forms of speech which are not marked as stories at all.

Let me sketch roughly what I think narrative thought involves. It is a capacity to cognize not merely immediate relations between oneself and another, but many-sided human interactions carried out over a period of time. We might say: humans understand *character*, a notion which embodies the understandings of rights, obligations, expectations, propensities, attitudes and intentions in oneself and many different others; and *plot*, which shows the consequences of those characteristics in a multifarious flow of actions. To put it another way, human beings can perceive any current action within a large temporal envelope, and within that envelope they can perceive any given action, not only as a response to the immediate circumstances, or to the perceived current mental state of an interlocutor or of oneself, but also as part of an unfolding story. (I owe this latter formulation to Paul Harris (personal communication).)

I use both *plot* and *character* here as terms of art. I think it essential that character be conceived very broadly, since it must comprehend simultaneously individuals as having statuses and roles – that is, as standing in well-precedented relation to one another – and individuals as having idiosyncratic histories and propensities. There must be some room for abstraction, so that people can be understood as acting with a generic set of obligations and rights: as, for example, a lawyer, or a king, or a mother acts with obligations and rights toward clients, subjects, or sons and daughters. But the particularity of one person rather than another, of Hannah rather than Amy, must also be grasped at the same time. We must understand not just the type of the grandfather, for example, with all the relevant expectations about how he should act within a family, but also *this* grandfather's individual propensities: mellowness or irascibility, friendliness or aloofness, wisdom or foolishness, and so forth. Whether or not the western notion of an individuated personality really grew out of a much earlier sense of people as personae as Mauss suggested (see Carrithers *et al.* 1985), narrative understanding must comprehend both of those possibilities and many others as well. In this respect the notion of character resembles that of Schutz's 'type'.

But characters, with their relationships, are also set in a flow of events, a plot, with its sense of plans, goals, situations, acts, and outcomes. As Bruner (1986: 13) puts it, narrative thought concerns 'intention and action and the vicissitudes and consequences that mark their course'. Plots embody what a character or characters did to, or about, or with, some other character or characters, for what reasons; how people's attitudes, beliefs, and intentions thereby changed, and what followed on from that. To comprehend a plot is therefore to have some notion of the changes in an inner landscape of thought in the participants as well as the outer landscape of events. Indeed the two are inseparable, because the metamorphosis of thoughts entails the metamorphosis of social relations and vice versa.

This metamorphosis arises from the fact that people do things because of what others feel, think, and plan. I may apologize *because* she was *angry*. Or I may buy her a Michael Innes thriller *because* she will *enjoy* it. I may explain why I made that remark in a department meeting *because* my colleague apparently *misunderstood* it. Savage repression may be started *because* a rival faction *plans* to overthrow the government. Many, perhaps all, forms of law are based upon the attribution of intentions or knowledge to those held accountable. In war, deeds are done because of what the enemy think or believe. And it is difficult to conceive of conducting the most elementary interaction of everyday life without attribution of intentions and knowledge to others: for example, even the simplest conversation is based on mutual attribution of states of mind to each other by interlocutors (Bennett 1976; Brown and Levinson 1987; Whiten 1991).

So when we understand a plot, we understand changes of mind and of relationship, changes brought about by acts. Moreover, we are able to link acts, thoughts, and their consequences together so that we grasp the metamorphosis of each other's thoughts and each other's situations in a flow of action. In this perspective character and plot are indivisible, for we understand character only as it is revealed to us in the flow of action, and we only understand plot as the consequence of characters acting with characteristic beliefs and intentions. With such narrative understanding people orient themselves and act in an accountable manner, sensibly, effectively, and appropriately, creating and re-creating complex skeins of social life.

There is one further trait of narrative thinking worth mentioning, and that is its specificity: narrative is not, in my understanding, a generalizing mode of thought, but one which works from particular to particular. It may seem that this makes narrative thought rather like that great invention of Alfred Jarry, namely 'pataphysics' or the science of the particular, whose purpose is to produce scientific statements like 'I have just taken a small bite out of this apple.' The delightful irony in this idea derives from a contrast with a notion of abstract qualities being shared by objects and of proper knowledge as knowledge couched in such abstractions. On this view it might even be thought improper to dignify with the name 'thought' anything which did not use abstract classification. But I suggest, to the contrary, that narrative thought, like metonymic and metaphoric thought (see Lakoff and Johnson 1980; Lakoff 1987; Fernandez 1974; Sperber 1975), works more in a pataphysical than a metaphysical way. This is perhaps clearest in the case of specific characters: to understand, for example, the assertion that 'Saddam Hussein is a Hitler' may require little or no abstraction at all, but only a sense of what Hitler's character was in his own very specific plot.

I write as an anthropologist, not as a cognitive psychologist, so there are some issues on which I cannot decisively pronounce. Is narrative thought wholly distinct or is it made up of cognitive abilities used in other ways as well? For my purposes the suggestion of Feldman *et al.* (1990: 3) is adequate: 'the cognitive processing that we use to interpret human intentionality in stories is related to the processes we use to understand human intentionality in life encounters with other people'. The stories which I will discuss here are indeed closely related to the conduct of actual life, and they seem to suggest that any sharp distinction between narrative and other socially applied thought would be artificial.

A Jain tale

I want to set out two illustrations, ethnographic snapshots of the territory of story in social life. The first stems from an episode which occurred while I was doing fieldwork among Jains in Kolhapur, Maharashtra State, India.

Jains are a severely ascetic minority sect who hold that souls cycle in endless torment from birth to birth. The cause of this eternal suffering is the physical and mental pain we inflict on other beings, for by such deeds we cause defilements to adhere to our own souls, and these defilements lead inexorably, with law-like regularity, to further painful rebirth. We may prevent defilement by living a strict life of vegetarianism, celibacy, truthfulness, and non-attachment to belongings, and we can cleanse ourselves of already accrued defilement by practising self-mortification. Jains are thus celebrated for the doctrine of harmlessness or non-violence, *ahiṃsā*, which had great influence on Gandhi. They are celebrated likewise for the austerities of their *munis*, monks or ascetics. The *munis* of the Digambar sect (the sect with whom I worked in Kolhapur) go permanently naked, eat once a day, walk the length and breadth of India, and from time to time remove their head hair by plucking it out with their own hands. This strenuous spiritual heroism is held in profound reverence by lay Jains.

The Jains among whom I worked were mostly urban businessmen who were eager to speak of Jainism, and I was frequently offered a long impromptu religio-philosophical lecture – a well-marked local communicative genre. On the occasion in question I was sitting in the office of a dealer in agricultural supplies, Mr P (the 'P' stands for 'philosophy'). The following is from my field notes. Mr P spoke in English.

He began treating me to a sermon. Did I know about Jainism? Not much. He told me that the essence of Jainism is *ahiṃsā*. This is non-violence, and Gandhi was really a Jain ... Did I know what *ahiṃsā* means? I did not. *Ahiṃsā* is the essence of all religions, he said. We must do no harm, we must help all beings. Did I eat meat? I used to, but no longer. Good, he said, that is *ahiṃsā*. *Ahiṃsā* is always a profit to yourself. . . . *Ahiṃsā* means that we must say ill of no-one, because we might harm them, but we would anyway harm ourselves. Why? Because to speak ill or to lie is to speak out of greed and hatred, and these harm ourselves. *Ahiṃsā* means no harm to others, and that means no harm to yourself. Did I think fasting was bad for health? I hesitated. No! he said. Fasting is good for self, fasting is *ahiṃsā*, because it harms no-one and helps only self . . .

Mr P seemed to be hitting his stride when someone called on a business matter, and Mr P asked me to stay for tea, saying that he had to go out but would be right back. He left, and after a pause a shabby older man who had been sitting in the corner spoke in Marathi. He was a farmer perhaps, perhaps a poor relation or had come about a loan. Did I speak Marathi? A little. This, he said, is a story my grandfather told me. This is very important. Write this down, he said, pointing to my notebook. There was a great man, a hero, a *mahāpuruṣ*, who lived right near here, and one time that man went out to the bulls. While (doing something unknown to me) to the bulls one of them stood on his hand. What did he do? He did nothing! He waited and waited, and finally the bull's owner came and saw what was happening! The owner struck the bull to make it move, and the great man told him to stop, that the bull did not understand! *That* is dharma [true religion], he said, that is genuine *jainadharma* [Jainism]!

The man – I will call him Mr S for 'story' – told the tale with marked fervour, but fell silent when Mr P returned and did not speak again. I took it that he was rebutting or improving on Mr P's account (which I have very considerably abridged). I later discovered a printed biography of one Siddhasagar which contained the episode of which Mr S spoke. Siddhasagar lived into the first decade of the twentieth century. Late in life, after many notable religious deeds as a layman, he became a *muni*, naked ascetic, and continued to live an increasingly ascetic life until his death. His printed biography (Shaha 1983) informs us that he was removing dung from beneath the bulls when the reported incident happened.

What is the difference between Mr P's philosophical account and Mr S's story? Let me begin by pointing out an important dimension in which they do *not* differ, namely, they both rely on *implicit inference*. By implicit inference I mean that these slices of talk, like all discourse, require a substantial amount of background knowledge and alertness to context to be intelligible. For example, neither Mr P nor Mr S actually explained the Jain theory of rebirth. I had to know it, and to infer that it was relevant (on relevance see Brown and Yule 1983: 68ff.; Sperber and Wilson 1986). Moreover, when Mr S began to speak I had to infer that he was referring to what Mr P had said and not striking out on another topic altogether, such as 'awful things that can happen to you with bulls'. It was only later that he made the connection outright: 'that is true religion'. Moreover, both slices of talk presupposed a knowledge of everyday assumptions – that food, rather than its absence, is good for you, or that one would do just about anything to get a bull off one's hand.

Explicit inference, on the other hand, marked Mr P's, but not Mr S's, discourse. That is, Mr P's account was organized to demonstrate a particular process of reasoning and a particular set of propositions about the world. After the preamble (i.e., after 'we must help all beings') each segment of the talk had roughly the form: 'you might think X is good for you, but in fact Y is good for you, because of the entailments of the theory of rebirth and *ahiṃsā*'. Though the talk was impromptu, it was recognizably patterned after typical Jain ethical reasoning such as has been cultivated by Jain scholars and philosophers for more than two millennia. And in fact Mr P was setting out an example of what Bruner (1986) called the 'paradigmatic mode of understanding', the mode of understanding of logic and impersonal abstraction, which Bruner contrasts with the narrative mode of understanding.

I have already suggested that narrative thought differs from such paradigmatic thought by its plot-like organization, its characters, and its specificity, but now I want to go a bit further. It is my view – and I think that of Mr S – that narrative thought is, for some purposes, superior to paradigmatic thought. For paradigmatic thought, I suggest, cannot so easily be applied to one's own actual life; it is less persuasive, less vivid, and less informative. In practice, story is easier to use, conveys more, and does so more effectively. Narratives have a capacity to move people and, in so doing, to make things happen.

There are a number of reasons for attributing such potential to narrative thought. Levinson suggests in this volume (Chapter 11) that humans have an interactive bias in thought, and part of that bias is a propensity to regard phenomena as having intentions, that is, as being, in my terms, characters. Dennett (1987) has made a similar point in regard to the 'intentional stance'. If this is so, then we might expect listeners to understand a point more readily through what happens to a specific character with his or her characteristic intentions. Moreover, Lakoff (1987), Winograd and Flores (1987), Bourdieu (1977) and many others have suggested that humans tend to think in specifics, in images, metonyms, and metaphors, and in terms intelligible through corporeal rather than ratiocinative experience. And finally Bruner (1987) has proposed that people generally see themselves in their own lives in narrative terms, as having a specific character and a specific life plot. For all these reasons story seems more intimately connected to our fundamentally social and embodied nature than derived forms of abstract and general reasoning.

The writer of the preface to the biography of Siddhasagar saw the virtue of narrative clearly. 'It is our experience', he wrote, 'that the life stories of great men are attractive, *informative*, and inspiring to people . . . The readers' minds are so concentrated that they attend to nothing else.'

(Shaha 1983: 1; my translation, my emphasis.) One part of the extra knowledge gained here, knowledge that no ethical reasoning could adequately convey, is that Jains find it admirable when someone goes to such extreme lengths to achieve the project of Jainism.

Short sharp stories

Let me look more closely at Mr S's discourse. For the moment I will speak of that part of it that was straightforwardly narrative, namely the account of Siddhasagar and the bull. The plot of this was minimal, but it was a plot all the same because (1) it shows a flow of events, (2) it concerns specific characters, (3) it displays the attitudes, beliefs and intentions of the characters and (4) it reveals the relationship between events and those intentions and attitudes.

But however spare, the story was not really straightforward. Take, to begin with, the purpose of Mr S's discourse, which was to reveal Siddhasagar's spiritual heroism. This evidently involved attributing character, with typical intentions and attitudes, to Siddhasagar – yet there was in the telling no *explicit* attribution to him of any mental qualities at all. The only mental attribution, indeed, was to the bull, which 'did not understand'. So the story, as told, required background information, and in fact the entire import of the narration had to be inferred. However this story meant what it meant, it did not do so by putting thoughts directly into words.

I make this point partly because an important view of narrative, that set out by Bruner (1986; see also Feldman *et al.* 1990), suggests that narratives might be divided into different kinds according to their verbal form: one kind possesses a 'landscape of action', the other a 'landscape of consciousness'. On this view some stories, such as the Russian folk tales analysed by Propp, comprise largely a description of events, but contain few or no attributions of attitudes, beliefs, and intentions. Modernist stream-of-consciousness stories, on the other hand, are quite the opposite, being full of mental description and very little action.

But what I suggest is rather different. Verbal form may be decisive for certain forms of fiction or for certain genres, and these may perhaps stress one or the other of the landscapes. But stories that are closely connected to the conduct of life must necessarily concern both landscapes, for narrative is about orienting people in a stream of events constituted of both action and consciousness. And so we have a story such as that of Siddhasagar and the bull, which on the surface consists almost solely of action but which in fact concerns – and must concern, to be of any use – the union of consciousness and action.

These considerations of verbal form suggest, I think, that there can be no minimal definition of what constitutes a narrative apart from its setting. Gergen and Gergen (1984), for example, have suggested that an utterance such as 'I thought she was my friend' could be a complete story – but of course it presupposes an implied setting of friendship and disappointed expectations. Similarly, the words 'I came, I saw, I conquered', if uttered to the right people by the right person at the right time, are a complete story, rich with mental and character attribution (especially by the speaker to himself).

These examples have at least a temporal reference marked by a past tense or by word sequence in the sentence, but what about the warning 'don't be a Miss Bossy!', as issued to my daughter, with whom I had recently read a story by that name (Hargreaves 1981)? This has no temporal marker at all, but I suggest that it is an important example of narrative all the same, for by mentioning a character it also evokes acts, attitudes, and the relationship between the two. Sperber and Wilson (1986: 48–51) and Bakhtin (in Holquist 1990: 62) give examples of slight signals – a movement, a phatic utterance – which are barely verbal but which are nevertheless richly communicative and precise, and I see no reason to exclude narrative from the sorts of significance that could be so sketchily conveyed. To accept that a story could be evoked rather than told is no more than a corollary of the observation that implicit inference is necessary to all stories. My point is not that such compact utterances should be regarded solely and exclusively as narratives, but rather that to see them as narratives is to show how they orient people to events and intentions in a flow of action. I will refer to brief, un-story-like evocations as *minimal narratives*.

Planning my future

I want now to pursue the nature of implicit inference further, and propose that the implied meaning in Mr S's telling of the story arose in part through the collaboration of us interlocutors rather than merely through individual ratiocination. The flow of action of the story, that is, was understood partly through the flow of action of its telling.

Let me begin with the events in which Mr P and I were already involved before Mr S spoke. My own part in them had a well-established background, in that I was understood among local Jains to be a student of Jainism and a researcher of the Jain community, intent on recording these important matters for posterity in a complimentary light. In the foreground I demonstrated, by quick and encouraging responses and by writing in my notebook as the encounter progressed, that I valued Mr P's opinion. Mr P, for his part, fell into the advisory, admonitory tone of the impromptu lecture. And so we established that his utterances were for the record, for my notebook; and that as such they were authoritative, important, and reasonable. So if he said things that might seem to run against the grain of (some assumed) common sense, then we would both know that good reason for such assertions would be forthcoming.

When Mr P stepped out of this flow, Mr S stepped in. He said, and did, this:

Did I speak Marathi? A little. This, he said, is a story my grandfather told me. This is very important. Write this down, he said, pointing to my notebook. There was a great man ... who lived right near here ...

Note first the parts of this utterance that were directed toward continuing the flow of action and preserving the generous interpretation of utterances in the same terms. Mr S required me to speak Marathi, to agree on the worth of what was to be said, and to record it for posterity. For my part I had to assent to these terms, which I did by complying. So we established a commonality of understanding that might otherwise, had the interlocutors been closer in experience, have been left unsaid.

The other part of Mr S's prelude was this:

This, he said, is a story my grandfather told me ... There was a great man ... who lived right near here ...

This part of the prelude might seem formulaic, but in the setting it had a particular force. I took it at the time, and it was subsequently confirmed by finding Siddhasagar's biography, that Siddhasagar's life may have overlapped with that of Mr S's grandfather. Moreover Siddhasagar lived and travelled among the villages just to the south of Kolhapur. So his was not a story of remote, unreckonable antiquity, as so much of Jain story literature is, but one which occurred within Mr S's known world. Mr S was bound to his grandfather, and his grandfather was bound through further (inferrable) connections, the connections which bore the tellings and re-tellings of the story, to Siddhasagar himself. So in effect the prelude was part of the story. It gave the tale further characters, the grandfather and the younger Mr S, who were implicitly assigned the intention to speak and listen most gravely, concerning issues of the highest import. The appended incident was set half-way between Siddhasagar's deed and the present, in Mr S's childhood, and it added to the plot an account of how a famous deed passes among people, one authoritative speaker to the next, as the discourse of the ends of life. In the present telling, implied Mr S, he was playing the role toward me that his grandfather had played toward him in the earlier telling.

So on the one hand Mr S was urging me to consider a specific past flow of events in which present action was to be oriented. On the other hand, this account of the past was directed toward the future as well. Mr S's intention was to produce in me, with my compliance, an understanding of Jainism and an emotional orientation informed by Jain values. This could reasonably be regarded as interactive planning, even though Mr S was working not on an egalitarian but on a hierarchical notion of interaction. And in fact it might be better to speak, not of planning, but of *deuteroplanning*, planning how to plan, suggesting a general orientation to life that would mould any later episode of specific planning. Mr S was not proposing specific actions in the short or medium term, but rather a wholesale reorientation of how to plan altogether.

Kaluli stories

I have considered this Jain material because it illustrates many things: the distinction between narrative and other forms of thought, the allusive and cooperative nature of story, and its power to call into relevance events long past and to adumbrate flows of action on a very large scale. But the mutually planned outcome was purely a change in attitude and understanding and so does not show one of the most important features of narrative thought, namely its close integration with social action. For that I turn now to E. Schieffelin's (1976) ethnography of the Kaluli, a people of the Papua New Guinea plateau. These narratives are much closer to an immediate flow of events and therefore illustrate more plainly how people use narrative thought to construct their mutual life.

The ethnography of the Kaluli recapitulates many themes found throughout Papua New Guinea. They are shifting cultivators who supplement their diet by hunting, fishing, and pig raising. Their social intercourse is dominated by exchange and reciprocity. Such reciprocity may create and reaffirm friendly relations, and Schieffelin makes clear that, in such exchange, the expression of sentiment is at least as important as material considerations. But Kaluli also reciprocate violence with violence, and the abiding threat of conflict influences many of their institutions.

Kaluli live in large communal longhouses distributed over their territory. But though the most immediate way of identifying a Kaluli is by identifying his or her longhouse, large-scale social events are not necessarily organized according to longhouse membership. Nor do the Kaluli possess superordinate coercive institutions. Hence their domestic and kinship arrangements are relatively fluid, and most of their collective life – work, play, ceremony and fighting – is achieved by groups assembled *ad hoc* for an occasion. Schieffelin represents the organizing of *ad hoc* groups as largely a male matter, and I will therefore be concerned chiefly with relations between adult men (for a complementary and corrective viewpoint see B. Schieffelin 1990).

Schieffelin stresses that even though the group formed on a particular occasion may appear to come together through ties of kinship or friendship, there is no sense in which mutual aid is obligatory or automatic. On the contrary, Kaluli styles of interaction assume that interlocutors are autonomous, that participants in a common activity are equal, and that any cooperation arises out of freely chosen fellow feeling. Thus a group gathered for a collective purpose, such as damming a river for fishing,

takes cognizance of itself according to the task to be performed, not the social relationships involved. The result, in most group activity, is visible in the posture of autonomy preserved by each man engaged in the common project. (1976: 132.)

How do the Kaluli manage collective action in such an aggressively egalitarian milieu, where 'any appearance of compulsion infringes on one's sense of personal autonomy and invites an angry reaction, even between children and adults' (p. 129)? Schieffelin explains that Kaluli have two modalities or styles of addressing requests for action to each other: assertion and appeal. Assertion takes the form of loud, imperative statements which have the appearance of orders or demands, even though in fact they can count as no more than forceful requests. Assertion appears to be used most frequently with close relatives and friends. It works most effectively, suggests Schieffelin, against a background of excitement, helping to initiate action by being itself 'exciting, noisy, and dramatic' (p. 129). Appeal, on the other hand, is most often used between people who are more distant, or in moods or circumstances that are more sombre, and it may be conveyed either explicitly or nonverbally, as by sighs or a dejected posture, for example. But however a request for help is framed, Kaluli describe their reasons for responding 'in terms of sympathy and compassion – "I felt sorry for him so I went" – or supportive outrage – "I was angry when those people killed his pig" ' (p. 130).

Schieffelin provides us with an example of these processes in action. To understand what follows it is necessary to know that a *sei* is a witch, a person deemed responsible for causing or promoting another's death by supernatural means. Before pacification, *seis* used to be killed by bereaved relatives of their victims.

When Dasemi of Olabia [longhouse] died from snake bite, Jomo of Ferisa was publicly identified as the *sei* responsible. At the funeral ... Dasemi's husband, Beli, sat forlornly in the rubbish near the back of the [longhouse] ... Around him visiting men seated on the sleeping platforms shouted speeches of outraged sympathy. The children had no mother now and Beli had no one to cook for him, they yelled at me in anger and dismay. Others shouted at newcomers that Jomo had taken Beli's wife and should be made to give return. If it were not for the government, they declared, they would go right out and kill him. This was how support for the murder of [an alleged *sei*] had materialized almost of itself twelve years before. (p. 130.)

Here I am concerned with the narrative thought conveyed in the assertions made to Schieffelin and the newcomers. One assertion was that, because of Jomo's act, 'the children had no mother now and Beli had no one to cook for him'. The other was that 'Jomo had taken Beli's wife and should be made to give return. If it were not for the government . . . they would go right out and kill him.'

Of course these are not stories in a conventional sense. Unlike the story of Siddhasagar and the bull, these utterances are not preceded by a 'once upon a time . . .' marker. Nor are they placed entirely in the past tense: some of the utterances concern recent past events, but others concern the present or future. From a strictly linguistic point of view, these utterances are a different genre, quite unlike that of Siddhasagar and the bull. But on the other hand they do act as I have suggested narrative must: they show how people coming upon the scene were informed of the flow of events in terms of previous events – Jomo's mystical deed, Dasemi's death – and previous and present mental states – Jomo's evil attitude, Beli's grief, others' anger. In other words, these speeches evince narrative thought without having narrative form. To that extent they may be regarded as (among other things) minimal narratives, and as minimal narratives they connect closely to ongoing events (as did that other minimal narrative, 'I thought she was my friend.').

Minimal narratives plainly depend on inference, and some of the intentions evoked by these were certainly implicit: for example, to speak of *sei* at all is to evoke his or her evil attitude. But some mental states were made explicit, and were perhaps more explicit in the event than in Schieffelin's brief depiction of it. For as he makes clear elsewhere, and may suggest here with the words 'they yelled at me in anger and dismay', Kaluli both display their feelings openly and say explicitly that they feel 'angry' or 'sad' (see E. Schieffelin 1976: 135).

It would be quite contrary to what Kaluli say and do on such an occasion to divide speech marked by reference to the past – Dasemi's death, Jomo's alleged activity as a *sei* – from that which describes present circumstances or proposes future action – people's anger, a proposed demand for compensation. As Schieffelin depicts the speeches, they move effortlessly and naturally from showing what has happened to what people now feel, and from what people now feel to what should happen. Here, *in medias res*, narrative thought welds the past seamlessly to the present and future, such that what to do seems to follow inevitably from what has happened. Indeed by suggesting appropriate action (to go to Jomo and demand compensation) Kaluli were commenting on the past (the evil of Jomo's deed) as much as they were deriving present plans from that past. Similarly, it would be a distortion to divide too sharply the saying from the doing: where Schieffelin writes that men 'shouted speeches of outraged sympathy', I suppose him to reflect that people were both showing themselves to be emotionally excited and going on record as being angry.

I make these points in order to suggest how closely narrative thought can be bound up with action. The immediately proposed plan, to go to Jomo with demands, derived its sense from the flow of events which led up to it. Without understanding these events, present proposals would be senseless. Moreover people were both acting angrily and immediately reflecting that anger as part of their narrative of events, so their anger continually became a recorded, significant part of the flow. These continual re-tellings then pointed forward compellingly to the rest of the story, the future, just as Siddhasagar's story pointed toward a desired result. We might say: as people composed the immediate past and present for each other, they composed the future as well. Their speech had a cognitive and an emotive or evaluative element, but also a conative element, an element of will and determination. In the excitement, each re-telling of events demonstrated the speaker's own willingness to face the consequences. Each invited others to join in, and each contributed to the growing consensus over what had, and what should, happen. Esther Goody suggested to me the term 'confabulation' to cover this process.

The long term

Schieffelin argues not just that Kaluli confabulate their response to events, but that they do so in a particular way, and I want now to look at their style in the more leisurely creation of long-term relationships. Schieffelin makes abundantly clear that material gifts and material help are regarded by them straightforwardly as signs of love, affection and esteem. Thus their sentimental dimension is much more salient than we would easily recognize. He also shows that relatively formal gifts between future in-laws initiate a marriage, and that continued gifts sustain both the marriage and the newly created relationship between brothers-in-law, real and classificatory. Indeed the greater part of work done by Kaluli in mature life to gain their livelihood and feed their children is done by men and women labouring together within the affinal relationship thus created. The relationship between marriage partners and between affines is therefore both sentimental and urgently practical. The consequence of all this, writes Schieffelin (p. 25), is that

A man's relations with, interactions with, and affection for his affines ... are so bound up with situations of reciprocal gift-giving and mutual help that he tends to think of his life with his wife, on reflection, in terms of the situations in which he worked cooperatively with her and reciprocally with her relatives and exchanged countless minor gifts of food.

In this light – and 'on reflection' – an older man, Sialo, of Bona longhouse, told Schieffelin the story of his marriage:

(After a ceremony at Tusuku longhouse I met a woman.) I told her to wait. Later Tusuku (people – his future in-laws) brought her to (my longhouse) Bona for a formal wedding.

Well, we went down and planted pandanus and bananas. Then my brother-in-law Kiliyae called us to plant bananas. We went to Tusuku and planted many, many bananas, and cut many trees.

Later Tusuku brought a cassowary. I brought them bananas I cut from my garden. I went to (Mt.) Bosavi and hunted for animals. I got many, many animals, and also sago grubs and brought them to Tusuku. Then Tusuku went to (Mt.) Bosavi and hunted animals and got sago grubs and brought them to Bona as return. That's the way it was!

Well we went down to Alimsak (a garden place). We planted okari nuts. We called Tusuku, 'Come plant bananas!' We planted bananas one day, two days, five, six days. Then we cut trees. Being hungry we said, 'You take this sago.' 'You go pick bananas and pandanus.'

We were hungry for meat. We (invited Tusuku) to the Walu (stream). We caught crayfish. We dammed the Isawa, and beat poison and caught many, many fish. We went to the gardens. Tusuku said, 'Bring bananas!' So we brought bananas. 'Bring more'; so we brought more.

At Balasawel the woman died. I gave it up. (*Ibid*.: 26.)

B. Schieffelin (1990: 246) gives a clue to the narrative style of Kaluli in general. She remarks that Kaluli story-tellers 'can evoke the sentiments of the participants in a compressed discursive space ... and while there is provided an outcome to which a response is certain, response is not given by an authoritative or judgmental stance of the teller'. The style of Kaluli narrative is not to draw moral points explicitly, but to show the texture of human life by a muted narrative, a relatively bare reflection. They are more modernist than homiletic, more in the style of Hemingway than of the preacher Jonathan Edwards. So a story such as that of Sialo is very differently framed from that of Mr S, for whom the establishing of authority was one of the main concerns. But not just any evocation would do, and as B. Schieffelin makes clear, and as E. Schieffelin (1976) and Feld (1982) agree, the theme of interdependence and its difficulties would be uppermost in Kaluli reception of the story. They would understand the importance of these events to Sialo, the way in which they stood as landmarks on the course of his life.

The measure of that importance depends critically on the sheer scale of what is being narrated. Sialo's story frames the whole of his adult life. The gain of a wife and in-laws created Sialo's very character as an adult, and their loss marked his transition to another stage of life: 'I gave it up.' Within that frame, moreover, acts of reciprocity and their accompanying intentions of amity created not just a series of atomic situations, but rather a developing narrative of increasing affection, esteem, and mutual reliability, of characters mutually made and tested in work and appreciation. It was the cumulative effect of all those acts of trust in the developing plot of their relationship which created the sentiment which bound Sialo, his wife and her brothers; and it was a sense of that amassed value of feeling that created the sense of loss with which the story ends. If the relationships described in the story were not more than the sum of their individual occasions, the story could not have had such force.

How was this narrative understanding used interactively? Schieffelin reports (personal communication) that Sialo told him the story early in their acquaintance when they were getting to know one another. He also reports that the story was consistent with such a situation, namely that it was offered as something like a brief *curriculum vitae*. The incidents chosen to illustrate his life by Sialo were conventional in that they were the sort of events commonly used by Kaluli as chronological markers in veridical narratives, though other stories would be likely to be more digressive and less concentrated, less full of such markers. The effect was to orient Schieffelin to the plot of Sialo's life and thereby to inform him of Sialo's character. This, Sialo implied, is the way a Kaluli life, my life, works out, this is the way I laboured and showed proper affection to my fellows, this is the way relationships, and gardens, are rightly made and cultivated.

So Sialo's autobiography was offered as part of a mutual informing which would subsequently allow the two to work together – as, says Schieffelin, they eventually did. It was a self-revelation which formed the basis of a bond. We can understand, too, that this cannot have been the only such occasion: there would have been other, earlier, fragmented tellings of the autobiography *in medias res*, tellings of successful exchanges by Sialo and his in-laws while he was young and his wife was prospering. Those tellings would have drawn others in, carrying forward the process of forming and cementing relationships just as this one did.

Confabulation

So people confabulate society using stories. The word 'confabulate' in its common acceptation means just chatting together, with a suggestion perhaps of yarning, gossiping, or story-telling. I suggest that we should add a further implication to its sense, namely that of making together, 'confabrication' if you will. What is thus made is characteristically human social action, with its large temporal and causal perspective and its cognizance of many related characters with their richly imagined mental states. Godelier remarks that 'human beings, in contrast to other social animals, do not just live in society, they produce society in order to live'

(Godelier 1988: 1). The sense of this is well illustrated by the Kaluli, who form work groups along affinal lines to produce their livelihood. But the Kaluli also produce stories in order to live in society. Stories of conflict constitute society through a conflictual understanding, stories of amity constitute it through a cooperative understanding. In either case, the mutual knowledge created through narrative thought ensures that subsequent action by partners to a relationship will act appropriately and with mutual regard – even where that regard is mutually destructive.

Finally I want to point out that stories and story consciousness help to confabulate not just action, but more or less predictable action in a familiar style. I have argued that stories and narrative consciousness are specific, particular, effectively 'pataphysical' in their form and application. It has however also been implicit in my presentation that there are differences of culture or social structure which set apart one style of story or story consciousness from another. The Kaluli have a different view of what makes a good or intelligible story, and of what makes an appropriate response in life, than do the Jains, and the ethnographic literature could be consulted for many more variants. E. Schieffelin has captured the style of story and action specific to a society in the phrase 'cultural scenario', which is recognizable in the way 'a people repeatedly approach and interpret diverse situations and carry them to similar types of resolution' (1976: 3). In this respect Kaluli or Jain stories have a generic character, not just a specific, pataphysical one.

Now the features of a cultural scenario may be largely implicit for the people themselves, as they seem to be for Kaluli. In that case, ethnographers are left to produce a theoretical gloss, their own paradigmatic thought, which describes the generic element in Kaluli narrative and social dispositions. In other cases, such as among the Jains, the people themselves may cultivate their own commentary with great industry. But in either case, narrative thought allows people to weld the general disposition to the particular action, the general aesthetic feeling for outcomes to the particular story, the generic role to the particular player.

In this perspective the central characteristic of story is neither its predictability nor its originality, but rather its ability to combine the two. Stories must be intelligible, but within the bounds of intelligibility they may still tell a story which interlocutors have never heard before. Indeed, as Chafe argues, people tell stories in order to say something new: 'narratives that entirely fit expectations are not really narratives at all'. (Chafe 1990: 83) Consequently, I suggest, we may in future want to look more closely to story to see more clearly how people mutually construct a social world that resembles the past while still creating new inventions and new responses.

Consolidated bibliography

Abrahams, R.G. (1989) Law and order and the State in the Nyamwezi and Sukuma area of Tanzania. *Africa* 59: 356–70.

Ahern, E.M. (1973) *The Cult of the Dead in a Chinese Village*. Stanford, Calif.

Alhonsaari, A. (1973) *Prayer; an analysis of theological society*. Publication of the Luther-Agricola Society: B8. Helsinki.

Allen, J. (1983) Recognizing intentions from natural language utterances. In M. Brady and R.C. Berwick (eds.) *Computational Models of Discourse*. Cambridge, Mass.

Alverez, T. (1980) *Living with God: St. Theresa's concept of prayer*, edited by T. Curran. Dublin.

Anderson, J.R. (1984) Monkeys with mirrors: some questions for primate psychology. *Journal of Comparative Psychology* 99: 211–17.

Anesaki, M. (1918) Buddhist prayer. In J. Hastings (ed.) *Encyclopedia of Religion and Ethics*, Vol. X. Edinburgh.

Argyle, M. (1968) *The Psychology of Interpersonal Behaviour*. London.

Aristotle [1962] *The Nichomachean Ethics*. Indianapolis, Ind.

Arundale, R.B. (1993) Cultural assumptions in conceptualizing face. Paper presented to the International Communication Association, Washington D.C., May.

Atkinson, J.M. (1984) *Our Master's Voices: the language and body language of politics*. London/New York.

Atkinson, J.M. and Drew, P. (1979) *Order in Court: the organisation of verbal interaction in judicial settings*. London.

Atkinson, J.M. and Heritage, J. (eds.) (1986) *Structures of Social Actions: studies in conversation analysis*. Cambridge.

Atlas, J. (1989) *Philosophy without Ambiguity*. Oxford.

Atlas, J. and Levinson, S. (1973) The importance of practical reasoning in language usage: an explanation of conversational implicature. Unpublished manuscript, Department of Linguistics, University of Cambridge.

  (1981) It-clefts, informativeness and logical form. In P. Cole (ed.) *Radical Pragmatics*. New York.

Austin, J.L. (1962) *How to do Things with Words*. Oxford.

Averna, G. (1977) Italian and Venetian profanity. *Maledicta* 1.

Avramides, A. (1989) *Meaning and Mind*. Cambridge, Mass.

Bailey, R. *et al.* (1989) Hunting and gathering in tropical rain forest: is it possible? *American Anthropologist* 91: 59–82.

Bakhtin, M.M. (1965) *Rabelais and his World*. English translation, 1968. Cambridge, Mass.

(1986) *Speech Genres and Other Late Essays*. Austin, Texas. (Partial translation of *Estetika slovesnogo tvorchestva*. Moscow, 1979.)

(1986) [1952–3] The problem of speech genres. In C. Emerson and M. Holquist (eds.) *Speech Genres and Other Late Essays*. Austin, Texas.

Baldi, C. (1623) *Delle Mentite*. Bologna.

Barnard, A. (1981) Universal categorization in four Bushmen societies. *L'Uomo* 5: 219–37.

Barnes, J.A. (1994) *A Pack of Lies*. Cambridge.

Baron-Cohen, S., Leslie, A.M. and Frith, U. (1985) Does the autistic child have a theory of mind? *Cognition* 21: 37–46.

Barth, F. (1966) *Models of Social Organization*. Royal Anthropology Institute occasional paper no. 23. Glasgow.

Bascom, W.R. (1954) Four functions of folklore. *Journal of American Folklore* 67: 333–49.

(1969) *Ifa Divination: communication between gods and men in West Africa*. Bloomington, Ind.

Bauman, R. (1983) *Let Your Words Be Few: symbolism of speech and silence among seventeenth-century Quakers*. Cambridge.

Bauman, R. and Sherzer, J. (eds.) (1974) *Explorations in the Ethnography of Speaking*. Cambridge.

Beattie, G.W. (1979) Planning units in spontaneous speech: some evidence from hesitation in speech and speaker gaze direction in conversation. *Linguistics* 17: 61–78.

(1983) *Talk*. Milton Keynes.

Beattie, J.H.M. (1964) Divination in Bunyoro, Uganda. *Sociologious* 14: 44–61.

(1966) Consulting a diviner in Bunyoro: a text. *Ethnology* 5: 202–17.

(1967) Consulting a Nyoro diviner: the ethnologist as client. *Ethnology* 6: 57–65.

Beavin, J.H., Jackson, D.D. and Watzlawick, P. (1969) *Menschliche Kommunikation, Formen, Störungen, Paradoxien*. Bern, Stuttgart and Vienna.

Bell, D.E., Raiffa, H. and Tversky, A. (eds.) (1988) *Decision Making: descriptive, normative and prescriptive interactions*. Cambridge.

Bennett, J. (1976) *Linguistic Behaviour*. Cambridge.

Berger, P.L. and Luckmann, T. (1966) *The Social Construction of Reality: a treatise in the sociology of knowledge*. New York.

Bergmann, J.R. (1993) *Gossip*. New York. German edition, 1987. Berlin.

Bickerton, D. (1990) *Language and Species*. Chicago.

Binsbergen, W. van and Schoffeleers, M. (eds.) (1985) *Theoretical Explorations in African Religion*. London.

Bird, N. (subsequently Bird-David) (1982) 'Inside' and 'outside' in kinship usage: the hunter-gatherer Naiken of South India. *Cambridge Anthropology* 7(1): 47–57.

(1983a) Conjugal families and single persons: an analysis of the Naiken social system. Ph.D. dissertation, University of Cambridge.

(1983b) Wage-gathering: socio-economic change and the case of the Naiken of South India. In P. Robb (ed.) *Rural South Asia: linkages, change and development*. London.

Bird-David, N. (1987a) The Kurumbas of the Nilgiris: an ethnographic myth? *Modern Asian Studies* 21: 173–89.

(1987b) Single persons and social cohesion in a hunter-gatherer society. In P. Hockings (ed.) *Dimensions of Social Life: essays in honour of David Mandelbaum*. Berlin.

(1988) Hunter-gatherers and other people: a re-examination. In T. Ingold, D. Riches and J. Woodburn (eds.) *Hunters and Gatherers*, Vol. I: *History, Evolution and Social Change*. Oxford.

(1989) An introduction to the Naikens: the people and the ethnographic myth. In P. Hockings (ed.) *Blue Mountains: the ethnography and biogeography of a South Indian region*. New Delhi.

(1990) Giving environment: another perspective on the economic system of gatherer-hunters. *Current Anthropology* 31: 189–96.

(1992a) Beyond 'the original affluent society': a culturalist reformulation. *Current Anthropology* 33: 189–96.

(1992b) Beyond 'the hunting and gathering mode of subsistence': observations on Nayaka and other modern hunter-gatherers. *Man* (n.s.) 27: 19–44.

(1994) The Nayaka. *Encyclopedia of World Cultures*. Human Relations Area File: New Haven, Conn.

Boesch, C. (1991) Teaching in wild chimpanzees. *Animal Behaviour* 41: 530–2.

(forthcoming) *Teaching in Wild Chimpanzees*.

Boesch, C. and Boesch, H. (1989) Cooperative hunting among wild chimpanzees in the Tai National Park. *American Journal of Physical Anthropology* 78: 547–73.

Bourdieu, P. (1977) *Outline of a Theory of Practice*. Cambridge.

Boyce, M. (1979) *Zoroastrians: their religious beliefs and practices*. London.

Boyd, R. and Richardson, P. (1985) *Culture and the Evolutionary Process*. Chicago.

Briggs, J.L. (1970) *Never in Anger: portrait of an eskimo family*. Cambridge, Mass.

Britton, B. and Pellegrini, A. (eds.) (1990) *Narrative Thought and Narrative Language*. Hillsdale, N.J.

Brother, O.P. (1979) *The Little Way: the spirituality of Thérèse of Lisieux*. London.

Brown, G. and Yule, G. (1983) *Discourse Analysis*. Cambridge.

Brown, P. (1979) Language, interaction and sex roles in a Mayan community: a study of politeness and the position of women. Ph.D. dissertation, University of California, Berkeley.

(1980) How and why are women more polite: some evidence from a Mayan community. In S. McConnell-Ginet, R. Borker and N. Furman (eds.) *Women and Language in Literature and Society*. New York.

(1990) Gender, politeness and confrontation in Tenejapa. In D. Tannen (ed.)

Gender and Conversational Interaction, special issue of *Discourse Processes* (Spring). Reprinted in D. Tannen (ed.) *Gender and Conversational Interaction.* Oxford.

Brown, P. and Levinson, S. (1978) Universals in language use: politeness phenomena. In E. Goody (ed.) *Questions and Politeness: strategies in social interaction.* Cambridge.

(1987) *Politeness: some universals in language usage.* Cambridge.

Bruner, J.S. (1972) Nature and uses of immaturity. *American Psychologist* 27: 687–708.

(1978) From communication to language: a psychological perspective. In I. Markova (ed.) *The Social Context of Language.* Chichester.

(1986) *Actual Minds, Possible Worlds.* London.

(1987) Life as narrative. *Social Research* 32: 11–32.

(1990) *Acts of Meaning.* Cambridge, Mass.

Bruner, J.S. and Sherwood, V. (1976) Peekaboo and the learning of rule structures. In J.S. Bruner, A. Jolly and K. Sylva (eds.) *Play: its role in development and evolution.* Harmondsworth.

Buber, M. (1900) *I and Thou.*

(1970) *Between Man and Man.* New York.

Burke, K. (1945) *A Grammar of Motives.* New York.

Burke, P. (1987) Insult and blasphemy. In P. Burke, *The Historical Anthropology of Early Modern Italy: essays on perception and communication.* Cambridge.

Byrne, R.W. and Whiten, A. (eds.) (1988) *Machiavellian Intelligence: social expertise and the evolution of intellect in monkeys, apes and humans.* Oxford.

(1990) Tactical deception in primates: the 1990 database. *Primate Report* 27: 1–101.

(1991) Computation and mindreading in primate tactile deception. In A. Whiten (ed.) *Natural Theories of Mind: evolution, development and simulation of everyday mindreading.* Oxford.

(1992) Cognitive evolution in primates: evidence from tactical deception. *Man* (n.s.) 27: 609–27.

Carrithers, M. (1988) Passions of nation and community in the Bahubali Affair. *Modern Asian Studies* 22: 815–44.

(1991a) Narrativity: mindreading and making societies. In A. Whiten (ed.) *Natural Theories of Mind: evolution, development and simulation of everyday mindreading.* Oxford.

(1991b). The foundations of community among southern Digambar Jains: an essay on rhetoric and experience. In M. Carrithers and C. Humphrey (eds.) *The Assembly of Listeners: Jains in society.* Cambridge.

(1992) *Why Humans have Cultures: explaining anthropology and social diversity.* Oxford.

Carrithers, M., Collins, S. and Lukes, S. (eds.) (1985) *The Category of the Person: anthropology, philosophy, history.* Cambridge.

Chafe, W. (1990) Some things that narrative tells us about the mind. In B. Britton and A. Pellegrini (eds.) *Narrative Thought and Narrative Language.* Hillsdale, N.J.

Chauvin, Y. (1988) Symbol acquisition in humans and neural (PDP) networks. Ph.D. dissertation, University of California, San Diego.

Chaytor, M. (1980) Household and kinship. *History Workshop Journal* 10: 25–51.

Cheney, D.L. and Seyfarth, R.M. (1988) Social and non-social knowledge in vervet monkeys. In R.W. Byrne and A. Whiten (eds.) *Machiavellian Intelligence: social expertise and the evolution of intellect in monkeys, apes and humans.* Oxford.

(1990) *How Monkeys see the World.* Chicago.

Chomsky, N. (1966) *Cartesian Linguistics.* New York.

(1968) *Language and Mind.* New York.

(1980) *Rules and Representations.* New York.

Cicero, Q. [1923] *De Senectute, De Amicitia, De Divinatione*, translated by W.A. Falconer: Loeb Classical Library, London.

Clark, H. (1992) *Arenas of Language Use.* Chicago.

Clark, H. and Carlson, T. (1982) Speech acts and hearer's beliefs. In N. Smith (ed.) *Mutual Knowledge.* London.

Clark, H. and Marshall, C. (1981) Definite reference and mutual knowledge. In A. Joshi, I. Sag and B. Webber (eds.) *Elements of Discourse Understanding.* Cambridge.

Clutton-Brock, T.H. and Harvey, P.H. (1980) Primates, brains and ecology. *Journal of Zoology* 190: 309–23.

Cohen, P., Morgan, J. and Pollock, M. (1990) *Intentions in Communication.* Cambridge, Mass.

Cole, M. (1985) The zone of proximal development: where culture and cognition create each other. In J.V. Wertsch (ed.) *Culture, Communication and Cognition.* Cambridge.

Connolly, P. (1978) *Hannibal and the Enemies of Rome.* London.

Corum, C. (1975) Basques, particles and babytalk: a case for pragmatics. *Proceedings of the Berkeley Linguistics Society* 1: 90–9.

Coulmas, F. (ed.) (1981a) *Conversational Routine: explorations in standardized communication situations and prepatterned speech.* The Hague, Paris and New York.

(1981b) Poison to your soul, thanks and apologies contrastively viewed. In F. Coulmas (ed.) *Conversational Routine: explorations in standardized communication situations and prepatterned speech.* The Hague, Paris and New York.

Cranach, M. von, Foppa, K., Lepenies, W. and Ploog, D. (eds.) (1979) *Human Ethology: claims and limits of a new discipline.* Cambridge.

D'Andrade, R. (1981) The cultural part of cognition. *Cognitive Science* 5: 179–95.

(1984) Cultural meaning systems. In R.A. Shweder and R.A. LeVine (eds.) *Culture Theory: essays on mind, self and emotion.* Cambridge.

(1990) Some propositions about the relations between culture and human cognition. In J.W. Stigler, R.A. Shweder and G. Herdt (eds.) *Cultural Psychology.* Cambridge.

Darwin, C. (1964) [1859] *On the Origin of the Species.* Cambridge, Mass.

Dasser, V. (1988) Mapping social concepts in monkeys. In R.W. Byrne and A. Whiten (eds.), *Machiavellian Intelligence: social expertise and the evolution of intellect in monkeys, apes and humans*. Oxford.

de Waal, F. (1982) *Chimpanzee Politics*. London.

Dennett, D.C. (1983) Intentional systems in cognitive ethology: the Panglossian paradigm defended. *Behavioral and Brain Sciences* 6: 343–90.

(1987) *The Intentional Stance*. Cambridge, Mass.

(1988) The intentional stance in theory and practice. In R.W. Byrne and A. Whiten (eds.) *Machiavellian Intelligence: social expertise and the evolution of intellect in monkeys, apes and humans*. Oxford.

Devisch, R. (1985) Perspectives on divination in contemporary sub-Saharan Africa. In W. van Binsbergen and M. Schoffeleers (eds.) *Theoretical Explorations in African Religion*. London.

Dhalla, M.N. (1922) *Zoroastrian Civilization: from the earliest times to the downfall of the last Zoroastrian Empire 651 AD*. New York.

Diaz, R.M. (1986) The union of thought and language in children's private speech. *Quarterly Newsletter of the Laboratory of Human Cognition* 8: 90–7.

Donald, M. (1991) *Origins of the Modern Mind*. Cambridge, Mass.

Donin, H.H. (1980) *To Pray as a Jew*. New York.

Dörner, D. (1987) *On the Logic of Failure: thinking, planning and decision making in uncertainty and complexity*. Working paper no. 54, Lehrstuhl Psychologie II, University of Bemburg.

(1990) The logic of failure. *Philosophical Transactions of the Royal Society* B327: 463–73. (Originally given as address to the Royal Society meeting: Human factors in high-risk situations, June 1989.)

Drew, P. (1984) Speakers' reportings in invitation sequences. In J.M. Atkinson and J. Heritage (eds.) *Structures of Social Actions: studies in conversation analysis*. Cambridge.

(1987) Po-faced receipts of teases. *Linguistics* 25: 219–53.

(1991) Asymmetries of knowledge in conversational interactions. In I. Markova and K. Foppa (eds.) *Asymmetries of dialogue*. Hemel Hempstead.

Drew, P. and Holt, E. (1988) Complainable matters: the use of idiomatic expressions in making complaints. *Social Problems* 35: 398–417.

Du Bois, J.W. (1987) Meaning without intention: lessons from divination. *IPJA papers in pragmatics* 1(2): 80–112.

Dunbar, R.I.M. (1992a) Why gossip is good for you. *New Scientist* 136 (1848): 28–31.

(1992b) Neocortex size as a constraint on group size in primates. *Journal of Human Evolution* 20: 469–93.

(1993) Coevolution of neocortical size, group size and language in humans. *Behavioral and Brain Sciences* 16: 681–735.

Enkvist, N.E. (1984) Text and discourse linguistics, rhetoric, and stylistics. In T. van Dijk (ed.) *Discourse and Literature*. Amsterdam.

Ervin-Tripp, S. (1979) Children's verbal turn-taking. In E. Ochs and B. Schieffelin (eds.) *Developmental Pragmatics*. New York.

Evans-Pritchard, E.E. (1937) *Witchcraft, Oracles and Magic among the Azande*. Oxford.

(1956) *Nuer Religion*. Oxford.

Fauconnier, G. (1985) *Mental Spaces*. Cambridge, Mass.

Feld, S. (1982) *Sound and Sentiment: birds, weeping, poetics and song in Kaluli expression*. Philadelphia.

Feldman, C., Bruner, J., Renderer, B. and Spitzer, S. (1990) Narrative comprehension. In B. Britton and A. Pellegrini (eds.) *Narrative Thought and Narrative Language*. Hillsdale, N.J.

Ferguson, C.A. (1981) The structure and use of politeness formulas. In F. Coulmas (ed.) *Conversational Routine: explorations in standardized communication situations and prepatterned speech*. The Hague, Paris and New York.

Fernandez, J. (1974) The mission of metaphor in expressive culture. *Current Anthropology* 15: 119–45.

Field, J. (1955) [1934] *A Life of One's Own*. London.

Finnegan, R. (1969) How to do things with words: performative utterances among the Limba of Sierra Leone. *Man* (n.s.) 4.

Flavell, J.H. and Ross, L. (eds.) (1981) *Social Cognitive Development*. Cambridge.

Fodor, J. (1983) *Modularity of Mind*. Cambridge, Mass.

Fortes, M.F. (1983) *Rules and the Emergence of Society*. Royal Anthropological Institute, occasional paper no. 39. London.

(1987) Ritual and office. In J.R. Goody (ed.) *Religion, Morality and the Person*. Cambridge.

Fouts, R.S., Fouts, D.H. and Van Cantfort, T.E. (1989) The infant Loulis learns signs from cross fostered chimpanzees. In R.A. Gardner, B.T. Gardner and T.E. Van Cantfort (eds.) *Teaching Sign Language to Chimpanzees*. New York.

Frankel, R. (1983) From sentence to sequence: understanding the medical encounter through microinteractional analysis. *Discourse Processes* 7: 135–70.

Gallup, G.G. (1970) Chimpanzees: self-recognition. *Science* 167: 86–7.

Gardner, H. (1983) *Frames of Mind*. New York.

Gardner, P. (1966) Symmetric response and memorate knowledge: the structure and ecology of individualistic culture. *Southwestern Journal of Anthropology* 22: 389–415.

(1991) Foragers' pursuit of individual autonomy. *Current Anthropology* 32: 543–73.

Garfinkel, H. (1967) *Studies in Ethnomethodology*. Englewood Cliffs, N.J.

(1984) [1967] Commonsense knowledge of social structures: the documentary method of interpretation in lay and professional fact finding. In H. Garfinkel *Studies in Ethnomethodology*. Cambridge.

Garfinkel, H., Lynch, M. and Livingston, E. (1981) The work of a discovering science construed with materials from the optically discovered pulsar. *Philosophy of the Social Sciences* 11: 131–58.

Geiss, M. and Zwicky, A. (1971) On invited inferences. *Linguistic Inquiry* 2: 561–5.

Gelb, N. (1986) *The Berlin Wall*. New York.

Gellner, E. (1975) Ethnomethodology: the re-enchantment industry or the Calif.n way of subjectivity. *Philosophy of the Social Sciences* 5: 431–50.

Gelman, R. and Spelke, E. (1981) The development of thought about animate and inanimate objects: implications for research on social cognition. In J.H. Flavell, and L. Ross (eds.) *Social Cognitive Development*. Cambridge.

Gergen, M. and Gergen, K. (1984) The social construction of narrative accounts. In K. Gergen and M. Gergen (eds.) *Historical Social Psychology*. Hillsdale.

Gibson, T. (1986) *Sacrifice and Sharing in the Philippine Highlands: religion and society among the Buid of Mindoro*. London School of Economics monographs on social anthropology, no. 57. London.

Gill, S.D. (1981) *Sacred Words: a study of Navajo religion and prayer*. Westport, Conn.

Ginsberg, M.L. (1987) *Readings in Non-monotonic Logic*. Los Altos, Calif.

Glickman, S.E. and Scroges, R.W. (1966) Curiosity in zoo animals. *Behaviour* 26: 151–8.

Godelier, M. (1988) *The Mental and the Material*. London.

Goffman, E. (1959) *The Presentation of Self in Everyday Life*. New York.

(1974) *Frame analysis*. Cambridge, Mass.

(1978) Response cries. *Language* 54: 787–815.

(1981) *Forms of Talk*. Philadelphia.

(1983) The interaction order. American Sociological Association 1982 Presidential Address. *American Sociological Review* 48: 1–17.

Good, D.A. (1989) The viability of conversational grammars. In M. Taylor, F. Neel and D. Bouwhuis (eds.) *Multi-modal aspects of Dialogue*. Berlin.

Goodall, J. (1986) *The Chimpanzees of Gombe: patterns of behavior*. Cambridge, Mass.

Goodenough, W.H. (1990) Evolution of the human capacity for beliefs. *American Anthropologist* 92: 597–612.

Goodwin, C. (1979) The interactional construction of a sentence. In G. Psathas (ed.) *Everyday Language*. New York.

(1981) *Conversational Organization: interaction between speakers and hearers*. New York.

(1986) Gesture as a resource for the organization of mutual orientation. *Semiotica* 62(1–2): 29–49.

(1993) Perception, technology and interaction on a scientific research vessel. Unpublished manuscript, University of South Carolina.

Goodwin, C. and Goodwin, M.H. (1986) Gesture and coparticipation in the activity of searching for a word. *Semiotica* 62(1–2): 51–75.

Goodwin, M.H. (1981) Searching for a word as an interactive activity. In J. Deely and M.D. Lenkart (eds.) *Semiotics*. New York.

Goody, E. (1972) Greetings, begging and the presentation of respect. In J.S. LaFontaine (ed.) *The Interpretation of Ritual*. London.

(1978a) Towards a theory of questions. In E. Goody (ed.) *Questions and Politeness: strategies in social interaction*. Cambridge.

(1978b) Introduction. In E. Goody (ed.) *Questions and Politeness: strategies in social interaction*. Cambridge.

(1982) Daboya weavers: relation of production, dependence and reciprocity. In E. Goody (ed.) *From Craft to Industry*. Cambridge.

(1987) Why must might be right? Observations on sexual Herrschaft. *Quarterly Newsletter of the Laboratory of Comparative Human Cognition* 9: 54–76.

(1989) Learning, apprenticeship and the division of labour. In M. Coy (ed.) *Apprenticeship: from theory to method and back again*. Albany, N.Y.

(1993) Informal learning of adult roles in Baale. In M. Fielous, J. Lombard and J-M. Kambou-Ferrand (eds.) *Images d'Afrique et Sciences Sociales: les pays lobi, birifor et dagara*. Paris.

(n.d.) Working papers in implications of a social origin of human intelligence. Berlin. Unpublished manuscript.

Goody, J.R. (1962) *Death, Property and the Ancestors*. Stanford, Calif.

(1977) *The Domestication of the Savage Mind*. Cambridge.

(1987) *The Interface between the Written and the Oral*. Cambridge.

Greenfield, P. (1991) Language, tools and brain: the ontogeny and phylogeny of hierarchically organized sequential behavior. *Behavioral and Brain Sciences* 14: 531–95.

Grice, H.P. (1957) Meaning. *Philosophical Review* 66: 377–88.

(1989) *Ways with Words*. Cambridge, Mass.

Gumperz, J.J. and Hymes, D. (eds.) (1964) *The Ethnography of Communication*. Special publication of *American Anthropologist*, vol. 66.

Haack, S. (1978) *Philosophy of Logics*. Cambridge.

Haiman, J. (1990) Sarcasm as theater. *Cognitive Linguistics* 1–2: 181–205.

Haimoff, E. (n.d.) Video analysis of Siamang call bouts. Unpublished manuscript, University of California, Los Angeles.

Hall, E.T. (1959) *The Silent Language*. Greenwich, Conn.

Harcourt, A.H. (1988) Alliances in contests and social intelligence. In R.W. Byrne and A. Whiten (eds.) *Machiavellian Intelligence: social expertise and the evolution of intellect in monkeys, apes and humans*. Oxford.

Harcourt, A.H. and de Waal, F. (eds.) (1992) *Coalitions and Alliances among Humans and other Animals*. Oxford.

Hargreaves, R. (1981) *Little Miss Bossy*. Bromley, Kent.

Harman, G. (1974) review of *Meaning* by S. Schiffer. *Journal of Philosophy* 71(7): 224–9.

Havelock, E.A. (1963) *Preface to Plato*. Cambridge, Mass.

Haviland, J.B. (1977) *Gossip, Reputation and Knowledge in Zinacantan*. Chicago.

Hayes, C. (1951) *The Ape in our House*. New York.

Hayes, K.J. and Hayes, C. (1952) Imitation in a home-raised chimpanzee. *Journal of Comparative Physiological Psychology* 45: 450–9.

Headland, T.N. and Reid, L. (1989) Hunter-gatherers and their neighbours from prehistory to the present. *Current Anthropology* 30: 43–67.

Heath, S.B. (1983) *Ways with Words: language, life and work in communities and classrooms*. Cambridge.

Henn-Schmölders, C. (1975) Ars Conversationis. Zur Geschichte des sprachlichen Umgangs. *Arcadia* 10: 16-33.

Heritage, J. (1984) *Garfinkel and Ethnomethodology*. Cambridge.

(1990/91) Intention, meaning and strategy: observations on constraints in interactional analysis. *Research in Language and Social Interaction* 24: 311–22.

Herskovits, A. (1986) *Language and Spatial Cognition*. Cambridge.

Hobson, R.P. (1984) Early childhood autism and the question of egocentrism. *Journal of Autism and Developmental Disorders* 14: 85–104.

Hollis, M. and Lukes, S. (eds.) (1982) *Rationality and Relativism*. Oxford.

Holquist, M. (1990) *Dialogism: Bakhtin and his world*. London.

Holton, G. (1981) Comments on Professor Harold Garfinkel's paper. *Philosophy of the Social Sciences* 11: 159–61.

Horn, L. (1989) *A Natural History of Negation*. Chicago.

Horton, R. (1967) African traditional thought and Western science. *Africa* 38: 50–71 and 155–87.

  (1982) Tradition and modernity revisited. In M. Hollis and S. Lukes (eds.) *Rationality and Relativism*. Oxford.

Howe, M. (1989) *Fragments of Genius: the strange feats of idiots savants*. London.

Humboldt, W. von (1988) [1836] *On Language*. Cambridge.

Humphrey, N.K. (1976) The social function of intellect. In P.P.G. Bateson and R.A. Hinde (eds.) *Growing Points in Ethology*. Cambridge. Reprinted in R.W. Byrne and A. Whiten (eds.) *Machiavellian Intelligence: social expertise and the evolution of intellect in monkeys, apes and humans*. Oxford, 1988.

  (1983) *Consciousness Regained*. Oxford.

  (1986) *The Inner Eye*. London.

Hutchins, E. (1991) Social organization of distributed cognition. In L. Resnick, J. Levine and S. Teasley (eds.) *Perspectives on Socially Shared Cognition*. Washington, D.C.

  (in press) *Cognition in the Wild*. Cambridge, Mass.

Hutchins, E. and Hazlehurst, B. (1991) Learning in the cultural process. In C. Langton, C. Taylor, D. Farmer and S. Rasmussen (eds.) *Artificial Life*, Vol. II. Redwood City, Calif.

Hutchins, E. and Klausen, T. (1990) *Distributed Cognition in an Airline Cockpit*. Department of Cognitive Science, University of California, San Diego.

Ingold, T. (1987) *The Appropriation of Nature: essays on human ecology and social relations*. Iowa.

Irvine, J. (1974) Strategies of status manipulation in Wolof greeting. In R. Bauman and J. Sherzer (eds.) *Explorations in the Ethnography of Speaking*. London.

Jackson, M. (1978) An approach to Kuranko divination. *Human Relations* 31: 117–38.

Jammer, M. (1974) *The Philosophy of Quantum Mechanics*. New York.

Jauss, H.-R. (1972) Theorie der Gattungen und Literatur des Mittelalters. In H.-R. Jauss and E. Kohler (eds.) *Grundriss der romanischen Literaturen des Mittelalters*, Vol. I: *Generalities*. Heidelberg.

Jefferson, G. (1975) Error correction as an international resource. *Language in Society* 4: 181–99.

  (1978) Sequential aspects of storytelling in conversation. In J. Schenkein (ed.) *Studies in the Organization of Conversational Interaction*. New York.

  (1984) On stepwise transition from talk about a trouble to inappropriately next-positioned matters. In J.M. Atkinson and J. Heritage (eds.) *Structures of Social Action*. Cambridge.

  (1988a) On the sequential organization of troubles-talk in ordinary conversation. *Social Problems* 35: 418–41.

  (1988b) Remarks on 'non-correction' in conversation. Unpublished paper: lecture given at Helsingen Yliopisto, Suomen Kielen Laitos, Helsinki (to appear in *Text*).

(1992) List-construction as a task and resource. In G. Psathas (ed.) *Interactional Competence*. Hillsdale, N.J.

Jerison, H.J. (1973) *Evolution of the Brain and Intelligence*. New York.

Johnson-Laird, P.N. (1983) *Mental Models: towards a cognitive science of language, inference and consciousness*. Cambridge.

Johnson-Laird, P.N. and Wason, P.C. (eds.) (1977a) *Thinking: readings in cognitive science*. Cambridge.

(1977b) A theoretical analysis of insight into a reasoning task, and Postscript. In P.N. Johnson-Laird and P.C. Wason (eds.) *Thinking: readings in cognitive science*. Cambridge.

Jolles, A. (1972) *Einfache Formen: Legende, Sage, Mythe, Rätsel, Spruch, Kasus, Memorabile, Märchen, Witz*. Tübingen.

Jolly, A. (1966a) Lemur social behaviour and primate intelligence. *Science* 153: 501–6. Reprinted in R.W. Byrne and A. Whiten (eds.) *Machiavellian Intelligence: social expertise and the evolution of intellect in monkeys, apes and humans*. Oxford.

(1966b) *Lemur Behaviour*. Chicago.

Judge, P.G. (1982) Redirection of aggression based on kinship in a captive group of pigtail macaques. *International Journal of Primatology* 3: 301.

Kahneman, D., Slovic, P. and Tversky, A. (1982) *Judgement under Uncertainty: heuristics and biases*. Cambridge.

Kant, I. (1934) *Religion Within the Limits of Reason Alone*. New York.

Katz, R. (1982) *Boiling Energy: community healing among the Kalahari !Kung*. Cambridge, Mass.

Keenan, E.O. (1977) Why look at unplanned and planned discourse? In E.O. Keenan and T.L. Bernett (eds.) *Discourse across Time and Space*. Los Angeles.

Keesing, R.M. (1982) *Kwaio Religion: the living and the dead in a Solomon Island society*. New York.

Kendon, A. (1976) Some functions of the face in a kissing round. *Semiotica* 17: 299–334.

Kenny, A. (1966) Practical inference. *Analysis* 26(3): 65–75.

Kolb, B. and Whishaw, I. (1990) *Fundamentals of Human Neuropsychology*. New York.

Kummer, H. (1967) Tripartite relations in hamadryas baboons. In S.A. Altman (ed.) *Social Communication among Primates*. Chicago.

Lafon, J.-C. (1968) Auditory basis of phonetics. In B. Malmberg (ed.) *Manual of Phonetics*. Amsterdam.

LaFontaine, J.S. (1978) Introduction. In J.S. LaFontaine (ed.) *Sex and Age as Principles of Social Differentiation*. London.

Lakoff, G. (1987) *Women, Fire and Dangerous Things*. Chicago.

Lakoff, G. and Johnson, M. (1980) *Metaphors We Live By*. Chicago.

Landau, T. (1989) *About Faces: the evolution of the human face*. New York.

Langacker, R. W. (1986) An introduction to cognitive grammar. *Cognitive Science* 10: 1–40.

(1987) *Foundations of Cognitive Grammar*, Vol. I: *Theoretical Prerequisites*. Stanford, Calif.

Lave, J., Murtaugh, M. and de la Rocha, O. (1984) The dialectic of arithmetic in grocery shopping. In B. Rogoff and J. Lave (eds.) *Everyday Cognition: its development in social context*. Cambridge, Mass.

Laver, J.D.M.H. (1981) Linguistic routines and politeness in greeting and parting. In F. Coulmas (ed.) *Conversational Routine*. The Hague, Paris and New York.

Lee, R.B. (1979) *The !Kung San: men, women and work in a foraging society*. New York.

(1984) *The Dobe !Kung*. New York.

Lee, R.B. and DeVore, I. (eds.) (1968) *Man the Hunter*. Chicago.

Lerner, G.H. (1987) Collaborative turn sequences: sentence construction and social action. Ph.D. dissertation. University of California, Irvine.

Leslie, A.M. (1987) Pretence and representation in infancy: the origins of 'theory of mind'. *Psychological Review* 94: 412–26.

Levine, L.W. (1977) *Black Culture and Black Consciousness: Afro-American folk thought from slavery to freedom*. New York.

Levinson, S. (1983) *Pragmatics*. Cambridge.

(1985) What's special about conversational inference? Paper presented to the Annual Conference of the British Psychological Society, Swansea, April.

(1987a) Minimization and conversational inference. In M. Pappi and J. Verscheuren (eds.) *The Pragmatic Perspective*. Amsterdam.

(1987b) Pragmatics and the grammar of anaphora. *Journal of Linguistics* 23: 379–434.

(1988) Putting linguistics on a proper footing: explorations in Goffman's participation framework. In P. Drew and A. Wootton (eds.) *Erving Goffman: exploring the interaction order*. Cambridge.

(1989) Review of Sperber and Wilson's *Relevance*. *Journal of Linguistics* 25: 455–72.

(1991) Pragmatic reduction of the binding conditions revisited. *Journal of Linguistics* 27: 107–61.

(in press) Three levels of meaning. In F. Palmer (ed.) *Grammar and Meaning*. Cambridge.

(forthcoming) *Generalized Conversational Implicature*. Cambridge.

Lévi-Strauss, C. (1969) *The Elementary Structure of Kinship*. London. French edition, 1949.

Lewis, D. (1969) *Convention*. Cambridge, Mass.

Lewis, I.M. (1971) *Ecstatic Religion*. Harmondsworth.

Liberman, R. (1985) *Understanding Interaction in Central Australia*. London.

Lieberman, P. (1968) Primate vocalizations and human linguistic ability. *Journal of the Acoustical Society of America* 44: 1157–64.

(1991) *Uniquely Human: the evolution of speech, thought and selfless behavior*. Cambridge, Mass.

Lieberman, P. and Blumstein, S. (1988) *Speech Physiology, Speech Perception, and Acoustic Phonetics*. Cambridge.

Lienhardt, G. (1961) *Divinity and Experience: the religion of the Dinka*. Oxford.

Lindblom, B., MacNeilage, P.F. and Studdert-Kennedy, M. (in press) *Evolution of Spoken Language*. New York.

Lloyd, G.E.R. (1979) *Magic, Reason and Experience*. Cambridge.

Luce, R.D. and Raiffa, H. (1957) *Games and Decisions*. New York.

Luckmann, T. (1979) Soziologie der Sprache. In R. König (ed.) *Handbuch der empirischen Sozialforschung*, Vol. XIII. Stuttgart.

(1982) Individual action and social knowledge. In M. von Cranach and R. Harré (eds.) *The Analysis of Action: recent theoretical and empirical advances*. Cambridge.

(1983) Elements of a social-theory of communication. In T. Luckmann *Life-world and Social Realities*. London.

(1986) Grundformen der gesellschaftlichen Vermittlung des Wissens: kommunikative Gattungen. In F. Neidhardt, M. Lepsius and J. Weiss (eds.) *Kultur und Gesellschaft*, Sonderheft 27 der *Kolner Zeitschrift für Soziologie and Sozialpsychologie*. (French: Les formes élémentaires de la transmission sociale du savoir: genres comunicatifs. To be published in *Sociétés*.)

(1987) Kanon und Konversion. In A. and J. Assman (eds.) *Kanon und Zensur*. Munich.

(1989) Prolegomena to a social theory of communicative genres. *Slovene Studies* 11(1–2), Toussaint Hocevar Memorial Issue: 159–66.

(1992) On the communicative adjustment of perspectives, dialogue, and communicative genres. In A. Heen Wold (ed.) *The Dialogical Alternative: towards a theory of language and mind*. London.

Luckmann, T. and Keppler, A. (1989) Weissheits-vermittlung im Alltag. Wer in den Augen eines anderen weise ist, ist weise. In W. Oelmuller (ed.) *Philosophie und Weisheit*. Paderborn.

Luria, A.R. (1979) *The Making of Mind*, edited by M. Cole and S. Cole, Cambridge, Mass.

(1981) *Language and Cognition*, edited by J.V. Wertsch. Washington, D.C.

Lynch, M. and Woolgar, S. (eds.) (1988) *Representation in Scientific Practice*. Cambridge, Mass.

Lyons, J. (1988) Origins of language. In A.C. Fabian (ed.) *Origins*. Cambridge.

Machiavelli, N. (1966) *The Prince*, translated by D. Donno. London.

MacNeilage, P.F. (1987) The evolution of hemispheric specialization for manual function and language. In S. Wyse (ed.) *Higher Brain Functions: recent explorations of the brain's emergent properties*. New York.

MacNeilage, P.F., Studdert-Kennedy, M. and Lindblom, B. (1987) Primate handedness reconsidered. *Behavioral and Brain Sciences* 10: 247–63.

Macphail, E.M. (1985) Vertebrate intelligence: the null hypothesis. In L. Weiskrantz (ed.) *Animal Intelligence*. Oxford.

Malinowski, B. (1927) The problem of meaning in primitive languages. In C.K. Ogden and I.A. Richards (eds.) *The Meaning of Meaning*. London.

Mandelbaum, J. and Pomerantz, A. (1991) What drives social action? In K. Tracy (ed.) *Understanding Face-to-Face Interaction: issues linking goals and discourse*. Hillsdale, N.J.

Marett, R.R. (1909) *The Threshold of Religion*. London.

Marshall, L. (1957) The kin terminology system of the !Kung Bushmen. *Africa* 27(1): 1–25.

(1976) *The !Kung of Nyae Nyae*. Cambridge, Mass.

Marslen-Wilson, W., Levy, E. and Tyler, L. (1982) Producing interpretable discourse: the establishment and maintenance of reference. In R. Jarvella and W. Klein (eds.) *Speech, Place and Action*. London.

Martin, C.E. (1990) Popular speech and social order in Northern Mexico, 1650–1830. *Comparative Studies in Society and History* 32: 305–24.

Martin, R.D. (1990) *Primate Origins and Evolution*. London.

Maupoil, B. (1943) La géomancie à l'ancienne Côte des Esclaves. *Trav. et Mem. de l'Inst. d'Eth*. 42.

McHugh, P. (1968) *Defining the Situation: the organisation of meaning in social interaction*. New York.

McNeill, D. (1985) So you think gestures are nonverbal? *Psychological Review* 92: 350–71.

Mead, G.H. (1967) [1934] *Mind, Self and Society*. Chicago.

Mervis, C. and Rosch, E. (1981) Categorization of natural objects. *Annual Review of Psychology* 32: 89–115.

Michaels, S. (1986) Narrative presentations: an oral preparation for literacy with first graders. In J. Cook-Gumperz (ed.) *The Social Construction of Literacy*. Cambridge.

Miller, G.A. (1956) The magical number seven, plus or minus two. *Psychological Review* 63: 81–97.

Miller, G.A., Galanter, E. and Pribram, K.H. (1960) *Plans and the Structure of Behavior*. New York.

Miller, G.A. and Johnson-Laird, P.N. (1976) *Language and Perception*. Cambridge.

Miller, R.A. (1967) *The Japanese Language*. Chicago.

Milton, K. (1988) Foraging behaviour and the evolution of primate intelli gence. In R.W. Byrne and A. Whiten (eds.) *Machiavellian Intelligence: social expertise and the evolution of intellect in monkeys, apes and humans*. Oxford.

Morris, D. (1979) *Gestures: their origins and distribution*. London.

Moulton, J.H. (1913) *Early Zoroastrianism*. (Hibbert lectures at Oxford and London 1912.) London.

Myers, F. (1982) Always ask: resource use and land ownership among Pintupi aborigines of the Australian Western Desert. In N.M. William and E.S. Hunn (eds.) *Resource Managers: North American and Australian hunter-gatherers*. Canberra.

Nadel, S.F. (1957) *The Theory of Social Structure*. New York.

Nelson, K. (1981) Social cognition in a script framework. In J.H. Flavell and L. Ross (eds.) *Social Cognitive Development*. Cambridge.

Nies, F. (1978) *Genres mineurs. Texte zur Theorie und Geschichte nichtkanonischer Literatur (vom 16 Jahrhundert bis zur Gegenwart)*. Munich.

Nishida, T. (1983) Alpha status and agonistic alliance in wild chimpanzees. *Primates* 24: 318–36.

Oldman, D. (1974) Chance and skill: a study of roulette. *Sociology* 8: 596–603.

Oxnard, C.E. (1981) The place of man among the primates: anatomical, molecular and morphometric evidence. *Homo* 32: 149–76.

Park, G.K. (1963) Divination and its social context. *Journal of the Royal Anthropological Institute* 93: 195–209.

Parkin, D. (1979) Straightening the paths from wilderness: the case of divinatory speech. *Journal of the Anthropology Society of Oxford* 10(3): 147–60.

Passingham, R.E. (1981) Primate specializations in brain and intelligence. *Symposia of the Zoological Society of London* 46: 361–88.

(1982) *The Human Primate.* New York.

Passingham, R.E. and Ettlinger, G. (1974) A comparison of cortical function in man and other primates. *International Review of Neurobiology* 16: 233–99.

Patterson, F.G. and Cohn, R. (in press) Self recognition and self awareness in lowland gorillas. In S. Parker, M. Boccia and R. Mitchell (eds.) *Comparative Reflections on Self Awareness in Animals and Humans.* Cambridge.

Patterson, F.G. and Linden, E. (1981) *The Education of Koko.* New York.

Perrault, C.R. (1987) *An Application of Default Logic to Speech Act Theory.* Stanford CSLI report.

Piaget, J. (1929) *The Child's Conception of the World.* London.

Pollack, M. (1986a) *A Model of Plan Inference that Distinguishes between the Beliefs of Actors and Observers.* Technical note 387, AI center, Computer Science Division, SRI International.

(1986b) *Inferring Domain Plans in Question-Answering.* Technical note 403, AI center, Computer Science Division, SRI International.

Pomerantz, A. (1978) Compliment responses: notes on the cooperation of multiple constrains. In J. Schenkein (ed.) *Studies in the Organization of Conversational Interaction.* New York.

(1980) Telling my side: 'limited access' as a 'fishing' device. *Sociological Inquiry* 50: 186–98.

(1984) Agreeing and disagreeing with assessments: some features of preferred/dispreferred turn shapes. In J.M. Atkinson and J. Heritage (eds.) *Structures of Social Actions: studies in conversational analysis.* Cambridge.

Premack, D. (1986) *Gavagai! or the Future History of the Animal Language Controversy.* Cambridge, Mass.

(1988) 'Does the chimpanzee have a theory of mind?' revisited. In R.W. Byrne and A. Whiten (eds.) *Machiavellian Intelligence: social expertise and the evolution of intellect in monkeys, apes and humans.* Oxford.

Quinn, N. and Holland, D. (1987) Culture and cognition. In D. Holland and N. Quinn (eds.) *Cultural Models in Language and Thought.* Cambridge.

Ransom, T.W. (1981) *Beach Troop of the Gombe.* East Brunswick, N.J.

Rappaport, R.A. (1988) Logos, liturgy and the evolution of humanity. Conference paper, Symposium, Zagreb, XII International Conference of Anthropological and Ethnological Sciences.

Rattray, R.S. (1927) *Religion and Art in Ashanti.* London.

Reason, J. (1987) The Chernobyl Errors. *Bulletin of the British Psychology Society* 40: 201–6.

Rehfisch, F. (1960) The dynamics of multilinearity on the Mambila Plateau. *Africa* 3: 246–61.

(1972) *The Social Structure of a Mambila Village.* Ahmadu Bello University Sociology Department, occasional paper 2. Zaria.

Reisman, P. (1977) *Freedom in Fulani Social Life: an introspective ethnography.* Chicago.

(1992) *First Find your Child a Good Mother: the construction of self in two African communities.* New Brunswick, N.J.

Richards, A.I. (1956) *Chisungu: a girls' initiation ceremony among the Bemba of Northern Rhodesia.* London.

Rogoff, B. (1990) *Apprenticeship in Thinking: cognitive development in social context.* Oxford.

Rommetveit, R. (1990) On axiomatic features of a dialogical approach to language and mind. In I. Markova and K. Foppa (eds.) *The Dynamics of Dialogue.* Hemel Hempstead.

(1992) Outlines of a dialogically based social-cognitive approach to human cognition and communication. In A. Heen Wold (ed.) *The Dialogical Alternative: towards a theory of language and mind.* London.

Rosaldo, M. (1980) *Knowledge and Passion: Ilongot notions of self and social life.* Cambridge.

(1984) Toward an anthropology of self and feeling. In R. Schweder and R. LeVine (eds.) *Culture Theory: essays on mind, self and emotion.* Cambridge.

Rosaldo, R. (1980) *Ilongot Headhunting, 1883–1974: a study in society and history.* Stanford, Calif.

Rosch, E. (1978) Principles of categorization. In E. Rosch and B. Floyd (eds.) *Cognition and Categorization.* Hillsdale, N.J.

Rumelhart, D., Hinton, G. and Williams, R. (1986) Learning internal representations by error propagation. In D. Rumelhart, J. McClelland and the PDP Group (eds.) *Parallel Distributed Processing,* Vol. I: *Foundations.* Cambridge, Mass.

Rumelhart, D., McClelland, J. and the PDP Group (1986) *Parallel Distributed Processing,* Vol. I: *Foundations.* Cambridge, Mass.

Sacks, H. (1986) [1973] On the preferences for agreement and contiguity in sequences in conversation. In G. Button and J.R.E. Lee (eds.) *Talk and Social Organization.* London.

(1989) Lectures 1964–1965. *Human Studies* 12, special issue, edited by G. Jefferson.

(1992) *Lectures on Conversation.* 2 vols. Edited by G. Jefferson. Oxford.

Sacks, H. and Schegloff, E.A. (1979) Two preferences in the organization of reference to persons in conversation and their interaction. In G. Psathas (ed.) *Everyday language: studies in ethnomethodology.* New York.

Sacks, H., Schegloff, E.A., and Jefferson, G. (1974) A simplest systematics for the organization of turn-taking for conversation. *Language* 50: 696–735.

Sacks, O. (1985) *The Man who Mistook his Wife for a Hat.* London.

Samarin, W.J. (1976) *Language in Religious Practice.* Georgetown, Washington, D.C.

Sanders, R.E. (1988) Review of Sperber and Wilson's *Relevance. Language in Society* 17: 604–9.

Sarich, V.M. and Wilson, A.C. (1967) Immunological time scale for hominid evolution. *Science* 158: 1200–3.

Savage-Rumbaugh, E.S. (1986) *Ape Language: from conditioned response to symbol.* New York. Accompanying film.

Savage-Rumbaugh, E.S. and McDonald, K. (1988) Deception and social manipulation in symbol using apes. In R.W. Byrne and A. Whiten (eds.) *Machiavellian Intelligence: social expertise and the evolution of intellect in monkeys, apes and humans.* Oxford.

Schank, R. and Abelson, R. (1977) *Scripts, Plans, Goals and Understanding: an enquiry into human knowledge structures.* Hillsdale, N.J.

Scheflen, A. (1972) *Body Language and Social Order.* Englewood Cliffs, N.J.

Schegloff, E.A. (1979) The relevance of repair to syntax-to-conversation. In T. Givon (ed.) *Syntax and Semantics 12: discourse and syntax.* New York.

(1980) Preliminaries to preliminaries: 'Can I ask you a question?'. *Sociological Inquiry* 50(3–4): 104–51.

(1984a) On some questions and ambiguities in conversation. In J.M. Atkinson and J. Heritage (eds.) *Structures of Social Action.* Cambridge.

(1984b) On some gestures' relation to talk. In J.M. Atkinson and J. Heritage (eds.) *Structures of Social Action.* Cambridge.

(1986) The routine as achievement. *Human Studies* 9: 111–52.

(1988a) On an actual virtual servo-mechanism for guessing bad news: a single case conjecture. *Social Problems* 35: 442–57.

(1988b) Presequences and indirection. *Journal of Pragmatics* 12: 55–62.

(1989) Harvey Sacks lectures: an introduction/memoir. In G. Jefferson (ed.) *Harvey Sacks Lectures 1964–1965*, special issue of *Human Studies* 12.

(1992a) Repair after next turn: the last structurally provided defense of intersubjectivity in conversation. *American Journal of Sociology* 97: 1295–345.

(1992b) Introduction. In G. Jefferson (ed.) *Lectures on Conversation*, Vol. I. Oxford.

(1992c) Reflections on language, development, and the interactional character of talk-in-interaction. In M. Bornstein and J.S. Bruner (eds.) *Interaction in Human Development.* Hillsdale, N.J.

Schegloff, E.A., Jefferson, G. and Sacks, H. (1977) The preference for self-correction in the organization of repair in conversation. *Language* 53: 361–82.

Schegloff, E. and Sacks, H. (1973) Opening up closings. *Semiotica* 7: 289–327.

Schelling, T. (1960) *The Strategy of Conflict.* Cambridge, Mass.

(1988) The mind as a consuming organ. In D. Bell, H. Raiffa and A. Tversky (eds.) *Decision Making.* Cambridge.

Scher, N.J.M. (ed.) (1962) *Theories of Mind.* New York.

Schieffelin, B. (1990) *The Give and Take of Everyday Life: language socialization of Kaluli children.* Cambridge.

Schieffelin, E. (1976) *The Sorrow of the Lonely and the Burning of the Dancers.* New York.

Schiffer, S.R. (1972) *Meaning.* Oxford.

Schöne, H. (1984) *Spatial Orientation.* Princeton.

Schrire, C. (1984) *Past and Present in Hunter-Gatherer Studies.* London.

Schutz, A. (1932) *Der sinnhafte Aufbau der sozialen Welt.* Vienna.

(1962) Choosing among projects of action. In A. Schutz *Collected Papers*, Vol. I: *The Problem of Social Reality.* The Hague.

(1970) *On Phenomenology and Social Relations.* Selected writings edited by H.R. Wagner. Chicago.

Schutz, A. and Luckman, T. (1973) *The Structures of the Life-World*, Vol. I. Evanston, Ill.

(1989) *The Structures of the Life-World*, Vol. II. Evanston, Ill.

Searle, J.R. (1969) *Speech Acts*. Cambridge.

Service, E.R. (1962) *Primitive Social Organization: an evolutionary perspective.* New York.

Seyfarth, R.M. and Cheney, D.L. (1988) Do monkeys understand their relations? In R.W. Byrne and A. Whiten (eds.) *Machiavellian Intelligence: social expertise and the evolution of intellect in monkeys, apes and humans*. Oxford.

Shaha, S. (1983) *Srī 108 Siddhasāgar Muni Mahārāj*. Kolhapur.

Sharpe, J.C. (1980) *Defamation and Sexual Slander in Early Modern England.* York.

Shaw, R. (1985) Gender and structuring of reality in Temne divination: an interactive study. *Africa* 53: 286–303.

Sibley, C.G. and Ahlquist, J.E. (1984) The phylogeny of the hominoid primates, as indicated by DNA–DNA hybridization. *Journal of Molecular Evolution* 20: 2–15.

Simon, H. (1981) *The Sciences of the Artificial*. Cambridge, Mass.

Smith, P.K. (1988) The cognitive demands of children's social interactions with peers. In R.W. Byrne and A. Whiten (eds.) *Machiavellian Intelligence: social expertise and the evolution of intellect in monkeys, apes and humans*. Oxford.

Smith, W.J. (1977) *The Behavior of Communicating: an ethological approach.* Cambridge, Mass.

Smuts, B. (1985) *Sex and Friendship in Baboons*. Chicago.

Solway, J. and Lee, R.B. (1990) Foragers, genuine or spurious? Situating the Kalahari San in history. *Current Anthropology* 31: 109–46.

Sperber, D. (1975) *Rethinking Symbolism*. Cambridge.

(1985) The epidemiology of beliefs. In C. Fraser and G. Gaskell (eds.) *Psychological Studies of Widespread Beliefs*.

(1990) The evolution of the language faculty: a paradox and its solution. *Behavioral and Brain Sciences* 13: 756–8.

Sperber, D. and Wilson, D. (1981) Irony and the use-mention distinction. In P. Cole (ed.) *Radical Pragmatics*. New York.

(1986) *Relevance: communication and cognition*. Oxford.

Stern, D.N. (1977) *The First Relationship: infant and mother*. London.

Steward, J.H. (1936) The economic and social basis of primitive bands. In R.H. Lowie (ed.) *Essays in Anthropology Presented to A.L. Kroeber*. Berkeley, Calif.

Strathern, M. (1988) *The Gender of the Gift: problems with women and problems with society in Melanesia*. Berkeley, Calif.

Strecker, L. (1988) *The Social Practice of Symbolisation: an anthropological analysis*. London School of Economics monograph on social anthropology, no. 60. London.

Streeck, J. (1988) The significance of gesture: how is it established? *Papers in Pragmatics* 2: 1–2.

(1989a) The social organization of self-adaptor sequences in conversation.

Paper presented at the annual meeting of the American Anthropological Association, Washington, D.C.

(1989b) On self-initiated repair in Ilokano conversation. Paper presented at the Annual Meeting of the Speech Communication Association, San Francisco.

(1992) The dispreferred other. In J. Searle *et al.* *(On) Searle on Conversation.* Amsterdam.

(1993) Gesture as communication I: its coordination with gaze and speech. *Communication Monographs* 60: 275–99.

(1994) Gesture as communication II: the audience as co-author. *Research on Language and Social Interaction* (Fall) Special issue *Is Gesture Communicative?* A. Kendon, ed.

Streeck, J. and Hartge, U. (1992) Previews: gestures at the transition place. In P. Auer and A. di Luzio (eds.) *The Contextualization of Language.* Amsterdam.

Stross, B. (1974) Speaking of speaking: Tzeltal meta-linguistics. In R. Bauman and J. Sherzer (eds.) *Explorations in the Ethnography of Speaking.* Cambridge.

Strum, S.C. (1983) Use of females by male olive baboons. *American Journal of Primatology* 5: 53–109.

Surgy, A. de (1981) *La Géomancie et le culte d'Afa chez les Evhe du Littoral.* Paris.

Talmy, L. (1985) Lexicalization patterns: semantic structure in lexical forms. In T. Shopen (ed.) *Language Typology and Syntactic Description,* Vol. III. Cambridge.

Tambiah, S.J. (1970) *Buddhism and the Spirit Cults in Northeast Thailand.* Cambridge.

(1985) *Culture, Thought and Social Action.* Cambridge, Mass.

Taylor, W.B. (1979) *Drinking, Homicide and Rebellion in Colonial Mexican Villages.* Stanford, Calif.

Terasaki, A. (1976) *Pre-Announcement Sequences in Conversation.* Social Sciences working paper, no. 99. University of California, Irvine.

Thomas, W.I. (1960) *On Social Organization and Social Personality. Selected Papers,* edited by M. Janowitz. Chicago.

Thompson, J.B. (1984) *Studies in the Theory of Ideology.* Cambridge.

Tomasello, M., Davis-Dasilva, M., Camak, L. and Bard, K. (1987) Observational learning of tool-use by young chimpanzees. *Journal of Human Evolution* 2: 175–83.

Tomasello, M., Kruger, A.C. and Ratner, H.H. (1993) Cultural learning. *Behavioral and Brain Sciences* 16: 495–552.

Tracy, K. (ed.) (1991) *Understanding Face-to-Face Interaction: issues linking goals and discourse.* Hillsdale, N.J.

Trevarthen, C.B. (1979a) Communication and cooperation in early infancy: a description of primary intersubjectivity. In M. Bullowa (ed.) *Before Speech: the beginning of interpersonal communication.* Cambridge.

(1979b) Instincts for human understanding and for cultural cooperation: their development in infancy. In M. von Cranach, K. Foppa, W. Lepenies and D. Ploog (eds.) *Human Ethology: claims and limits of a new discipline.* Cambridge.

(1988) Universal co-operative motives: how infants begin to know the language and culture of their parents. In G. Jahoda and I.M. Lewis (eds.) *Acquiring Culture: cross cultural studies in child development*. London.

Trexler, R.C. (1987) *The Christian at Prayer: an illustrated prayer manual attributed to Peter the Chanter (d. 1197)*. Birmingham, N.Y.

Turnbull, C. (1968) The importance of flux in two hunting societies. In R.B. Lee and I. Devore (eds.) *Man the Hunter*. Chicago.

Tversky, A. and Kahneman, D. (1977) Judgement and uncertainty: heuristics and biases. In P.N. Johnson-Laird and P.C. Watson (eds.) *Thinking: readings in cognitive science*. Cambridge.

Tyler, L.K. (1992) *Spoken Language Comprehension*. Cambridge, Mass.

Tylor, E.B. (1958) [1871] *Religion in Primitive Culture*. Part II of *Primitive Culture*, chs. 11–19. New York.

Ulmer, B. (1988) Konversionserzahlungen als rekonstruktive Gattung. Erzahlerische Mittel und Strategien bei der Rekonstruktion eines Bekehrungserlebnisses. *Zeitschrift für Soziologie* 17: 19–33.

Velmans, M. (1991) Is human information processing conscious? *Behavioral and Brain Sciences* 14: 651–726.

Vernant, J.P. (1974) Paroles et signes muets. In J.P. Vernant (ed.) *Divination et Rationalité*. Paris.

Visalberghi, E. and Fragaszy, D.M. (1990) Do monkeys ape? In S. Parker and K. Gibson (eds.) *'Language' and Intelligence in Monkeys and Apes: comparative development perspectives*. Cambridge.

Voosinov, V.N. (1973) *Marxism and the Philosophy of Language*. New York and London.

Von Wright, G.H. (1971) *Explanation and Understanding*. London.

Vygotsky, L.S. (1934) *Myshlenie i Rech': psikhologicheskie issledovaniy* (Thinking and Speech: psychological investigations). Moscow and Leningrad.

(1962) *Thought and Language*. Cambridge, Mass.

(1978) *Mind in Society: the development of higher psychological processes*, edited by M. Cole, V. John-Steiner, S. Scribner and E. Souberman. Cambridge, Mass.

Warren, J.M. (1973) Learning in vertebrates. In D.A. Dewsbury and D.A. Rethlingshafer (eds.) *Comparative Psychology: a modern survey*. New York.

Weber, M. (1922) *Wirtschaft und Gesellschaft*. Tübingen. English edition (1968) *Economy and Society*. New York.

Weiser, A. (1975) How not to answer a question: purposive devices in conversational strategy. *Proceedings of the Chicago Linguistics Society* 11: 649–60.

Welch, H. (1967) *The Practice of Chinese Buddhism 1900–1950*. Cambridge, Mass.

Werbner, R.P. (1989) Tswapong wisdom divination. In R.P. Werbner *Ritual Passage, Sacred Journey*. Washington, D.C.

Wertsch, J.V. (1985a) *Vygotsky and the Social Formation of the Mind*. Cambridge, Mass.

(ed.) (1985b) *Culture, Communication and Cognition: Vygotskian perspectives*. Cambridge.

Whiten, A. (ed.) (1991) *Natural Theories of Mind: evolution, development and simulation of everyday mindreading*. Oxford.

Whiten, A. and Byrne, R.W. (1988) Tactical deception in primates. *Behavioral and Brain Sciences* 11: 233–73.

Whiten, A. and Perner, J. (1991) Fundamental issues in the multidimensional study of mindreading. In A. Whiten (ed.) *Natural Theories of Mind: evolution, development and simulation of everyday mindreading.* Oxford.

Whiting, B.B. and Edwards, C.P. (1988) *Children of Different Worlds: the formation of social behavior.* Cambridge, Mass.

Wiessner, P. (1982) Risk, reciprocity, and social influence on !Kung San economics. In E. Leacock and R. Lee (eds.) *Politics and History in Band Societies.* Cambridge.

Wilkins, W. and Dumford, J. (1990) In defence of exaptation. *Behavioral and Brain Sciences* 13: 763.

Williams Jackson, A.V.W. (1899) *Zoroaster: the prophet of ancient Iran.* New York.

Wilmsen, E. and Denbow, J. (1991) Paradigmatic history of San-speaking peoples and current attempts at revision. *Current Anthropology* 31: 489–524.

Wilson, P.J. (1980) *Man, the Promising Primate: the conditions of human evolution.* New Haven, Conn.

(1988) *The Domestication of the Human Species.* New Haven and London.

Wimmer, H. and Perner, J. (1983) Beliefs about beliefs: representing and constraining function of wrong beliefs in young children's understanding of deception. *Cognition* 13: 103–28.

Winograd, T. and Flores, F. (1987) *Understanding Computers and Cognition: a new foundation for design.* Reading, Mass.

Wood, D.J., Bruner, J.S. and Ross, G. (1976) The role of tutoring in problem solving. *Journal of Child Psychology and Psychiatry* 17(2): 89–100.

Woodburn, J. (1968) Stability and flexibility in Hazda residential groupings. In R.B. Lee and I. DeVore (eds.) *Man the Hunter.* Chicago.

(1979) Minimal politics: the political organization of the Hadza of North Tanzania. In W.A. Shack and P.S. Cohen (eds.) *Politics in Leadership.* Oxford.

(1980) Hunters and gatherers today and reconstruction of the past. In E. Gellner (ed.) *Soviet and Western Anthropology.* London.

(1982) Egalitarian societies. *Man* (n.s.) 17: 431–51.

Young, J.Z. (1951) *Doubt and Certainty in Science.* Oxford.

Zeitlyn, D. (1983) Contradictions and alternative logics. *Man* (n.s.) 18: 788–9.

(1987) Mambila divination. *Cambridge Anthropology* 12(1): 21–51.

(1990a) Mambila traditional religion: Sua in Somie. Ph.D. thesis, University of Cambridge.

(1990b) Professor Garfinkel visits the soothsayers: ethnomethodology and Mambila divination. *Man* (n.s.) 25: 654–66.

(1993) Spiders in and out of court or 'the long legs of the law'. Styles of spider divination in their sociological contexts. *Africa* 63(2): 219–40.

Ziff, P. (1971) On H.P. Grice's account of meaning. In D. Steinberg and L. Jakobovitz (eds.) *Semantics.* Cambridge.

Zvelebil, K.V. (1981) Problems of identification and classification of some Nilgiri tribes. *Anthropos* 76: 467–528.

Index

Abrahams, R.G. 32 *n*21
action; AIP as prerequisite for 219;
accountability of 207; joint/
collaborative 6, 93–4, 106, 143–4;
logic of 230–1; primate 48–50;
projected/planned 23, 88–94, 98–9,
104–6, 128, 176–7; social 16, 184 *n*2,
270, 273, 275; strategies for 12, 22,
134; synchronization of 16, 21–2; *see*
also coordination, goal-directed
interaction, interaction, interaction
sequences, social interaction
activity theory 32 *n*14
adjacency pairs, in conversation 115, 139,
189
agonistic planning 226, 244
agreement, preference for in conversation
117–18
AIP *see* anticipatory interactive planning
Alhonsaari, A. 215
Allen, J. 240
allometric scaling 40, 43
ambiguity; of action in primates 49; in
conversation 23, 25; in divination 199;
of intended meaning 139, 141–3, 158,
164–9 *passim*, 170; of pre's 89, 235; *see*
also inference, intentionality,
intention-attribution, meaning
ancestor worship 209–10
Anesaki, M. 216–17, 218
animism 218, 224–5
anticipation limit (AL) 145, 148
anticipatory interactive planning (AIP)
2–3, 32 *n*16, 206; and conscious
strategy 111, 112, 114; and control
7–8, 129–132; evolution of 52, 68–9,
82–3, 140; and communicative
interaction 176; and intentionality 16,
24, 26, 112–14; and language 3, 6–9,
10–13, 16, 140, 206–7; in primates 18,
50–1, 68; and projectability 119, 121,
124, 127; and social roles and rules

6–7, 10, 14–15, 16, 68–9, 81–3, 183;
and temporality 139, 140, 144–5, 148;
see also AIP entries under separate
headings, and also agonistic planning,
confabulation, foresight, goal-directed
interaction, interaction sequences,
modelling, projection, strategy.
apes; and closeness to humans 39; and
intelligence 42–3, 44, 45; and
intention-attribution 47, 48–9;
teaching among 46; *see* also primates,
hominids
approval, desire for 26–7
Argyle, M. 32 *n*17
Aristotle 230
Ashanti prayer 209–10
Atlas, J. 259 *n*31
Austin, J.L. 142–3
autism 9, 45, 48, 222
autoassociation networks 56–8, 66 *n*2, *n*3
autobiography 275
awareness; and language 8–9, 19; and
relationship with intentionality 32
*n*16; self-awareness 8–9, 18, 19, 44,
148;- *see* also cognition, intelligence,
knowledge, social intelligence

Bakhtin, M.M. 108, 185 *n*12
Bayesian conjunction 243, 244, 247
Beattie, J.H.M. 144
Berger, P.L. 68–70, 77, 80, 82, 83
bias, of human intelligence; towards
animism 224–5; in cognition 221; and
interactive intelligence 224–5, 241–2,
245–7, 250–1, 253–4, 255 *n*6; in
judging probability 204 *n*4, 242–4,
253, 259 *n*38; against logical reasoning
13, 29, 221; against randomness
245–7; towards social interaction 27–9
Bickerton, D. 3, 6, 18
Bird-David, N. 19–20
Blumstein, S. 255 *n*2